The Sino-Soviet Dispute

Other books by Alfred D. Low:

Lenin on the Question of Nationality

The Soviet Hungarian Republic and the Paris Peace Conference

The Anschluss Movement in Austria and Germany, 1918-1919, and
the Paris Peace Conference

THE SINO-SOVIET DISPUTE
An Analysis of the Polemics

Alfred D. Low

RUTHERFORD • MADISON • TEANECK
Fairleigh Dickinson University Press
LONDON: Associated University Presses

© 1976 by Associated University Presses, Inc.

Associated University Presses, Inc.
Cranbury, New Jersey 08512

Associated University Presses
108 New Bond Street
London W1Y OQX, England

Library of Congress Cataloging in Publication Data

Low, Alfred D
  The Sino-Soviet dispute.
  Bibliography: p.
  Includes index.
  1. China—Foreign relations—Russia. 2. Russia—Foreign relations—China.
I. Title.
DS740.5.R8L68   327.51'047   74-2949
ISBN 0-8386-1479-5

To Hilda and Walter,
Helli and Marian,
Florence and Hans and their family.

Contents

Preface

The Sino-Soviet rift is a political reality of our day that cannot be denied. It is likely to remain the pivot of international relations in our lifetime. Whether it will lead to more serious clashes than those which occurred in 1969 is of course impossible to anticipate, though some Western observers have expressed the belief that war between Moscow and Peking is likely, if not inevitable. There can be little doubt about the giant preparations for defense or perhaps preventive war that are being made on both sides of the Sino-Soviet boundary.

The year 1949, when the People's Republic of China was proudly proclaimed and the USSR considered the expansion of Communism to the China Sea one of her greatest victories, seems to belong to the dim past. The very circumstance that such an assessment could have been made by people all over the globe without being seriously challenged appears incredible in these days of heightened Sino-Soviet tension. The Far Eastern victory of 1949 has, for the Soviet Union, turned into a nightmare and a source of most serious concern.

No one writing in the field of Sino-Soviet relations treads on entirely novel ground. This author owes much to some laborious and penetrating studies on some phases of the period in question, especially those by D. S. Zagoria, W. E. Griffith, J. Gittings, and H. C. Hinton. Every writer in this field must also be keenly aware of the serious limitations that the inaccessibility of archives and the contemporary nature of the topic impose. Yet it is unlikely that Soviet or Chinese archives will be opened to the scholar from abroad as long as the Communist regimes retain their grip over both states. In the meantime, reaching even the most tentative judgments about the character of the Sino-Soviet relationship is an obvious imperative.

The focus of this study is the polemics. This is the more necessary in the absence of types of sources such as are available in the West —memoirs and personal accounts of ministers, secretaries, presidents and premiers, and other high-placed policy-makers—and in the absence of confidential reports of the highest agencies of Party and government in the

9

USSR and the CPR. Yet an attempt has here been made to trace and analyze Soviet and Chinese policies toward each other on the basis of available documents and general evidence.

The polemics of course is an outgrowth of Moscow's and Peking's policies, though in turn it has also shaped these policies. Once issues came into the open and were publicly raked over, both parties were limited in their freedom to break away from the openly proclaimed course or alter radically the relationship to the other Communist Party and superpower. Making public the differences between them therefore represented, as both sides must have realized, a "point of no return." Thereafter they were on a downhill race, neither one able to stop.

There is an abundance of articles in dailies and journals, of pamphlets and, to a lesser degree, of books, both in Russian and Chinese, pertaining to the topic. This writer has been able to make use of Chinese sources only in English translation. Russian sources, often directly consulted, have been made accessible through the invaluable aid of the Current Digest of the Soviet Press.

In treating the subject matter I have deliberately chosen a combination of the chronological and topical approach. Since the dispute by its very nature took the form of a dialogue, I have also attempted to preserve this framework in order to give the escalating debate between the two world capitals of Communism the character of authenticity and immediate reality. This effect, I believe, is enhanced by numerous quotations, to convey to the reader the arguments and heated atmosphere of a direct confrontation.

I have confined myself to the task of analyzing only the last seventeen years of the conflict, providing in chapter 2 a brief survey of the important period between 1917 and 1921—the years of the Russian October Revolution and of the founding of the CPC respectively—and 1956, when the fateful Twentieth Party Congress of the CPSU was convened. This chapter gives a bird's-eye view of the relationship between the two Communist parties before the dispute, as a Chinese proverb has it, brought down the heavens. The first chapter aims at establishing the framework of the study and poses the questions as to the deeper causes of the dispute.

I am grateful to Marquette University for having given me a Faculty Summer Fellowship grant, which considerably speeded up the writing process. Marquette University Library was most helpful in securing interlibrary loans, and the University of Michigan Library in securing other badly needed materials during my stay in Ann Arbor during the summer of 1973. Professor John K. C. Oh of the Political Science Department of Marquette University was most helpful with the transliteration of a few names from the Chinese. My research assistant Dennis J. Mueller has assisted me conscientiously with the Bibliography and Mrs. Eleanor Sachs with part of the typing. As usual, I am indebted to my wife for patient listening, and this time also to my daughter Suzanne for critically reading the entire manuscript; both made numerous valuable suggestions. My daughter Ruth was helpful in a number of ways.

Alfred D. Low

Milwaukee, Wisconsin

The Sino-Soviet Dispute

Abbreviations

Central Committee	CC
Current Abstracts of the Soviet Press	CAPS
Current Digest of the Soviet Press	CDSP
Communist Party of China	CPC
Chinese People's Republic	CPR
Communist Party of the Soviet Union	CPSU
Peking Review	PR

1

The Sino-Soviet Dispute.
Roots and Theories

I would advise comrades to remain firm in the conviction that the masses of the Soviet people and of Party members and cadres are good, that
they desire revolution and that revisionist rule will not last long.

—Mao Tse-tung

Never have our fiercest enemies resorted to such odious devices on such
a scale as the Chinese leaders are now doing in order to denigrate the
activity of the Soviet Union.

—A. Gromyko

The dispute between Moscow and Peking that has raged in the open for
more than a decade burst upon a world little prepared for it. Not even the
shrewdest analyst or most farsighted prophet could have anticipated its
emergence and the scope and depth it would attain. With hardly a decade
after the proclamation of victory for Chinese Communism, Sino-Soviet relations have stunned the experts and perplexed the most acute political observers of virtually all countries and of the most diverse persuasions, as
well as the public at large. Sino-Soviet relations have taken a course that
nobody on either side of the iron and bamboo curtains anticipated.

The Sino-Soviet dispute is not a passing phenomenon but one of the
great schisms in history. The star of the Kremlin has long lost its radiance
for Peking. For Chinese Communism, Moscow is no longer the Mecca of
international Communism, but rather the cesspool of error, heresy, and
betrayal; what has occurred is a fundamental and irreparable break in world
Communism. The rift has radically altered the world political scene and
the foreign-policy course of the major and smaller powers. Peking has
leveled the accusation of "Soviet-American collusion" against the two
superpowers and Moscow has been made jittery about the relaxation of

15

tension between China and the U.S. and its implication for Soviet security.

The dispute has puzzled and continues to puzzle especially those who are inclined to overestimate the role of ideology in international affairs. Neither orthodox Marxists nor rabid anti-Communists find it possible that nations professing "the same" Communist philosophy could be deeply antagonistic and could go to war against each other, though this possibility can no longer be discounted. Major border clashes have taken place and a war psychology prevails along the Sino-Soviet border—the longest border on earth between two states. The new political facts of life have compelled the experts to reexamine basic problems of foreign policy. American foreign-policy-makers too have finally come to reassess and take advantage of the Sino-Soviet split. Driving a wedge between the two Communist superpowers, Washington has managed to obtain a limited rapprochement with both. Earlier, the assumption that world Communism was monolithic—perhaps with the exception of Yugoslavia—was the very cornerstone of American foreign-policy thought in regard to the Communist world. But today the world Communist movement is split into numerous parties and factions whose leaders brand each other as worse than heretics, as betrayers of the legacy of Marx and Lenin, and display toward each other not comradeship but unmitigated hostility and contempt.

The Sino-Soviet dispute ranges over a wide field. It is concerned with ideological differences, some seemingly abstruse, as well as with down-to-earth territorial disputes and the struggle for leadership and domination of the Communist Parties of the world. The dispute centers on questions of tactics and strategy, on the coordination of national Communist goals with those of Moscow and Peking, and on problems of Marxist exegesis and "theology." The dispute raged, and rages, around questions of economic and military help to China and to the underdeveloped countries of the Third World. It focuses on Stalin's role in history and on personality clashes between Mao Tse-tung and Khrushchev and his successors. The last, in Peking's view, pursue the policy of "Khrushchevism without Khrushchev."

The dispute is also a continuation of the centuries-old hostility between Russia and China. It is a clash of two great powers whose adoption of the ideology and language of internationalism scarcely hides their selfish nationalist drives. Their ideological supranationalism is only a poor camouflage for a most extravagant nationalism nurtured by both sides. In an era of decolonization, of the abolishment of the West's "unequal" treaties of the nineteenth century, the CPR has reminded the USSR of the continuation of Russia's "unequal" treaties of that time, of the vast territories that Tsarist Russia wrested from China and of the Soviet Union's most recent encroachments, and leveled the painful and embarrassing accusation of colonialism against Moscow—an accusation that the latter usually hurls against the West.

In the Chinese Communist view, the Soviet Union's strategy of world revolution is misconceived, since it reneges on sacrifice and repudiates war under all circumstances. The USSR herself continues to claim that she is going to win the economic competition with the United States and that all, or almost all, that is needed to revolutionize the world is to furnish the new nations of Asia, Africa, and Latin America with a helpful model and the proper diplomatic, moral, and economic support. The Russian October Revolution is generously offered as the classic example of the proletarian revolution, as the effective liberating cure for all the ills of the world. To the Chinese Communists, however, the USSR and her strategy appear an example of bourgeois softness, hypocrisy, and degeneration—of relinquishing world revolution in favor of peaceful coexistence. In this context they point to Soviet reluctance to take serious risks over Berlin, the Congo, Cuba, Taiwan, and Vietnam.

China's bark, on the other hand, has so far proved worse than her bite. Revolutionary and militant language is cheap, after all. Actually, China herself, in regard to the offshore islands, Hong Kong, India, and especially the war in Vietnam, has pursued a much more cautious policy than her reckless propaganda would indicate. Yet it is Peking's strident voice calling for instant revolution and support for national liberation movements at virtually any price, including thermonuclear war, that has aroused worldwide concern and brought upon the Chinese leadership charges by Moscow that it did not comprehend the frightful realities of such a war.

What is the essence of the Sino-Soviet dispute, which has shaken and irreparably split the world Communist movement and has radically altered the balance of power in the world? Let us turn to a brief analysis of the main reasons usually adduced for it, singly or in combination, to explain its development.

The dispute is considered by some the inevitable clash of two vigorous national movements that have come of age. Both the CPR and the USSR are multinational states. Yet while the dominant Han people make up 94% of the population of China, the Great Russians, the dominant nationality in the Soviet Union, form only about 50% of the entire population of the USSR. Even if one adds other Slavic nationalities such as the Ukrainians and Belo Russians to the Great Russian element, one obtains only between 3/4 and 4/5 of the population of the USSR. Aside from minorities that inhabit both the USSR and the CPR and that to a large degree are immediate neighbors across the extended Sino-Soviet border, the struggle between the CPR and the USSR represents the unavoidable confrontation of two major nations, both of which have pushed toward the border regions, have colonized them, and have attempted to assimilate the non-Han and and non-Russian peoples respectively. This thrust toward the border was generated long before the October Revolution in Russia and before Communism seized power on the mainland of China in 1949, and thus is unrelated to ideology. Its basic reasons were the drive to enhance national security and provide room for present and future colonization, and the desire for imperial assertion over the minor "breeds" or peoples of lesser civilization in the border areas. Whatever the original motivation, economic development in the border regions and military build-up brought Chinese and Russian colonists almost face to face, only to magnify fear and suspicion on both sides.

Both multinational Communist empires, insistent on defending their territorial legacy, spurn the suggestion of relinquishing extensive border territories or any portion of their empire. Neither is prepared to let any nationality living within its realm secede. Both the CPR and the USSR base their adamant stand on Marxist doctrine, which extols the large state as a stepping stone toward socialism, economic planning, and a higher living standard. Each claims to have solved the age-old nationality question within its realm and looks upon any inclination toward secession as plain treason, betrayal of international brotherhood, and repudiation of Chinese and Soviet patriotism respectively. The USSR, though permitting secession in its constitution, denies it in practice; even Lenin considered the very act of self-determination—such as, for instance, joining the Soviet Union—a single and irrevocable act, not a permanent national right.[1] According to an eminent Chinese expert, C. P. Fitzgerald, the Chinese view similarly was, and is, that territory once won for civilization—for China—"must be recovered at the first opportunity."[2] After the CPR and the USSR had embraced Communism, and nationalism and Communism had combined their forces, the stand of both ruling parties on territorial questions and numerous other issues separating them has grown even more inflexible. Two unyielding forces of tremendous power seem to be on a collision course. Only great wisdom and mutual restraint can prevent a conflagration between them.

The USSR is, territorially speaking, a satiated state, though intent on spreading her influence and power beyond her confines in accordance with both Marxist-Leninist doctrine and national self-interest. As far as the CPR is concerned, she is insistent upon incorporating Taiwan in due time —American long-range pledges along this line were given in Canton in February 1972—and upon revising substantially the extended Sino-Soviet frontier. She of course has global aspirations in addition. The territorial

---

1. A. D. Low, *Lenin on the Question of Nationality* (New York, 1958), p. 90.
2. C. P. Fitzgerald, *The Birth of Communist China* (Baltimore, Md., 1964), pp. 85-86.

thrusts of the two Communist giants are not only directed at the outside world; China's expressed territorial ambitions focus on Soviet Asia. The decision in favor of the latter region pits her hopelessly against the Soviet Union and leaves the latter no choice but a completely negative and hostile reaction. True, the CPR may at any time decide to tone down her territorial claims. But so far she has given no inkling in this direction. And it is doubtful whether the extensive claims pressed by Peking over a good many years will ever be completely forgotten by Moscow and whether the state of early innocence in the Peking-Moscow relationship can ever be restored.

Geographic proximity in past and present has often made for hostility of neighboring peoples in many parts of the globe. The persistent Russian push into Asia, in particular the nineteenth-century conquest of Chinese territories and their forced cession, has aroused Chinese bitterness and anger and the desire to roll the Soviet Union as far back as possible. To the angry puzzlement of the USSR, Communist China has presented her with exorbitant claims involving the return of Asian territories and has even charged violation of the imposed boundary lines. Taken by themselves, these claims, once derided by Khrushchev as "Old Testamentaric Boundaries," are indistinguishable from those of rapacious capitalist and imperialist states that have given battle to each other over disputed borders.

Nationalism in China acquired special force in view of the transgressions and encroachments of foreign imperialism upon an ancient and proud civilization and her subsequent humiliation in the course of the nineteenth century. During the same period, Russia pursued her expansionist objectives in the Balkans, the Middle East, and the Far East, alternately scoring victories and suffering setbacks, both of which tended to strengthen Russian nationalism and sharpen a Russian sense of mission at home and abroad. The October Revolution broadened and deepened the concept of mission, though secularizing it. Nationalism and internationalism closely merged with sentiments of patriotism and of proletarian brotherhood and in turn transformed Russian nationalism. Chinese nationalism after World War I, on the other hand, still suffering from the wounds inflicted earlier by Western imperialism and still battling this imperialism, found new nourishment in the Soviet example. This example was either wholly endorsed, as by the Chinese Communists, or, taken as its organizational model, was of great influence on the Kuomintang, first under Sun Yat-sen and then under Chiang Kai-shek.

After the Chinese Communist victory in 1949, traditional Chinese nationalism on the mainland wrapped itself in the garb of Marxism-Leninism. The rivalry of past Chinese and Russian nationalism and between their imperial ambitions was at first hardly noticeable, since the two Communist states seemed partners and fellow travelers on the road to socialism. The prestige and power of Moscow, to which Chinese Communism looked up; the unchallenged preeminence of Stalin; Communist China's apparent economic dependence and weakness in weaponry—all explain the apparently unquestioned acknowledgment by Peking of Moscow's leadership, at least during the first years. But the national self-assertion of China and the self-assurance, pride, and independence of Mao and the CPC became apparent as early as the twenties and thirties and later manifested themselves in frequent disregard of Moscow's advice. All this foreshadowed Peking's ultimate challenge of Moscow and unabashed rivalry with it.

Twentieth-century nationalist exaggerations and excesses were, in the case of China, the result of humiliation and overcompensation, an outgrowth of the sensation of national power after a catastrophic decline of political and military status. Tsarist Russia too had suffered setbacks and lost wars, in 1905 and 1917, and Bolshevik Russia had to lick the wounds inflicted on her during World War I and the civil war, trying to recover strength in the twenties and thirties. Following the Fatherland's War, the USSR indulged for several years in cultural propaganda of the most chauvinist type, magnifying especially Great Russian achievements. The disease of chauvinism has gripped both Communist superpowers, with each leveling this very charge, among many others, at the other—in both cases with justification. While professing internationalism, they have succumbed to extreme nationalism, but have attempted to refurbish it and give it a red coat. Both Communist superpowers are militarily stronger than their countries have ever been.

The dispute between the USSR and the CPR developed at a historic juncture that saw the elevation of both Communist giants to the rank of major military powers, the USSR becoming in the postwar era a world power, and the CPR—due to its sheer size, population, and new-won cohesion, as manifested during the Korean War—a power of impressive Asiatic dimension.

Nationalism and militarism are closely intertwined both in the CPR and in the USSR. National pride and military prowess march arm in arm. The growth of both in the two Communist superpowers, in combination with their memory of past weakness, makes it virtually impossible for either side to make meaningful concessions in the current dispute and makes a solution of their differences in the foreseeable future more difficult.

Common Marxist-Leninist ideology of both Communist powers had long convinced both Marxists and Western observers that Moscow and Peking were brothers-in-arms. The thirty-year alliance concluded between them in 1950, following the victory in the prolonged Civil War, was bound to strengthen their conviction as to the unbreakable solidarity of the two partners, a solidarity forged by joint ideals and common interests. But the Marxist-Leninist trappings that they both displayed made them only look alike. They actually were rather hostile brothers—not bound by common intellectual heritage, the ideology of Marxism-Leninism, but, rather, separated by their widely diverging interpretations of it. These divergences centered first upon a differing assessment of Stalin and Stalinism. Many in the Soviet Union, especially Khrushchev, were desirous of breaking with Stalinism, while official China clung desperately to Stalin's exalted image, seeing in it the very foundation upon which Mao's ideas rested.

Russian Marxists had always asserted that their version of Marxism-Leninism was the only correct one. Any other interpretation was faulty and heretical, the mere idea that anybody but Moscow could be guardian of the doctrine abhorrent and anathema. Peking vigorously denied that it bent doctrine to suit its own purposes, though the Chinese Communists had long talked about the need to "sinify" Communism. They claimed that their interpretation of Marxism-Leninism and their resulting policy was nothing but "creative application" of Marxism and that their version still had universal significance and applicability.

Thus nationalism was not eliminated but merely submerged in both the Soviet Union and the CPR, to surface with élan at the first opportunity. When it did, it faced, in the USSR, not only westward, toward Europe, and in the CPR not merely east and south, toward the Pacific, Indochina, and India, but also, in both cases the Sino-Soviet frontier, in a most serious and unexpected confrontation. Those who had resorted to ideology as the key to explaining friendships and hostilities on the international plane were stunned by this development.

Marxists in particular were, and many still are, at a loss to account for hostility between two allegedly classless socialist societies— the CPR and the USSR—that at the same time show a desire to conclude an "armistice" in the Cold War with the class enemy—the imperialist devil himself, the United States.

The most superficial glance at twentieth-century developments, not to mention world history in general, shows that alliances in different periods have been shaped not by ideological kinship, but rather by self-interest: monarchic interest in earlier ages, broad national interest in later times. It is imperatives of power, and the political and military balance of power, that have created blocs and alliances. Ideological affinity under some circumstances might give special impetus to these imperatives, but by itself it can not forge alliances. Nor will ideological dissonances prevent an alliance of powerful interests from working toward its own preservation. Yet in the Cold War atmosphere of the immediate postwar era, the intensity of anti-Communist sentiments and the power of propaganda were such that it seemed incredible, if not preposterous, that a system of alliances in disregard of strictly ideological lines—Communism versus anti-Communism—could ever emerge.

Some students of history and politics have been persuaded that power generates its own momentum. Endorsing a Macchiavellian point of view rather than an ideological one, they have claimed that every organization, party, nation, and individual is driven to the acquisition of power, toward holding onto the power that has been seized and toward increasing it. They hold that conflicts of power are unrelated to ideology and may be even fiercer among those of similar or almost identical political and social outlook, between ideological brothers and cousins, than between ideological opposites. The sharp differences that occasionally have arisen in the postwar world between De Gaulle's France and the United States, between Moscow and Belgrade, and later between Moscow and Peking, are all cases in point.

The ideological kinship of two groups, rather than making for unity, can be deeply divisive. The number of religious communities starting out from a joint religious base, common Holy Scripture, and ending up with different, sharply opposing theological conceptions, is legion; religious splinter groups, each claiming to be the sole correct interpreter of Holy Writ, may frequently be more hostile to yesterday's religious fellow traveler than to those of entirely different denominations and faiths and even to outright atheists. The religious and ideological deviant is often looked upon as worse than a "heretic" and is ruthlessly persecuted. The history of the relationship between anarchists, syndicalists, and between Marxists in the nineteenth century, Bernstein revisionists and orthodox Marxists, between social democrats and Communists after the formation of the Third International in 1919, between Stalinists and Trotskyites, and between numerous other socialists of diverse ideological colors is testimony to this truth.

The struggle between Tito and Stalin was largely a struggle over power, though one overlaid by ideological justifications on both sides. Tito, who had reached the apex of power through his own and the Yugoslav Communist Party's efforts rather than Soviet endeavors, balked at surrender to the control of Moscow. Though Yugoslav nationalism rallied to Tito in support and played a decisive role in this dispute, it merely reenforced the power aspect of the struggle. The dispute between Moscow and Peking is likewise overwhelmingly a struggle for power—for the recognition of Moscow's overlordship, for acknowledgment of the "socialist" or "limited" sovereignty (expounded and defended by Moscow ever since the invasion of Czechoslovakia in 1968) and of the overall direction of international tactics and strategy by the USSR. At the same time, this struggle is also a clash between two elemental national movements, each shaped by peculiar historical circumstances, and is also rooted in ideology.

What exactly is the relationship between ideology, Marxist-Leninist doctrine in particular, and national self-interest, as judged and implemented by the ruling Communist Parties of the two superpowers? Ideology is the guide to their action and policy, but it is given expression by leaders who can be depended upon never to act counter to their national interests and who are most adept in bending ideology to suit their purposes. The Communist leaders of the CPSU and the CPC can hardly publicly admit, nor are they probably able to discern, that they are primarily champions of the national interests of their respective countries. Though both may talk in terms of assisting the international proletarian revolution, and may be prepared to extend help to it within limits, they are at the same time ruthless contenders and competitors, each desiring to gain control of the international Communist movement, to defeat the rival, and to establish their own national leadership over other Parties and states.

If one is to believe Moscow and Peking, however, their dispute is nothing but ideological; both strongly deny that national and power aspects enter into it at all. But this is hardly persuasive. By necessity, following its own inherent logic, Communist ideology must disavow the existence of any but an ideological rift between Communist Parties. Thus, to believe Moscow and Peking, the difference between the two capitals of Communism is only one between those who are genuine Marxist-Leninists and those who falsely lay claim to be the true interpreters of the doctrine—in other words, between people who follow the Party line and are Marxist sages and saints, and their opponents, who are vicious and unrepentant sinners. Peking and Moscow differ, of course, in their views as to who is good and bad, who is the true guardian of doctrine, who the creative interpreter of the Holy Writ, but they agree as to the nature of the dispute, its theoretical, "theological," ideological character. Even if the issue in dispute concerns territorial concessions, the error is pronounced an outgrowth of wrong thinking, of wrong interpretation of Marxism-Leninism.

Geopoliticians and adherents of the school of international power politics generally disdain the role of theory and ideology and try to deflate it, priding themselves on their hardheaded realism. Americans are frequently inclined to take ideological disputes not too seriously. There is a propensity on this side of the Atlantic to look behind frightful words to what is hoped is perhaps a less shocking meaning. Such an attitude marked U.S. policy in the thirties toward the Nazi regime and Nazi ideology. There is a similar tendency, recently born of domestic political expediency and plain wishful thinking, to ignore, minimize, or interpret away the seriousness of the long-range Communist imperialist threat both to the West and to the uncommitted Third World. There is a related inclination to dismiss nonchalantly the depth of the differences between Moscow and Peking. Some people hold that foreign Communist propaganda ought to be taken as casually as American advertisements of products for sale. Ideological disputes, it is widely held, are an abstruse game, played only by a few isolated intellectuals who tend to take their own pronunciamentos too seriously. Repetition of ideological pet phrases, it is asserted, has only a limited ritual purpose.

There is a strong undercurrent of belief that all-knowing men of affairs and state had better ignore ideology, and Marxist-Leninist philosophy in particular, since even the leaders of the two Communist superpowers pay only lip-sercie to it.

While Communists themselves, as well as adherents of the ideological school, stress Marxist-Leninist doctrine as the key to the dispute, geopoliticians and the school of power politics represent the very opposite point of view, denying that ideology is the true cause of the dispute and acknowledging at best that arguments bared in its course are perhaps a clue to the real differences—which are to be found in geopolitics and power.

There can be no doubt that the Sino-Soviet dispute has not only ideological aspects but also ideological causes. It is difficult seriously to reject the proposition that the views put forth by the Soviets and the Chinese Communists in numerous statements and in mutual accusations are all meaningless and bear no relation to the deeper causes of the dispute. The passion generated by it and the energy and seriousness spent on the debate point to the very opposite. The issues taken up in the Sino-Soviet dispute are real live issues that have substantially contributed to the rift. The only point that might be conceded is that the divisive issues as listed by both parties may not be the only ones that have given rise to the split. But denying or belittling ideology as a very potent source of the conflict between Moscow and Peking is as unrealistic as to deny the moving power of religion in a deeply religious age.

The ideological factor, on the other hand, is inseparable from the factors of geopolitics and those of national power and nationalism, of mass psychology as well as of the psychological make-up of leaders such as Mao, Khrushchev, and his successors, and is inseparable from the historical past; it is partly a reflection of the difference of the historical routes that both Communist giants and both countries in their pre-Communist era have traveled. All these causes of the split are intricately linked with each other and, though in a critical analysis they must be dealt with separately, in actual life they are irretrievably bound together.

Ideology, in the apt words of a student of Chinese history, I. C. Ojha, is almost the sole vehicle through which the antagonisms can be articulated.[3] The man who refuses to listen to its voice arbitrarily and shortsightedly

3. I. C. Ojha, *Chinese Foreign Policy in an Age of Transition. . .* (Berkeley, Calif., 1969), p. 127.

cuts himself off from the very means of comprehending the issues that separate the two Communist rivals. In Communist circles, it is Marxist-Leninist theory and ideology, rather than theology or traditional philosophy as among other groups, that is the guide to "correct" policy and tactics. Politicians and statesmen in the Western world may be guided by pragmatic considerations and by voters' preferences. Communist leaders must be guided by the Party line, which is allegedly decided upon democratically by the Party membership in accordance with the tenets of Marxism-Leninism. Thus, Marxist-Leninist ideology, correctly interpreted and "creatively applied," is the very touchstone of Communist policy and tactics. And Marxist-Leninist objectives must be expressed in Marxist-Leninist thought and language. Therefore, the influence of Marxism-Leninism upon the minds of their followers, and their mode of expression, can hardly be exaggerated. It permeates their very being and their very action. It would be utterly unrealistic to ignore or even to attempt to minimize its impact upon Communists anywhere, including the top leadership of the CPSU and the CPC.

Throughout the ages, man has expounded ideas and doctrines and has shaped his own life and that of others in accordance with their precepts —religious, ethical, philosophical, social and political ones, noble and ignoble ones. The Nazi followers and leaders were as much captives of their own "philosophy," rhetoric, and propaganda as Communists, and even democratic leaders are captives of their own thought systems.

Moscow and Peking are clearly rivals in the world of Communism. Each aspires to be the leader, to wield the greatest influence, if not actually to dominate world Communism. For years each has thundered against capitalism, imperialism, and neo-colonialism, and against the United States in particular; the latter was and still is depicted as the embodiment and leader of all these currents, systems, and ideas. After the rapprochement of both Peking and Moscow with Washington during the last years, each continues to be careful to nurture good official relations with the United States, while in its propaganda, aimed for home consumption and for Communists abroad, it desires to give the appearance of utmost dedication to the struggle for revolution, and still violently denounces the evils of capitalism and imperialism. At the same time it questions the revolutionary zeal of the other Communist superpower and its tactics and methods.

This struggle has extended to international organizations, including Communists and fellow travelers, and to every Communist party in the world. While each Communist conference reasserts as a matter of ritual its faith and conviction that the international scale of Communism tilts increasingly toward socialism and against capitalism, each of the rivals wishes to make certain that the international scale of Communism tilts its own way and against the other Communist superpower. It thus works feverishly to disseminate its own conceptions among all Communist Parties of the world and to discredit and denigrate those of the Communist rival. It uses all instruments at its disposal to achieve this goal, namely, state and economic power, foreign aid programs, technical and propaganda experts, and foreign policy in and outside of the UN, and it unleashes an unceasing propaganda barrage in its own behalf and against the other Communist superpower. This extensive propagandistic effort of Peking against Moscow and vice-versa plays, of course, into the hands of their common enemies, variously called by them capitalist and imperialist countries, including, obviously, those practicing political democracy.

Garnering votes within the Communist bloc is as much a power play as gathering the necessary votes in any other body. There is at international Communist conferences a constant maneuvering for and wooing of votes. The Soviet Union is assured of the unquestioned loyalty and the votes of the East European Communist countries. Maverick Rumania, however, dissident Yugoslavia, and Albania—China's spokesman and stalwart follower on the European continent, herself in safe geographic distance from the USSR and thus enjoying a greater measure of security and elbow room—cannot be counted on by the USSR in a vote on an issue related to the Sino-Soviet rift.

Asian Communist countries, on the other hand, especially immediate neighbors of the CPR such as North Korea and North Vietnam, are, of course, susceptible to China's pressure, which they can never hope to escape. But they have been careful not to alienate the USSR in view of the vast benefits of an economic and military nature that technologically advanced Moscow is able to confer—or to withhold. Also, to increase their leverage upon the neighboring CPR, these Communist countries are vitally interested in dealing with the USSR to reduce to a minimum their geographic, economic, and military dependence on China and to secure more breathing space. They are in regard to China in a situation similar to that of Rumania and Yugoslavia vis-à-vis the Soviet Union; all are driven to deal with the other Communist superpower. Other large Communist Parties in Europe, such as the Italian and French, though either to the right of Moscow or Moscow-oriented, have found it advantageous to disapprove of Moscow's policy toward Peking at one time or the other—without endorsing in any way the latter's course of policy and action. They are basically interested in pursuing individual, divergent courses and, in some measure, in polycentrism. The dispute between Peking and Moscow has raised the bargaining power and prestige of even the smallest Communist-ruled state and Party, and has forever ended bipolarism within the Communist world. The struggle for domination of Communist Parties and world organizations in general, whether engaged in trade-union activities, concerned with peace, or directing a special appeal to youth, women, or geographic regions and races, is a war waged for power and control, and it adds a momentum of its own to the Sino-Soviet dispute.

There are elements of immaturity, if not outright irrationality, in the behavior of the CPC toward the CPSU. The anger and frustration of a junior partner that has acted repeatedly against the advice of Moscow, and whose ruling Party, of a country with an older civilization than that of the USSR, is balking at its minor role in world Communism, are psychologically understandable. Yet, the demand for sharing atomic weapons, made at the very birth of the conflict, should not have been allowed to play a central role in the emerging rift. Likewise, Peking's occasional claiming its right to share the benefits of the economically more advanced Soviet partner defies cool rational calculations; it is an upshot, however, of Communist fanaticism, of the combination of a literal belief in the Communist credo and a selfish naiveté. Yet the hard-boiled and Macchiavellian CPC, in spite of repeated exuberant professions of international comradeship, should not have permitted itself to become a prisoner of its own slogans about international brotherhood and solidarity. Did not pure sentimentality, even passion, here replace cold-blooded realism? The unceasing propaganda campaign minimizing the horrors of a hydrogen war was hardly designed to make friends among either the uncommitted Third World—the alleged beneficiary of Peking's radical and uncompromising policy on war and on social and national liberation—or even the saner elements of Communists and other revolutionaries fighting for national and social emancipation. These circles, while interested in national freedom and independence, want national life, not collective suicide, not dying with a beautiful proletarian slogan on their lips. Fanaticism of a revolutionary and chauvinist type, perhaps unmatched, certainly unsurpassed, in history, is the keystone of some of the horrendous aspects of Maoism (more recently soft-pedaled) and its implications for world affairs.

It is to the fusion of Marxist-Leninist theory and ideology, of the hunger for power in its domestic and international aspects, and of traditional and twentieth-century nationalism that the roots of the Sino-Soviet dispute must be traced.

Nationalist exuberance if not arrogance—the long-repressed pride of a people used to playing center stage but in its recent history pushed into the background—explains some of the mysteries of Chinese behavior and propaganda prior to and during the Sino-Soviet rift. The CPC could hardly expect that its excessive territorial claims, or any major claims of this sort, would be benevolently received by Moscow, already on the alert vis-à-vis a rival and upstart and probably both annoyed and puzzled by its impudent claims, claims completely unsupported by any corresponding military power. Did Peking really think that Moscow would rush to accommodate the Chinese comrades? Why then did it raise these territorial questions in the first place? Why did it blurt out its sentiments, revealing rage and fury, instead of adhering to the time-honored principles of oriental diplomacy and practice of concealing one's thought and saving face? What practical advantages could Peking expect from letting all Communists and the entire world take a close look into the long-guarded secret of the nature of the relationship between the two largest Communist parties on earth? Was it purposeful for Peking to raise territorial questions at all, especially in view of the circumstance that the USSR had not yielded an inch on any other issue raised previously? True, Peking had become the challenger and Moscow the challenged party. But was it tactically advisable to challenge Moscow on virtually every ground, on issues on which the USSR, relative power aside, could never make any significant concessions?

Peking did not see, or did not wish to see, that the point of no return had been reached. Apparently the CPC entertained the hope that, by its raising the banner of revolution, Communist and national revolutionaries the world over would break with the CPSU and rush to the support of Peking, provincial and isolationist though it was, and impoverished, internationally inexperienced, economically backward, and militarily potent only within a narrow geographic range. Was it a chauvinist blindness, in combination with revolutionary intransigence and an all-pervasive personality cult, that had seized and dazed Peking?

True, in the case of totalitarian powers such as the CPR and the USSR, one must sharply distinguish between propaganda and deed, both at home and abroad. Both countries have shown somewhat greater circumspection in their actual foreign policy than in their reckless propaganda and mutual accusations designed to whip up frenzy within China and the Soviet Union respectively and among revolutionaries and members of Communist parties all over the globe. The invasion of Czechoslovakia, and earlier the Cuban missile crisis, renewed threats to Berlin, and Soviet naval moves in the Mediterranean, are among the boldest and most reckless moves of the Soviet Union beyond her frontiers, while the intervention in Korea and the invasion of India were among the most venturesome and risky thrusts of the CPR. Still, Peking's challenge thrown down to Moscow is the most dangerous of all Peking-initiated moves, surpassing any made previously against any foreign power. Were the gains expected from this policy likely to outweigh the disadvantages and risks that Peking took? Or was the challenge thrown at Moscow the result of a horrendous miscalculation on Peking's part?

Could not Peking have swallowed its pride and suppressed its anger, as it must already have done for a good number of years, if not decades? Marxism-Leninism surely had little to do with the decision to wash dirty linen in public, Maotsetungism probably everything! It is just possible that Mao and Khrushchev especially may have escalated the dispute to a point far beyond genuine Soviet or Chinese interests, that it has reached Frankenstein dimensions, and that both sides find it virtually impossible to extricate themselves from the deep morass of the rift without loss of face and general serious harm.

The CPR and the USSR represent different stages of social and economic development. The outlook of their ruling elites is influenced by the circumstance that their peoples in 1917 and 1949 each started out from a different level; a comparison of the economic stage of the Soviet Union's development in 1917 with that of the Chinese Communists in 1949 shows the former far advanced. The peoples of the USSR had made further striking industrial progress before World War II, and in spite of painful wartime losses had quickly rebuilt and even increased their industrial potential. The living standard in the Soviet Union has been slowly raised and a new class society, though embarrassingly protesting its classless character, has emerged in the USSR. Modest Soviet comforts appear highly suspect to the spartan Chinese, with their still underdeveloped economy and their strong egalitarianism, which is reminiscent of the Russian civil war period. The Chinese Communists, whose industrial power grows at a more moderate pace, judge Soviet economy with a good deal of envy and claim to detect in it sure signs of the bourgeoisification of Soviet society, for which they profess nothing but disdain. To the Chinese Communists the USSR appears an increasingly rich country with a much higher living standard and higher level of modernization than the CPR and, apparently, a higher standard than in their eyes befits a revolutionary and proletarian nation.

The Soviet Union, in its alleged selfishness, is unwilling to share its prosperity, not to mention its weaponry, with poorer and underdeveloped countries, even though they are ruled by socialist comrades. Communist China is interested in arousing, and politically exploiting, the envy of other poor, underdeveloped nations against the USSR. The different notions about Soviet and Chinese tactics and strategy, about peaceful coexistence, the apparently greater willingness of the Chinese Communist leadership to move, at least theoretically, to the very brink of war, is to a large extent rooted in the relative poverty of China and the relative wealth of the USSR. The poverty of China explains to a large part the greater preparedness of the Chinese Communist leadership to assume dangerous risks. The very wealth laboriously accumulated in the Soviet Union after the destruction in World War II tends to restrain the Soviet peoples and its leadership from an adventurous policy that would threaten to destroy once more such material progress as has been achieved. Because of her advanced economic level the Soviet Union has much more to lose in an atomic war than underdeveloped China.

Only in manpower is China richer than the USSR. But this is a kind of wealth that makes for recklessness rather than restraint. Mao and the Chinese Communist leadership, ruling the most populous country in the world, seem prepared to make sacrifices in an atomic war before which smaller peoples tremble, fearing complete destruction and annihilation of their very physical and national existence. The prospect of atomic war frightens even the USSR, with only a third of the population of the CPR. Though China has experienced a long civil war and the war of resistance against Japan, her losses have been relatively small compared to those suffered by the Soviet Union in manpower and facilities during the Russian Civil War and the Great Fatherland War. China's very backwardness has set limits to the amount of destruction that could be wreaked upon her. Khrushchev, with some justification, derided the Chinese Communist leadership's one-sided and provincial conception of war, based upon the limited Chinese experience of guerrilla war against the Kuomintang and Japan.[4] The concept of guerrilla war itself is tied up with underdeveloped nations and a backward economy, rather than with an economically highly developed society, the urban industries of which can be pulverized at a moment's notice at the very outbreak of an atomic war.* The distance that separates the CPR from the Soviet Union in regard to their economic and social development explains to a large degree the difference in their political and tactical outlook, their views on war and peace, revolution, coexistence, and national liberation.

Finally, Communist China and the Soviet Union are in different stages of the proletarian revolution. The CPR's Revolution of 1949 is almost a quarter of a century old. Due to the longevity of Mao and other Chinese Communist leaders, to their unbroken revolutionary zeal, to the turmoil of the recent Great Proletarian Cultural Revolution, and to the numerous hints of similar revolutions to follow, the CPR today still seems to live in the frenzied atmosphere of 1949, and the Chinese masses, seemingly willing and obedient, are on the march toward total reform of life and society. In the Soviet Union, however, the revolutionary ardor has long since cooled down; the leadership has frequently changed; bureaucrats and planners, builders, and engineers, rather than revolutionaries, are in political and economic control. Only lip-service is paid to further revolution at home and abroad.

The Sino-Soviet rift has a long history. But if we limit our vision to the

4. J. Crankshaw, ed., *Khrushchev Remembers* (Boston, 1970), pp. 467, 470-71.
*Though the Soviets encouraged guerrilla warfare during the Great Fatherland War, it was to supplement, not to supplant the regular war against the Nazi armies.

time span since about 1956, when the Twentieth Party Congress of the CPSU and the Eighth Party Congress of the CPC were held, certain major phases seem to stand out clearly, marked respectively by the years 1958 and 1960, 1962-63, 1966 and 1969. The years 1958 and 1960 marked the incipient stages of the dispute which, though repressed, could no longer be hidden and was openly debated in party forums. In the years 1962-63 the dispute burst into the open and definitely shattered the myth of the Communist monolithic bloc. These years saw the two Communist superpowers in sharpest ideological, organizational, and tactical confrontation with each other. With 1966, the beginning of the Great Proletarian Cultural Revolution, the dispute was further exacerbated, though the CPR reentered the international arena with a vengeance. But it did so hardly in a true spirit of internationalism—which did not motivate the USSR either—but to intensify the competition and the struggle with Moscow and to strengthen its own position in Asia and the world.

Until the late fifties both the CPC and the CPSU, seemingly marching shoulder to shoulder toward the joint goal of Communism, agreed in the main as to direction, speed, the major enemies and obstacles on the road, and the tactics to be pursued. They had every interest in suppressing points of differences between themselves in regard to their own people and the world at large.

For a considerable length of time the dispute between Peking and Moscow was a war by proxy. Each had a whipping boy; Peking had Yugoslavia, Moscow had Albania. Each advertised its likes and dislikes to the other Communist superpower, and admonished and warned it, indirectly still, but in an unmistakable manner. The disagreements first centered on the role of Stalin and on Stalinism, China's "Great Leap Forward," and her claims to greater prominence and equality, which were embedded in her domestic program; on the question of the extent of economic and military help to the CPR; and on the question of Communist tactics, war, and peaceful coexistence; the differences broadened subsequently.

For a time Moscow's and Peking's criticism of each other took the high road of pure theory and was esoteric in character. Increasingly, however, imperious, brutal, and vicious verbal assault took its place. The two Parties, which for a long time had refrained from attacking and insulting each other, resorted to these very devices. By 1963 the war against straw men such as Albania and Yugoslavia had turned into a bitter struggle involving the two main contenders directly. And the acrimony and fury aimed against the other Communist superpower often exceeded that against the imperialist archenemy itself, the U.S. The comparison with Hitlerism and fascism made by both Peking and Moscow, plainly unthinkable in the early stages of the Sino-Soviet conflict, became more frequent.

The Moscow-Peking alliance of 1950 had gradually been transformed into a cold war between them, just as the military alliance between East and West during the Great Fatherland War had given way to the cold war in 1945-46. As in Europe, the cold war at a few critical moments threatened to turn into a shooting war; the Sino-Soviet border clashes in 1969 constituted a menace to the peace of Asia.

The major turning points in the Sino-Soviet dispute are probably the years 1958, when the first hints of a serious dispute emerged, and 1960, when the withdrawal of the Soviet experts from China occurred. The dispute reached a new stage with the publication in China of the long essay *Long Live Leninism* in 1960. Differences between Peking and Moscow were now gradually revealed, but still with great circumspection and caution on both sides, and within Party forums, in words that could be fully comprehended only by those initiated. Both sides held the view that baring the dispute was in the interest of neither Party, and both feared to cross the Rubicon. Only gradually did the rift grow in scope and depth, the criticism become more direct and pointed, and the language used become sharper and more vitriolic.

W. E. Griffith, one of the leading authorities on the Sino-Soviet rift, holds that the "point of no return" was reached in 1959.[5] It rather appears that the Cuban missile crisis and the subsequent revelation of the Sino-Soviet differences and the bursting of the schism into the open in 1962-63 presented the crucial divide in the dispute. Once the rift was revealed to the Soviet and Chinese masses, it gained a momentum of its own, playing upon xenophobia and mistrust in both countries, and it was then virtually impossible to find the way back to diminish tension.

Open and sharp verbal warfare followed only in the wake of the missile crisis in 1962. After the dispute about the Test Ban Treaty in 1963, no holds were barred. By the time of the beginning of the Great Proletarian Revolution, virtually all divisive issues had been fully explored and revealed by both sides, but the rift grew still wider and deeper. The border clashes of 1969 represented the final climax. In spite of the absence of such clashes since, there is no assurance that similar incidents threatening to explode into an atomic holocaust might not reoccur. In any case, the last years have seen no let-up in the Sino-Soviet dispute, no demonstration of a genuine will to coexistence.

5. W. E. Griffith, *Peking, Moscow and Beyond* (Washington, D.C., 1973), p. 2.

2

From Unequal Partnership
to "Friendship and Alliance,"
1917-1956

China, Chinese Communism, and the USSR, 1917-1945

The October Revolution directed the attention of the Soviet leadership to the spread of revolution not only in Europe but also in Asia. Frustrated in the West in the early postwar period, Soviet Russia turned her eyes increasingly eastward. As early as 1919 Trotsky considered China "an important base for world revolution." The Soviets saw there the most populous country in the world, which in 1911 had toppled the foreign Manchu dynasty and ushered in a republic. China then was plagued by internal confusion and warlordism and a series of so-called governments in Peking that were unable to control the entire country and to come to grips with a multitude of pressing political, economic and social, national and international problems. Between September 1920 and 1922-23 the Soviets, sensing their opportunity, staged three major conferences that dealt with China. One, the Congress of Oriental Nations, met in Baku in September 1920; another one convened in Moscow in January 1921. In 1922 the Congress of Far Eastern Toilers focused also on China.

Interest in closer relations between China and Soviet Russia was mutual. Sun Yat-sen, leading figure in the Kuomintang, held that China was badly in need of foreign aid and advice relating to the organization of a modern army. Rebuffed by the United States, Great Britain, and Germany, he turned to Russia for help. At first the Russian Revolution had not struck any responsive chord in China. But the Soviets, after regaining control of Siberia during the Civil War in 1920, approached China with the seemingly generous proposition of renouncing the extraterritorial rights and special privileges in North Manchuria that Tsarism had wrested from her. This renunciation, especially if contrasted with the attitude of the Western powers, which continued to cling to their privileges, made an extremely favorable impression upon China and created a propitious atmosphere for cooperation between the two governments. The Russian envoy Adolph Joffe, dispatched to Peking, was given a cordial welcome in the Chinese capital both officially and in intellectual circles.

On the international plane, both revolutionary Russia and revolutionary China were rather isolated. Moscow had been invited neither to the Paris Peace Conference in 1919 nor to the Washington Conference in 1921-22, and China too was rather ignored; at the Washington Conference the West dealt only with the militarist regime in Peking. Both Russia and China were overwhelmingly peasant countries, economically underdeveloped and eager for rapid industrialization; both, until recently, had suffered from monarchist absolutism and in both countries a recent revolution had swept away the monarchic foundations. While in Russia the Bolsheviks, the most radical party, had already seized power, in China social and economic revolution had merely caused ripples in the huge waves that swept over China. Revolution in China was still rent by political disunity, territorial divisions, and social cleavages, and was hampered by general backwardness.

Though Sun Yat-sen was anxious for Russian help, he by no means trusted Russia fully. But in a joint Sino-Russian Manifesto of January 26, 1923, Sun Yat-sen asserted his opinion that "the communistic order or even the Soviet system" could not be introduced in China, since she lacked suitable conditions for the successful establishment of either. Joffee expressed full agreement with this view and held that "China's paramount and most pressing problem" was to achieve national unification and to attain full independence, and he assured Peking of Moscow's support. Joffee also reaffirmed an earlier Soviet pledge, contained in the message of September 27, 1920, that Soviet Russia was prepared to annul all treaties concluded by Tsarist Russia with China and to surrender all concessions granted to Imperial Russia. He also promised that Russia would not pursue an imperialist policy in Outer Mongolia, one aiming at the separation of this province from China.[1] In spite of misgivings about the possibility of Russia's interference in China's affairs, Sun signed the treaty. In the name of his party, now renamed the Kuomintang (Nationalist) Party, Sun not only thus received aid from Soviet Russia abroad, but also concluded an alliance with the nascent CPC domestically.

1. C. Brandt, B. Schwartz, J. K. Fairbank, *A Documentary History of Chinese Communism* (Cambridge, Mass., 1952), pp. 70-71.

Implementing the treaty, Sun, in August 1923, sent Chiang Kai-shek, his chief-of-staff, to Moscow for a close study of the organization of the Red Army. After a stay of four months in the Soviet Union, Chiang returned home to head the Whampoa Military Academy. The Russian General Galen (alias Bluecher) became one of the first foreign military advisers in charge of training cadets, the first of altogether more than 30 Russian advisers sent to reorganize the Chinese army.

The Comintern too sent its agent Michael Borodin, who arrived in October 1923 to help reorganize the Chinese government and party structures.* Having been appointed High Councilor of the Cantonese government, he advised Sun how to transform the Kuomintang into a mass organization. The first national Kuomintang Congress in 1924 deliberately appealed to China's downtrodden millions, proclaiming that the national revolution would be victorious if only peasants and workers would join in the national effort. Both foreigners, who controlled much of Chinese industry, banking, and shipping, and China's propertied classes became increasingly alarmed about the Kuomintang's collaboration with the Bolsheviks. Sun, on the other hand, thundered against the foreign governments that sent remittances of Cantonese custom revenues to Peking, thus giving moral prestige to the Peking authorities. Continuing to work for the unification of China, he aimed at the reconciliation of hostile groups, extending from conservatives to the extreme Left. Sun was a man dedicated to Western ideals and to Western concepts of liberty and democracy, but toward the end of his life he had come to lean heavily toward Moscow. He had come to suspect that the West feared the formation of a strong, united, and nationalistic China.[2]

The Kuomintang was reorganized after the pattern of the Russian Communist Party; strict discipline, mass propaganda, and all other paraphernalia of Communist political organization and activity, as distinguished from Communist doctrine, were copied by the Chinese nationalist party organization. At the same time the Kuomintang Party turned away from democracy and leaned increasingly toward authoritarianism. Sun's stress on a merely temporary dictatorship—a period of tutelage by the Party for a number of years—was abandoned. The Kuomintang tended in practice to perpetuate its monopolistic power.

The new relationship between Moscow and the Kuomintang entailed a change also in the policy of the CPC. The third Congress of the CPC, which met in Canton in 1923, had established an alliance with the

*Other leading Comintern agents in China between 1920 and 1931 were Grigorii Voitinskii, the Dutch agent, G. Maring, the Indian M. N. Roy, Heinz Neumann, and Pavel Mif, formerly Director of the Sun Yat-sen University in Moscow.

2. *Ibid.*, pp. 72-73.

Kuomintang.[3] Mao himself worked in the executive committees of both parties in Shanghai. Later he also became a member of the Communist Politburo. His experiences in his native Hunan between 1925 and 1926 opened his eyes to the revolutionary potentialities, especially of "poor peasants."[4] He formed more than 20 peasant unions, the nucleus, as he called it later, of "a great peasant movement." Abandoning rigid Marxist conceptions, he conceived new and independent ideas about the role of the peasantry in the Chinese revolution. Contrary to the views of the Chinese communist leaders and the Russian advisers, Mao urged the adoption by the CPC of a radical land policy and the concentration of efforts upon the peasants rather than upon the small and vulnerable Chinese proletariat.

Sun, pursuing his policies of "Alliance with Russia" and "Admission of the Communists," was convinced that the Kuomintang would be able to control the Communists. Soviet and Communist policies in turn were based upon Lenin's "Theses on the National and Colonial Question" of the Second Comintern Congress in 1920, which had demanded temporary agreements or even alliances with bourgeois-democratic and national liberation movements in dependent countries, though never specifying their character and duration. Each side aimed at having the other perform coolie services for itself.

The collaboration of the Kuomintang with the Communists until early 1927 was mutually profitable. The Kuomintang, with Soviet help, obtained an efficient party apparatus, strengthened the organization of the army, and secured a foothold among the peasant masses. Through the Kuomintang armies, the Communists in turn, gained enormous influence over numerous workers' and peasants' organizations in South and Central China. In 1927 their contest climaxed in Chiang's victory and the Communists' debacle. Yet, while Chiang fulfilled the task of national unification and later brought about the abolition of the unequal treaties, the task of social and economic reform, the program enshrined in Sun's "People's Livelihood," remained an unfulfilled legacy; this shortcoming ultimately was to play into the hands of the CPC.

In the wake of the successful Northern Expedition, which established the Nationalists in Peking, came the break of the Kuomintang-Communist entente. Mao returned to Hunan, continuing to incite the peasants to revolt. After one of these revolts, "the Autumn Crop Uprising," was crushed, Mao lost his seat in the Politburo and perhaps was even expelled from the Party; his unauthorized activities, challenging Party doctrine itself, were "repudiated." Yet the Russian-oriented leadership of the CPC, which after

3. *Ibid.*, pp. 71-72.
4. Stuart R. Schram, *The Political Thought of Mao Tse-tung* (New York, 1969), pp. 241f.

the 1927 split with the Kuomintang moved toward a workers' revolution in the cities, failed disastrously. At the same time Mao's revolutionary efforts in the countryside were crowned with success. Thus Mao's prestige in Party circles rose, while Russian-sponsored leaders like Li Li-san suffered in comparison.[5]

Between 1928 and 1930, a nucleus of the Red Army was created and Communist power was consolidated in the Hunan-Kiangsi border districts and a Soviet Republic proclaimed. There Soviets were formed, land was redistributed, and guerrilla bands of armed peasants were organized. While Li Li-san was still supported by Moscow and the Comintern, his failure to take Changsha resulted in his demotion. He lost his seat in the Politburo and was sent for "reeducation" to Moscow, where he remained for fifteen years. Mao's leadership, on the other hand, was no longer disputed.[6] Like Tito later, Mao, though a dedicated Communist, had never been Moscow's agent in the true sense of the term, but in the last resort was a self-made and independent man.

By defying, or at least ignoring, Moscow at crucial stages and over significant issues in his rise to power, Mao and the CPC avoided the stigma of being a mere instrument and the stooge of a foreign power. Mao rejected the course charted by the Comintern, though often paying lip service to it, and adopted a policy suited to Chinese conditions. He emphasized the need for peasant and army support and stressed the necessity of a domestic four-power bloc, which actually included about 99 percent of the Chinese people.[7] By later adopting also a strong anti-Japanese national stand, the CPC appealed powerfully to the masses of the Chinese people and thus acted as a unifying rather than a divisive force. At the same time, the Kuomintang, which had failed in the twenties to assert itself strongly against Western imperialism, failed also after 1931 to take a strong national stance against Japanese aggression. Furthermore, it called a halt to social and agrarian reforms and also alienated the intelligentsia, traditionally a most important segment of Chinese society. Whatever the Kuomintang's achievements in the twenties and thirties, Chiang and his party neglected to offer the Chinese people a truly inspiring ideology and did not live up to Sun's promise of democracy. These failures of the Kuomintang contributed to the ultimate success of the CPC.

Between 1930 and 1934 the Kuomintang made several attempts to crush the Kiangsi Soviet and other soviets. The Communists broke through the Kuomintang blockade that had been erected around them, marched first southwest and finally north into the Shensi province that adjoined the

5. Brandt, Schwartz, Fairbank, pp. 165-66, 179-84.
6. *Ibid.*, p. 217.
7. Schram, p. 48.

Mongolian steppe region. After this arduous Long March, they arrived in North Shensi only 20,000 men strong[8] and were soon calling for national unity against Japanese aggression. Once again they organized new soviets, redistributed land, and built a new Soviet state, similar to the one that had been destroyed in Kiangsi.

After 1935, when they had moved their forces to the north, the Communists were in a better position to establish close contact with Moscow. Yet there is little evidence of the presence of Russian Communist agents in Shensi. Though the USSR, with an eye on Tokyo, was clearly interested in preserving the united front in China and in influencing the CPC along these lines, she may have been hesitant to reestablish in the thirties the close relationship with the CPC that had ended on an unhappy note in the twenties. There were also increasing indications that the CPC, while perhaps not challenging Moscow directly, was likely to pursue its own course, and that the usual kind of comradely persuasion or pressure would be of little avail.

In December 1936 Chiang, having been taken prisoner at Sian, pledged resistance to Japan and peace with the Communists, which the latter demanded as price for his release. Chiang granted amnesty to the rebels and the Communists thereupon acknowledged his authority. A united front was agreed upon, which was to oppose any future Japanese aggression. Nominally, the Communists abolished their independent state, calling it now the Border District Administration, and suspended further land distribution though they continued to insist on rent reduction. The Red Army was renamed the Eighth Route Army and placed under the strategic direction of Chiang. As one keen student of Chinese politics remarked, Chiang saved "face," but the Communists obtained the substance of their demands.[9] They had forced Chiang to change the character and course of his domestic policy as well as his policy toward Japan.

Mao's rise in the Communist movement, which gave him a commanding role in the early thirties, took place without any aid or encouragement from Moscow and the Comintern. On the other hand, Mao at no time was scorned or criticized in the Soviet press or the Comintern. A student of Soviet policy toward China in the thirties has reached the conclusion that Moscow's estimate of Mao, prior to 1935, appeared to have been most cautious. He also held that Mao's position in the CPC and relationship to existing Party leadership was "left obscure" in Soviet writings of the period, probably either to acclaim him if it became necessary, or repudiate him as a mere peasant leader if he should fail.[10] Officially at least, the

    8. Charles B. McLane, *Soviet Policy and the Chinese Communists 1931-1946* (New York, 1958), pp. 53-58.
    9. Fitzgerald, *The Birth of Communist China*, p. 82.
    10. Brandt, Schwartz, Fairbank, p. 184.

Comintern tried long to ignore rivalries within the leadership of the Chinese Party. Between 1931 and 1935, Stalin himself made only one passing reference to the soviets in China and no reference at all to the Communist movement as such.[11]

Compared to the twenties, Comintern influence in the Chinese Communist movement continued to decline during the Kiangsi period. This may be attributed to several circumstances: First, the international revolutionary movement had generally become more an instrument of the Soviet Union's national policy, in accordance with Stalin's proclamation of the need to establish "Socialism in one country" and in accordance with the change in Soviet priorities. Also, Japanese aggression in Asia and Hitler's rise to power in Germany created a new and dangerous situation for the Soviet Union. The Soviets responded by establishing diplomatic relations with the Kuomintang government in Nanking in 1932[12] and with the U.S. the following year. In 1934 the USSR entered the League of Nations and in 1935 signed defensive alliances with France and Czechoslovakia. These diplomatic and military arrangements took precedence over spreading world revolution; revolution held out little likelihood of success and would only defeat the chances of rapprochement with the West and, in Asia, with the Kuomintang.

At the time of the Sian incident, Soviet Russia was friendly disposed toward the Kuomintang. On December 14, 1936, *Pravda* commented that the Nanking government, despite earlier waverings, had shown ability to "lead the defense" against Japan.[13] A definite agreement between the Kuomintang and the Communists, however, was concluded only after the Japanese had launched their assault on China on July 7, 1937. Soon thereafter, in August 1937, followed the Sino-Soviet nonaggression pact, and in September came the formal announcement of the United Front in China.

According to the terms of the United Front of September 1937, which partly repeated the agreement of December 1936, the Communists agreed to fight for the Three People's Principles of Sun Yat-sen, to give up armed rebellion, red propaganda, land confiscation, and the soviets. The Soviet Chinese government was nominally abolished, the name of the Red Army was abandoned, and its forces were to be reorganized as part of the troops of the National Government.

Yet the objectives of the Chinese Communists and of Soviet Russia were by no means identical. The Communists had not abandoned their revolutionary program for the sake of collaboration with the Kuomintang and of the United Front policy; many of their concessions were rather sham than reality. There was never any intention on the Communist side to re-

11. McLane, p. 47.
12. *Ibid.*, pp. 11-12.
13. *Pravda*, Dec. 14, 1936.

linquish the identity of the CPC.[14] The "Propaganda Outline" of June 1938 upheld the ultimate Communist goals of the revolution. Another pamphlet of the CPC of May 1838 had appealed to Party members not only to fight Japan "but also to struggle for communism."[15]

Soviet Russia, on the other hand, was primarily interested in an effective all-Chinese resistance, which was likely to diminish Japanese pressure on Russia's exposed eastern frontier. *Pravda* frequently singled out Chiang for special praise and even assured the Kuomintang that the new policy of the Chinese Communists was not merely tactically motivated. In 1938 the CPC sent Chou En-lai as liaison officer to Chungking and there he entered the national government.

For strategic reasons, Soviet Russia was deeply interested in preserving the United Front policy in China, as was revealed by Wang Ming following his return from Moscow at the end of 1937 as the official emissary of the Comintern. A regular and respected contributor to Comintern publications, he had the reputation of being one of the leading experts on colonial affairs. Quite in accord with the Soviet point of view, he asserted that leadership in the war should be exercised by the Kuomintang rather than by the CPC. Most important, Wang Ming favored a course that would have resulted in the complete and permanent subordination of the CPC to the Kuomintang, the submerging of its independence, and would have precluded any significant future role for the CPC. Mao, however, weathered the crisis and emerged victorious over Wang Ming and the Russian and Comintern point of view. The official CPSU history, published in 1951, denounced what it then considered as a "Right opportunist standpoint," by implication criticizing Mao.[16]

Moscow's United Front policy of the thirties was born of the Soviet desire to gain security and protection against Germany and Japan. The Soviet Union's sudden interest in the League of Nations, formerly denounced as an imperialist tool, and in collective security was of course indissolubly linked with this main objective. The USSR strove for diplomatic alliances with capitalist states that were resolved to oppose fascist aggressor states and encouraged political alliances between Communists and non-Communists in democratic countries. While Soviet Russia clung to the hope of collective security in Europe until 1939, in the Far East she had to abandon every hope in regard to it as early as 1937, when Japan launched her full-scale aggression against China.

The USSR frequently proposed a nonaggression pact to Japan. Numerous petty grievances, which in the aggregate had a very divisive impact,

14. Mclane, p. 106.
15. Brandt, Schwartz, Fairbank, pp. 258-59.
16. Quoted by McLane, pp. 119, 120-23.

delayed, however, the signing of this treaty. These grievances centered on Japanese fishing rights along the Soviet coast line north of Vladivostok, on payments to the Soviet Union for the Chinese Eastern Railway, on oil and other concessions in North Sakhalin and, last but not least, on border violations along the Amur and along the Mongolian-Manchukuan border region. A number of clashes between June 1937 and the summer of 1939, the latter definitely provoked by Japan, left no doubt about increasing Russian preparedness.

The Sino-Soviet nonaggression pact of August 21, 1937, was supplemented by secret agreements pledging Soviet economic aid to the Nanking government. Moscow extended considerable aid to the Kuomintang for the purpose of encouraging and sustaining resistance against Japan. Two years later followed the Nazi-Soviet pact of August 1939, in which the USSR and Nazi Germany pledged not to attack each other; this pact actually flung open the doors to the European war. Both Chiang and Mao reacted relatively mildly to the Nazi-Soviet pact, after having apparently been assured by Moscow that its aid to China would continue.

Having signed a pact with Nazi Germany, the Soviet Union, on April 13, 1941, signed a similar pact with Japan. Following the pattern of the Sino-Soviet pact of 1937, the treaty pledged respect for the territorial integrity of the other party and neutrality in the event the other side should become involved in war. Both the USSR and Japan apparently aimed at limiting their risks and at avoiding a two-front war. There was no reference to China whatsoever in the treaty.

This time, however, Chinese reaction varied. The Chungking press seemed disturbed, though Chiang himself was confident that Russian aid would continue; the Chinese Communists appeared similarly hopeful. Soviet aid to Chungking indeed continued for at least two years, even after Kuomintang-Chinese Communist relations began to worsen. In Moscow's view, the Nationalists formed the focal point of resistance to Japan and aid to China was thus imperative. By 1941, Comintern publications, just like Soviet publications, were primarily concerned about bolstering Chungking and the Kuomintang rather than the CPC.[17]

When war with Japan broke out in 1937, both Communists and Nationalists fought the invader. Yet, after the first two years of the war against Japan, clashes also took place between the Kuomintang and the Communists. In January 1941 Kuomintang troops in the Yangtse valley destroyed Communist guerrilla troops, the so-called New Fourth Army; according to Yenan, 6,000 Communist soldiers were killed on that occasion. Mao bristled with indignation and most solemnly warned Chungking of

17. *Ibid.*, pp. 136-37.

dire consequences. The Soviet and Comintern press, however, waited ten days before even mentioning the incident, and then refrained from editorial comment.[18] Yet the CPC remained confident that in the end it would overcome both the Japanese invaders and the rival Kuomintang.

The Nationalists, driven from their capital, Nanking, and later from Hankow, found refuge in the western mountainous regions, choosing Chungking in the Szechwan Province as capital. The Chungking government was remote both from the eastern Japanese-occupied seaboard and from the north, where the Communists had entrenched themselves. It was unable to assert its control over the Communists, who retained the Red Army as well as their soviet type of government. The Chungking government also made no effort to recover lost territories and, unlike the Communists, did not engage in extensive guerrilla warfare behind the Japanese lines. Nor did the Kuomintang carry out far-reaching land reforms or introduce other social and political changes in response to urgent popular demands.

Mao and the Chinese Communists never questioned Moscow's rapidly alternating and often puzzling tactics in Asia and Europe, nor the basic and ultimate community of interests between Chinese Communism and the USSR.[19] But they always feared a Nationalist capitulation to Japan. Though not challenging Moscow outright, Mao was pursuing his own course. For the CPC the struggle for postwar control of all of China had already begun.

After Hitler's attack in 1941, Soviet Russia faced mortal danger. At the same time, her Far Eastern front remained quiet. The Soviets' main interest during this period, until the spring and summer of 1945, was to continue to encourage China's national struggle against the Japanese invader, to prevent Chungking's capitulation, and to maintain the uneasy alliance between Chungking and Yenan—all likely to lessen the chances of a Japanese thrust into Siberia. And the Kuomintang, rather than the Chinese Communists, was considered the kingpin of the Chinese resistance struggle. The Soviets' state Encyclopedic Institute, in a survey of Chinese history, centered its attention on the Kuomintang and almost ignored the activities of the CPC after 1935.

Yet the CPC seemed little concerned about this lack of interest on the part of its Soviet mentor. It seemed also to care little when in May 1943 the Comintern was dissolved, largely in deference and as an assurance to the Western powers. To the contrary, Mao, though acknowledging the "great assistance" rendered by the Comintern in the past, underlined that the Chinese Communists had "long since been able to determine their

18. *Ibid.*, p. 149.
19. *Ibid.*, p. 148.

political line independently and to carry it out in accordance with the concrete situation and the specific circumstances in their country."[20] The disbandment of the Comintern did not weaken, but according to Mao, rather strengthened the CPC, making it more national and more suited to the necessities of the war against fascism. The ties between Moscow and Yenan had worn thin and the relations between the two parties after the dissolution of the Comintern continued therefore without change.

The war years represented an extraordinary growth for Communist China. While in 1937 the total Party membership was estimated to be 40,000, by 1942 it had increased to 800,000. The concern for quality and theoretical indoctrination and purity was demonstrated by the reform movement of 1942, which became known as the cheng feng movement. It aimed at, actually meant, "correction of unorthodox tendencies," and its major goal was to make "Marxism Chinese," an idea expressed by Mao as early as 1938. Some theoreticians in Yenan went so far as to assert that the Chinese Communist experience had no peer in the world revolutionary movement. And Liu Shao-ch'i claimed in 1943 that the "Chinese Communist Party has in its 22 years passed through more great events than any other Party in the world and has had richer experience in the revolutionary struggle."[21]

During the war the Soviets, understandably, minimized or deliberately ignored such views. But after the war they once again stressed the unique value and the primacy of Bolshevik experience for revolutionary movements everywhere. The Chinese, on the other hand, never went so far as to press their claims to the extent of alienating Moscow and seemed fully aware of the continuing basic identity of interests between Yenan and Moscow. In important matters there would be no doubt as to the loyalty of Yenan and to the deference, at least in matters of vital interest, to the Soviet point of view.

During the last two years of the war, when differences between the two Chinese parties escalated and the United Front was virtually destroyed, the Soviet government began critically to reappraise the role of the Kuomintang. At the same time, Soviet-Kuomintang relations once again grew tense over Sinkiang, which had long been a source of dispute. Later, in Teheran in 1943, Stalin revealed privately to Roosevelt his own low opinion of China's fighting capacity. The following year the Soviets ceased to suppress the reports of internal divisions in China and shed some of their enthusiasm about the role of Chiang and especially of the Kuomintang in the anti-Japanese struggle in China. Still, Moscow did not demonstrate any

20. Decisions by Communist Parties, *Kommunisticheskii Internatsional*, nos. 5-6 (May-June 1943), p. 23.
21. Quoted by McLane, p. 163.

growing interest in or appreciation of the services rendered by the CPC for the cause of international Communism or that of national liberation. The USSR virtually ignored the Seventh Congress of the CPC held in Yenan in April and May 1945, though this was the first full Congress convened since 1928! At this time, which marked the end of the war in Europe and Soviet preparations for entry into the war against Japan, the USSR thought more about regaining her own geopolitical, military, and economic position in the Far East than about decisively influencing the outcome of the impending struggle between Chungking and Yenan.

At the Yalta Conference, Roosevelt and Churchill, anxious to have Russia enter the war in Asia as soon as possible after the termination of the war in Europe, gave Stalin far-reaching concessions in the Far East. The concessions included the preservation of the status quo in Outer Mongolia, a joint Sino-Soviet operation of the Chinese Eastern and South Manchurian Railway through a joint company, and naval bases in South Manchurian ports of Dairen and Port Arthur. In a subsequent Treaty of Friendship and Alliance between Russia and China, concluded on August 14, 1945, Chiang confirmed the Yalta agreements as far as they related to China and even extended them by consenting to a plebiscite in Outer Mongolia on the very question of her independence.[22] On the other hand, the USSR assured China that she would not interfere in Sinkiang, in which she had shown great interest between 1934 and 1942. The Soviet Union also pledged noninterference in China's internal affairs and "moral and military assistance" to Chiang as the central government in China. In return for such substantial concessions from the Kuomintang government, the Soviet Union seemed to write off her Chinese comrades. Contrary to apparent Chinese Communist expectations, such as reported by American Ambassador Hurley one month earlier, in July 1945, the USSR dealt then with Chiang and not with Mao and the CPC.

Mao's Thought and Leninism

Mao was born in Hunan in 1893. The son of a poor peasant who had risen to become a rich peasant and a grain merchant, he was early exposed to Westernizing influences; he avidly read works by Adam Smith, John Stuart Mill, Herbert Spencer, Darwin, Rousseau, and Montesquieu. But an equal if not greater impression upon him was made by tales from Japan, which he heard from one of his teachers who was returning from the Japanese isles; his acquaintance with the Japanese military code bushido;

22. Tien-Fong Cheng, *A History of Sino-Russian Relations* (Washington, D.C., 1957), pp. 271f.

and by books on Napoleon, Peter the Great and other military and political heroes.[23] When on May 4, 1919, a movement of Chinese students was launched against the decision of the Paris Peace Conference to cede former German concessions in Shantung to Japan rather than returning them to China, Mao too gave it strong support. He was then filled with concepts of a vigorous, strident nationalism and the conviction that what China needed was military strength and a heroic posture in order to pull herself out of the mire of backwardness, political dependence, and national disgrace.

A tradition-oriented conservative nationalism thus combined with a revolutionary and Westernized outlook to permeate his thought. Characteristic of the latter strain of his philosophy was a strong individualism and the un-Chinese notion that man, though part of nature, had the power to influence and determine the latter, rather than the mere ability to adapt himself to it.

In his autobiography Mao has described his ideas in the spring of 1918 when he received his diploma from the Normal School of Changsha. His mind then was a "curious mixture of the ideas of liberalism, democratic reformism and utopian socialism." He rejected the so-called three bonds, the very foundation of Confucian morality, but still harked back to China's past, with its legends and its glorification of military valor.

Already on the eve of the foundation of the CPC in 1921 there existed in China a fundamental cleavage between the champions and adherents of Western democracy and those of radical Leninism. Even within the camp of Chinese Communism there were significant differences between the two founders of the Chinese Communist Party, Ch'en Tu-hsiu and Li Ta-chao, reflecting an incipient East-West conflict. The first-named was above all a Westernizer, who was attracted to Communism as the seemingly most efficient instrument for modernizing Chinese society. The latter was a chauvinist, who embraced the Leninist theory of imperialism as a theoretical tool to defeat barbarian imperialism. Mao was indebted to both men, but more to Li than to Ch'en. Like Li, Mao was a genuine Communist revolutionary, his basic outlook being Marxist-Leninist; but restoration of China's glory was to him at least as important as the success of world revolution.[24]

In an article written in 1920, Li had hailed the Russian Revolution as being superior even to the French Revolution of 1789 and, reversing the traditional Marxist view, had voiced the opinion that Russia's very cultural backwardness was in a way advantageous for the cause of progress, since it gave Russia a "great surplus energy." Li imbued Mao with a faith and fervor, and a belief in the revolutionary importance of the peasantry that is

23. Schram, p. 22.
24. *Ibid.*, pp. 41-42.

strongly reminiscent of Russian populism; in view of his peasant upbring-
ing, it was to strike in Mao a responsive chord.

European prewar socialism had assigned backward colonial peoples only
a minor role in the socialist revolution. It had held that they could be
helped only by the revolutionary European proletariat. Lenin had overcome
this Europocentrism; according to him, Asia was to play a much more active part in the world revolution. In his work on imperialism he had developed the idea that the colonies could substantially contribute to the outbreak of revolution in the mother country. The view that revolutions in the
colonies were possible and might speed the outbreak of revolution in
Europe became firmly entrenched in Bolshevik thought during World War
I and found clear expression in Lenin's address to the Second Congress of
the Comintern in July 1920. On the eve of the foundation of the CPC in
1921, these ideas served as guideposts to the Chinese Party.

But the Second Comintern Congress revealed sharp differences within
international communism, which were highlighted by the Italian delegate
Serrati, the Indian communist M. N. Roy, and Lenin himself.[25] Serrati
represented the European or Western point of view, tending to minimize
the importance of underdeveloped countries for the success of world revolution. Roy expressed an opposite Oriental point of view, underlining
the significance of colonial revolution for the proletarian revolution; and
Lenin, the official rapporteur on the national and colonial question, took an
intermediate position. Yet, while prepared to acknowledge that Asia might
play an important role in the coming revolution, one perhaps equal to that
of Europe, he rejected the extreme position of Roy, who asserted that
without a revolution in Asia none could occur in Europe. Many Asian
Communists continued to cling to this view that gave primacy to Asia,
though the Second Comintern Congress, as expected, endorsed Lenin's
stand. The position of the CPC today harks back directly to Roy.

The second Congress also came to grips with the question of the relations of Communist Parties with bourgeois revolutionaries. While Roy insisted on the leadership of the proletariat even in the incipient stages of the
revolutionary movement, Lenin, pragmatist and leader of a primarily European Party, was inclined to leave the leadership of the revolution in the
colonies under some circumstances to the bourgeoisie. The final position of
the Congress was not conclusive in this matter. Again, however, the debate between Lenin and Roy was a kind of forerunner of the contemporary
dispute and current differences between Moscow and Peking.

At its First Congress in 1921 the CPC, aiming at a social rather than a
national revolution and virtually ignoring the decisions adopted at the Sec-

25. *The Second Congress of the Communist International. . . ;* also C. Brandt, *Stalin's Failure in China,* pp. 3-5.

ond International Congress, assumed a rather intolerant attitude toward other revolutionary groups.[26] Some criticized Sun Yat-sen as being hardly better than the northern warlords in China. Mao himself, though of a revolutionary bent, appeared to have been a strong proponent of the alliance with the Kuomintang and the bourgeoisie. Since early 1924 Communists entered the Kuomintang as individual members, and some leading Communists occupied top posts in the Kuomintang Party. This policy, while desired by Moscow, grew also out of calculations of the Chinese Communist leaders themselves. Mao's teacher Li Ta-chao, for instance, had earlier propounded the thesis that the Chinese people constituted in its entirety a "proletarian nation," and in 1922 he had already demanded a "democratic united front." Mao himself, similarly, was to hold that as many as 395 million out of a total of 400 million Chinese were exploited masses. Thus the Chinese people was almost in its entirety a "proletarian" nation; the true revolutionary was thus bound to be a revolutionary nationalist!

Li's influence upon Mao appears to have extended further. In the twenties Li went through an ultra-nationalist phase, accusing Europeans of considering themselves the upper classes and the colored peoples of the world the lower classes. Thus the race struggle actually was only a thinly disguised class struggle. Racial and ethnic animosity was thus given a seemingly Marxist blessing. Li called upon the other races of the world to enter into a class struggle against the white race, an appeal that again was to be heard aloud from Peking in the sixties.

In the twenties Mao demonstrated zeal in cooperating with the Kuomintang; he became known as "Hu Han-min's secretary," the latter being a member of the right wing of the Kuomintang. Mao was convinced that the CPC would ultimately take over the Kuomintang from within. In accordance with the CPC program of 1922 to propagate revolution among the peasants, whose support was considered essential to its success, Mao, like Lenin before him, also rediscovered the revolutionary potential of the peasantry, overcoming both the young revolutionary intellectual's aversion to his youthful peasant surroundings as well as Marxist prejudices against the peasants and the countryside. In 1924 and 1925 Mao spent a few months organizing peasants in Hunan and thereafter played a leading role in the Kuomintang's effort to establish a Peasant Movement Training Institute. While the Communist leadership condemned the peasant riots in China as excesses by paupers, loafers, and gamblers, Mao saw in the stirring of the peasant masses "the rising up of democratic forces in the countryside," praised the leadership of the Peasant Associations by the poor

26. Brandt, Schwartz, Fairbank, pp. 51-52.

peasants, and warned that rejection of the poor peasants meant rejection of revolution itself.[27]

Later Mao credited 70 percent of the accomplishments of the Chinese Revolution to the peasantry. In the Hunan Report he stressed that the peasants must constitute the chief force of the Asiatic revolution.[28] Altogether he conceded to the peasantry a revolutionary initiative and drive that went far beyond what Lenin and Stalin were prepared to acknowledge.

Mao was then clearly reaching out not only for the poor peasants but also for the bourgeoisie, and was by no means repudiating, but rather acknowledging, Chiang Kai-shek's leadership. In early 1926 he saw Chiang as leader of the "red banner of revolution." In a speech at the Second Kuomintang Congress in January 1926, he was still bent on creating the widest possible united front in China for the sake of national revolution. This position was partly due to his always strong nationalist sentiments and outlook, but also, it has been suggested, to his deficient grasp of Marxism and of its class analysis.[29]

In 1926 Chiang laid the foundation for his northern expedition, which was to reunify China. While Stalin for a time opposed the concept of "military expeditions of an offensive character" by the Kuomintang regime in Canton, Mao heartily endorsed Chiang's plan from the beginning and, even after his coup of March 26, 1926, went on collaborating with him longer than did any other leading communist. The very nationalism that led Mao seemingly to subordinate Communist activities to Chiang's national goals made him, however, shift his ground in 1927, when it appeared that Chiang and the Kuomintang were ready to compromise with foreign powers.

Nationalism, the tactics of a United Front, and the appeal to poor peasants aside, Mao's thought, as the Hunan report revealed, was marked by appreciation of the role of organization and of its crucial importance in the political struggle—what one writer called "natural Leninism," because it preceded Mao's acquaintance with Lenin's doctrine. He was also convinced that political struggle was the key to economic struggle.[30] This, of course, was hardly Marxism, though surely theoretical and practical Leninism.

Stalin had given strict orders to the CPC to "restrain" the peasants, in order to avoid a break with the Left Kuomintang. But the pressures mounted to widen the gulf between Chiang and the Communists, and finally even between the Left Kuomintang and the CPC. While Stalin prohi-

27. *Ibid.*, pp. 83-85.
28. *Ibid.*, pp. 53, 79, 83.
29. Schram, p. 47.
30. *Ibid.*, p. 55, 106.

bited the formation of soviets in China until a later stage, Mao called for the immediate setting-up of soviets. He also espoused a more radical agrarian line than Stalin, calling for confiscation of all land, even of that of the smallest peasant landholder, before dividing it up again. Once one of the staunchest proponents of the alliance with the Kuomintang, he was now one of the first and most resolute advocates of a break with it. He also began to conceive the importance of a Red Army for the victory of revolution in China.

Mao bent his efforts toward preparing a revolution that would develop and expand in the countryside and ultimately conquer the cities. Instead of following the familiar Marxist-Leninist prescription, creating a "proletarian" revolution in the urban centers and then establishing control over the entire country, Mao actually reversed the pattern. In the decade 1927-37 he created an organization made up of peasant and rural vagabonds, which, however, called itself the party of the proletariat. In the end Stalin and the Comintern leadership gave their approval to Mao's strategy, though they also supported the Central Committee under Li Lisan and, later, Wang-Ming, whose revolutionary strategy was rather based upon primary reliance on the urban working classes and the conquest of the great Chinese cities. The Comintern continued to raise questions about the inadequate number of proletarians in the CPC. But, as one student of Chinese affairs aptly remarked, the more unconventional Mao became in his tactics and strategy—his actual stress on the peasant base of the Communist movement—"the more impeccably orthodox he became in words."[31]

After the Japanese attack and conquest of Manchuria and the establishment of the puppet regime of Manchukuo, the CPC began to display even more flexibility and greater independence vis-à-vis the Communist International and Moscow. According to a declaration of January 10, 1933, to which Mao also attached his signature, the Red Army proclaimed its readiness to enter into domestic agreements "with any armed force." The CPC, while still adhering to the policy of "united front from below," moved toward the national policy of a "united front from above" to reach agreements with the leadership of established national organizations. Clearly, Japanese military pressure and the need for establishing an anti-Japanese front with the rival Kuomintang were primarily responsible for the shift of the Chinese Communist line. But the rapprochement with Chiang did not come about rapidly. At various phases of the long march toward political power, Mao's tempo, if not political direction, was frequently at variance with that advised by Moscow and the Comintern. Even during the long

31. *Ibid.*, p. 60.

years when Mao had not yet thought of challenging Moscow and its policies outright, the CPC under his leadership showed increasing autonomy in many areas of policy. The relative differences on many issues may not appear to have been striking, but in their totality they were substantial enough. Considering these differences, it is impossible to speak of monolithic Communism as then holding the USSR and the CPC indissolubly together like an iron clasp.

In the thirties the USSR was concerned not only with world revolution, which loomed only on the distant horizon, but also with national security, which was threatened along its frontiers. While Soviet interests dictated cooperation and a "united-front-from-above" policy for China against the growing Japanese danger—a threat to both China and the USSR—the CPC could never forget Chiang's anti-Communist military moves in 1927-28 and thereafter. Nevertheless, Mao accepted the "united-front-from-above" policy and cooperation with the "national bourgeoisie," and even predicted a "brilliant future" for Chiang and the Kuomintang. As he developed in a report in December 1935, it was necessary to create a "four-class bloc" composed of workers, peasants, the petty bourgeoisie, and the national bourgeoisie.[32] While Stalin considered such collaboration to be only a fleeting moment in the course of the revolutionary struggle, Mao looked upon it as likely being of longer duration.

In September 1937 the CPC had concluded an anti-Japanese united front with the Kuomintang. Units of the Red Army were at least theoretically under order from the Nanking government and renamed the "Eight-Route Army." Establishing guerrilla bases behind the Japanese lines, they not only began to fight Japanese troops, but also exercised control over the population. The people responded positively to the CPC, since the call for agrarian reform as well as that for national liberation had strong appeal. Both these currents swelled the stream on which Mao and the CPC were sailing ahead.

There were, in spite of a similarity of outlook, substantial theoretical and practical differences between the CPSU and the CPC in their relationship to the masses, especially peasants. Lenin had seized power in the cities, being supported by a segment of the working class. Though Lenin had come to appreciate the revolutionary potential among the peasants, he like his comrades looked upon the Russian peasants, the bulk of the Russian population, as the "dark people," as backward and ignorant. Mao and his comrades, on the other hand, had established their power base in the countryside, moving among the peasant masses like fish in water, to use Mao's phrase.

32. *Ibid.*, pp. 67, 76-77.

Both the CPSU and the CPC have theoretically and practically aimed at transforming men's minds. The CPC's most ambitious effort along this line prior to the seizure of power was the Rectification Campaign of 1942. Its goal was not only to furnish basic training in Marxism-Leninism, but also to provide one adapted to Chinese conditions. Such a call for the "Sinification of Marxism" had been made by Mao in his report of October 1938, when he demanded "concrete" rather than abstract Marxism, meaning Marxism that had adopted definite "national form" and had taken account of "Chinese peculiarities."[33] Of course, it was only one logical step from adaptation of Marxism to the national scene in China to the claim that all other interpretations of Marxism were meaningless to China, even harmful, and a further step to the assertion that the Chinese variety of Marxism—the only proper one for China, the largest nation on earth—was valid for many, if not most other peoples. This view was in due time to blossom forth during the Great Proletarian Cultural Revolution.

There are striking differences between revolutionary Russia in 1917 and revolutionary China in 1949. Russia, basically a European country, was geographically and culturally never a closed region as China had been, but was penetrated and shaped by ideas from the West. Russia was also industrially a much more developed country and had in 1917 a stronger industrial base than China in 1949. Militarily too, Russia was superior to China. At no time was she in serious danger of being carved up, as China was at the turn of the century. The tsarist Empire, in spite of military setbacks in Asia in 1905 and in Europe in 1917, was still a formidable state, retaining many of the fruits of both her peaceful expansion and her military conquests of former centuries. China's history in the nineteenth and much of the twentieth century was, on the other hand, one of defeat and national humiliation; her misfortunes had thrust China from the heights of national pride into the abyss of despair. The Russian intelligentsia, absorbing progressive Western thought, had become alienated long before 1914, and seeds of the Revolution had been implanted that were to sprout in 1917. In China, centuries of subjection to the family elder, landowner, and bureaucrat had strengthened among the masses the habits of submission that the teachings of Confucianism had only deepened. Obedience to authority rather than continuous rebellion was taught as the supreme obligation of the individual.[34]

Proletarian victory in Russia had first been achieved in the city and then spread to the countryside; in China the process had been in reverse. In Russia there had been a relatively short civil war, which had followed the Bolshevik seizure of power. In China, Mao had come to power in the

33. Mao Tse-tung, *Selected Works* (Peking, 1967), 2:195-211.
34. Schram, p. 75.

wake of a civil war that had lasted for decades. In view of all these differences it was to be expected that the tactics and strategy of the CPC would
never be a mere replica of the Russian example, however high the prestige
that Communist Parties all over the world attached to the pioneering Soviet
achievement.

The USSR and the Last Phase of the Chinese Civil War

While Nazi Germany was in its death throes and the outcome of China's
Patriotic War against Japan was no longer in doubt, the Seventh National
Party Congress of the CPC was held in Yenan from April 24 to June 11,
1945.[35] On the eve of its meeting an Enlarged Plenary Session of the Sixth
Central Committee had produced a remarkable document, "Resolutions on
Questions in Party History." These resolutions, passed only four days before the opening of the Seventh Congress, were a triumph for Mao, sanc-
tioning all of his policies and warning of past "right" and "left" deviations in the CPC. The resolution proclaimed that the practice of the
Chinese Revolution during the last twenty-four years had proved that the
line represented by Mao was "entirely correct"; the document also be-
stowed praise upon Liu Shao-ch'i, whom Peking has bitterly since denounced.

In his report to the Congress itself, Liu showered more praise, even outright adulation, upon Mao. Mao's name was invoked in Liu's address
more than 100 times! He compared Mao, a "creative and talented Marxist," to Lenin and Stalin, and gave him credit for uniting the theories of
Marxism with the actual practice of the Chinese revolution, "thus giving
rise to Chinese communism."[36] Liu hailed Mao not only as "the greatest
revolutionary and statesman in Chinese history but also as its greatest
theoretician and scientist." In the field of political theory Mao had been
"boldly creative," discarding Marxist principles that were "obsolete and
incompatible" and replacing them with principles that were compatible with
China's new historical conditions." Liu also disclosed that the constitution
of the CPC would be derived from the practical experience of the Chinese
Revolution, from "the ideas of Mao." Cult of personality was thus in full
swing. It no doubt was all designed to give Mao status and power comparable to that of Stalin in the USSR, especially before the entry of the USSR
into the Far Eastern War.

It was on August 8, 1945, that this momentous event took place. In a

35. Tien-Fong Cheng, pp. 236-37.
36. L. Fessler, *The Party Comes of Age* (American University Field Staff, East Asia) 16,
no. 8, (n.d.): 10.

quick nine-day war Russia occupied all of Manchuria, with the exception of the province of Jehol in the southwest. The Allied High Command, instructed on highest authority to have Chiang decide upon the disposition of all Allied forces in China, responded to his demand for lifting his troops to the regions occupied by Japanese troops. These troops, which still controlled all the cities in northern and eastern China, and many along the Yangtze and their puppet Chinese units, were ordered to surrender only to the Kuomintang forces, not to the Communists. This American policy appeared to the Communists as an outright intervention in behalf of the corrupt Kuomintang, which was thus able to extend its operations to the north and was anxious to halt the land reform and other reforms that the Communists had introduced. In the immediate postwar period many Chinese, especially the educated class, already alienated from the Kuomintang but not yet ready to endorse Communism, preferred a coalition government to a reoccupation of the North by Chiang's forces; such an occupation might only unleash full civil war.

The USSR could have turned over Manchuria, the most industrialized province in China, intact to the Communists.[37] Had Russia adopted this policy, the Communists, who already controlled the rural areas in the north and east of China, would have been able to lay their hands on a considerable industrial potential and could soon have defeated the Kuomintang.

Yet, the Soviet Union kept the Chinese Communists at arm's length. The USSR was not to recognize Communist China until 1949. In 1945 she negotiated only with Chiang and his government. Contrary to the belief in a worldwide Communist conspiracy, which then and for years to come dominated Western public opinion and political thinking, Soviet Russia and the Chinese Communists were by no means working hand in glove. The USSR gave full support neither to Chiang nor to the Communists, but pursued a contradictory policy which, lacking inner consistency, left most bystanders puzzled.

It has been suggested that Russian lack of knowledge of China and of the Far East, Stalin's prejudices, and his fears of Communist China's likely independent stance and of her future competition were responsible for this policy. To this must be added the lack of any long-range Soviet policy planning, resort to improvisation, and the consistent underestimation of Mao and the CPC. Finally, the Chinese Revolution had gone on for more than a generation and the likelihood that the Communists were on the eve of winning the civil war appeared slight to Stalin. According to one story current in Peking at the end of World War II, Stalin is supposed to have sent to Peking a Russian book on partisan warfare. This only amused

---

37. Fitzgerald, p. 97.

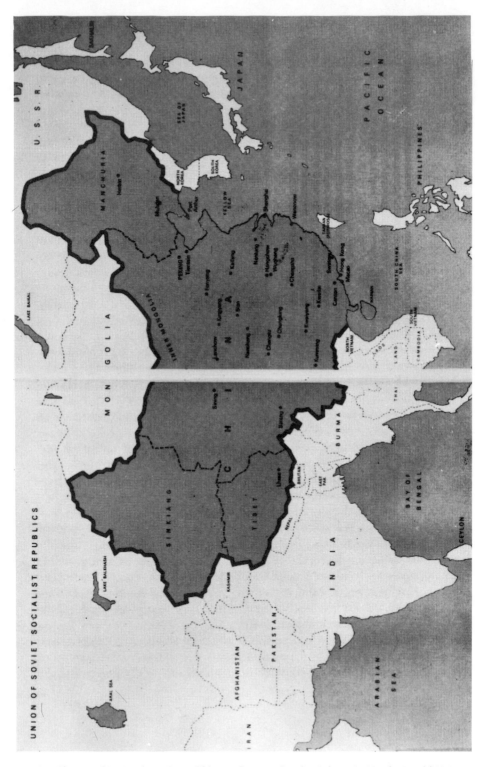

1   China and Its Borders. From *Chinese Communism* by Robert C. North. World University Library. Copyright 1966 McGraw-Hill Book Company, New York and Toronto. Used with permission of McGraw-Hill Book Company.

the Chinese comrades, since Stalin apparently did not conceive the basic difference between the struggle in Russia and that in China: Russian partisans operated during the war in conjunction with regular Russian army forces, while the Chinese Communists in the civil war had long no regular forces and no fixed bases at all.[38]

The Russians began gradually to evacuate Manchuria, turning the cities over to the Kuomintang troops who were flown in to take control. But the Manchurian countryside was occupied by Chinese Communist troops from North China. Even if the Soviets had been genuinely interested in preventing the latter occupation, they would have been unable to do so. By returning the cities to the Nationalists and leaving the countryside to the Communists, they followed what was probably the line of least resistance and, considering their relations with the West and with Chiang, a course likely to produce the least friction with their allies. At the same time, however, the Russian troops, by stripping Manchuria of industrial equipment and carrying it off, gratified their own national desires, though definitely weakening the CPC in its continuing struggle for power. Though the Chinese Communists did not criticize then Russian policy in Manchuria, it must have bitterly disappointed them. The agreement reached later between Stalin and Mao to return Manchurian industrial equipment to China was both a vindication of the justice of Communist China's claims and an embarrassment to Soviet Russia, since she had to admit having taken this equipment illegally. By having deprived the Communists of these materials at a crucial stage in their combat with Chiang, Soviet Russia served ill the interests of an allegedly close comrade-in-arms.

In 1947 Chiang failed to conquer Shantung, to establish the connection with the north, and to expand control of the Kuomintang in Manchuria. Still, in July 1948 at a Communist conference in South Hopei, Liu Shao-ch'i, who had returned from Russia, expounded Stalin's recommendation that the Chinese Communists refrain from mounting a major offensive to bring the civil war to a rapid conclusion and, rather, continue guerrilla war. Other Chinese leaders, including Chou En-lai, held, however, that the war should be pressed till final victory was won. Actually, within a few weeks the Nationalists lost all of Manchuria and North China. After the fall of Mukden, Chiang left Peking. On February 3, 1949, the Communists entered Peking; no Russian weapons were seen when the Communist troops paraded through the city.

After 1945 the Soviets had rather favored accommodation of the Chinese Communists with Chiang, the establishment of a coalition government with the Kuomintang, or some kind of viable agreement. Tito's biographer, V.

38. *Ibid.*, pp. 93-94.

Dedijer, has revealed Stalin's remarks on China to Tito in February 1948. According to Stalin, after the war the Russians had invited the Chinese comrades to visit Moscow "to discuss the situation in China." "We told them bluntly that we considered the development of the uprising in China had no prospect and that the Chinese comrades should seek a modus vivendi with Chiang." Yet the Chinese comrades, while agreeing with the view of the Soviet comrades, "went back to China and acted quite otherwise."[39] Now they were beating the army of Chiang. And Stalin admitted that the Russians had been wrong.

Knowing the extent of the ravages the Soviet Union had suffered during the war and its exhaustion at war's end, Stalin was probably fearful that the Soviet Union could be sucked into the Chinese civil war, a war in which the U.S. was already heavily engaged. He wanted to avoid an American confrontation in China. The Soviet policy debacle in China in 1927, which strongly militated against further intervention in China, had also never been forgotten by the Kremlin. In the immediate postwar period, Russia's hands were tied in Eastern Europe, where she constructed a vast new Empire and erected new defense lines against a resurgent Germany, ostensibly Russia's main enemy in the twentieth century. A strongly assertive Soviet policy in Asia seemed then neither timely nor propitious. The realization and fear that Communist China, in view of the sheer size of the country and the independence displayed by Mao, would never play the role of a submissive satellite such as, for instance, Bulgaria or Poland, pointed no doubt in the same direction. Everything seemed to admonish Soviet Russia to move with caution in Asia.

The Treaty of Alliance, 1950, and Economic and Cultural Exchange

Mao has frequently attempted to justify his "leaning-to-one-side," leaning-to-Russia policy. He claimed that Communist China had "no other choice," since the USSR was "our best teacher from whom we must learn."[40] Communist ideology aside, the CPC repeatedly underlined the systematic and rapid industrialization of the USSR and especially of Siberia, which because of its proximity had special interest for the CPR, as a case in point. Also, American hostility to Communism and Communist China in particular had become quite obvious during the last phase of the civil war.

The Moscow-Peking alliance, forged in February 1950, seemed in the best interests of both Soviet Russia and Communist China. It furnished the

39. V. Dedijer, *Tito Speaks* (London, 1953), p. 322.
40. H. G. Callis, *China Confucian and Communist* (New York, 1959), p. 383.

Soviet Union a junior partner against the U.S. America had led the resistance against further expansion of the USSR in Europe and had established NATO as first line of defense and a means of containing Russia. The U.S. was also the dominant nation in the Pacific and, as occupying power in the Japanese islands, was a virtual neighbor of the Soviet Union in regard to both the Far Eastern Province and Sakhalin. Thus the alliance with China would strengthen the USSR against the American threat of encirclement in Europe and in Asia. The alliance promised to end Russia's isolation in the world and especially to protect the long-vulnerable Siberian coast line.

As far as China was concerned, she probably needed the alliance even more than the USSR. In 1949-50, Communist China, though she had won the civil war, appeared dangerously isolated and in urgent need of a powerful military ally. Her political and military gains at home might again be challenged by the U.S. China needed help in the creation of a modern military establishment. The alliance with Russia might enable Communist China to learn more quickly about Western science and technological "know-how." By sending technicians and experts, Soviet Russia might help China bridge the gulf between its underdeveloped condition and the rapid and advanced industrialization that was her goal. A strengthened China would be able to regain influence in the lost border regions and to restore the traditional power that its predecessor, the "Middle Kingdom," had exerted in these strategic areas.

The Sino-Soviet Treaty of February 1950, called a Treaty of Friendship, Alliance and Mutual Assistance, pledged the two partners to far-reaching cooperation for at least three decades along ideological, political, economic, cultural, and, last but not least, military lines. The very preamble of the treaty asserted the determination of the two signatories to oppose jointly the rebirth of Japanese imperialism as well as aggressive moves of other states in collaboration with Japan. This, unmistakably, was aimed against the U.S. Though Communist China was not a member of the U.N., the preamble of the treaty promised that the two powers would always act in conformity with the aims and principles of the world organization. Article 1 pledged the two signatories to come to each other's military assistance in the event that peace should be violated by Japan or any state collaborating with her directly or indirectly. Both sides promised in Article 3 not to take part in any coalition or action against the other signatory. Article 4 required the two Communist powers to coordinate their foreign policies and the Soviets to support the entry of Communist China into the U.N. Article 5 finally pledged both powers to develop and strengthen their economic and cultural ties. Yet economic assistance must be "in conformity with the principles of equality, mutual benefit and of mutual respect for the national sovereignty, territorial integrity and non-interference in internal affairs" of the other party.[41] In theory at least, the treaty was based upon the assumption of full equality between the two Communist powers. Though defensive in form, many believed they discerned in the treaty a grand plan to expel the U.S. from the mainland of Asia and even from the western Pacific.

In a covenant signed simultaneously with the Sino-Soviet Treaty, the USSR renounced its old sphere of influence in Manchuria. Though the Chinese Eastern Railway and the South Manchurian Railway, Port Arthur, and Dairen were not turned over to China forthwith, Russia pledged to do so within the next years. This pledge, however, was somewhat qualified: Soviet Russia, jointly with China, could use Port Arthur for conducting joint military operations in the event of aggression by Japan or any power that might collaborate with Japan. Still, there could be little doubt that Russia had been compelled to promise to return to China shortly most of the gains she had wrested from Chiang in 1945. Russia's far-reaching privileges in the Far East, which she had acquired after the turn of the century, had soon lost to Japan, but, recovered in 1945, now had to be returned to the Chinese comrades. No comparable concessions—excepting perhaps the return of some Finnish bases acquired during and after World War II—were made by Soviet Russia to any of her European neighbors and comradely Parties. The preamble of the ancillary agreement with China asserted that these changes were possible in view of the "new situation" that had arisen in the Far East: the policy of friendly cooperation between China and the USSR made special Soviet safeguards in the Far East superfluous.

Of special significance for China was the Soviet Russian pledge to turn over to China the Manchurian "war booty" that the USSR had seized from the Japanese in 1945. This was to be done without compensation, just as the Manchurian railways were to be returned without any indemnification—clear admission that Russian seizure of these properties from the Kuomintang government had had no legal or moral basis. There were also to be established Sino-Soviet joint stock companies to operate in Manchuria and Sinkiang, and a rather niggardly loan of 300 million dollars was to be granted to Peking.

In an exchange of separate notes, Communist China acknowledged "the independent status of the Mongolian People's Republic." Here was one area that the USSR had effectively detached from China in the twenties. The Mongolian People's Republic had gained independence in 1945, an arrangement quite favorable to Soviet Russia. Communist China failed, how-

41. *Ibid.*, pp. 386-88.

ever, to regain it in 1950, as with other territories. The Soviets no doubt could hide behind the assertion that the final separation of Outer Mongolia in 1945 had not led to its incorporation into the USSR but to its independent status, and that it was beyond the power and outside the jurisdiction of the Soviet Union to reverse a process that affected only Outer Mongolia and China and not herself. Actually, in the mid-fifties, Khrushchev, when confronted by Mao regarding Outer Mongolia, advised the Chinese leader to deal with Ulan Bator directly.

The Sino-Soviet Treaty of February 1950, concluded after a stay of unusual length by Mao and the Chinese Delegation in Moscow and only a few months after the proclamation of the CPR, left little doubt about the equality or near-equality of the two Communist partners. No similar treaty had been signed by Soviet Russia and her European communist satellite neighbors. The provisions then made for Sino-Soviet joint stock companies to exploit nonferrous and rare minerals in Sinkiang and to extract and refine petroleum in Chinese Central Asia turned out to come to an end after only a few years. The same held true for joint stock companies to build and repair ships in Dairen and jointly operate civil airlines for the purpose of linking the two countries. By 1954 the two governments announced that beginning January 1, 1955, the Soviet shares in these mixed companies would be transferred to China, which in turn would compensate the Soviet Union with "usual export" goods. Perhaps this included food from Manchuria and uranium from Sinkiang.

Yet, whatever the provisions of the Sino-Soviet treaty of 1950, the Russians in China did not move into top administrative posts in the government. To the contrary, Mao and the Chinese leadership seem to have been bent on removing Moscow-trained leaders from positions of highest responsibility. Li Li-san, the most prominent of the Russian-oriented Chinese Communist leaders lost his eminent stature and soon after Stalin's death was unceremoniously dismissed from his posts. Simultaneously, Deputy Foreign Minister V. V. Kuznetsov, Soviet ambassador in Peking, was recalled to Moscow. The dismissal of Li was an unmistakable warning to Moscow that the Peking government was no longer disposed to accept directives from the USSR.

On October 11, 1954, another Sino-Soviet treaty was signed which elaborated and partly implemented the earlier pact of February 1950.[42] The treaty contained new concessions to Peking. While under the earlier agreement China, through joint stock companies, close technical, and thus economic supervision and military control in some strategic areas was in a

42. *Ibid.*, p. 392.

state almost approaching tutelage vis-à-vis the USSR, the new treaty pledged Soviet evacuation of Port Arthur by the spring of 1955 and the dissolution of the joint stock companies. The "unequal treaty" of 1950 was substantially modified. In Chinese eyes, however, it was merely a beginning.

The period after the conclusion of the Sino-Soviet Treaty of February 1950 was marked by an enormous increase in cultural, economic, technical, military, and political exchanges between Moscow and Peking. They were based upon China's eagerness to learn as much as possible from the Soviet partner, to strengthen her economic and military stance in the world at large, not excluding that vis-à-vis Soviet Russia herself, and to bridge as rapidly as possible the gulf between herself and the technologically advanced countries of the world. They were also rooted in Soviet Russia's willingness to help less-fortunate China in the expectation that her own eminent stature as the Mecca of world Communism and as the economically and culturally leading country in the Communist bloc would not be seriously jeopardized in the eyes of the world, but rather enhanced by the spectacle of seeming selfless comradely help.

There followed many high-level meetings between the USSR and the CPR, which partly continued and implemented, partly departed from, the pattern of cooperation and collaboration established in February 1950. Most important was an agreement signed by Khrushchev and Bulganin in Peking in 1954. It provided for greater exchange of scientific information and personnel between the two countries, for further Russian credit, for the dissolution of the joint stock companies, and for the construction of railroads through Mongolia and Sinkiang. Another visit to Peking by Mikoyan in 1956 produced additional economic agreements and raised to 211 the number of industrial projects in China for which Russia offered assistance.

To further Sino-Soviet relations, Peking sponsored the Sino-Soviet Friendship Association.[43] Founded on October 5, 1949, only five days after the proclamation of the CPR itself, it was headed by Liu Shao-ch'i. The Association claimed a membership of 40 million, distributed articles praising the USSR, and published a surprisingly large number of special magazines and books year after year. It sponsored and organized numerous speeches and rallies in behalf of Sino-Soviet collaboration and distributed Soviet films and plays. It helped arrange tours through China for Soviet trade, technical, political and sport organizations, and artistic and theater groups. It was responsible for programs in the Russian language over Peking radio and encouraged the adoption of Soviet educational methods and

43. *Ibid.*, p. 394.

curricula in the country's schools. With its counterparts in the USSR, it provided for a continuous exchange of cultural delegations, scientists, lecturers, writers, and actors between the two countries.

The War in Korea

Following the proclamation of the CPR in Peking in October 1949 and the flight of Chiang to Taiwan and the establishment there of his government, the U.S. under President Truman refused to give support to Chiang and, in the words of the President on January 5, 1950, to become involved "in the civil conflict in China." Both the President and Secretary of State Dean Acheson considered Taiwan an integral part of China. Though the U.S. did not move toward recognition of Mao and his government, neither did they at first contemplate furnishing aid or advice to Chinese military forces on Taiwan.

In a speech on January 12, 1950, Secretary Acheson drew a line of America's primary defense in the Far East, clearly differentiating between regions of primary and secondary interest to the U.S. He significantly did not include Korea within the American "military perimeter."*[44] At the very time Acheson gave this address, Mao was in Moscow for a visit that lasted two full months. Though the conclusion of the Sino-Soviet treaty on February 15, 1950, struck fear into some Western circles and evoked demands in the U.S. that the policy of "containment," which had been successfully applied to Europe to meet the mounting Soviet threat be now extended to Asia, there seemed to be little immediate and effective response. In another speech, on March 15, 1950, again about Asia and the Pacific, Dean Acheson suggested no changes in regard to America's defense perimeter in Asia. For the moment, tension in Korea neither abated nor increased and both North and South Korea continued to display aggressive hostility. In mid-June, John Foster Dulles, on a personal mission to Asia in behalf of Secretary Acheson, visited the 38th parallel, still without an inkling of the coming attack.

The attack came on June 25th. President Truman responded immediately by declaring that the U.S. would defend South Korea. Because of the United Nations' refusal to seat Communist China, Soviet Russia, boycotting

*While Acheson in his *Memoirs* insisted that he did not intend to exclude Korea, this interpretation appears doubtful. On the other hand, the later Republican critics preferred to ignore that, when Acheson made this speech, no Republican leader in or out of Congress criticized his omission.

44. D. Acheson, *Present at the Creation* (New York, 1969), p. 66.

the Security Council, was absent when the attack on South Korea started. Thereupon the Security Council denounced North Korea as aggressor. The Korean War was in full swing.

Could it be assumed that the North Korean aggression had been planned during the extended talks in Moscow between December 1949 and February 1950? Or was it China alone or the USSR alone that triggered the gun, or perhaps North Korea that forced the hands of the two other Communist powers?

America's responses were based on the assumption that behind North Korea stood Communist China, not the USSR. In a note to Moscow President Truman pleaded with the Russians to persuade the North Korean leader Kim Il Sung to withdraw his invading troops from the South.[45] After the start of the Korean War the American President promptly gave Chiang full support—which so far he had refused to do. He ordered the Seventh Fleet to sail into the Taiwan straits to protect Taiwan from a mainland attack. At the same time military aid was dispatched to the Philippines. The President even sent a military mission to Indochina to lend assistance to the French, who were already in dire straits. All American moves seemed to be designed to block China on all sides. But was there sufficient reason to assume that China had plotted and abetted the Korean attack and was at the point of plunging into further adventures?

It can hardly be assumed that North Korea undertook the attack without advance notice to the Soviet Union, without having consulted her and having received the promise of help if it should be needed. Kim Il Sung, who had spent many years in Russia, was a confidant of the Soviets and had been placed by them in power in Pyongyang. Though Soviet troops had been withdrawn from North Korea in January 1949—earlier than American troops from South Korea—numerous Russian advisors were left behind to continue training the North Korean troops. In 1950 North Korea was still, for all practical purposes, a satellite of Moscow. By the time of the outbreak of the Korean War, the regime of Communist China was less than a year old; it had not even yet established diplomatic relations with North Korea. Such ties, however, were knit in August 1950, two months *after* the outbreak of the Korean War.

It appears most likely that the North Korean attack was agreed upon in Moscow by the North Koreans and Russians, probably *after* Mao's visit to the Soviet capital. Secretary Acheson's omitting to include Korea within the American defense perimeter may have contributed to the misunderstanding by North Korea and Soviet Russia. Perhaps the Communist victory in China was interpreted in North Korea as a defeat for the U.S., Chiang's

45. Fitzgerald, p. 215.

friend and ally, and may have given encouragement to her own aggressive designs. It is quite likely that the North Korean attack caused as much surprise in Peking as it did in Washington, D.C.

At the time of the outbreak of the war, Stalin held strong positions in North Korea, Mongolia, and Manchuria. He had his own man, Kao Kang. in control in strategic and resource-rich Manchuria.[46] Peking accused him later of having aspired to establish a separate "kingdom" of his own in Manchuria and to detach the province from China and denounced him as a traitor. (Not long after Stalin's death, Kao Kang was to commit suicide.) In 1949, before the CPR was proclaimed, Kao had indeed attempted to set up the Northeast China Region. He then had rushed to Moscow and signed a treaty for Manchuria as if the latter were an independent country. The Northeast China Region for a time survived the proclamation of the CPR in October 1949.

There seems little doubt that Stalin and Kao collaborated and that they wanted to place before Mao the fait accompli of an independent Manchuria. While Kao posthumously was condemned by Peking, Moscow kept strangely silent about him. Later, however, Moscow "rehabilitated" Kao, promoting him from the oblivion of a nonperson to the honorable status of a loyal patriotic Chinese, a picture quite at variance with that painted by Peking.

Seen against the background of Russian interests in the Chinese border regions, stretching from Sinkiang to Manchuria and beyond it to Korea, the outbreak of the Korean War had special meaning and significance. A control of Korea through Stalin, according to H. Salisbury, would "place Mao in a nutcracker."[47] Obviously, Stalin proved to have been mistaken. He did not anticipate the American and the United Nations' intervention. When in the course of the war all of North Korea seemed to be lost and Americans were approching the Yalu river, Soviet Russia, which had furnished arms and equipment for the North Koreans, continued to hold back Russian troops and specialists, except for a few. Surprisingly enough, it was China that intervened, thus transforming the Korean conflict into a Sino-American war. And at the end of the fighting, it was China that appeared as the most loyal and trustworthy ally of North Korea, as her savior.

The Korean War does not offer evidence of a very close collaboration between the two Communist giants, though this was the picture the West then painted. The war was rather the consequence of a power play engaged in by Stalin against Mao soon after the latter had come to power; but it failed. It was a kind of chess game that Stalin began without knowing who

46. Harrison E. Salisbury, *War between Russia and China* (New York, 1969), p. 74.
47. *Ibid.*, p. 76.

his opponent would be. When he learned that it would be the United States, he promptly withdrew without even making the first move. Mao took his place and finished the game. It ended in a draw, and thus boosted China's prestige immensely.

After Stalin

The death of Stalin on March 5, 1953, was to have a significant impact upon the further development of Sino-Soviet relations. Mao himself did not attend Stalin's funeral. Perhaps he recalled grievances nurtured earlier with regard to Stalin's imperious attitude toward China and Chinese communism, or he might have wished to demonstrate his new status vis-à-vis the new ruling group in the Kremlin—mere epigones as compared to himself, a charismatic and undisputed leader in his own Party and country, now a senior Communist in the world Communist movement. He sent Chou En-lai to the funeral, while he himself remained in Peking. On the other hand, the new Soviet leaders, in order to boost their relative position in the struggle for power, attempted to create the impression of being on best terms with Mao. Beria and Malenkov, riding high in the first days after Stalin's death, displayed a photograph depicting the signing of the Sino-Soviet alliance on February 1950 that placed Malenkov next to Mao himself. The alleged closeness of the Chinese Communist leadership to the new rulers in the Kremlin was to give an air of legitimacy to them! As late as February 1955 Molotov referred to the socialist camp as being "led by the Soviet Union and China,"[48] a statement that gave China an unprecedented and, as a matter of fact, never-repeated recognition.

The years between 1953 and 1955 witnessed the emergence of a "collective leadership" in the Soviet Union and the gradual rise of Khrushchev to the headship of both Party and state. During this period, when a struggle for power gripped the Soviet leadership, a decisive change in the Sino-Soviet relationship was not in the offing. Also, after the end of the "hot" war in the Far East, the USSR, deeply involved in the cold war with the West, then faced problems of greater importance in Europe than in Asia. In 1954 she energetically pushed her plans for the introduction of international socialist division of labor in the Council for Mutual Economic Assistance (CMEA) and was deeply concerned about the German problem and the West's attempts to integrate Bonn militarily into NATO and economically and ideologically into the West European system.

The most immediate result of the death of Stalin was the resumption of

48. H. C. Hinton, *China's Turbulent Quest* (Bloomington, Ind., 1972), p. 62.

truce negotiations in Korea. The UN General Assembly had come out unanimously in favor of negotiations and had expressed hope in an early armistice in Korea. After a threat by Secretary John Foster Dulles, transmitted to Peking through the Indian ambassador, to use atomic bombs against China in the event of further obstructions in Panmunjom, the armistice was signed on July 27, 1953.

After the end of the Korean War, the consolidation in the CPR and the diplomatic successes at Geneva in 1954 and at the Bandung Conference in 1955 that were to come her way, Communist China's self-confidence grew by leaps and bounds. Despite her inability to crush the boastful and hostile Taiwan regime, the CPR displayed a new pride and self-assurance. The adoption of a new constitution in September 1954 by the First National People's Congress was as much an expression of her revolutionary ardor as of her nationalist exuberance. Her nationalist intransigence, now showed itself in increasing toughness during the negotiations with the USSR, in her insistence for modification of numerous clauses, if not entire treaties, that had been concluded with the Soviets only a few years before. Communist China clearly flexed her muscles. Mao had become increasingly critical of the value of the "mixed companies" that the USSR had established in China just as she had in her East European satellites. The CPR, jealous of her "sovereign" economic rights and resentful of the "privileged" position of any foreign power in China—even though it was that of a friendly, "comradely" state like the USSR, the fatherland of socialism itself —pressured the Soviet Union into relinquishing some of the concessions granted to her earlier.

After the signing of the armistice in Korea, Peking had seemed determined to dispatch military equipment to the Viet Minh. But after American threats of "massive retaliation" uttered early in 1954 were followed by US thermonuclear tests in the Pacific, the Geneva Conference soon settled the Indochina question in May 1954. Despite Peking's frequent references later to the American "paper tiger," the CPR was not prepared to test the sharpness of the "tiger's" teeth. Also, differently from Korea, there were then no American ground forces in Indochina and no immediate threat of the US staging an all-out attack on China from the Indochina base.

Chou En-lai's role at the Geneva Conference, the first major international gathering in which the CPR participated, turned into a personal diplomatic triumph for him and a national one for the CPR. The settlement was distasteful to Hanoi, seemingly snatching victory from her or at least postponing it until the projected election of 1956. The Viet Minh thus felt abandoned by both the USSR and Communist China.[49] Yet the US, while not

49. *Ibid.*, p. 65.

affixing her signature to the final declaration, was to have no bases and troops in Indochina—a reassurance pleasing especially to the CPR. On the whole, both the Soviet Union and Communist China were then bent on ending the war; their national interests ran parallel, and their positions throughout the last negotiations differed little from each other, though at times they differed sharply from the position of the Democratic Republic of Vietnam.

Chinese self-confidence found full expression in a joint Sino-Soviet communique, signed in Peking in October 1954. It ominously stressed that after the termination of the war in both Korea and Indochina the "defense potential" of the CPR had been strengthened, and announced the withdrawal of Soviet military forces from the area of the Port Arthur naval base.[50] The CPR, which in 1949-50 had been anxious to conclude the military treaty of alliance with the USSR against Japan and any power allied with Japan, had met the enemy on the Korean battlefield and thereafter felt confident enough to ask for the liquidation of Soviet military establishments on Chinese soil. Thus Communist China was on the march to assert her economic and military independence; in her infancy, when she was weak and the US hostile, she had been compelled to mortgage it to the Soviet Union.

Following the end of the war in Indochina, American Secretary of State Dulles in September 1954 actively sponsored and organized the Southeast Asia Treaty Organization (SEATO); the move could be interpreted as designed either to block China's further expansion and contain her, or to threaten her integrity and her Communist regime. To counter this threat Peking launched a campaign against the Taiwan regime. Due to the objections of the European partners of the U.S. in SEATO, Taiwan had been excluded from the alliance and Peking, on this ground, might have considered her vulnerable. Thus, in the spring of 1955, the first Taiwan Strait crisis developed.

Actually, Peking's foreign policy now entered a more pacific phase. This coincided with the first five-year plan, the prospectus of which was completed by February 1955, though not yet published; the plan, for which additional Soviet economic aid was promised, corresponded in its major outlines to Soviet models and desires. In April 1954 China had signed an agreement with India that acknowledged the former's position in Tibet and terminated New Delhi's special rights there. In July 1954 Chou En-lai and India's Prime Minister Jawaharlal Nehru proclaimed the Five Principles—Panch Shila—which extolled economic cooperation and peaceful coexistence. These were the very guidelines that the post-Stalinist Soviet leadership accepted for the new Soviet foreign policy.

50. *Ibid.*, p. 70.

The CPR also substantially modified her line of policy toward neutral countries, following an earlier change of policy by the USSR. In the vital areas of economic policy and international relations, Peking and Moscow thus seemed to march side by side. And the crisis in the Taiwan Straits rapidly evaporated into thin air, which must have pleased the Soviet leadership. In January 1955, Moscow announced that it had made to a number of East European Communist states, as well as to China, a proposal to extend to them scientific and technological assistance for developing atomic energy for peaceful purposes.

On the other hand, Khrushchev's activist policy toward the Third World, which commenced immediately after the Bandung Conference, testifies to Soviet concern over Peking's making headway among the underdeveloped countries. This new, worldwide activity of the USSR under Khrushchev was for Peking an unwelcome contrast to the more limited and cautious Soviet Foreign policy under Stalin; Peking could hardly appreciate what threatened to develop into a brisk competition. Still, after its long perilous voyage, the ship of Sino-Soviet friendship seemed finally to encounter good weather conditions.

Even the Bandung Conference in 1955 did not appear to disturb the basic relationship of the USSR and the CPR as comrades and allies, though China's sudden rise to diplomatic eminence and her apparent claim to leadership in Asia and Africa must have produced angry shock waves in the USSR. After Chou's role at the Geneva Conference, his star performance at the Bandung Conference no doubt aroused envy and concern in Moscow, even if, as some assume, between 1950 and 1955 Moscow and Peking did arrange between themselves for some sort of division into spheres of influence and activities.[51]

In any case, between 1949 when the CPR was proclaimed and 1955 when the Bandung Conference was held, Communist China appeared to have completed a full circle. Starting out with a revolutionary foreign policy sharpened by the early confrontation with the U.S. in Korea, she ended by eagerly embracing the principles of peaceful coexistence and actually reconciling herself to the domination of imperialism in many parts of the world. At Bandung Chou hobnobbed with the representatives of bourgeois Asian and African states, already hopeful of in due time becoming their champion and leader. Chou attempted to persuade the neutralist countries that the CPR was a firm believer in "peaceful coexistence," trying to make them forget that she had ever talked, thought, or acted to the contrary. To the surprise of many participants at the Conference and other observers, Chou outshone even Nehru. The USSR, though also an Asiatic

51. Edmund Clubb, *China and Russia: the "Great Game"* (New York 1964), pp. 408-9.

power, was not represented at this Afro-Asian conference, probably to her lasting disadvantage.

Were the preoccupations of the USSR with Europe responsible for the neglect of her interests in Asia? After West Germany joined the NATO pact, the USSR was busily engaged in taking appropriate countermeasures. In May 1955 there was created the Warsaw Pact, providing for mutual defense and military aid among the Eastern bloc countries. The same eight countries that formed the economic group called the CMEA (Council for Mutual Economic Assistance) now pledged mutual military defense to the Soviet Union and to each other. China, however, was neither a member of the CMEA nor of the Warsaw Pact. Distant from Europe, the CPR was also in other respects in a category *sui generis,* in a situation that was not comparable to that of any of the European satellites of the USSR.

3

The Seeds of the
Disagreement, 1956-1959

The Twentieth Congress of the CPSU, February 1956

The year 1956 represented a turning point in the domestic history of both the USSR and the CPR. It was the year of the Twentieth Congress of the CPSU at which Khrushchev denounced Stalin, and the year of the Eighth Congress of the CPC which, half a year later, reaffirmed the basic policies of Moscow and diminished Mao's exalted status. Though it represented a stage of seeming agreement between Moscow and Peking, in the light of subsequent developments it proved to be one of the last fleeting moments of harmony and concordance.

The Twentieth Congress of the CPSU, which opened in February 1956, launched a two-pronged program, the policies of so-called de-Stalinization and peaceful coexistence, both of which had large domestic and foreign implications. De-Stalinization produced the effect of a bombshell in the USSR, shocked the Communist world to its foundation, and was also to affect adversely Sino-Soviet relations. The other theme, of peaceful coexistence, taking account of the worldwide longing for peace, had obvious propagandist significance, but also reflected the Soviet desire to avoid an unnecessary war; it was to have a decisive impact upon Soviet-Western, as well as Soviet-Chinese relations.

The downgrading of Stalin had already begun soon after his death, but it was an embarrassed, stealthy, and ambiguous undertaking, rather than an open criticism of Stalin and frank admission of the errors and crimes the Soviet government had committed under his leadership. Therefore Khrushchev's blunt and uninhibited accusations against Stalin at the Twentieth Congress, even though coming three years after his death, represented a bold, unprecedented move and ushered in a revolution in the political and intellectual climate of the USSR. Peking, however, was to become increasingly suspicious of de-Stalinization.

The theme of peaceful coexistence, though proclaimed at the Twentieth Party Congress, had at various earlier moments been given greater emphasis, most recently by Malenkov at the Nineteenth Party Congress in October 1952, at which Stalin was still present. In the years immediately thereafter, Peking too seemed to have endorsed the principles of peaceful coexistence, which were also incorporated in an agreement between China and India signed on April 29, 1954. In April 1955, at the Bandung Conference of Afro-Asian states, Chou repudiated the concept of war with the United States and declared his readiness to enter into negotiations with the American government for purposes of lessening tension in the Far East.[1] Peking did not then spurn the concept of peaceful coexistence.

But Khrushchev's views, as expressed at the Twentieth Party Congress, were sharply criticized by Peking, especially his concept that transition from capitalism to socialism could be effected "through the parliamentary road." Khrushchev, according to Peking, had also questioned the continued validity of Lenin's teachings on imperialism and on war and peace. Distorting Lenin's correct principle of peaceful coexistence between countries with different social systems, Khrushchev, Peking asserted, had in practice excluded from the foreign policy of the socialist countries their mutual assistance and cooperation as well as assistance by them to revolutionary struggles of the oppressed peoples and nations. He had sacrificed these struggles at the altar of so-called "peaceful coexistence."[2]

In his report to the Congress as First Secretary of the Central Committee of the CPSU, Khrushchev made repeated reference to the CPR, singling her out from among all people's democracies, but leaving no doubt as to her subordinate position in regard to the USSR. The CPR had set about building socialism later than had the other people's democracies, yet it had made outstanding progress. While the CPSU noted the CPC's achievements in socialist industrialization with great satisfaction, it did not omit congratulating itself: "Never before in history has a highly industrialized country [the USSR] voluntarily helped other countries to become industrialized." The USSR would continue, Khrushchev pledged, to give all around assistance in economic, technological, scientific, and cultural development in accordance with "our fraternal duty."[3] The stronger the entire socialist camp, the more reliable would be the guarantee of the free-

1. J. Rowland, *A History of Sino-Indian Relations* (Toronto, 1967), pp. 91-99.
2. *Statements by Khrushchev* (Peking; World Culture Press, 1965) (*PR*, Apr. 30, 1965).
3. *Pravda.*, Feb. 15, 1961 (Khrushchev's speech), pp. 1-11 (*CDSP* 8, no. 4 [March 7, 1956]: 3-15, 29).

dom, independence, and economic and cultural progress of each of the countries making up this great camp.

The imperialist colonial system, Khrushchev continued, was disintegrating and a new period of history was being ushered in in which "the peoples of the East play an active part in deciding the destinies of the whole world." Though in their later dispute with Communist China the Soviets were to accuse her of racism, Khrushchev then made a clear bid to the peoples of the East. International relations, he assured and flattered them, were "no longer determined by countries inhabited chiefly by peoples of the white race," but were beginning to become genuine worldwide relations.

Peaceful coexistence, Khrushchev asserted, had always been and remained the general line, the fundamental principle of the Soviet Union's foreign policy; it was not growing out of merely tactical considerations, not out of expediency. In the past the precept that wars were inevitable as long as imperialism existed was absolutely correct. But war is no longer a "fatalistic inevitability." "Whether there is to be a war or not depends in large measure on the correlation of class, political forces, the degree of organization and the awareness and resolve of the people." In certain conditions, moreover, the struggle waged by progressive social and political forces could play a decisive role.

While discussing forms of transition to socialism in different countries, Khrushchev devoted much attention to Chinese Communism. Much that was unique in socialist construction was being contributed by the CPR, which had inherited an "exceedingly backward" semi-feudal and semi-colonial economy. In the days before the "Great Leap," Khrushchev credited China with pursuing a policy of "gradual transformation" of private industry and trade into components of socialist economy. Her policy, and that of the other people's democracies, represented "creative Marxism in action."

Khrushchev's speech, as well as the Resolutions of the Twentieth Congress of the CPSU, revealed a paternalistic attitude toward Communist China. No threat to Soviet Russia's undisputed preeminence among the Communist-led nations was yet in sight. The concepts of peaceful coexistence, evitability of war, of peaceful transition to socialism—all soon to be questioned by Peking—were here elaborated. At the Twentieth Congress of the CPSU, the CPR evidently stood out clearly among all People's Republics. She was given credit for her pioneering experience, her role in international affairs, and her likely importance for the further expansion of Communism among the peoples of the East. Yet the generous assistance by the USSR to the CPR and to fraternal Communist Parties and underdeveloped nations in general was not forgotten.

The denunciation of Stalin followed in a speech by Khrushchev that was not published in the Soviet Union, though its contents became known to leading party members. When it was published months later in *The New York Times,* the Soviets made no attempt to disavow the authenticity of the *Times* version.

When the Twentieth Congress of the CPSU opened its doors, Chou, the Chinese delegate to the congress, read a message from Mao that praised the CPSU, "created by Lenin and reared by Stalin and his close comrades-in-arms."[4] Ten days later, Khrushchev, then leader of the CPSU, denounced his predecessor and master, the man who had "reared" the Party. Moscow's apparent lack of previous consultation with Mao and the CPC must have been most embarrassing to them. Or was Mao's praise a last-minute attempt to halt the impending criticism by Khrushchev? The Chinese opposition to the Soviet denigration of Stalin, in combination with the still-strong Stalinist influences in the USSR and the unexpected repercussions of de-Stalinization in Hungary and Poland in 1956, compelled Khrushchev to retreat significantly the following year.

But a few weeks after Khrushchev's denunciation of Stalin, *Pravda,* on March 28, 1956, had openly attacked the "cult of the individual." It criticized it as an "inordinate glorification of individuals. . .making them almost miracle workers and worshipping them. Such incorrect conceptions of man, and specifically of J. V. Stalin, which are alien to the spirit of Marxism-Leninism, developed and were cultivated among us for many years."[5]

The cult of the individual, *Pravda* continued, was "alien and repugnant" to the founders of Marxism-Leninism, Marx, Engels, and Lenin. It was "indisputable" that Stalin had rendered great services to the Soviet Union. Yet "lacking personal modesty, he did not cut off the glorification and praises addressed to him, but even supported and encouraged them in every way." As time went on, this cult of the individual assumed ever more monstrous forms and did serious harm to the cause.

The Chinese view of Stalin and of Khrushchev's criticism of him at the Twentieth Party Congress was expressed in an article of *People's Daily,* "On the Historical Experience of the Dictatorship of the Proletariat," on April 5, 1956. It called Stalin "an outstanding Marxist-Leninist fighter," though he had "erroneously exaggerated his own role and counterposed his individual authority to the collective leadership," as a result of which "certain of his actions were opposed to certain fundamental Marxist-Leninist concepts."[6] Thus Stalin, "during the later part of his life," had

4. *CDSP*, no. 4 (March 14, 1956): 11.
5. *Pravda,* March 28, 1956, "Why is the cult of the individual alien to the spirit of Marxism-Leninism?", pp. 2-3 (*CDSP* 8, no. 9 [Apr. 11, 1956]: 3, 6-7).
6. *People's Daily,* Apr. 5, 1956.

found himself in contradiction, in a discrepancy between theory—that inner-Party democracy and self-criticism and criticism from below must be developed—and practice.

Though *People's Daily* underlined that the masses were the "maker of history," it claimed at the same time that, according to Marxism-Leninism, leaders played a "big role in history." It was "utterly wrong" to "deny the role of the individual, the role of forerunners and leaders. . . ." But, of course, no leader should place himself over and above the Party and the masses, instead of in their midst. On certain important matters Stalin, admittedly, had made unrealistic and erroneous decisions; he had, during the latter part of his life, taken "more and more pleasure in this cult of the individual and violated the Party's system of democratic centralism and the principle of combining collective leadership with individual responsibility." Among his "serious mistakes" listed were that he broadened the scope of the counterrevolution, that he lacked the necessary vigilance on the eve of the anti-fascist war, that he failed to pay proper attention to the further development of agriculture and the material welfare of the peasantry, that he gave certain wrong advice on the international Communist movement and, in particular, made a wrong decision on the question of Yugoslavia. Following this pattern of deliberate understatement in regard to the most crucial problems that the USSR had faced, the author of the article concluded that Stalin had fallen victim to "subjectivism and one-sidedness"—was the "victim," rather than the perpetrator of monstrous errors and crimes.

The author of the article even attempted to give a historical explanation for the phenomenon of Stalin's shortcomings. The cult of the individual was "a foul carry-over" from the long history of mankind. "Naive ideas" seem to suggest that contradictions did not exist in a socialist society. As a matter of fact, even under a Communist society "not everybody will be perfect." In spite of its deceptive appearance of objectivity, the article was an obvious attempt to cling desperately to the elusive phenomenon of Stalin's pervasive greatness, conceding merely a few weaknesses.[7]*

7. *Ibid.;* also *PR*, Sept. 20, 1963, "On the Question of Stalin." *People's Daily* and *Red Flag.*

*As time went on, however, and the rift between Moscow and Peking deepened, the Chinese objections to the denigration of Stalin were uttered more strongly and with less inhibition. In September 1963 the editorial department of *People's Daily* called Stalin, in reply to the recent Soviet Open Letter, "a great Marxist-Leninist, a great proletarian revolutionary." Then, countering the Soviet charges that the CPC after 1956 had long remained quiet about Soviet criticism of Stalin, the Chinese article pointed out that, in internal discussions after the Twentieth Congress of the CPSU, prominent Chinese comrades had frequently "solemnly criticized" the errors of the CPSU leadership. As early as April 1956, less than two months after the Soviet Party Congress, Mao, conversing with A. Mikoyan and the Soviet ambassador to China, had expressed his own differing views on Stalin, and he took a similar position on October 23 and on November 30, 1956. At no time and in no place had the CPC

In spite of serious past differences between Stalin and the CPC, and Mao in particular, both before the victory in the Chinese Civil War and thereafter, the harsh and ruthless aspects of Stalinism did not repel the CPC. In addition, the Soviet struggle against the personality cult had, whether intended or not, all-too-apparent anti-Maoist implications. It went straight against the glorification and deification of the Chinese leader himself. As such, it was plainly intolerable to Mao and his followers. In fighting for the historic place of the dead Stalin, Mao was fighting for his political life and his own preeminent role in history.

As the Soviets later pointed out, the personality cult had already assumed "a truly unheard-of magnitude in China." Nobody in China actually read the works of Marx and Engels any longer. The infinitesimal number of copies of Lenin's works published in China made them practically inaccessible to readers at large. But the works of Mao Tse-tung, which were issued in more than 380 million copies, were spoken and written about everywhere "as the sun illuminating the road, as the ultimate wisdom."[8] "Keep Mao's works in three places—at home, in the pocket, and at your place of work, and recall Mao's behest at least three times every day," party members were urged. A pious attitude toward Mao's personality was also manifested in that he was thanked for the food the Chinese received, for the health of the family, for the stroke of luck. It was not hard to understand why the Chinese leaders, having created such a mystical atmosphere around Mao's personality, opposed the CPSU, which had boldly combated Stalin's personality cult and demonstrated the incompatibility of any personality cult with Marxism-Leninism.

As Peking revealed in 1963, the attack against Stalin appeared to it as

completely affirmed the Twentieth Congress of the CPSU; as was known, it had continued to display the portrait of Stalin along with those of Marx, Engels, and Lenin. *People's Daily* admitted that Stalin had made "certain mistakes." But his merits outweighed his faults. August Bebel and Rosa Luxemburg had also made mistakes, but were still "eagles" in the working-class movement; and their role was not comparable to that of Stalin.

About two weeks later, the editorial departments of *People's Daily* and *Red Flag* wrote as follows in an article "On the Question of Stalin. Comment on the Open Latter of the C.C. of the CPSU" (*P.R.*, Sept. 20, 1963. No. 38): "There is virtual agreement among the majority of the international working class and of revolutionary people who disapprove of the complete negation of Stalin and more and more cherish his memory." To the CPSU and Khrushchev in particular were ascribed "ulterior motives" in completely negating Stalin. Stalin was credited with having fought resolutely both internal and external foes of the CPSU and the Soviet people, of having upheld the line of socialist industrialization and agricultural collectivization and having led the CPSU and the Soviet army to the great victory of the anti-fascist war. He had made "an indelible contribution" to the Communist movement in a number of theoretical writings that are "immortal" Marxist-Leninist works, had pursued a foreign policy that on the whole was in keeping with proletarian internationalism, and had assisted the revolutionary struggles of all peoples, including the Chinese people.

8. *Partiinaya Zhizn*, no. 8, Apr. 1964; *Pravda*, Apr. 22, 1964 (*CDSP*, 16, 16 [May 13, 1964]).

criticism of a foe rather than that of a comrade-in-arms and friend, as complete negativism and as an attack against the dictatorship of the proletariat and the Communist movement itself.[9]* Peking apparently feared that Moscow's attempt at self-purification would irretrievably sully revolutionary socialism.

On September 6, 1963 *People's Daily* emphasized that the questions the Soviet Leadership had raised at the Twentieth Congress were "by no means simply internal affairs of the CPSU." But, "without any prior consultations" with the fraternal parties, the Twentieth Party Congress of the CPSU had forced these parties to accept a *fait accompli* and thus in effect had "crudely interfered" in the internal affairs of the fraternal parties and countries and subverted their leaderships. Out of these "errors" had grown, as subsequent events showed, the revision and betrayal of Marxism-Leninism.

In 1963 and thereafter the CPC preferred to look upon the Twentieth Party Congress of the CPSU as the root from which stemmed all the evils done by the Khrushchev revisionists. In particular, the Twenty-Second Congress of the CPSU and a number of revisionist doctrines propagated in the later fifties and sixties were traced back to the Twentieth Congress.[10]

The Soviets countered the later criticism of the Twentieth Congress by the Chinese leadership by reminding the CPC that they had fully endorsed the thesis of the Twentieth Soviet Party Congress. They also drew attention to the circumstance that Mao himself, when opening the Eighth Congress of the CPC in September 1956, had praised the work of the Twentieth Party Congress of the CPSU and that on the same occasion Liu Shao-chi in

---

9. "Origin and development of the Differences. . . , "*People's Daily,* Sept. 6. 1963. (Editorial Departments of the *People's Daily* and *Red Flag* [Peking: Foreign Language Press, 1963]).

*On September 6, 1963, *People's Daily* wrote as follows:

It was necessary to criticize Stalin's mistakes. But in his secret report to the Twentieth Congress, Comrade Khrushchev completely negated Stalin and in doing so defamed the dictatorship of the proletariat, defamed the socialist system, the great CPSU, the great Soviet Union and the international communist movement. Far from using a revolutionary proletarian party's method of criticism and self-criticism for the purpose of making an earnest and serious analysis and summation of the historical experience of the dictatorship of the proletariat, he treated Stalin as an enemy and shifted the blame for all mistakes on to Stalin alone. . . . Stalin's life was that of a great Marxist-Leninist, a great proletarian revolutionary. For thirty years after Lenin's death, Stalin was the foremost leader of the international communist movement and the standard-bearer of the world revolution. During his lifetime Stalin made some serious mistakes, but compared to his great and meritorious deeds his mistakes are only secondary. . . .

In completely negating Stalin at the Twentieth Party Congress of the CPSU, Khrushchev in effect negated the dictatorship of the proletariat and the fundamental theories of Marxism-Leninism which Stalin defended and developed.

10. Publisher's Preface to *Statements by Khrushchev*, World Culture Press, Apr. 1965, p.v. (*PR*, Apr. 30, 1965).

particular had endorsed the condemnation of the "cult of the individual." In a widely noted article on April 5, 1956, *People's Daily* similarly expressed the belief that "all those positive factors" which previously were suppressed in the USSR will, as a result of the sharp·criticisms made at the Twentieth Congress, "inevitably spring to life and will become more firmly united in the struggle to build a communist society."[11]

Actually, many doctrines propounded at the Twentieth Congress did not seem to be so divisive at the time as they were to become late in 1957 and thereafter, following the radicalization of China's policies at home and abroad. It should also be pointed out that Khrushchev in 1956 was to a lesser degree the initiator of a new course than Peking later made it appear. In several respects it was Stalin's death rather than the Twentieth Party Congress that was the decisive turning-point in Soviet policy, though a radical Soviet turn was not made until February 1956. The "thaw" set in much earlier; in matters of foreign policy as well as in regard to de-Stalinization and domestic policy in general, the process began right after Stalin's death.*

In the view of some, de-Stalinization became identical with Khrushchevism; this deepened the gulf between Khrushchev and Mao and, as long as Khrushchev held the reins of power, between the USSR and the CPR. Yet Khrushchev's overthrow, eight years after the Twentieth Congress, did not lessen the deep differences between Moscow and Peking.

Only a few months after the Twentieth Congress of the CPSU, the Eighth Party Congress of the CPC convened, on September 8, 1956. Eleven years had elapsed since the Seventh Party Congress in 1945. In the meantime, the forces of the Kuomintang had lost the civil war and the Chinese People's Republic had been proclaimed. Communist China, in spite of her backwardness, had shown herself an equal to American forces on the Korean battle front and had laid the economic foundation for a new surge forward.

On September 15, 1956, Liu again presented the political report to the Eighth Party Congress.[12] But unlike the 1945 address, when Mao's name had been listed more than 100 times, in this report his name was mentioned only four times, a clear indication of his much more modest role and foreshadowing perhaps a further loss of status. Now there was also no allusion in the new Party constitution to Mao's thought as a guide to the actual practice of the Chinese Revolution and hardly any reference to him

11. See n 6 above.

*Also, the rapprochement with Belgrade and a different approach toward problems of the East European neighbors of the USSR and toward disarmament and the West—all these rather preceded than followed the Twentieth Party Congress.

12. L. Fessler, *The Party Comes of Age,* pp. 6f.

in the political report. In Liu's address words like "world peace" or "peaceful coexistence" or "peaceful settlement" appeared more than 35 times and specific reference was even made to "more somber-minded" people inside the ruling circles of the U.S. who were becoming aware that the policy of war was not to America's advantage. The revised Party constitution also emphasized the need for greater "democracy" in the CPC.

The deemphasis of Mao and the implied criticism of "personality cult," the insistence on Party democracy and, in foreign affairs, the stress on peaceful coexistence—all this was of course quite in line with the policies proclaimed by the Twentieth Party Congress of the CPSU earlier that year. The Eighth Party Congress of the CPC seemed to be a worthy sequel to the Congress of the CPSU, reaffirming some of its basic policies and toeing its line. Mao personally may not have liked this course, but the CPC clearly ranged itself at the side of the CPSU. Both parties and countries seemed to march shoulder to shoulder and to follow a more "liberal" Communist line. Moscow then approved of Peking's course and continued to do so even later, though its own policy was to become less "liberal." The CPC's Eighth Party Congress has always pleased the CPSU, since it acknowledged the theme of "peaceful coexistence" with the West, recognized Moscow's leadership within the Communist bloc, and assigned a more modest role to Mao than the Seventh Congress had done.

China's Intervention in the Polish and Hungarian Crises and the USSR, October-November 1956

After Stalin's death both the USSR and its satellite Empire went through a period of prolonged crisis. Khrushchev's momentous denunciation of Stalin at the Twentieth Congress of the CPSU had unleashed a veritable storm and giant waves swept throughout the Communist world. In October 1956 both Hungary and Poland were gripped by revolution, Moscow was faced with one of the most crucial decisions in its history—military intervention or the defection of Hungary, and China, in a stunning turn of events, was called upon to play the role of moderator.

On October 31, 1956, *Pravda* published a "Declaration by the Government of the USSR on the Principles of Development and Further Strengthening of Friendship and Cooperation between the Soviet Union and Other Socialist States," bearing the date of October 30.[13] The declaration, referring to the Polish and Hungarian events of late October 1956, freely

13. "Declaration by the Government of the USSR on the Principles of Development and Further Strengthening of Friendship and Cooperation between the Soviet Union and other Socialist States, *Pravda*, Oct. 31, 1956 (*CDSP* 8, no. 45 [Nov. 14, 1956]: 10-11).

admitted that in the process of the rise of the system of people's democracies after the Second World War many different unresolved problems and downright mistakes, "including mistakes in the mutual relations among the socialist countries," had occurred—"violations and errors which demeaned the principle of equality in relations among socialist states." The Soviet government declared itself ready to review jointly with the people's democracies the question of the expediency of the further presence of Soviet advisors and of Soviet military units in these countries. In reference to Hungary in particular, the Soviet Government voiced its "deep regret" for the bloodshed that had taken place.

This declaration by the Soviet Government was hailed in the people's democracies and in the CPR. On November 2, 1956, *People's Daily,* the organ of the Central Committee of the CPC, in the article "Long Live the Great Unity of the Socialist Countries," called the Soviet declaration a highly significant document.[14] The socialist cause, new in man's history, could not be immune from errors of one kind or another. But all the errors made in the mutual relations between the socialist countries could be corrected and eliminated. Therefore, this could never be a pretext for breaking the unity of the socialist countries and friendship with the Soviet Union. The Chinese people, it said, "hope that their comradely influence can help the cause of socialism in Hungary in its present serious condition and by positive action can safeguard the great internationalist solidarity of the socialist countries with the Soviet Union at the center." The CPR stood firmly inside the Socialist camp headed by the Soviet Union. The friendship with the USSR was "forever unshakeable."

Simultaneously with this authoritative article was published the official Peking Statement on the Declaration of the Soviet Government on Relations Among Socialist States, November 1, 1956.[15] The government of the CPR asserted therein that the five principles of mutual respect for the sovereignty and territorial integrity of states—nonaggression, nonintervention in each other's internal affairs, equality and mutual benefit, and peaceful coexistence—should be the principles governing the establishment and development of mutual relations among the nations of the world and should certainly govern relations among socialist countries. Referring to the admission by the Soviet government of mistakes committed and resulting misunderstandings and estrangements, the Chinese Statement illustrated them by pointing specifically to the 1948-49 Yugoslav situation and the most recent happenings in Poland and Hungary. The demands raised by the people of Poland and Hungary that democratic independence and equality

14. *People's Daily,* Nov. 2, 1956, quoted in P. E. Zinner, *National Communism and Popular Revolt in Eastern Europe* (New York, 1956), pp. 492-95.
15. *Ibid.*

be strengthened and the material well-being of the people be raised were completely proper and their satisfaction would have a favorable impact upon the unity of the socialist countries. The Polish leaders were praised because they wisely differentiated between the just demands of the people and conspiratorial activities of an extremely small number of reactionary elements.

It often happened that certain personnel of socialist governments neglected the principle of equality among nations in their mutual relations. "Such a mistake, particularly the mistake of chauvinism by a big country," the Statement continued, resulted in serious damage to the solidarity and common cause of the socialist countries.

The Statement of the Chinese Government drew the conclusion that leading members of the Peking government and the people of the entire country must at all times be vigilant to prevent the error of big-nation chauvinism in relations with socialist countries and others, and carry out appropriate education. Thus Peking seemingly refrained from adding its own criticism to Soviet self-criticism. But this, of course, was deceptive. Under the guise of approving the most recent Soviet statement, the CPC actually castigated Soviet policy. Referring to the Soviet-Yugoslav dispute of 1948-49, it expressed the view that the errors that led to the crisis in Poland and Hungary were of long standing and that the post-Stalin regime had not improved on Soviet conduct with socialist states; it was actually guilty of an unforgivable crime—of "bourgeois chauvinism," of "big-nation chauvinism."

Peking had not challenged the USSR at the moment of acute crisis in Eastern Europe; on the contrary, it had appeared fearful of its possible consequences for the entire socialist bloc, including Communist China. But it came out strongly for the just demands of the peoples of Hungary and Poland and for their "democratic independence" and equality. Peking held that these demands could be satisfied within the socialist bloc without destroying its unity.

The Chinese leaders appear to have given encouragement to the movement of the East European peoples for greater autonomy from Moscow. Mao is alleged to have urged the Poles not only to develop greater "autonomy" but also to model their social system after the Yugoslav pattern. During the October crisis, after Khrushchev's sudden appearance in the Polish capital, Warsaw quickly appealed to Peking, and with apparent success: Peking let Moscow know of its opposition to Soviet armed intervention in Poland.[16]

Much later, in 1963, *People's Daily* and *Red Flag*, while blaming the

16. *New York Times,* Nov. 4 and 12, 1956.

Twentieth Party Congress of the CPSU for the deluge of revisionist ideas sweeping Europe, pointed to other "grave errors" of the Soviet leaders. "By moving up troops in an attempt to subdue the Polish comrades by armed force, it [Moscow] committed the error of great-power chauvinism. And at the critical moment when the Hungarian counterrevolutionaries had occupied Budapest, it intended to adopt a policy of capitulation and abandon socialist Hungary to counterrevolution."[17] Thus the USSR was accused both of chauvinism—in the case of Poland—and insufficient revolutionary fervor in the case of Hungary, the latter accusation being based upon mere temporary vacillation. Ideological inconsistency aside, Moscow appeared to Peking tactically indecisive and floundering.

Communist China's ambivalent tendencies and contradictory interests were clearly reflected in Peking's wavering attitude toward Hungary. Peking showed early sympathy for Budapest's demand for national autonomy, which was manifested in the early phase of the Hungarian Revolution. When, however, the government headed by Imre Nagy unfurled the flag of neutrality and made clear its resolve to withdraw from the Warsaw pact, Peking took this as an unmistakable sign of the victory of counterrevolution in Hungary and of the country's impending defection from the socialist camp and applauded Soviet intervention. As *People's Daily* and *Red Flag* put it later: "We insisted on taking all necessary measures to smash the counter-revolutionary rebellion in Hungary and firmly opposed the abandonment of socialist Hungary."[18] In the end Peking supported bloc unity under Moscow's leadership, not a national revolution leading to separation and thus to the weakening of the socialist commonwealth. This very position was reaffirmed by Chou En-lai during his tour of Hungary and Poland in January 1957; while he still pledged assistance to both countries, he made clear his own acceptance of Moscow's preeminence.

Communist China's position toward the Hungarian and Polish revolutions was of course an ambiguous one. On the one hand, Peking was favorably inclined toward polycentrist tendencies in Communism which, if successful, were likely to strengthen her own position vis-à-vis the USSR. On the other hand, as a major state with vast human, natural, and geographic resources, the CPR was in a different position from that of the smaller East European satellites of the USSR and might have anticipated the time when she herself would be the center of a satellite empire, similar to the one the USSR had created in Europe after World War II. She also might have feared the impact of a successful Hungarian and Polish challenge to the Soviet Union and of the possible defection of either from the socialist camp.

17. See n 9 above.
18. *Ibid.*

Communist China, taking advantage of the crisis in Europe, threw, to the amazement of the entire world, her weight into the European scales. She thus accomplished an unprecedented feat, one of the greatest and one not yet fully appreciated diplomatic revolutions in modern times. China's voice suddenly was attentively listened to in Europe. Peking then appeared to some as the very champion of national equality in the socialist camp. Her role, however, due to the generally obsequious tone and behavior toward the USSR and continuing recognition of her overall leadership, was apparently not resented by the latter.

Moscow was probably not entirely happy about China's continued forays into Europe, but might have considered her diplomatic and comradely ventures in East European affairs helpful to a degree. Poland, at least, seemed to be appreciative of China's role as a reliable "good and tried friend," though Hungary's hopes of Chinese assistance were rather disappointed.[19]

The Moscow Meeting and the Declaration, November 1957

In November 1957, delegations from all Communist countries except Yugoslavia converged upon Moscow for the celebration of the fortieth anniversary of the Bolshevik revolution. The Chinese delegation was headed by Mao Tse-tung himself.

The Moscow meeting of 1957 consisted of two parts. First was a meeting of the twelve "socialist," actually Communist-ruled countries, which adopted the Moscow Declaration (November 14-16); then followed the full session of the sixty-four parties, which endorsed the Moscow Peace Manifesto (November 16-19). On November 18 Mao delivered a speech that for the first time revealed to many delegates China's unique position.

After the launching of the first Sputnik on August 26, 1957, Mao was under the strong impression that the Soviets possessed great military strength. He considered the Soviet space achievement, at a time when the United States "had not yet got up a potato," a striking illustration of a major scientific and potential military breakthrough, an assessment that conflicted with the more modest Soviet evaluation of the significance of the first Sputnik launching.[20] In his address at the Moscow meeting, Mao asserted that the international situation had reached a critical point. The East wind now prevailed over the West wind: "That is to say the forces of socialism are overwhelmingly superior to the forces of imperialism." On the other hand, "war maniacs" might drop atomic or hydrogen bombs.

19. Gomulka's speech, Nov. 26, 1956, quoted by J. Gittings, *Survey of the Sino-Soviet Dispute* (London, 1968), p. 69; also BBC Summary of World Broadcasts, pt. 2a, no. 782.
20. Quoted in Gittings, p. 80; Report by Ebert, *Neues Deutschland*, Nov. 30, 1957.

As Mao recounted:

> I debated this question with a foreign statesman. He believed that if an
> atomic war was fought the whole of mankind would be annihilated. I
> said that if worse came to worst and half of mankind died, the other
> half would remain while imperialism would be razed to the ground and
> the whole world would become socialist; in a number of years there
> would be 700 million people again and definitely more. We Chinese
> have not yet completed our construction and we desire peace. However,
> if imperialism insists on fighting a war, we will have no alternative
> but. . .to fight to the finish before going ahead with our construction.[21]

According to the later voiced Moscow view, this speech signified a tendency to underestimate the consequences of a hydrogen war; in Peking's
opinion, such a war would merely delay the return to "construction."
Furthermore, while, according to the Soviets, their technological accomplishments enhanced the prospects for peace by tilting the balance of power
in their favor, in the Chinese view the spectacular Soviet achievements justified greater militancy by the USSR and the socialist bloc in pursuing their
just objectives.[22]

The Moscow Meeting of Representatives of Communist and Workers'
Parties produced a significant document, the Moscow Declaration, which
since has figured large in the history of the world Communist movement
and forms an important page in the Sino-Soviet dispute in particular.[23]
Though the Chinese delegation had few outright supporters, it did exercise
an important role at the meeting. In the debate the noted heroine of the
Spanish Civil War, La Pasionara, in spite of her unquestionably pro-Soviet
stance, freely conceded the weight of a delegation that spoke for 600 million people! China's role at the meeting reflected her growing influence in
world Communism at a time when, following Stalin's death and the crisis
of 1956, the East European Empire of the USSR had been shaken to its
very foundation and Soviet prestige had suffered a major blow.

It was noted that at the Moscow Conference Mao gave strong support to
Soviet bloc leadership, reversing his position of the preceding year when
he had stressed equality within the bloc. In 1964 *People's Daily* and *Red
Flag* conceded that Mao in 1957 had acknowledged Moscow's leadership,
but asserted that this had never signified an abandonment of the principle

21. The Statement by the Spokesman of the Chinese Government—A Comment on the
Soviet Government's Statement of Aug. 21, *People's Daily*, Sept. 1, 1963 (*PR*, Sept. 6,
1963).

22. Moscow was to charge subsequently that Mao's inclination to consider his opponents,
including the U.S.A., only "paper tigers" was as ludicrous as his claim that the "only result" of a Third World War would be to hasten the complete destruction of the world
capitalist system.

23. Declaration of the Conference of twelve Communist Parties, *Pravda*, Nov. 14-16,
1957, Nov. 22, pp. 1-2 (*CDSP* 9, no. 47 [Jan. 1, 1958]: 3-7).

of equality among fraternal parties; it merely meant that the CPSU was to "carry greater responsibility and duties on its shoulders."[24] In any case, Mao's recognition of Moscow's leadership stemmed from both realistic and opportunistic considerations.

A bilateral agreement between the USSR and the CPR had been concluded prior to the Moscow Meeting, on October 18, 1957. After the Conference, on January 18, 1958, the two powers signed a protocol that provided for a five-year program of cooperation along scientific lines. Mao's move at the Moscow Conference to flatter the Soviet ego was apparently made in exchange for what he considered all-important military and economic aid. It was also made in return for substantial theoretical concessions to the Chinese point of view. The all-important Declaration, drafted at the Moscow Conference, was, as finally accepted, a compromise between the Moscow and Peking points of view. Actually, the Declaration contained irreconcilable positions. But for this very reason both Moscow and Peking, alleged "revisionists" and "dogmatists," could subsequently turn to it for inspiration, for the justification of their policies, and for the condemnation of their "heretical" opponents.

People's Daily and *Red Flag,* long after the Moscow Conference, have depicted the violent struggle behind the scenes of the 1957 Moscow meeting and the major role then played by the Chinese delegation in drafting the Declaration. The papers also claimed that the Chinese spokesman made concessions out of regard for the "different position" of the CPSU:[25] the latter on a number of points insisted on the Declaration's being compatible with the resolutions of the Twentieth Congress of the CPSU in 1956.

Whatever the deeper reasons for the concessions, they were mutual. In his speech on November 14, Mao, in a rather self-deprecatory and submissive vein, insisted on the need for Soviet leadership of the socialist camp and in the world Communist movement. According to him, "the CPC is not worthy of this function [leadership]. . . . China has not even a quarter of a sputnik, whereas the Soviet Union has two."[26] Mao's stress on Moscow's Communist bloc leadership displeased even Kadar and Gomulka, and may have accounted for Yugoslavia's absence from the Meeting.*

24. Editorial Departments of *People's Daily* and *Red Flag, People's Daily,* Feb. 4, 1964 (*PR*, Feb. 7, 1964).

25. See n 9 above.

26. Report by Ebert, *Neues Deutschland,* Nov. 30, 1957.

*About Gomulka's alleged reproaches to Mao for having sold out to Moscow in exchange for Soviet economic and military aid, see *Le Monde,* December 19, 1957. Gittings, in his thorough study of the Sino-Soviet rift, which focuses on the years 1962-63, holds that Mao's line on Soviet primacy in 1957 at the Moscow conference was "more anti-Yugoslav than pro-Soviet." In any case, he could not have overlooked the apparent anti-Chinese implication of Mao's stand.

The Declaration proclaimed that "the main content of the present epoch was the transition from capitalism to socialism, which actually had begun by the Great October Socialist Revolution in Russia. More than a third of the population of the world—more than 950,000,000 people—had since taken the road of socialism and were building a new life. The tremendous development of the forces of socialism had stimulated tempestuous growth of the anti-imperialist national movement in the postwar period." Besides the Chinese People's Republic, the Democratic Republic of Vietnam and the Korean People's Democratic Republic, altogether more than 700,000,000 people, had shaken off the colonial yoke and established national independent states during the past twelve years. The peoples of the colonial and dependent countries, still languishing in slavery, were intensifying the struggle for their national liberation. The victory of the USSR in 1945 and the development of socialism and of the national liberation movement had sharply accelerated the disintegration of imperialism. Imperialism had lost its one-time domination over the greater part of mankind.

From the pages of the Declaration Soviet Russia emerged in splendid preeminence; the exemplary role of the Russian October Revolution and the decisive importance of Soviet experience for all socialist states were duly stressed. The Chinese People's Republic was listed side by side with other socialist states, including the Democratic Republic of Vietnam and the Korean People's Republic. While the Soviet Union's great successes in economic, scientific, and technical progress were singled out, China was not even specially mentioned in these respects, but figured anonymously among "other socialist countries" that were achieving, it was benevolently conceded, "results" in socialist construction.

The Declaration went on to stress that world development was now determined by the course and results of the competition between two diametrically opposed social orders. During the last 40 years socialism had proven superior to capitalism as a social system. It was on the upgrade, while imperialism was heading toward decline. Nevertheless, aggressive imperialist circles of the United States were pursuing the policy of the so-called position-of-strength, attempting to bring most countries of the globe under their sway and to place a new form of colonial yoke on the liberated peoples. "In the postwar years the American, British, French, and other imperialists and their lackeys have conducted or are conducting wars in Indochina, Indonesia, Korea, Malaya, Kenya, Guatemala, Egypt, Algeria, Oman, and Yemen."

The question of war or peaceful coexistence had become the fundamental problem in world politics. The forces of peace had grown so formidable that there was a real possibility of averting war, as was demonstrated by the failure of the imperialists' aggressive designs in Egypt and by the failure of their plans to use counterrevolutionary forces for the overthrow of the people's democratic system in Hungary. The cause of peace was now upheld by powerful forces, by the camp of socialist states headed by the Soviet Union, by the peace-loving anti-imperialist states of Asia and Africa which, together with the socialist countries, formed "a large peace zone"; by the international working class and "above all, its vanguard, the Communist Parties"; by the liberation movement of the peoples of the colonies and semicolonies, the mass peace movement, the neutral European countries and the peoples of Latin America, and the masses in the imperialist countries themselves. The alliance of these mighty forces was strong enough to prevent the outbreak of war. It is to this very concept that war is not inevitable but can be averted that the Soviets in their later open dispute with Communist China harked back repeatedly.

The Leninist principle of peaceful coexistence of the two different social systems was the firm foundation of foreign policy of the socialist countries. The five principles advanced jointly by the Chinese People's Republic and the Republic of India, and the program adopted by the Bandung Conference of African and Asian countries, were listed as corresponding to the interests of peaceful coexistence—the program now of the broad masses in all the countries of the world. On the whole, however, China's role in foreign affairs was toned down; such honors as there were in Asia were shared by several countries, including India. In the struggle for peace and for peaceful coexistence, Communist China still played only a subordinate role as compared to the USSR.

In its reference to the role of the national-liberation and democratic movements in the world, the Conference again underlined the preeminence of Soviet Russia and the lesser role of China. The working class, the democratic forces and the working people of all countries were interested in defending the historic political and social gains effected in the Soviet Union, "the first and mightiest socialist power," in the Chinese People's Republic, and in all the socialist countries. The victory of socialism in the USSR and the successes in socialist construction in the people's democracies evoked ever deeper sympathy among the broad masses of working people of all countries. Again, the Declaration left no doubt about the CPSU being the leader of the assembled Communist parties and of world Communism in general.

The Declaration considered revisionism "the main danger" to the international Communist movement, though it already warned that dogmatism might become the main threat, an ominous notice to Peking. The Declaration underlined the necessity of resolutely overcoming both revisionism and dogmatism in the ranks of Communist and Workers' Parties. Dogmatism and sectarianism hindered the creative application of Marxist-Leninist theory in concrete, changing conditions, "replacing study of the specific situation with quotations and pedantry" and leading to the Party's isolation from the masses. Yet each Communist Party was to determine which deviation, revisionism or dogmatism, was the main danger at a given time.

The forms of the transition of different countries from capitalism to socialism might vary. The working class and its vanguard—the Marxist-Leninist party—sought to bring about socialist revolution by peaceful means. Under present-day conditions the working class in a number of capitalist countries might be able to unite the majority of the people, win a firm majority in parliament, and with mass support from outside the parliament bring about the socialist revolution peacefully. Yet it was necessary to bear in mind another possibility, "non-peaceful transition to socialism."

Toward the end the Declaration acknowledged the likelihood that the Communist movement might encounter difficulties and obstacles. In spite of absurd assertions of imperialism regarding the so-called crisis in Communism, the Communist movement would, it was boldly asserted, undoubtedly hasten "great new victories for the cause of peace, democracy, and socialism on a world scale." Yet even in regard to "socialism" the Declaration stressed Soviet rather than Chinese experiences. The historic decisions of the Twentieth Party Congress, it asserted, were not only of great importance for the Communist Party of the Soviet Union and the building of Communism in the USSR; they had also laid the basis for a new stage in the international Communist movement and contributed to its further development on the basis of Marxism-Leninism. The ruling CPC in this context was merely compared to the still struggling French and Italian Communist Parties.

In spite of many compromises in the Declaration, there could be no question as to the relative roles and importance of Moscow and Peking, as to which of the two powers was preeminent and where the ultimate leadership was located. Nor was Soviet leadership of the socialist camp seriously questioned during the double crisis over Taiwan and the Middle East in the summer of 1958, though the differences that then emerged between Moscow and Peking were never fully erased.

The Taiwan Straits Crisis (August-October 1958) and Intervention in the Middle East (July-August 1958)

In the summer of 1958 two major crises, one in the Far East, the other in the Middle East, brought the world to the brink of war. The first-named crisis threatened a confrontation between the United States and Communist

China over Taiwan. The second pitted the United States against the Soviet Union. When the revolution in Baghdad threatened to spill beyond its borders and the entire Middle East teetered on the brink of chaos, American and British troops landed in Lebanon and Jordan respectively. Fear prevailed that Soviet Russia too might actively intervene and a military clash become unavoidable.

But it soon became evident that the USSR would not respond in kind. Khrushchev, in a relatively mild note of protest against the American and British military intervention forwarded to President Eisenhower, proposed a summit meeting between the heads of government of the USSR, the United States, Britain, France, and India, with the participation of the Secretary General of the United Nations. Khrushchev stressed the Soviet view on peaceful methods of solving the pressing problems of the Near East and Middle East. He assured the Western Powers of their continued access to the oil and other raw materials of that part of the globe and also urged the heads of states of the concerned nations to consider the question of stopping shipments and arms to the countries of the Near and Middle East. The Soviet government was prepared "to go anywhere,"[27] but the Party Secretary proposed a meeting in Geneva to start two days later.

Khrushchev had not insisted on the participation of the United Arab Republic or of any other Arab state, nor of that of Communist China in spite of the latter's apparent aspirations in the Middle East. Later he accepted an American amendment to the effect that the meeting take place within the framework of the United Nations Security Council. Peking apparently was disturbed over these developments, which would have excluded her, and warned against "yielding to evil."[28]

Two weeks after Khrushchev's proposition, on August 4, the Russian press, following a meeting between Soviet and Chinese political and military leaders which, ominously, had been held in Peking, published a joint communiqué by the USSR and Communist China on the Middle East. This communiqué was phrased incomparably more sharply than the earlier Soviet protest. The Soviets therein went far in acquiescing to the Chinese point of view. The communiqué spoke of the "exceptional cordiality and warmth" of the meeting and the comprehensive exchange of views that had extended to a number of major questions confronting both sides in Asia and in Europe. The earlier Soviet proposition for a Summit conference that would have banished China was not again repeated. But in spite of Moscow's change in tactics, the Soviets avoided any firm pledge in regard to the Middle East or, for that matter, in regard to Taiwan.

27. *Pravda* and *Izvestiia*, July 20, 1963, p. 1 (*CDSP* 15, no. 29 [Aug. 14, 1963]: 4-5).
28. *People's Daily* editorial, July 20, 1958, quoted in D. S. Zagoria, *The Sino-Soviet Conflict 1956-1961* (Princeton, N.J., 1962), p. 196.

On August 6 Khrushchev dropped his proposal for a Summit conference within the framework of the Security Council, since, as he now recalled, China would not be represented on it. In spite of his yielding to Peking's pressure, the Chinese press continued its implicit criticism of a soft Soviet policy in the Middle East.

Clearly, Peking had no interest in abating the tension in the Middle East so long as tension in the Taiwan Straits was acute. On the contrary, a lessening of America's preoccupation in the Middle East was likely to strengthen America's hand in the Taiwan Straits. Also, differently from Moscow, Peking suggested that ''international assistance'' be extended to Lebanon and Iraq, a help that no doubt would take the form of dispatching arms and volunteers from the Soviet bloc. Communist China, going thus beyond what the USSR considered advisable, struck a radical, ultra-leftist pose.

On July 23 the CPR once again raised the call for the liberation of Taiwan. The situation surrounding Taiwan had remained quiet for about three-and-one-half years. Alarmed at the unexpected worsening of the situation, and fearful that China might accelerate military preparations in the Taiwan Straits, Khrushchev, as mentioned, flew to Peking for talks with the Chinese leaders (July 31-August 3), apparently with little advance notice to his hosts. The final communiqué issued after their conference was vague about the Middle East and had nothing at all to say about Taiwan. A few days after Khrushchev's departure, Peking unleashed once again a vigorous propaganda about the liberation of Taiwan. And on August 23 the Chinese began the shelling of Quemoy. During the ensuing verbal duel between Peking and Washington, Moscow remained rather silent. American Secretary of State John Foster Dulles warned that any attempt by Peking to change the status quo by force would bring prompt American retaliation. In response, China let it be known that she would not be deterred in her attempts to liberate Taiwan and the offshore islands. But on September 6 Chou-En-lai consented to ambassadorial talks with the United States, thus indicating Peking's willingness for a peaceful settlement.

The diplomatic game as played by the Soviets was compounded of utmost caution and reluctance to be drawn into an atomic war for the liberation of Taiwan and the desire to appear as a true friend and loyal ally of the Chinese comrades, though the latter were already suspect on several grounds. This Soviet attitude was clearly reflected in Soviet press statements.

On August 31 *Pravda* published an article, entitled ''Dangerous Playing with Fire,'' criticizing American military preparation on Taiwan.[29] The island, occupied by the United States, had been, it was said, an integral part

29. *Pravda*, Aug. 31, 1958, p. 4 (*CDSP* 10, no. 35 [1959]: 16-17).

of China for many centuries, long before Columbus discovered the American continent. In 1950, President Truman had tried to depict the United States' action as designed to "neutralize" Taiwan for the period of the Korean conflict. Though the conflict had long been ended, Dulles, discarding all camouflage, had bluntly referred to Taiwan as a "strategic island." The American imperialists should stop trying the patience of the Chinese people. The Soviet people, like all the peoples of the mighty socialist camp, supported the just struggle of the fraternal Chinese people for the restoration of their legal rights on Taiwan and the other offshore islands. The Soviet Union would render the CPR "the necessary moral and material aid in its just struggle." The organizers of the armed provocations deceived themselves by thinking that they would be able to localize the conflict. In spite of these threats, neither the writer of the article nor the Soviets in subsequent declarations gave a definite pledge to China to come militarily to her assistance in the event of a Sino-American conflagration.

On September 5 *Pravda* similarly charged that American diplomats and generals were shouting that even the small Chinese offshore islands were of great importance to the defense and security of the United States herself. The Soviet Union could not remain indifferent to clashes along the very border of her great ally and would "not sit by quietly while United States military preparations unfold in the Pacific whose waters also wash Soviet shores." Bound to the CPC "by ties of fraternal friendship and mutual aid," the Soviet people, *Pravda* asserted, would give their brothers "all possible aid" to curb adventurers and warmongers. In spite of the threatening language, the USSR again fell short of pledging outright military assistance to the CPR.

On September 20 *Pravda* published another note from Khrushchev addressed to President Eisenhower, asking for the withdrawal of American warships from the Taiwan Straits and of American troops from Taiwan. Otherwise Peking would have "no other recourse" but to drive the armed forces of the enemy from its territory, which had been transformed into an arsenal for the attack against the CPR. The Soviet Union, *Pravda* pledged, would continue to support Peking's policy. Soviet promises had at times a flamboyant streak, but in their essence remained vague and empty.

Moscow's refusal to give Peking vigorous support was the primary reason for Communist China's abandoning her military stance toward Taiwan. On October 6 China proclaimed a unilateral ceasefire. The Taiwan crisis had died a natural death.

What remained very much alive, however, was a dispute over the role of the Soviets during the height of the crisis and the extent of their assistance to the CPR.

The Soviets made the most of two communications from Khrushchev to Eisenhower, dated September 7 and 19, in which they had asserted their support for their ally. The Chinese, however, later pointed out correctly that the Soviets had waited with their declaration until after the apex of the crisis had been reached and a peaceful settlement assured. In his first letter to the American President, Khrushchev warned that an attack on China was identical with an attack on the USSR, but avoided spelling out whether Soviet Russia would resort to nuclear weapons in the defense of the CPR. Only in his second letter, after the resumption of the ambassadorial talks between Peking and Washington, did Khrushchev refer to the 1950 Sino-Soviet Treaty; then he went further, hinting at the possible use of atomic weapons, without, however, clearly and irrevocably committing himself to it.

The outcome of the Taiwan crisis may have been a diplomatic defeat for Peking, but it strengthened its desire for its own nuclear deterrent. Also, it must have raised many a doubt in the Chinese mind about the reliability of the Sino-Soviet military tie-up, and especially about its possible use in wresting concessions from the United States. On these grounds the Taiwan crisis worsened the relationship between Peking and Moscow. The subsequent Russian claims, greatly exaggerated, did not help to improve this relationship.[30] *Krasnaya Zvezda's* assertion that the nuclear might of the USSR had "saved millions of Chinese from nuclear death and defended the sovereignty, security, and independence of their country" must have been galling to the utmost to Peking.[31] Moscow presented a bill for services it had never rendered, for saving China from an illusory nuclear holocaust. Peking asserted with ample justification that, though the Taiwan situation had become tense, outbreak of nuclear war had been quite unlikely.

The Soviets, on the other hand, pointed to a letter from the CC of the CPC, dated October 15, 1958, and signed by Mao himself, expressing his "gratitude" for help rendered and his confidence that the Soviet Union would unfailingly render assistance. This, however, could be interpreted as an expression of hope for the future rather than one of full gratification for actions already taken. By the time this letter was written, Peking had already announced a unilateral ceasefire.

The Twenty-First Congress of the CPSU (January-February 1959)

In spite of the differences that had arisen between Moscow and Peking

30. Soviet Government Statement, Aug. 21, 1963, and "Statement by the Spokesman of the Chinese Government—a comment on the Soviet Government Statement of August 21," *People's Daily,* Sept. 1, 1963 (*PR*, Sept. 6, 1963).
31. *Krasnaya Zvezda,* Aug. 25, 1963, p. 3 (*CDSP* 15, no. 34 [Sept. 18, 1963]: 32).

on foreign and domestic policy, both sides were long concerned with concealing their serious rift from their own peoples and the world at large. Thus at the Twenty-First Congress of the CPSU, which opened its doors on January 29, 1959, open disagreements between the USSR and the CPR were avoided. But Khrushchev's emphasis on peace, his cautiously critical remarks about the Great Leap Forward, his denial of, though giving close attention to, Yugoslav charges of alleged differences between the CPSU and the CPC, and his stress on the recognition of the CPSU as "the first" among all fraternal parties, were all quite ominous—at least they must appear so to today's analyst of Sino-Soviet relations.

Turning first to the domestic scene, Khrushchev linked internal endeavors to Soviet foreign policy and the pursuit of peace in particular. The significance of the Seven-Year Plan lay, he asserted, in that it was imbued with "the spirit of peace."[32] The plan would so greatly increase the economic potential of the USSR that it would work to the advantage of the forces of peace in the international arena and thus improve conditions for averting a world war. Khrushchev came out for the prohibition of atomic and hydrogen weapons and for peaceful coexistence. He propagated the concept of an atom-free zone in the Far East and in the entire Pacific basin. Chou En-lai, however, in his later address to the Soviet Congress, did not dignify Khrushchev's suggestions by making any comment.[33]

The Congress referred to the Conferences of representatives of Communist and Workers' Parties in November 1957, especially to its Declaration, which had condemned revisionism as the principal danger but had also denounced dogmatism and sectarianism. Since then, the revisionist "scum" had not succeeded in turning a single fraternal Party from the Marxist-Leninist path. However, revisionism was not yet dead, and it was up to the Yugoslav League of Communists to turn toward rapprochement. Then, however, the Congress pointed its finger eastward to Communist China, though without mentioning her by name. There was "also the need to combat dogmatism, sectarianism," which impeded the development of Marxist-Leninist theory and its creative application and caused the Communist parties to lose contact with the masses.

The Yugoslav Communists, according to Khrushchev, charged Moscow with "hegemonism" in the world Communist movement, and the foreign reactionaries similarly spoke of the "dependence" of Communist and Workers' Parties on Moscow. In making their accusations, both referred to the well-known thesis from the Declaration of the Moscow conference that the camp of socialist states was "headed" by the Soviet Union. But this was merely "a tribute to our country" and to the CPSU as "the first Party

32. *Pravda*, Jan. 28, 1959, pp. 2-10 (*CDSP* 10, no. 4 [1959]: 17-25).
33. *Ibid.*

to carry out the socialist revolution, the first to take power.'' And Khrushchev expressed ''sincere gratitude'' to the fraternal parties for this recognition of the historic role of the Soviet Union. ''As regards the Soviet Union, its role. . .consists not in controlling other countries, but in having been the first to blaze the trail to socialism for mankind, in being the most powerful country in the international socialist system and the first to have entered the period of extensive building of communism.''

There seems to be little doubt that the adoption by the Twenty-First Congress of the Statement on Problems of Theory was prompted by the Chinese challenge, especially the policy of the ''Great Leap Forward.'' The Twenty-First Congress of the CPSU had stated explicitly that the transition from the socialist stage of development to the higher phase was ''a logical historical process that one cannot arbitrarily violate or bypass.'' While the building of a Communist society was considered the ultimate goal of Communist parties, society ''cannot leap from capitalism to communism,'' skipping the socialist stage of development. Some comrades might say that the principles of Communism should be introduced sooner, yet passing prematurely to distribution according to needs would harm the cause of building Communism. ''Gradual'' transition to Communism should not be understood as a slowed movement; on the contrary it was a period of ''rapid revelopment.''

Communism was linked first of all to the further development of productive forces, to the increase in the production of goods and especially to the level of production in the developed capitalist countries. (The last-named factor, a rather extraneous one for judging Communism, was apparently introduced to establish a more definite yardstick, one applicable to the USSR but virtually excluding China.) All socialist countries were building socialism, but they were not doing it by stereotype. The CPC was employing many original forms of socialist construction. ''But we have no disagreements with this party, although in many respects its methods of building socialism do not resemble our own.'' China had its specific features of historic development and its own national culture. ''Therefore it would be a mistake to ignore these specific features and to copy what is good for one country, but unsuitable for another.'' There was no dispute between the CPSU and the CPC, because they shared the same class approach and class conception.

The section on ''Theory'' ended with an appeal to the Yugoslavs not to look for ''cracks where they don't exist.'' Yet the mere fact that Khrushchev dealt with Sino-Soviet differences rather extensively, and his repeated assurances that they were insignificant and only historically and culturally rooted, lent substance to their reality. Whatever the roots of these differences, they sank deeper as a result of Peking's ''Great Leap Forward.''

"The Great Leap Forward"

After the failure of the One Hundred Flowers Movement in 1957, China decided to turn radically to the left. This resolve found expression in the "Three Red Banners" program for the construction of socialism. Peking then unfurled the flag of the "Great Leap Forward," which demanded rapid industrial development, the People's Commune's Movement in the field of agriculture, and the "Everyone a Soldier" Movement, which meant expansion of the popular militia throughout all of China.

The Chinese leadership under Mao was driven by a curious combination of revolutionary ardor and national pride. Inspired by her long and heroic struggle, it seemed gripped by the fervent belief that the CPR would overcome all obstacles on the road to rapid economic and social progress toward Communism by the sheer will power of her millions of people, little Marxist as this faith seemed to be. Also, Peking seemed plainly averse to tying itself too closely to Moscow.

At the same time the USSR, while giving extensive loans and aid to Third World countries, especially India, treated China rather niggardly. The Soviet unwillingness to come forth with adequate economic and military aid, in spite of the promises that had already been made, contributed to Peking's decision to "go it alone." Once the policy of the Great Leap Forward was adopted, Chinese "self-reliance" acquired a momentum of its own. Economically, this expressed itself in resistance to associating the CPR with Comecon plans for economic integration.

First the Soviets gave the new Peking policy scant attention. Soon, however, they steadily mounted their criticism. It was clear to Soviet Russia that the Chinese claim to leapfrog certain stages of economic and social development and to be shortly within reach of "Communism" would deprive Soviet Russia of her status as the most advanced of all socialist countries and of her claim to leadership in the Communist bloc. This claim found expression in the thesis that the USSR was in the early phase of constructing Communism, while all the other Communist-ruled states were still constructing socialism. First Soviet Russia voiced a disguised, esoteric kind of criticism of the Great Leap Forward, but in informal talks with Chinese comrades soon offered it in blunter form. Moscow bared its critical attitude toward Peking's policies even to visiting Americans. In hardly camouflaged utterances Khrushchev warned against "economic maladjustment" and "over-arrogance," aiming unmistakably at Peking.

There were in 1958 and early 1959 some indications of an improvement in Sino-Soviet relations: praise for Soviet help to China, Chinese retractions of their earlier excessive claims about the People's Communes, and Khrushchev's admission that all the socialist countries would make the transition to Communism "more or less simultaneously." The latter prognosis acknowledged indirectly the "equality" of all fraternal parties, though of course it relegated it to a more distant future.

In 1963-64, when their quarrel had reached a new height, both Peking and Moscow revealed more about their differences in regard to the Great Leap Forward, which had separated them ever since 1958. Khrushchev had early accused the Chinese leaders of attempting to skip a whole stage in the building of a new society and had also denounced their "equalitarian Communism." In their statement of September 21, 1963, the Soviets similarly disclosed their concern about Peking's proclamation in 1958 of its line of the "Three Red Banners," since they considered it as leading to a "road of dangerous experiments, a road of disregard for economic laws and for the experience of other socialist states."[34] The excessive Chinese production goals were, in their view, not supported by sound economic calculations. The Soviets became alarmed when the CPC seemed to violate the Leninist principles of material incentive, abandoned the principle of remunerating labor, and went over to equalitarian distribution in People's Communes. Everything else aside, Peking's new economic policies could not have been understood by Moscow as anything but an indirect rebuke of her own different policies.

The CPSU, according to the foregoing Soviet Statement, could not come out with open criticism of the CPR. "We regarded it as our duty to tell the Chinese leaders in a comradely way as early as 1958 about our doubts concerning such 'innovations.' " Khrushchev personally told this to Mao in the summer of 1958, but the Chinese leaders, according to his account, turned a deaf ear to the remonstrations from Moscow. As a result, China's industry and agriculture were "seriously upset."[35] Originally the Chinese leadership had envisioned fifteen years as the time necessary for setting up the base for socialism in China. In 1958, however, they proclaimed that a period of only three years would be adequate for the transition to Communism. The so-called Great Leap, a political-economic adventure unprecedented in both design and scale, was based upon the desire, the Soviet statement acidly observed, "to solve grandiose tasks faster and to 'teach' others the newly invented methods of building socialism and communism."[36]

In the Soviet view, the Chinese leaders with the aid of fraternal socialist countries, had scored notable successes by 1958. These very successes in economic construction, however, had made them "dizzy, intoxicated." " 'China can do anything'—such was the official conclusion." The

34. Soviet Government Statement, Sept. 6, 1963, in *Pravda,* Sept. 21 and 22.
35. Ilyichev, "Revolutionary Science and the present day. . . ," June 1964; also *Kommunist,* no. 11, July 1963.
36. See *ibid.*

Chinese leaders, it was conceded, had been under heavy pressure to "hurry along," considering the magnitude of the task still ahead of them. When by the end of 1959 they found themselves confronted with the most serious economic difficulties, they once again produced a "sharp reversal," declaring agriculture to be the foundation of the economy. Having failed to outstrip the most highly developed countries, they attempted to score heavily on the political plane. According to the Soviets, the Chinese leaders' "hegemonic" pretensions grew directly out of their economic debacle.

The Chinese, on the other hand, have ascribed the difficulties they encountered in pursuing their policy of the Great Leap Forward to various causes: to serious natural calamities between the years 1959-61, to their own admitted shortcomings and mistakes, and, last but not least, to the selfish and vengeful policies of the Soviet Union, in particular to the withdrawal of Soviet experts in 1960. But they claimed to have triumphantly overcome all these difficulties.

According to the Chinese account, the Great Leap Forward was questioned by a minority in their own party.[37] At the Lushan meeting in 1959, in the official view of the CPC, "a handful of ambitious bourgeois careerists and schemers who had wormed their way into our party" launched "a ferocious attack" upon the Party's Central Committee headed by Mao and put forth a "revisionist program." These right opportunists had the alleged support of Khrushchev and the Soviet Party. The opposition was led by Defense Minister P'eng Teh-huai and included also his Chief of Staff Chang Wen-t'ien, a Vice Minister of Foreign Affairs and former Ambassador in Moscow. The Chinese charged then that P'eng had established contact with Khrushchev while the latter had visited Tirana. The CPC was infuriated at what it regarded as Khrushchev's interference in its internal affairs.

Apparently the policies of both the USSR and the CPR had found adherents in the other country and a minority of uncertain strength in either state questioned the adopted policies of the CPSU and CPC respectively. On the basis of the available evidence it is difficult to assess with any degree of accuracy the relative strength of such opposition in either party and country.

Nuclear Weapons and the Disarmament Problem, 1958-59

The first Chinese efforts in the field of nuclear science, according to their own accounts, were undertaken long before 1955. Thereafter, China

37. *People's Daily*, July 1, 1966; (*PR*, July 1, 1966), "Long Live Mao's . . . Thought,"

showed increasing desire to gain nuclear status. Perhaps all she may have wanted from the USSR was a moderate amount of nuclear aid to assist her in accelerating her own effort and to avoid needless and expensive research and experiments of her own. As late as September 1958, Mao himself held that China need not organize the production of such nuclear weapons, "especially considering the fact that they were very costly."[38]

At first, China's efforts appeared to be crowned with success. In 1955 the Soviets agreed to furnish aid to China for the construction of research reactors and for the training of nuclear scientists. On October 15, 1959, there was concluded another Sino-Soviet agreement on new technology for national defense, which was to furnish the CPR a sample of an atomic bomb and technical data concerning its manufacture. The Chinese leaders were to charge later that the Soviet government unilaterally tore up this agreement.[39] It appears that no subsequent agreement could be reached on the vital questions of control and command of nuclear weapons, including joint planning and command in the Far East. The Chinese later accused the Soviets of having put forward unreasonable demands designed to bring China under military control. The Soviets, on the other hand, appear to have been concerned that China might be inclined to take the military initiative against Taiwan and drag the Soviet Union into a war for the liberation of the island.

In 1958, the Chinese leadership embraced intransigent policies against the Offshore Islands. It vigorously promoted the "Everyone a Soldier" Movement, which aimed at nationwide expansion of the militia, and also unleashed a campaign of relying on China's own resources.[40] These policies were probably largely the result of China's disillusionment with Soviet Russia concerning assistance in the development of nuclear weapons. Military negotiations between Moscow and Peking seem to have continued during the year 1958, though without success. P'eng Teh-huai, the Chinese Minister of Defense, appears to have been a spokesman and ardent partisan of greater military interdependence with the USSR and the Warsaw Pact Nations. His activities, increasingly suspect, may have contributed to his abrupt dismissal as Minister of Defense late in September 1963.

Like many other differences between Peking and Moscow, those relating to nuclear weapons were not divulged until 1963-64. But on August 20 and 21, 1963, *Pravda*, in reply to a Chinese Government Statement of

38. Statement by Spokesman of Chinese Government, Sept. 21, 1963, *Pravda*, Sept. 21 and 22, 1963 (*CDSP* 15 (Oct. 16, 1963]: 3-15).
39. Statement by the Spokesman of the Chinese Government. . . , Aug. 15, 1963 (*PR*, Aug. 16, 1963).
40. New China News Agency, June 17, 1967 (*PR*, June 23, 1967).

August 15, published a Soviet Government Statement. According to the Soviets, Peking had shown keen displeasure at having been denied promised samples of atomic weapons. Perhaps the CPR, the Soviet statement ventured the opinion, "by overstraining her economy," might finally be able to produce a few atom bombs. But their number would be small compared to those aimed by the imperialists at the CPR. The Soviet statement denounced the practice of making public classified information relating to the defenses of the socialist commonwealth, a practice that raised questions about the Chinese Party leaders' reliability in general. The Soviet document further asserted that spreading nuclear weapons was against the interests of all socialist countries, including the CPR. "As history would have it[!], the Soviet Union is the only socialist country that produces nuclear weapons." Even if the CPR were to produce two or three bombs, this would not solve anything, but would only bring about a great exhaustion of China's economy. The most reasonable policy for the CPR would be to devote her efforts to her economic, scientific, technological, and agricultural development, and to the improvement of the well-being of the Chinese people and to meeting their vital needs.[41]

A few days later, on September 1, 1963, the Chinese leaders responded to the foregoing Soviet document with a "Statement by a Spokesman of the Chinese Government," which threw additional light upon the nuclear weapons dispute between the two powers in 1958-59.[42] The Chinese rejected the "slander" that the CPR had opposed the tripartite test-ban treaty between the United States, Great Britain, and Soviet Russia because they had been denied the atom bomb. But the Peking statement left no doubt that the Soviets' refusal to live up to their 1957 promise of rendering assistance in the development of the atom bomb, while at the same time lending assistance to nonsocialist India, was a turning point in Sino-Soviet relations. "Not only have you perfidiously [!] and unilaterally scrapped the agreement on providing China with nuclear technical data, but you have blatantly given more and more military aid to Indian reactionaries, who are hostile to China. . . . The real point is that the Soviet leaders hold that China should not, and must not, manufacture nuclear weapons, and that only the few nuclear powers, and particularly United States imperialism, . . . are entitled to continued production of nuclear weapons. . . . If the Soviet leaders practiced proletarian internationalism, they would have no reason whatever for obstructing China from manufacturing nuclear weapons." True, China was very poor and backward. "Soviet leaders say, how can the Chinese be qualified to manufacture nuc-

41. *Pravda*, Aug. 20 and 21, 1963.
42. Statement of the Chinese Government, *People's Daily*, Sept. 1, 1963 (*PR*, Sept. 6, 1963).

lear weapons when they eat watery soup out of a common bowl and do not even have pants to wear?'' The Soviet Leaders were perhaps too hasty in deriding China for its backwardness. But even if the Chinese people were unable to produce an atom bomb for a hundred years, "we will neither crawl to the baton of the Soviet leaders nor kneel before the nuclear blackmail of United States Imperialism.''

In their rejoinder of September 21, 1963, the Soviet Government statement voiced the fear that the Chinese desire to provide themselves with the atom bomb at all costs was bound to give rise to grave doubts regarding the aims of the foreign policy of China's leaders.[43] Such bombs were not needed for the defense of China and of the socialist camp. The Soviets, of course, would indignantly have rejected the argument that their own earlier development of the atomic bomb was an indication of anything but defensive military planning.

In any case, the events of 1959 enhanced Moscow's suspicions regarding the aims of Peking's foreign policy and raised the most serious questions about its subordination to the Kremlin.

The Sino-Indian Border Controversy, August-October 1959, and Peaceful Coexistence between East and West

During the summer and fall of 1959, Sino-Soviet relations worsened markedly. This came as a result of developments that affected the relationship between the USSR and the United States and that between China and India. Soviet Russia under Khrushchev was bent on improving relations with the United States, while China was willing to resort to force in her border conflict with India. The CPR, for patent reasons, was fulminating over the attempts of the Soviet Union to seek rapprochement with Washington. The USSR, on the other hand, suspected the CPR of wishing to destroy the chances for improving her relations with the United States. Moscow was indignant over Communist China's aggressive thrusts against India; such senseless aggression was bound to sully the image of Communism in the eyes of all, not only the United States but also the nonaligned Third World. Peking in turn bitterly resented lack of Soviet support in its border controversy with New Delhi; it later conceded that the difference on the Sino-Indian boundary question figured large in the unfurling of the Sino-Soviet dispute.[44]

43. Soviet Government Statement, Sept. 21, 1963, *Pravda*, Sept. 21 and 22, 1963; also ''A reply to Peking,'' Soviet Booklet no. 122, Sept. 1963.
44. Editorial Department, *People's Daily*, Nov. 2, 1963, ''The Truth about how the leaders of the CPSU have allied themselves with India against China'' (*PR*, Nov. 8, 1963, pp. 18-27).

In both August and October 1959 there occurred minor skirmishes along the Sino-Indian border. Each side accused the other of responsibility for these clashes, claiming that its territory had been violated. The incidents took place in an area claimed by both sides. The Chinese appear to have encroached upon the region before 1959, especially by constructing a road across the Aksai Chin region without knowledge of the government of New Delhi.

In the past Peking's relations with New Delhi had been quite good. But since the mid-fifties the Chinese leaders preferred to look upon India as a capitalist country lorded over by a reactionary bourgeoisie. Whatever India's former services to the cause of peace, progressivism, and anti-imperialism had been, New Delhi, according to Peking, had turned more and more toward Western imperialism and had allegedly abandoned its policy of nonalignment. Moscow, however, did not accept this view. After Stalin's death it had come to look upon the national-liberation movement and India in particular with friendly eyes. Since Khrushchev's tour of India in 1955, Soviet-Indian relations had steadily improved.

It was the Chinese repression of the Tibetan uprising that brought the threat from the north menacingly home to India. China, on the other hand, looked upon the Tibetan uprising not, like the West, as a national-liberation struggle, but as a rebellion caused by "the reactionary clique of the Tibetan upper strata."[45] The CPR suspected India of lending assistance to the Tibetan resistance movement, especially after the Dalai Lama's flight to India in the spring of 1959. The Indian government, *People's Daily* later charged, in staging the Tibetan provocation, wanted to oppose China *and* Communism. Whatever role Tibet played in the deterioration of Sino-Indian relations, the first claim for a revision of the Sino-Indian boundary had been made by Chou En-lai in a letter to Nehru dated as early as January 23, 1959. He had reminded Nehru that the border between their two countries had never before been delimited.

On August 25 and 26, 1959, the frontier post of Longju, which the Indian government claimed lay within the North-East Frontier Agency, was occupied by Chinese troops. In a note to Delhi, Peking had presented the counterclaim that Longju was rightfully Chinese territory. On September 9 the Tass Agency, reporting on the incident, attempted to divert attention from the clash to the "noisy campaign" of certain political circles in Western countries that were anxious to drive a wedge between the two largest states in Asia, the CPR and the Republic of India. The USSR expressed regret over the incident, especially since she enjoyed friendly relations with both states. The Chinese and Soviet peoples were, Moscow proclaimed, "tied together by indestructible bonds of fraternal friendship

45. *Ibid.*

based on the great principles of socialist internationalism."[46] Friendly cooperation between the USSR and India according to the ideas of peaceful coexistence was developing successfully. The report of Tass was virtually identical to a formal proclamation of Soviet neutrality.

Later, at the Moscow Conference of 1960, Teng Hsiao-ping, general secretary of the CPC, publicly accused the CPSU that this "tendentious" communiqué had first "revealed our Sino-Soviet differences" to the world at large. According to Peking,[47] Moscow's statement on the Sino-Indian border incident became a turning point in Sino-Soviet relations. As Peking bitterly remarked, this was the first instance in history in which a socialist country, "instead of condemning the armed provocations of the reactionaries of a capitalist country, condemned another fraternal socialist country when it was confronted with such armed provocation."

On November 2, 1963, *People's Daily,* in an article "The truth about how the leaders of the CPSU have allied themselves with India against China," underlined again the great importance that Peking had attached to the Tass Statement and the efforts it had made to prevent its publication, since it considered the revelation of Soviet neutrality on this issue embarrassing and harmful.[48] On the morning of September 9, 1959, according to *People's Daily,* the Soviet Chargé d'Affaires had informed the Peking leaders that his government would issue a Tass statement on the Sino-Indian boundary question the following day and delivered a copy of it. On the afternoon of September 9, the Soviet Chargé in Peking was handed a copy of Premier Chou's letter, dated September 8, which was addressed to Prime Minister Nehru and contained proposals for a friendly settlement of. the boundary question through negotiations. Peking apparently hoped that this move (which perhaps involved predating Chou's letter to Nehru) would persuade Moscow to withhold the publication of the Tass statement.

That very evening the government of the CPR again pleaded with Moscow through the Soviet Chargé not to issue the statement. Ignoring China's advice, however, *People's Daily* reported later, the Soviets published the Tass statement ahead of time, on the night of September 9, and thus disclosed the differences on this issue between China and the Soviet Union. In Peking's view, the Soviet government, assuming a façade of neutrality, thus "actually favored India and condemned China." On October 2 the Chinese leaders personally gave Khrushchev an "explanation" of the true situation along the border and of the background of the Sino-Indian border hostilities; Khrushchev, however, continued to insist that it was wrong to kill people.

Another serious incident in the Sino-Indian northwestern border region

46. *Pravda* and *Izvestiia,* Sept. 10, 1959, p. 3 (*CDSP* 21, no. 36 [1959]: 14).
47. *People's Daily,* Feb. 27, 1963 (*PR,* March 1, 1963, pp. 7f).
48. *People's Daily,* Nov. 2, 1963 (*PR,* Nov. 8, 1963, pp. 18-27).

took place on October 20-21 inside Ladakh when, during a clash with Chinese troops, nine members of an Indian police patrol were killed and about ten were taken prisoner; one Chinese soldier was shot. While Delhi claimed that the incident had occurred forty miles inside Ladakh, Peking asserted that an intrusion into Chinese territory had taken place. Khrushchev continued to maintain a neutral line. The Soviet press reported simultaneously the Chinese and Indian versions of the incident without taking sides.

At a session of the Supreme Soviet on October 31, 1959, Khrushchev, though voicing "regret" and "distress" over the new incident and border conflict in the Ladakh region, brushed aside India's responsibility for the provocation. On November 7, while receiving a correspondent of the Indian weekly *New Age*, he called the border incident "sad" and "stupid." Pointing to the settlement of the Soviet-Iranian boundary question, he said: "What are a few kilometres for a country like the Soviet Union?," suggesting that China abandon some of her border claims to satisfy India's demands.[49] The Chinese leaders talked with the Soviet Ambassador as often as six times in the period between December 10, 1959, and January 30, 1960, in a vain attempt to reverse the Soviet stand on this issue.*

In his report to the Supreme Soviet on October 31, 1959, Khrushchev expressed his special grief "over the losses on both sides," recalling the ties that bound the USSR to both China and India.[50] There was no hint that the USSR would relinquish her official neutrality policy in regard to this conflict.

In 1959 Moscow seemed convinced that Chinese militancy against India was aimed as much, if not more, at the USSR, in particular at "torpedoing the relaxation of international tension" by the lessening of the cold war between the Soviet Union and the United States, especially in view of Khrushchev's impending trip to the United States of America.[51] This was no doubt an exaggeration due to the Soviets' at times myopic and fre-

49. *Ibid.*

*On February 6, 1960, according to *People's Daily,* in a verbal communication to the CC of the CPC the CC of the CPSU had categorically asserted that "one cannot possibly seriously think that such a state as India, which is militarily and economically immeasurably weaker than China, would really launch a military attack on China and commit aggression against it." The CC of the CPSU bluntly charged that China's policies were the outgrowth of "a narrow nationalist attitude." Finally on June 22, 1960, Khrushchev told the head of the delegation of the CPC that "since Indians were killed, this meant that China attacked India." He also stated: "We are Communists, for us it is not important where the frontier line runs." As far as her own frontiers were concerned, the USSR has, of course, given the most detailed attention as to where her boundaries run, as her military and diplomatic efforts during and after World War II in both Europe and Asia testify. The Soviets have also shown great determination in resisting any efforts of Peking to redraw the Sino-Soviet boundary.

50. *Pravda* and *Izvestiia,* Nov. 1, 1959, pp. 1-3 (*CDSP* 11, no. 44, pp. 3-11, esp. 7-8).

51. Soviet Government Statement, Sept. 21, 1963; *Pravda,* Sept. 21, pp. 1-2 and Sept. 22, 1963, pp. 1-2.

quently distorted vision of the world at large, which rivaled that of Peking, but may have contained a grain of truth. According to the foregoing Soviet account, Moscow had warned Peking that the aggravation of the dispute and its development into a large-scale armed conflict was undesirable and "fraught with negative consequences" not only for Chinese-Indian relations but for the whole international situation. The conflict was likely to harm the unity of the anti-imperialist front in Asia. Looking back, the Soviet government statement disclosed: "It was with a feeling of bewilderment and bitterness that the people saw one of the socialist countries which had recently become independent and served as a model for them, get itself involved in a military conflict with a young neutralist state, and, using its military superiority, endeavor to gain for itself in that way a favorable solution of the problem of a certain part of territory."

The Chinese leaders, however, ignored the comradely advice of Moscow and were bitter about its unwillingness to lend them support. In the article "What is the cause of the Dispute?" the Chinese communists even traced the beginning of their wide-ranging differences with the USSR to the Soviet failure to give unconditional support to China's stand in the Himalayan conflict. Peking pointed an accusing finger at Moscow not only for refusing them moral and material aid but also for giving such aid to India.[52]

Such help as had been given by the USSR to India, the Soviets countered, was in the interests of peace and socialism. China herself, until 1959, had pursued the same kind of policy toward India. According to its own account, Moscow had viewed with approval the earlier friendly contacts between Chinese and Indian leaders, their joint statement in favor of peace, and especially the Pancha Shila principles proclaimed by the Premiers Chou En-lai and Nehru. In light of all this, Moscow asserted, the Chinese-Indian armed conflict came as a complete surprise both to the Soviet people and to the whole world public. The Soviets also rejected the Chinese accusation that India in waging war on China was using Soviet armaments, as being "essentially not true"; to follow this kind of logic, the Indian government, according to Moscow, had a great deal more reason to complain that the Chinese troops, equipped with Soviet weapons, were battling India.

Khrushchev's Visit to the United States and to Peking, September-October 1959

Between the two incidents along the Sino-Indian frontier, Khrushchev

52. Editorial, *People's Daily*, Feb. 27, 1963 (*PR*, March 1, 1963).

had journeyed both to the United States and to Peking. Accompanied by Soviet Foreign Minister Andrei Gromyko, Khrushchev arrived in New York on September 15, 1959, and stayed until September 28. The journey was climaxed by three days of talks with President Eisenhower at Camp David. Khrushchev himself was in an ebullient mood. He was quoted as saying that "the ice of the cold war has not only cracked, but has begun to crack up."[53] The Soviet press echoed his high expectation and even reflected his enthusiasm. Khrushchev's visit to the United States, *Izvestiia* wrote, opened up "wonderful opportunities" for consolidating the changes that have begun and "ensuring the peaceful coexistence of the Soviet Union and the United States and of all states."[54]

From America Khrushchev flew to Peking via Moscow, "literally alighting," as he disclosed in the Chinese capital, "from one plane and boarding another." Arriving at Showtu airport in Peking on September 30 on the occasion of celebrations for the tenth anniversary of the CPR, Khrushchev was welcomed by Mao himself.[55] He was under heavy pressure to smooth ruffled feathers and calm the aroused leaders of the CPC at that critical moment. While insisting that the talks in the United States had proven "useful" and would "undoubtedly lead to an improvement" of Soviet-American relations, Khrushchev also asserted the Soviets' great interest in ensuring peace "throughout the world" and attaining complete and universal disarmament. On the other hand, he profusely flattered the CPR as being "such a great power" and spoke of her right to take her lawful place in the United Nations.

On the occasion of a visit to Peking a year earlier, he had made significant concessions to the Chinese point of view. This time, however, flatteries notwithstanding, differences went so deep that not even an agreement on a joint communiqué could be reached and none therefore was issued. Repeatedly during his visit Khrushchev emphasized peaceful coexistence and made no secret of Soviet opposition to "wars of conquest": "That would be wrong; the peoples would never understand and would never support those who took it in their heads to act in this way."[56] Also, Khrushchev came out for "ending the cold war" and continued to express his confidence in President Eisenhower and the possibility of gaining a rapprochement between the USSR and the United States of America.

Publicly, Chou congratulated Khrushchev on the "success" he had scored while visiting the United States "as an emissary of peace."[57] He also acknowledged the enormous support given to China by the Soviet

53. *Pravda*, Sept. 18, 1959, p. 1 (*CDSP* 11, no. 38, p. 3).
54. *Izvestiia*, Sept. 18, 1959 (*CDSP* 11, no. 37, p. 4).
55. *Pravda*, Oct. 1, 1959, p. 1 (*CDSP* 11, no. 39 [Oct. 28, 1959]: 19f).
56. *Ibid.*, pp. 20-22.
57. Quoted in *ibid.*, p. 20.

Union and the other socialist states. But other high-placed Chinese officials were critical of the recognition accorded to the American government. On October 4, the very day Khrushchev departed from Peking to return to Moscow, the Chinese Foreign Minister called upon all peoples in the world to engage in "an unrelenting fight against United States imperialism."[58] And at the Moscow Conference in 1960, Teng Hsiao-ping found "Khrushchev's tactless eulogy of Eisenhower and other imperialists" inexcusable.[59] Nothing was more revealing of the depth of the rift between the two Communist giants than the difference in their actual assessment of the United States and her objectives.

58. *People's Daily*, Oct. 4, 1959 (*PR*, Oct. 6, 1959, p. 35); also Chou, "A Great Decade," *People's Daily*, Oct. 6 (*PR*, Oct. 13, 1959, pp. 14f).
59. Keesing's Research Report; *The Sino-Soviet Dispute* (New York, 1967), p. 20.

4
The Development of the Dispute, 1960-1962

"Long Live Leninism"

An article published by *Red Flag* on April 16, 1960, and possibly authored by Mao himself, was the first in a series entitled "Long Live Leninism." This publication was to play a major role in the unfolding of the Sino-Soviet dispute. In publishing this series, Peking still deliberately refrained from openly criticizing the CPSU.[1] It was rather against the imperialists and the Yugoslav revisionists that it seemed to direct its strongest arrows. But it was actually Moscow which, in its view, created "serious confusion" in the ranks of the international Communist movement and was the real target.[2]

In the forty years and more since the October Revolution, "Long Live Leninism" asserted, tremendous new changes had taken place in the world centering on Russia, China, and imperialism. From an economically and technically very backward country, Russia had developed into a first-rate world power with the most advanced technology. "By its economic and technological leaps [!] the Soviet Union has left the European capitalist countries far behind and the United States behind, too, in technology." The great victory of the Chinese people's revolution had broken the chain of imperialism on the Chinese mainland. Imperialism rotted with every passing day while for socialism things were daily getting better.

While, according to the author, the old revisionism of Eduard Bernstein

1. *"Long Live Leninism,"* Red Flag, no. 8, Apr. 16, 1960 (*PR*, Apr. 26, 1960). The Soviets later claimed that it was written by Mao himself.
2. Editorial Departments of *People's Daily* and *Red Flag, People's Daily,* Sept. 6, 1963 Peking: Foreign Language Press, 1963).

had attempted to prove that Marxism was outmoded, modern revisionism attempted to demonstrate that Leninism was no longer relevant. The author of "Long Live Leninism" denied that because of rockets and atomic bombs and great technical progress in general Marxism and Leninism had become obsolete. He was not terrified by what he called the United States' atomic and "imperialist blackmail." To make a case for greater revolutionary militancy on the part of the USSR, the author exaggerated Soviet technological and military progress. The USSR, Peking claimed, "clearly holds the upper hand in the development of new techniques." Besides, China's revolutionary experience, especially during the War of Resistance to Japanese Aggression, had demonstrated that it was not technique but man, the masses of people, who determined the fate of mankind. In the Chinese war against Japan the "weapons-mean-everything theory" had been disproven.

Communist China had always struggled against imperialist war, advocated banning of atomic and nuclear weapons, and championed the defense of world peace. Of course, whether or not the imperialists will unleash a war "is not determined by us." Should they start a war, "on the debris of a dead imperialism the victorious people would create very swiftly a civilization thousands of times higher than the capitalist system and a truly beautiful future for themselves."[3]

There followed a sharp criticism of the views of the "revisionists" on questions of violence, war, and peaceful coexistence. The foreign policy of socialist countries could only be a policy of peace. Such peaceful coexistence as prevailed between the wars between the USSR and imperialism, however, was won by the Soviet Union "entirely through struggle," beginning with the Civil War. In the postwar period the obstacle to peaceful coexistence was the imperialism of American capitalists, the American network of military bases, and guided missile bases everywhere along the periphery of the Soviet Union and the entire socialist camp. The imperialist system was the cause of modern war, including the American wars in Asia.

The major thrust of the article was a criticism of modern revisionism, as exemplified by the doctrines of Tito. The CPC, it was asserted, was the true heir of Lenin's legacy, while the CPSU was held as having betrayed it, jettisoned it as mere cumbrous ballast. The world was once again assured that socialist countries "never permit themselves to send, never should and never will send their troops across their borders, unless of course they were subjected to aggression from a foreign enemy." Since the Armed forces of the socialist countries fought for "justice," it was only

3. See n 1 p. 105.

natural that they should exert an influence when they have to go beyond their borders to counterattack a foreign enemy. Still, the emergence of a socialist system would depend on the will of the masses of the people of the countries affected. This assurance to the West, if it was any, was further qualified: "The spread of revolutionary ideas knows no national boundaries."

As far as the transition from capitalism to socialism was concerned, Marxists had always wanted to follow the peaceful way, though Lenin had made it clear that Marx's reference to the possibility of peaceful transition to socialism for the United States and Great Britain in his time was no longer valid because the bourgeoisie had strengthened a powerful militaristic and bureaucratic machine of oppression. It was apparent that the Chinese writers, aware of the concessions made by the CPR in the 1957 Declaration on the possibility of peaceful transition to socialism, did not wish to repudiate it, but also that they actually had no faith in the so-called peaceful way of transition. Revolutionary parties should take part in the parliamentary struggle, but have no illusions about the bourgeois parliamentary system.

In conclusion, the USSR was given full recognition for being the first socialist state, now "headed by comrade Khrushchev," in which a great period of extensive building of communism had definitely begun. Among China's accomplishments, despite their already apparent failures, were mentioned the Great Leap Forward and the People's Communes, since they had inspired the initiative and revolutionary spirit of the Chinese masses.

Countering the argument of some that revisionism, differently from the Declaration of 1957, was no longer the main danger within revolutionary ranks, the Peking writers insisted that it was still the main threat, and underlined the need to utterly "smash" all attempts of the modern revisionists "to distort and carve up the teachings of Lenin."

A prompt answer to the first articles in the series "Long Live Leninism" was Kuusinen's speech on the anniversary of Lenin's birth, delivered at a formal meeting in Moscow.[4] Just as Peking's criticism was still restrained and of an indirect nature, Moscow's reply followed the same pattern; both parties carefully avoided criticizing the other openly. But Kuusinen's emphasis on peaceful coexistence, his praise for Khrushchev as its champion, his virtual omission of war in his prognosis of outstanding trends for the rest of the century and his support of aid to underdeveloped, including nonsocialist countries, ran counter to some of the main theses of the recent Chinese publications.

According to Kuusinen, Lenin had favored peaceful coexistence, con-

4. *Pravda* and *Izvestiia*, Apr. 23, pp. 1-3 (*CDSP* 12, no. 17 [1960]: 8-12).

trary to "glib publicists" in the West who disputed this. While Kuusinen conceded that imperialism was aggressive, he held that socialists, rather than endlessly repeating it, should "take advantage of new factors in favor of peace and of sparing mankind the catastrophe of a new war." He came close to directly naming Peking as the main ideological culprit, and prophesied that the struggle for lasting peace would "intensify."

A similar indirect Soviet reply to the Chinese series "Long Live Leninism" was offered by *Pravda* in an attack on "Leftists" in the Communist Movement. On June 12 N. Matkovsky, on occasion of the fortieth anniversary of the publication of Lenin's book *Left Wing Communism, An Infantile Disorder,* published the article "Ideological Weapon of Communism."[5] The author pointed to the dangers of "left-sectarian sentiments and tendencies," against which Lenin's book was leveled and which occasionally found their manifestation "even in our day." Some people mistakenly found the policy of working for the peaceful coexistence of countries with different political systems, of struggling to put an end to the arms race and to strengthen peace and friendship between the leaders of the socialist system and capitalist countries, as "a kind of departure" from the positions of Marxism-Leninism. Lenin had also stressed that the Russian model was "an essential part" of the lessons for every revolutionary proletariat.

Moscow, while then fighting against Belgrade *and* Peking—openly against the first, still in a stealthy manner against the latter—was insistent on keeping the proper ideological distance from both. Therefore, when the leading Yugoslav politician and theoretician, Kardelj, wrote the book *Socialism and War,* the main target of which was Peking, Moscow, though it may have sympathized with some tenets of the publication, seemed primarily concerned about maintaining her middle-of-the-road position, avoiding what it considered both extremes, right opportunism and leftist adventurism. Also, it could not accept Kardelj's thesis that all military groupings contributed equally to the cold war tension. An analysis of a review article in *Pravda* shows that the daily, while seemingly defending Peking against the charges hurled from Belgrade, did by no means endorse Peking's views on peace and war. Kardelj was criticized for repeating the "slander" spread by American imperialists about the Chinese people, especially its alleged aggressiveness. It found Kardelj's thesis that a socialist state could be the bearer of an aggressive war "monstrous." Actually, Khrushchev personally had accused the Chinese leaders of having provoked the clashes along the Sino-Indian frontier. But publicly at least, Moscow still refrained from condemning China and even made it appear as if it were prepared to come to its rescue against unjust accusations.[6]

5. *Pravda,* June 12, 1960, p. 3 (*CDSP* 12, no. 24 [1960]: 3-5).
6. *Pravda*, Sept. 2, 1960, pp. 4-5 (*CDSP* 12, no. 35 [1960]: 7-8).

The Bucharest Conference, June 1960

The differences between the two great "fraternal" parties had reached such depth that both sides agreed to hold an international conference to attempt to narrow the dangerous gap that separated them. The third Congress of the Rumanian Workers Party in Bucharest, held between June 20 and 26, 1960, was not originally intended to serve this purpose. But Khrushchev decided at the Bucharest conference to strike a "surprise" blow against an uninstructed and unprepared Chinese delegation. Among the many issues raised in the Rumanian capital were military cooperation, the Sino-Indian border dispute, and the "Great Leap Forward."

Khrushchev may have counted on the absence of most Asian parties from Bucharest to play into his hands. In his speech of June 21 he revealed that in spite of the breakdown of the Paris Summit Conference his overall assessment of the international situation and his precept for coexistence had basically not changed. While he had reversed his view of Eisenhower as a partisan for peaceful coexistence, he seemed to set his hopes upon the next President of the United States.[7] The thesis that wars were not inevitable, enunciated at the Twentieth and Twenty-first Congresses of the CPSU, had "still immediate bearing." In conclusion, Khrushchev denied, though he knew better, that there existed different points of view on pressing international problems or problems relating to the revolutionary workers' movement among the socialist parties and socialist states.

The head of the Chinese delegation, P'eng Chen answered Khrushchev the following day, pointing to the U-2 incident as a clear lesson that imperialism could never be trusted.[8] With the break-up of the Paris Conference following this incident, a good lesson had been given to the peoples of the whole world. "In the end imperialism remains imperialism and the honeyed speeches of the imperialists must never be believed."

There followed a distribution of letters and documents that raised tempers at the Congress. The Chinese delegation protested that Khrushchev had violated the "long-standing principle" in the international Communist movement that questions of common concern should be settled "by consultation" among the fraternal Parties.[9] He had completely broken a prior agreement to confine the meeting to an exchange of views and had resorted

7. *Khrushchev Remembers,* pp. 463f. Khrushchev's speech, June 21, 1960, *Soviet News* June 22, 1960.

8. *Pravda,* June 24, 1960, pp. 3-5 (*CDSP* 12, no. 26 [1960]: 11); P'eng Chen, June 22; (*PR,* June 28, 1960).

9. Statement of the Delegation of the CPC, June 26, 1960, also "The origin and development of the Differences between the leadership of the CPSU and ourselves, "Comment on the Open Letter of the CC of the CPSU, Sept. 6, 1963, by the Editorial Departments of *People's Daily* and *Red Flag* (*PR,* Sept. 13, 1960, pp. 6-23, esp. pp. 10, 20-23).

to "surprise attack." Khrushchev had adopted a "patriarchal, arbitrary, and tyrannical" attitude toward the fraternal parties.

The delegates of the twelve ruling parties then affixed their signatures to a communiqué reaffirming the 1957 Declaration and the Peace Manifesto. In 1957, the Chinese delegation, though reluctantly, had also signed these documents. As lone defender of the Chinese point of view at the Bucharest conference appeared Albania, though at the time its ruling Communist Party still included partisans of the Moscow orientation.

The Moscow Conference, November 1960

The Bucharest Conference of June 1960 turned out to be the curtain-raiser for the Moscow Conference of eighty-one Communist and Workers' Parties that was held from November 11 to 25, 1960. This gathering, even more than the Moscow meeting of 1957, was dominated by the Sino-Soviet conflict. Never before were the divisive issues debated in so great detail and with so much passion. The Conference was actually preceded by bilateral Sino-Soviet talks, which were initiated in September. These in turn were continued in October by the work of the Drafting Committee, which consisted of twenty-six representatives and was in session for three and one-half weeks, a measure of the tough bargaining and hard in-fighting between the parties concerned.

The Sino-Soviet dispute, far from being settled at the Moscow Conference, was actually deepened. The final Statement that the Conference adopted was a document containing disparate elements that lent themselves easily to the justification of different, even contrary, political courses. If the Soviets scored a "victory," it was a Pyrrhic one, since it made clear to all concerned that individual parties could no longer be compelled blindly to follow Soviet leadership and to accept Moscow's dictate. The Chinese delegation impressed upon the Soviet leadership and the entire conference that the old Comintern discipline could not be revived in the new postwar era, in which Communist parties were no longer linked by a "centralized organization" such as the Comintern had been.[10]

The Soviet point of view came forth more strongly at the Conference than the Chinese position. On the issue of fractionalism the Chinese, realizing that at stake was the right of free expression and the defense of a minority viewpoint, fought hard and succeeded in having the final Statement avoid this question. Though China again was supported only by Albania, many Asiatic parties inclined toward the Chinese point of view,

10. See n 8 above; see also Zagoria, *Conflict,* pp. 455-58.

notwithstanding their determination to maintain a safe and advantageous neutrality between Moscow and Peking. Some European Communist parties, such as those of Poland, Hungary, Italy, Great Britain, and Sweden, while on the whole backing the Russian position, showed, nevertheless, a great deal of independence. The revelation of the full extent of the split between the giants seemed to encourage and invigorate the movement toward greater freedom and independence among the other Communist parties. Monolithic unity appeared to be a thing of the past, and polycentrism the wave of the future.

When Khrushchev, delivering a report on January 6, 1961, was asked who won at the 1960 Moscow conference, he avoided giving a clear-cut answer. One should not talk about victory or defeat, he admonished, but rather about the "solidarity of the international Communist movement."[11] This was hardly modesty, nor did it represent primarily a tactical move. What was at stake after the Moscow conference was the question of the extent of unity among the communist parties; both sides had an interest in keeping the non-Communist world guessing.

Both Moscow and Peking, when referring to key documents of present-day Communism, have pointed not only to the Declaration of 1957 but also to the Statement of November 1960. These documents were drafted and approved at Conferences that had convened in the capital of the USSR; the very site of the two conferences highlighted of course the leading position of the CPSU in international Communism. The Communist parties from all over the world approved the largely Moscow-inspired formulation of Communist goals and means, the most authoritative pronunciamentos of strategy and tactics of the international Communist movement of recent times.

The participants of the 1960 conference reaffirmed in the Statement first their "allegiance" to the Declaration and the Peace Manifesto that had been adopted in 1957. Looking back the road that had been traveled, they claimed great progress: "The chief result of these years is the swift growth of the might and international influence of the world socialist system, the active process of disintegration of the colonial system under the blows of the national liberation movement, the growth of class struggles in the capitalist world, and the further decline and decay of the world capitalist system."[12] The superiority of the forces of socialism over imperialism in the world arena was becoming increasingly evident. The rapid progress of the national-liberation movement was largely attributed to the new interna-

11. "Marxism-Leninism is the basis for the unity of the communist movement," *Kommunist*, no. 15, Oct. 1963.
12. Statement, *Pravda*, Dec. 6, 1960, pp. 1-4 (*CDSP* 12, no. 48 [1960]: 3-9; no. 49, pp. 3-8.

tional balance of power which, it was held, inclined in favor of the socialist camp. This of course redounded to the credit of the USSR, which militarily and economically was far ahead of China.

The leading role of the USSR in the socialist commonwealth was clearly spelled out. While the USSR was already building Communism, other Communist-controlled countries had either laid the foundations of socialism or had already started construction of socialism; no indication was given to which of the latter two groups Communist China belonged, but about its lesser role as compared to the USSR there was no shadow of a doubt. One may compare the following two paragraphs:

> The Soviet people, successfully fulfilling the seven-year plan for the development of the national economy, are rapidly creating the material and technical base of communism. . . . The Soviet Union is the first country in history to pave the way to communism for all mankind. It is the most vivid example and the most powerful bulwark for the peoples of the whole world in their struggle for peace, democratic freedoms, national independence, and social progress.
>
> The people's revolution in China dealt a crushing blow to the positions of imperialism in Asia and greatly contributed to a change in the correlation of world forces of socialism. By giving a strong new impetus to the national liberation movement, it exerted enormous influence on the peoples, especially the peoples of Asia, Africa, and Latin America.

While Chinese Communism was given generous recognition, it was no equal of the CPSU and the USSR in accomplishment and historic and revolutionary significance. In another context China was simply listed along with other people's democratic republics, and her achievements in the building of socialism were not considered more outstanding than those of any of her other fellow-travelers.

The Statement referred to the continued existence of nationalist prejudices in the socialist camp, which constituted an obstacle to further progress. The antagonism among nations diminished with the decline of the antagonism among classes, it was hopefully held out. However, "manifestations of nationalism and national narrowmindedness do not disappear automatically with the establishment of a social system." An "internationalist policy" on the part of the Communist and Workers' Parties and a resolute struggle were needed to "overcome the survivals of bourgeois nationalism and chauvinism." Chauvinism, it was implied, survived in some Communist and Workers' Parties. No parties were mentioned in this context, but it must have been disturbing to many participants that the conference had felt compelled to point to the danger signs.

Like the Declaration, the Statement considered the problem of war and peace "the most burning problem of our time." Monstrous means of mass annihilation and mass destruction had been developed. Imperialism represented a grave danger to all mankind, and American imperialism constituted the main force of aggression and war. Though the aggressive character of imperialism had not changed, war was "not fatally inevitable." The time was past when the imperialists could decide whether or not there was to be a war. World war could now be prevented by the united efforts of the world socialist camp, by the international working class, the national liberation movement, all countries opposing war, and all peace-loving forces. The superiority of the forces of socialism, of peace and democracy over those of imperialism, reaction, and aggression had become increasingly apparent. The first-named forces included "the mighty Soviet Union," "the entire socialist camp"—China was not specifically mentioned in this context—the peace-loving states of Asia, Africa, and Latin America, the international working class, and the national liberation movement.

"The struggle against the threat of a new war must be developed without waiting until the atomic and hydrogen bombs begin dropping. . . . The main thing is to curb the aggression in good time, to prevent war and not to let it break out." Communists must consider the struggle for peace "their primary task" and must be militant in behalf of peace and peaceful coexistence. If in spite of all efforts on the part of "Communist parties the "imperialist maniacs start a war, the peoples will sweep away and bury capitalism."

The Leninist principle of peaceful coexistence and economic competition between the socialist and capitalist countries was the firm foundation of the foreign policy of the socialist countries. "Under peaceful conditions" socialism will increasingly reveal its advantages over capitalism in economics, science, and technology. "The USSR will become the first [!] industrial power of the world. China will become a powerful [!] industrial country, the socialist system will account for more than half of the world industrial production." Under these conditions it will be possible to exclude world war from the life of society "even before the complete victory of socialism on earth, with capitalism still existing in part of the world."

We get a glimpse here of the very essence of the theoretical dispute between Moscow and Peking as far as peace and peaceful coexistence are concerned. Peking in its bitter exchange with Moscow was later to stress that the nature of imperialism had not changed. Therefore war and imperialism were indissolubly tied together. Moscow, referring to the Declaration and the Statement, was then to remind Peking that all Communist Parties, including the CPC, had subscribed to the view that a real possibility of banishing war would arise "even before" the complete victory of socialism, before victory on a global scale.

The Statement imposed upon Communists of the whole world the obliga-

tion to struggle vigorously to prevent war. "Communists must work untir-
ingly among the masses in order to prevent an underestimation of the possibility of preventing world war, underestimation of the possibility of
peaceful coexistence and, at the same time, underestimation of the danger
of war." "Peace is the true ally of socialism." This, clearly was not
Peking's formulation nor the main thrust of its views on the triad of
socialism, peace, and war.

Peaceful coexistence of states, however, did not signify renunciation of
the class struggle. It did not mean a reconciliation between socialist and
bourgeois ideologies. To the contrary, it meant an "intensification of the
struggle" for the triumph of socialist ideas. "But ideological and political
disputes among states must not be resolved by war." The Statement supported the Soviet Union's program for general and total disarmament.
Communists regarded it as their historic mission to abolish exploitation and
poverty and to "deliver mankind from the nightmare of a new world war
even in the present epoch."

The complete collapse of colonialism was inevitable. *The downfall of
the system of colonial slavery under the impact of the national-liberation
movement is a phenomenon ranking second in historical importance after
the formation of the world system of socialism.*" National-liberation
movements had triumphed in vast areas of the world, and the peoples of
Asia, Africa, and Latin America had begun to take an active part in international politics. Yet these victories of the national-liberation movement
were not achieved in a vacuum; they would not have been possible without
the inspiration of and the support extended by the socialist camp and particularly the USSR, without the change in the international balance of
power—the latter again a result of the growing strength of the socialist
commonwealth. It was a Soviet claim to which the Statement thus gave
acknowledgment.

Though the Soviets recognized the importance of the progress of the national liberation movement, it was still in their view only "second" in importance to the victory of socialism. This formulation was of Moscow's
rather than Peking's making. The CPC, which aspired to the leadership of
the international Communist movement, was, in the view of the CPSU,
merely exaggerating the strategic importance of the national liberation
movement for apparent opportunistic reasons; flattery would win it over to
its side.

The Socialist Revolution, the Statement asserted, was not imported and
could not be imposed from without. Communist Parties had always opposed "export of revolution." At the same time, they resolutely struggled
against imperialist export of counterrevolution. Communist Parties func-
tioned now in 87 countries of the world and included 36 million Party

members. They had, it was claimed, ideologically defeated the revisionists in their ranks. Just as in the Declaration of 1957, there followed a sharp denunciation of revisionism, which was "Right opportunism" and had found concentrated expression in Yugoslav theories. The Yugoslav revisionists were engaged in subversive work against the socialist camp and the world Communist movement. Yet Communists must fight not only against revisionism—which "remains the principal danger"—but also "against dogmatism and sectarianism," which "can also become the principal danger at a given stage." The 1960 Statement, just as had the 1957 Declaration, sharply denounced revisionism of the Titoist variety. On the other hand, it did not step up its denunciation of "dogmatism" of the Peking variety, in spite of the apparent escalation of the Sino-Soviet dispute.

Again, no doubt was left as to the continued preeminence of the USSR in the socialist camp: "The Communist and Workers' Parties unanimously declare that the CPSU has been and continues to be the universally recognized *vanguard* of the world Communist movement, being the most experienced and most thoroughly tempered detachment of the international Communist movement." The experience of the CPSU was of fundamental importance for the entire Communist movement. "The example of the CPSU and its fraternal solidarity inspired all Communist parties." And the historic decisions of the Twentieth Congress of the CPSU were not only of great importance for the USSR, but also initiated "a new stage" in the international Communist movement.

The Withdrawal of Soviet Technical Aid, July-August 1960

The conflict between Moscow and Peking took on new aspects during the summer and autumn of 1960; it grew in intensity along both political and economic lines. Once again Moscow apparently underestimated Chinese pride, determination, resourcefulness, and her resistance to economic mishaps—the "Great Leap" and the unexpected natural calamities, especially bad weather. These reverses, in combination with Soviet pressure, resulted in stiffening Communist China's resistance and deepening her resolve to persevere in her theoretical position and political isolation.

To understand why the conflict that emerged seemingly suddenly in the summer of 1960 took on primarily economic aspects, it is necessary to see Sino-Soviet economic relations in the proper historical perspective. In the early 1950s China had been an extremely backward country as far as science, economy, and technology were concerned. The Korean War, in which the CPR had taken part, and the economic blockade organized by

the United States had seriously hindered the elimination of this backwardness. In its first years the CPR had needed huge quantities of modern industrial equipment, as well as experienced cadres of engineers and technicians and skilled workers. The help rendered by the USSR along
economic, scientific, and technological lines was, according to the Soviets,
"unprecedented" in scope and effectiveness.[13] This aid came at a most
difficult period for the CPR and proved to be a "determining factor" in
the solution of the most complex political, social, and economic problems.
The USSR generously shared with the CPR goods that it sometimes badly
needed itself.

In the short span from 1950 to 1959, the CPR, with the help of the
USSR, rehabilitated her national economy and created industries that were
completely new for China, including the aircraft, automobile, tractor,
power and heavy machine-building, instrument-making, electrical and radio
engineering industries, and also important branches of chemical production. Yet, in planning the rehabilitation of its economy and the implementation of a broad program of economic development, China faced a serious
situation, having virtually no cadres of engineers, technicians, or scientists
with adequate technical knowledge and experience. It was the USSR that
in the fifties sent to China over 10,000 highly skilled Soviet specialists and
organized the training of Chinese scientists, technicians, and workers at
Soviet enterprises, advanced training schools, and research organizations.

Between 1951 and 1962 more than 8,000 Chinese citizens received training in industrial production in the USSR and more than 11,000 Chinese
students engaged in undergraduate and graduate studies in educational institutions of the Soviet Union. Another 1,000 scientists of the Academy of
Sciences of China studied at research institutions of the USSR Academy of
Sciences. Over 1500 Chinese engineers, technicians, and scientists visited
the USSR to acquaint themselves with Soviet technological achievements.
In the period of 1954-59 the Soviet Union transmitted to China more than
24,000 complete sets of scientific and technical documentation. There was,
the Soviets claimed, not a single branch of industry in the CPR that did
not produce output in accordance with blueprints and technical specifications developed in the USSR. In addition, between 1950 and 1961 the
Soviet Union granted China long-term credit on favorable terms, totaling
1,816 million foreign-currency rubles. The CPR began to repay its debts to
the Soviet Union in 1956. Beginning with that year, Chinese exports to the
USSR began to exceed Chinese imports. A large part of Chinese imports
from the Soviet Union consisted of goods intended to enhance the defensive capability of the CPR.

13. *Voprosy istorii*, no. 6, 1969, pp. 46-62.

The CPC was later to charge that the prices on many goods and items of equipment imported from Russia were much higher than in the world market and that Soviet goods were of a low quality.[14] The Soviets countered that as far as the latter charge was concerned, the USSR had often sent the very latest Soviet equipment, which had not undergone a sufficiently long testing period. Such shortcomings as came to light, the Soviets asserted, had been corrected. Since Chinese economic policy was basically a component of its foreign-policy course, the anti-Soviet course of the Chinese leadership resulted in a sharp reduction in Soviet exports to China. Between 1959 and 1966 the goods turnover between the CPR and the USSR had decreased by almost 85%.

In considering the size of the Soviet credit and financial assistance to the CPR, the Soviets underlined that the USSR had never claimed that it was fully providing China with the means necessary for the fulfillment of the entire program for the industrialization of China—"a vast country with a huge population."[15] It was merely aiming at helping the Chinese people to create "the initial base for socialist industrialization." The Chinese finance minister had pointed out that the proportion of Soviet loans in the total volume of financial receipts during the first ten years of the CPR's existence was only 2%. However, the Soviets countered, this did not mean that the Soviet Union played a small role in the industrialization of the CPR, since her funds were spent in a very concentrated manner.

The Moscow-Peking economic relationship took a turn for the worse in 1960. Battling what seemed to the USSR to be Peking's anti-Leninist, chauvinist, and adventurist policy, the Soviet press in the aftermath of the Bucharest Conference had mounted a new campaign against "Left Phrase-Mongers," comparing them to the Trotskyists and followers of Bukharin during the Russian Revolution. This was promptly followed by an article by S. Titarenko in *Sovetskaya Latvia* (August 16, 1960) on the Soviet technical experts in China—an article in the regional press that was given unusual spread throughout the entire Soviet Union—and by simultaneous threats of abrupt cessation of aid to Peking. The author questioned whether even as great a country as China could carry on "in a state of isolation" without the assistance of other socialist countries.[16] The Chinese press, however, did not share the doubts of the Soviet press. *Red Flag* considered China's self-sufficiency as a definite practical possibility. Chinese readers were reminded that the CPC had consistently urged the Chinese people to rely on their own efforts.

14. Correspondence between CC, CPC and CC, CPSU (Peking: Foreign Language Press 1964), p. 33 or *People's Daily*, May 9, 1964 (*PR*, May 8, 1964).
15. *Kommunist*, no. 9, 1968.
16. *Sovetskaya Latvia*, Aug. 16, 1960 (*CDSP* 12, no. 33 [Sept. 14, 1960]).

In August 1960 the Soviet Union rather suddenly decided on the withdrawal of 1,390 Soviet specialists from China. This was no doubt a severe blow to the CPR, though the Chinese leadership may have exaggerated its impact for propagandistic purposes, to place Soviet Russia in an unfavorable light. According to a later Chinese account, dated 1964, Peking had always highly appreciated the conscientious work of the "overwhelming majority" of Soviet experts.[17] But in spite of Chinese objections, the Soviets had abruptly turned their backs on the principles guiding international relations and "unscrupulously" withdrew the 1,390 Soviet experts working in China. They tore up 343 contracts and supplementary contracts concerning experts, and scrapped 257 projects of scientific and technical cooperation, all within the short span of a month. These experts had been posted in over 250 enterprises and establishments in the economic fields and fields of national defense, culture, education, and scientific research. As Peking later accused Moscow: "As a result of your preemptory orders to the Soviet experts to discontinue their work and return to the Soviet Union, many of our country's important designing and scientific research projects had to stop half-way, some of the construction projects in progress had to be suspended, and some of the factories and mines which were conducting trial production could not go into production according to schedule. Your perfidious[!]action disrupted China's original national economic plan and inflicted enormous losses upon China's socialist construction." This action, "going completely against Communist ethics," was a mere instrument for exerting political pressure on fraternal countries.

In the Soviet account of Sino-Soviet relations—also given much later, in February 1964, when relations between the two countries had reached an all-time low—Suslov and later the Novosti Press Agency presented an entirely different picture of the Sino-Soviet economic relationship. According to Suslov, Communist China in 1960, on the eve of the Moscow meeting of fraternal parties, had demanded that the USSR revise all agreements and protocols earlier concluded on economic, scientific, and technical cooperation; the USSR had "no choice but to consent to it."[18] To erase the memory of Soviet assistance from the minds of the Chinese people, the Chinese leaders had gone so far as to give orders to remove Soviet trade marks from the imported machinery and to charge that the Soviets had delivered obsolete equipment. According to Suslov: "On the one hand they try to blame the USSR for reducing its assistance and creating serious difficulties for China's economy. On the other hand, they spread rumors that Soviet assistance was 'ineffective and insignificant.' "

17. CC,CPC, Feb. 29, 1964, *People's Daily,* May 9, 1964 *(PR.,* May 8, 1964).
18. Suslov, "The Struggle of the CPSU for Unity." Report to Plenary Meeting of the CC, Feb. 14, 1964, *Pravda,* Apr. 3, 1964.

A few months later, on August 14, 1964, Novosti Press Agency extolled the work of Soviet specialists in China in the fifties as constituting a "glorious page" in the history of the fraternal relations of the Soviet people. It revealed that as early as 1956, and again in 1958, in view of the "outstanding progress" socialist countries had achieved in training their own engineers and technicians, the USSR had approached China with the suggestion that Soviet specialists, and particularly advisors, be recalled. Any further stay might only "hold up" the development of Chinese personnel. Moreover, the Soviet Union's stand was based "on the need to remove all causes [!], even the slightest, that might harm the unity of the two countries." Yet, at the special request of Peking, Soviet specialists then remained in China. But later in the year 1958 and in 1959, according to Novosti, the conditions for Soviet aid to China became "complicated."[19]

In 1958 Peking had proclaimed the slogan "Struggle against blind faith in established technical standards and regulations and in foreign experience." This was interpreted by Soviet specialists as a criticism of their work and their scientific and technical experience. Soviet experts in China became increasingly alarmed at these attacks and at the flagrant disregard of correct production technology, and also over the dangerous deterioration of the quality of work and the slackening of factory discipline. "The Chinese, on the other hand, accused the Soviet specialists of 'conservatism,' 'bureaucracy,' and 'loss of revolutionary spirit,' maintaining that they were putting spikes in the wheel of the 'Great Leap.' " It became increasingly clear that the warnings of Soviet specialists in China were ignored, that the attitude toward them became more and more a "political question," and that the Chinese authorities were aiming to "discredit" Soviet technicians and their economic experience and to cast doubts on Soviet motives in aiding China.

To cap all this, beginning with 1960, lectures were arranged for the Soviet specialists in the CPR, and Chinese publications attacking Soviet foreign policy were circulated among them. Faced with the urgent plea of Soviet personnel for a recall, the Soviet government, anxious to remove still another pretext for the deliberate worsening of Chinese relations with the USSR, acceded to the request of the specialists "to bring them back to their own country where they could be really useful." When the Chinese leaders expressed concern about this recall, A. Mikoyan toward the end of 1960 promised that Soviet specialists would return to China provided they were permitted to work under normal conditions.[20] In any case, the Soviets

19. "Soviet Aid to the CPR," Novosty Press Agency, Aug. 14, 1964; *Soviet News,* Aug. 14 and 17, 1964.
20. *Ibid.*

did not yet terminate the training and education of thousands of Chinese workers, engineers, technicians, and scientific workers living in the USSR.

It is quite possible that responsibilities for the sudden termination of the contracts and for the abrupt recall of Soviet experts may have been divided: that the technical and nationalistic arrogance of some Soviet experts and the chauvinistic pride and xenophobic sentiments of many Chinese, in combination with the increasing political alienation of the two countries, with the difference in the cultural and historic background and in the history of the revolutionary struggle of both countries, finally produced the inevitable collision. In any case, the sudden recall of the Soviet experts in July 1960 and the simultaneous cessation of the publication of the Soviet magazine *Druzhba* (Friendship) by China in the Soviet Union and of *Su Chung You Hao* (Soviet-Chinese Friendship) by the Soviet Union in China marked a turning point in Sino-Soviet relations.

In spite of the "Great Leap" and Soviet reservations about Chinese economic adventures, mutual trade until 1960 was not affected by the political and theoretical divergencies between the leadership of both countries. Thereafter, however, Sino-Soviet trade very much declined. By 1961 it had already dropped by over fifty percent and in the following years it continued to decrease. While in 1955 seventy percent of Chinese foreign trade went to the USSR and the East European socialist states, by 1963 this figure had been cut down to about thirty percent.

After the virtual breakdown of economic relations between the USSR and the CPR, Moscow and Peking disagreed as to the extent of the "aid" that had been given by the USSR to China, a disagreement that added a new dimension to their dispute. Soviet economists have tended to equate trade and aid, while Chinese writers have denied that free aid was given to China except in a very limited scope. Moscow did turn over to Peking industrial blueprints without charge. It also presented no bill to Peking for the costs of part of the training of Chinese specialists in the USSR. Aside from these and similar exceptions, however, Chinese assertions that alleged Soviet aid was overwhelmingly normal trade appear to be true; otherwise it would be incomprehensible how the CPR could already have repaid all Soviet debts by 1965.

The Soviets, of course, have been as interested in magnifying their aid to China as the Chinese Communist leadership has been in minimizing it. On a per capita basis the Soviets gave to China definitely less aid than to other Communist countries. Also, China, while a recipient of aid, has herself given aid to underdeveloped countries on more generous terms than those she received from the USSR.

Politics aside, the decline in trade between the two Communist giants can be partly explained also by China's economic distress between 1960 and 1962, her unfavorable balance of payments, and her need therefore to substantially reduce imports from abroad. Real or imagined Soviet "blackmail" in 1960 may have persuaded Communist China to diminish her overwhelming economic dependence on the Soviet Union to attain true political independence.

The Twenty-Second Congress of the CPSU, October 1961

After the Moscow conference an uneasy quiet marked the relations between Moscow and Peking. Soviet-Albanian relations, however, continued to deteriorate. In May 1961, in a spectacular move, the USSR withdrew eight Soviet submarines that had been stationed at an island off the Albanian coast. This was followed by the imposition of economic sanctions upon Tirana by Moscow and its satellites. But the increasing pressure upon Albania by her former East European friends and comrades was partly balanced by closer economic, diplomatic, and ideological relations with the CPR. It was not before the Twenty-Second Soviet Congress that Albania was proclaimed a real outcast. It was a blow that was meant for Peking and was deflected upon Tirana.

The Twenty-Second Congress of the CPSU, held between October 17 and 31, 1961, sharpened the differences between the Soviet Union and the CPR. As usual, Communist Parties from all over the world sent their leading representatives to Moscow. Albania and Yugoslavia, however, had not been invited and were absent. The Congress adopted a much-heralded new Party program, which was later sharply criticized by Peking on several grounds. Peking especially objected that the concept of the dictatorship of the proletariat had ceased to be indispensable to the USSR from the point of view of the tasks of her internal development and that the CPSU had become, as it boasted, the vanguard of the *entire* Soviet people. After another sharp denunciation of Stalin and condemnation of the personality cult by Khrushchev, the Congress passed a resolution to remove Stalin's coffin from the Lenin Mausoleum, as it was now officially called, because of his "abuses of power" and "serious violations of Lenin's behests."[21] These and other views went straight against cherished notions of Peking and of its "mouthpiece," Tirana.[22] But only Tirana served as the whipping boy for Khrushchev. Communist China, though already guilty in Moscow's eyes, was still spared, for apparent tactical considerations. In a later Peking view, Khrushchev then went so far as to call for an "over-

---

21. *Pravda*, Nov. 1, 1961. p. 6 (*CDSP* 12, no. 44 [Nov. 26, 1961]: 20).
22. *Pravda*, Oct. 15, 1963 (*CDSP* 15, no. 43 [Nov. 20, 1963]).

throw'' of the Albanian leadership under Enver Hoxha and Mehmet Shehu.[23]

In September 1963 the CPC revealed that at the Twenty-Second Congress of the CPSU it had resolutely opposed the Soviet "errors." Chou, who headed the CPC delegation to Moscow, criticized from the forum of the Congress the "open unilateral condemnation of a fraternal party," a procedure that did not make for unity or resolve any issues. Such disputes, he had insisted, should be resolved patiently "and by the principles of equality and the achievement of unity through consultation." "Openly exposing disputes between fraternal parties and fraternal countries for enemies to see cannot be regarded as a serious, Marxist-Leninist approach."

Chou's criticism in October 1961 of Soviet maltreatment of Albania was also a warning to Moscow to refrain from similar castigations of other fraternal parties and of the CPC itself. In subsequent conversations with Khrushchev and other Soviet leaders, he "frankly criticized" the mistakes of the Soviet leadership. Without waiting for the Congress to complete its work, Chou then returned to Peking. For his daring challenge of Khrushchev, he was given a hero's welcome in Peking by Mao himself and other Chinese leaders.

But Khrushchev and other Soviet leaders at the Twenty-Second congress of the CPSU continued to press the attack against the Albanian leadership,[24] denouncing the "provocative actions" of Hoxha, his continued adherence to the cult of personality, and especially his criticism of the new Soviet Party program, which he and his friends were also accused of "concealing" from their Party and their people.[25]

A two-thirds majority of the 80 Party delegations that attended the Congress ultimately took the Soviet side against Albania, though all the Asian Parties remained silent. Subsequently Moscow must have brought considerable pressure to bear upon them, since several of the Asian Parties soon thereafter made public a condemnation of Tirana.

Following the Twenty-Second Congress, attacks both by Russia upon Albania and by China upon Yugoslavia mounted. The two Communist giants still refrained from coming directly to grips with each other, though skirmishes between them did take place at meetings of the World Peace Council and the World Federation of Trade Unions in December 1961.

23. "Open Letter of CC of CPSU to Party Organizations," *Pravda,* July 14, 1963; Soviet Booklet no. 114, July 1963.

24. Khrushchev's Report at 22nd Congress of CPSU, *Pravda,* Oct. 18, 1961, pp. 2-11 (*CDSP* 12, No. 43 [Nov. 22, 1961]: 3-5).

25. Khrushchev's Report on the New Party Program, *Pravda,* Oct. 19, 1961, pp. 1-10.

5

The Open Conflict, 1962-1963

Moscow, Belgrade, Tirana, and Peking

During the autumn of 1962 Soviet and Chinese foreign-policy thrusts deepened the differences between Peking and Moscow and set the stage for the explosive war of words between the two Communist rivals that was to erupt in 1963. Divisive issues that dominated the stage and were to extend into 1963 and even beyond it were the Soviet-Yugoslav rapprochement, the Cuban missile crisis and, simultaneously with the latter, the Sino-Indian border conflict.

The break between Stalin and Tito in 1948 was never repaired as long as Stalin was alive. But under Khrushchev a rapprochement with Yugoslavia was vigorously pushed; it crystallized in his visit to Belgrade in May 1955. But in spite of the unquestionable improvement of Soviet-Yugoslav relations, their patched-up friendship continued to face critical times and to register many a setback. The Polish and Hungarian Revolutions of 1956, the Soviet repressive reaction, and Belgrade's criticism of some of Moscow's countermeasures widened the rift anew. The Declaration of the Moscow Meeting of Representatives of Communist and Workers' Parties in November 1957 aimed its major thrust at Yugoslavia by proclaiming the danger of revisionism the main peril to the Communist movement and by denouncing the policy of nonalignment. Tito, apparently aware of the new unfavorable trend of events, had refused to attend the Moscow Meeting and refused to sign the Declaration. The dispute between Moscow and Belgrade once again assumed threatening dimensions when in April 1958 the Soviet leadership subjected the Yugoslav Party Draft Program to sharpest criticism and openly announced that no Soviet delegation would attend the impending Yugoslav Party congress in Belgrade.[1]

The first significant Chinese criticism of Yugoslavia seems to have been published on May 5, 1958. Mao, particularly after the disappointments of the Hundred Flowers episode, was dead set against Yugoslav ''revisionism.'' Yet at the time Peking was not out of step with Moscow, but rather marching at its side. There was, nevertheless, a perceptible difference in their criticism of Belgrade. The USSR definitely held out hope for an improvement of her relations with Yugoslavia, while the CPR not only seemed disinterested in such a prospect but also determined to close the door to such a possibility. Peking considered the positions of Moscow and Belgrade irreconcilable[2] and accused Belgrade of betrayal of Marxism-Leninism. It also began to criticize the USSR's ''go easy'' policy in regard to Yugoslavia.[3] Further Chinese attacks on Belgrade reached their climax in the abrupt withdrawal of the Chinese ambassador from that city.

In their Open Letter of July 14, 1963, the Soviets raised the question as to why the Chinese leaders who in 1955 had followed the Soviet policy of normalizing relations with Yugoslavia had drastically changed their position on the Yugoslav question, and replied that the Chinese leadership saw in it an ''advantageous pretext'' to discredit the policy of the CPSU. The Soviets, as they now revealed, in spite of acknowledged differences with Yugoslavia, considered it ''wrong to excommunicate Yugoslavia from socialism,'' to cut her off from the socialist countries, and to push her into the camp of imperialism,'' as the CPC leaders are doing.''[4] That was precisely, the Soviets explained in 1963, what the imperialists had wanted.

The Chinese Communists in turn explained in 1963 that, though in the mid-fifties they had followed Khrushchev's proposal to improve relations with Yugoslavia, they ''did not entertain very much hope for the Tito clique even then.''[5] The Yugoslav rulers were accused of having gone ''farther and farther along the path of revisionism.'' Peking escalated the charges by claiming that the Belgrade leadership was bent on ''restoring capitalism''—an accusation later to be leveled against Moscow itself. Internationally too, Peking asserted, the Tito clique was serving more and more energetically as a counterrevolutionary special detachment of US imperialism. Thus it should no longer be considered a fraternal Party; it should not be won over, but should be thoroughly exposed and firmly combated as a gang of renegades. The Peking article pointed finally to the 1960 Statement, which was quite clear on this point. According to other

1. Zagoria, *Conflict,* pp. 176f.
2. *Refutation of Modern Revisionism* (Peking, 1963), p. 49.
3. Zagoria, pp. 183f.
4. ''Open Letter,'' *Pravda,* July 14, 1963.
5. *People's Daily,* Sept. 26, 1963 (*PR*, Sept. 27, 1963).

Chinese accounts Peking, as early as the late fifties, had also privately criticized Soviet Leaders for their continued concessions to Belgrade and for their "cringing" attitude toward it.[6]

At the eighty-one-party Moscow meeting in 1960, Khrushchev adopted a less hostile position toward Yugoslavia than Mao had wanted. Khrushchev appreciated Yugoslavia's strategic importance in Europe and the Mediterranean world and the political influence she wielded among the neutralist states. For him both de-Stalinization and a new, not necessarily equalitarian, but less rigid and authoritarian, relationship between the socialist states and the fraternal Parties, including Yugoslavia, were basic elements in post-Stalinist Soviet foreign policy, especially in view of rising differences with Peking on ideological and organizational grounds. Tito too, repudiating liberalization at home—he had his critic and former close associate Milovan Djilas, who was considered in Moscow violently anti-Russian, arrested—moved toward rapprochement with Moscow. In April and May of 1962 both Khrushchev and Gromyko expressed their gratification at the new reconciliation with Belgrade.[7]

The wide gap between Moscow and Belgrade seemed once again to be narrowed. On the occasion of a visit of Brezhnev, then Head of State, to Yugoslavia between September 24 and October 4, 1962, the joint communiqué in Belgrade spoke of "identity or closeness of the views of both sides."[8] Peking thereupon was highly provoked. On September 28 the CPC's Central Committee let loose a broadside against the "Tito clique."[9] Perhaps the Russo-Yugoslav communiqué, which had stressed the determination of the two parties to achieve "further expansion of economic cooperation"—at a time when economic help for China had been substantially reduced—aroused the special ire of Peking. Also, Mao Tse-tung, who had been pushed into the background in 1958, began his climb back into power at about this time. This development was accompanied by a sharpening of the ideological differences and of the general dispute with Moscow.

The rapprochement between Moscow and Belgrade alone would have been enough to alarm Tirana also. But Albania, already painfully isolated, was further excluded from the Council for Mutual Economic Aid and from the Warsaw Pact. Faced with the possible threat of a Belgrade-Moscow axis, pointed at Albania's heart, her leaders during the summer of 1962 began to attack Khrushchev directly. Brezhnev's visit in Belgrade on September 24 added to Tirana's discomfort.

For a full understanding of the two crises that gripped the CPR and the

6. G. F. Hudson, *The Sino-Soviet Dispute* (London, 1961), pp. 225f.
7. *Pravda*, Apr. 25, 1962 and May 17, 1962.
8. *Pravda* and *Izvestiia*, Oct. 5, 1962, pp. 1-2 (*CDSP* 14, no. 40 [Oct. 31, 1962]: 6-7).
9. CC, CPC, Sept. 28, 1962; *People's Daily*, Sept. 29, 62 (*PR* Sept. 28, 1962).

USSR in the fall of 1962, it is essential to realize the growing darkening of the clouds over the Sino-Soviet firmament during the preceding months. In August and September 1962 the relations between the USSR and the CPR were sharply exacerbated when Moscow secretly informed Peking of its interest in halting the proliferation of nuclear weapons. In a secret rejoinder—the entire correspondence was disclosed only a year later —Peking protested Moscow's reply and threatened to denounce it publicly.[10]

At the same time, Communist China and Albania found it mutually advantageous to work hand in glove. Many an article outlining China's position was first launched in Albanian dailies and journals. The Moscow-Belgrade alliance was increasingly opposed by a Peking-Tirana axis. On October 13, 1962, the Albanians called openly for a split in the international Communist movement "in spite of the terrible pain" this operation might cause.[11] OnSeptember 5, 1962, the Chinese ambassador in Moscow, Liu Hsiao, was recalled. About two weeks later it was reported in Moscow that Peking had requested the USSR to close all its consulates in China.

The Sino-Indian War and the Cuban Missile Crisis, 1962

The Cuban crisis and the outbreak of the Sino-Indian war virtually coincided. The first crisis pitted the USSR against the United States of America, the second juxtaposed Communist China against the next most populous country in the world, India, leader of the uncommitted Third World. Chinese criticism of Soviet policy in the Cuban confrontation and Soviet criticism of Indo-Chinese hostilities were bound to deepen the chasm between the two "fraternal" parties and leave permanent wounds.

The criticism of Soviet policy during the Cuban missile crisis in October 1962 was no doubt galling to the Soviets and to Khrushchev personally, who boasted of having single-handedly saved global peace.[12] At the same time, China's attack upon India, a nonaligned country with which the Soviets maintained good relations and whose stance in international affairs seemed often to serve Moscow's purposes, appeared to Soviet Russia's leadership most unfortunate,[13] an example of the Chinese People's Republic's aggressive and chauvinist policy.

Aggression against India, a nonimperialist state that had only recently

10. CPR government statement, *People's Daily,* Aug. 15, 1963 (*PR,* Aug. 16, 1963, pp. 7-15).

11. Quoted by Griffith, *Albania and the Sino-Soviet Rift,* Document 32.

12. B. Ponomarev, *Pravda,* Nov. 18, 1962.

13. *Pravda* editor., Nov. 5, 1962; see also Suslov, "The Struggle of the CPSU for the unity. . . ," Feb. 14, 1964, *Pravda,* Apr. 3, 1964.

emerged in a national-liberation struggle from its colonial yoke, was likely to undermine the prestige of socialism throughout the world and push India, not to mention other neutrals and peoples who were still struggling for liberation, into "imperialist" arms. Yet, the Soviet Union was in a quandary, for unwillingness to support China, on the other hand, would deepen, perhaps hopelessly, the division between the two Communist giants and irreparably split the socialist commonwealth from top to bottom.

Chinese suppression of the Tibetan uprising in 1959 and the Dalai Lama's flight to India had heightened Indian fears of ultimate Chinese intentions. In a letter dated January 23, 1959, written to Nehru, Chou En-lai had for the first time presented China's claims to a new Sino-Indian boundary line, pointing out that no boundary had ever been formally agreed upon. The conflict had grown sharper in July 1962, when armed clashes occurred in the frontier region. Each country then raised accusations of provocations and intrusions across the border against the other. In mid-August Prime Minister Nehru secured *carte blanche* from the Indian parliament for his dealings with the northern neighbor, and on October 12, 1962, he revealed that the Indian army had received instructions to push the Chinese forces, which allegedly had encroached on Indian territory, behind the McMahon line.[14] India was seemingly resolved to regain territory that had been lost during the last years and China appeared determined to defend what she considered a favorable status quo, if need be by resorting to aggression and force.

But while preparing for war with India, Communist China seemed to have no illusions about the atittude of the USSR. An article in the Albanian press charged Moscow with supporting India in the Sino-Indian border conflict and of selling weapons and planes to the "Indian reactionaries." Actually, during the preceding summer, the Indian government had signed an agreement with the Soviets for the delivery of Soviet MIG fighters and for the construction of a factory in India to produce these aircraft. But the first Soviet planes did not arrive before February 1963.

The outbreak of the Indo-Chinese hostilities occurred on October 20, 1962. Fighting erupted in the North-East Frontier Agency, where the rapid advance of the Chinese troops posed the most serious threat to the plain of Assam, and in Ladakh along the northwestern frontier of India.

A year after the crisis, Peking made public a detailed account of the then-secret Moscow-Peking exchanges that took place on the very eve of these hostilities. According to it, a Chinese leader had informed the Soviet ambassador in Peking of a planned "massive attack" against the Indian

14. *Zeri i Popullit,* Sept. 19-20, 1962, quoted by Griffith, *Albania,* Document 31, pp. 364, 54; about Nehru, *The Hindu,* Oct. 12, 1962.

position and strongly implied that Soviet military help to India would arouse sharp Chinese reaction: Indian use of Soviet-built planes was already making a "bad impression" upon Chinese frontier guards.[15] According to the Chinese account, on October 13 and 14 Khrushchev informed the Chinese ambassador in Moscow that the Soviet Government had received similar reports about the Himalayan developments. He had added that if the Soviets were in the position of China, "they would have taken the same measures."[16] This Chinese version of the occurrences prior to the outbreak was not contradicted by the Soviets. It clearly indicated a measure of Soviet advance approval such as did not come forth once the hostilities erupted. It also explained why the Chinese, when actually launching their attack, did not consider it necessary to give Moscow additional advance information.

The Soviet Union's position at the outbreak of hostilities was first one of neutrality, though slightly favoring China. But on October 25, *Pravda,* while voicing concern over the eruption of hostilities—"which benefit only the common enemy of these states," international imperialism—approved the Chinese three-point program for settling the dispute. The McMahon line, *Pravda* asserted, had been imposed on the Chinese and Indian peoples; the Chinese government had never recognized it.[17] The Soviet people, like all who loved peace, were "concerned" over the tense situation that had led to clashes on the Indo-Chinese border. Both the Soviet people and the Soviet government had always stood for the settlement of the border dispute "by peaceful means through negotiations." What was now needed was an "internationalist approach," not actions aimed at fanning animosity. The Soviet people saw in the Statement of the Chinese government evidence of a sincere concern to bring the conflict to a halt. In its view, Peking's proposals of October 24 constituted an acceptable basis for negotiations. An amicable settlement of the issue would once again demonstrate the great power of the principles of peaceful coexistence and cooperation of states with different systems.

The relative meagerness of *Pravda's* comment was quite revealing. Despite some advance warning on highest levels, the eruption of hostilities had caught the Soviet press, that is, the Soviet government, in an embarrassed and perplexed state of mind, especially in view of the simultaneous escalation of the Cuban conflict.

Chinese criticism of the Soviet Caribbean policy in late October may

15. *People's Daily*, Nov. 2, 1963, "The truth about how the leaders of the CPSU have allied themselves with India. . . ." (*PR*, Nov. 8, 1963).

16. *Ibid.*

17. "In the Interest of the People, in the Name of Universal Peace," *Pravda*, Oct. 25, 1962, p. 1. Reprinted in *People's Daily,* Oct. 26, 1962, also in *Soviet News,* Oct. 25, 1962; statement of the Government of China, *Izvestiia,* Oct. 25, 1962, p. 3.

have led to the lifting of any Soviet restraints on comments on the Sino-Indian boundary clashes. On November 5, 1962, *Pravda* warned both Peking and New Delhi that the Soviet people could "not remain indifferent when the blood of our brothers and friends—the Chinese and Indian peoples—is being shed" and, reverting to its previous policy of scrupulous neutrality, urged that a cease-fire be arranged and immediate and unconditional negotiations be commenced.[18] At the same time, Khrushchev allegedly apologized to Nehru for "certain misrepresentations" in the earlier *Pravda* editorial.[19] Finally, on November 21, Peking proclaimed a unilateral cease-fire and began the withdrawal of her military units from India. Moscow's change of policy on the Sino-Indian conflict was definitely linked to Peking's disillusionment with and open criticism of Soviet policy in the Caribbean.

The Chinese were bitterly disappointed over what seemed to them a Soviet retreat in the Caribbean, Soviet hesitancy and apparent unwillingness to shoulder the risks of a major conflagration. They were also disillusioned about the lack of support for a fraternal socialist country in the struggle against a nonsocialist state. Peking had merely to contrast what it proudly considered its heroic victory along its Indian border with Moscow's seemingly cowardly avoidance of giving battle in the Caribbean. It may have ignored that the respective risks in the Himalayan mountains and the Caribbean differed rather sharply and that the military power of India and America were not comparable. Griffith holds that the Soviet retreat in the Cuban crisis worsened Sino-Soviet relations "even more rapidly and drastically than the Chinese attack on India."[20] Both crises explain why, in the acrimonious and protracted dispute in 1962 and 1963, the issues of war and peace and peaceful coexistence figured as large as they did.

First, however, the Chinese supported Khrushchev's moves in the Caribbean, and it appeared as if the aggressive Soviet policy would bring Russia and Communist China together again, narrowing the gap between them.[21] But when Khrushchev seemed resolutely determined to avoid a collision course and pulled the missiles back, the Chinese were once again up in arms. With no effort at concealing their real target any longer, they accused Khrushchev of having staged "another Munich" and sacrificed Cuban independence and the international Communist movement.[22]

18. *Pravda,* Nov. 5, 1962.
19. Quoted by A. Dallin, *Diversity in International Communism* (New York, 1963), p. 660.
20. Griffith, *The Sino-Soviet Rift*, (Cambridge, Mass., 1964), p. 60.
21. *People's Daily,* Oct. 31, 1962 on Cuban Revolution (*PR*, Nov. 2, 1962, p. 5).
22. *People's Daily,* Nov. 5, 1962, "The Fearless Cuban People" (*PR*, Nov. 9, 1962, pp. 12-13).

Mass demonstrations in China pledged support for Cuban sovereignty;[23] they were meant to be a reproach to the USSR, which allegedly had betrayed the defense interests of sovereign socialist Cuba. The withdrawal of the Cuban missiles unquestionably lowered Soviet prestige in the eyes not only of radical communists but also of neutralists and the Western world. In the USSR, however, the withdrawal of the Soviet missiles was greeted as assuring the continuation of peace. The apparent Soviet-Cuban differences in the wake of the peaceful settlement merely corroborated the worldwide interpretation of the outcome of the Cuban affair as a Soviet retreat in the face of acute danger. The recent Soviet escalation in the Caribbean thus seemed utterly purposeless.

The major guns in defense of Soviet policy during the recent Cuban crisis opened up in Moscow itself. In a major speech to the Supreme Soviet on December 12, 1962, Khrushchev offered the official Soviet version of the puzzling Caribbean policy of the USSR. In this context, while mentioning Communist China only in an oblique manner, he left no doubt as to his bitter disappointment over Peking's attitude toward the USSR. But it was the Albanian leaders who bore, as before, the brunt of Khrushchev's attacks. Khrushchev compared them to "unreasoning boys" who used foul language against the USSR and were the more rewarded by their masters the cruder and stronger the language they used. They had shouted especially loudly during the Cuban crisis. At that time it was Yugoslav leaders—though criticized by "some people" who contended that Yugoslavia was not a socialist country—who took a correct stand, while the "dogmatists," who posed as true Marxists-Leninists, took a "provocative one."[24]

The repercussions of the Cuban crisis were so deep and long-lasting that almost a year later the Soviets felt it still necessary to deal with the issue in an Open Letter of the CC to Party Organizations, dated July 1963.[25] The Soviet statement underlined that there had existed a "real danger" of a thermonuclear war and that the missile weapons were only removed in return for the United States government's pledge not to invade Cuba. The Soviets thus deserved credit for saving both peace and Cuban independence. But the Chinese comrades had stubbornly ignored the positive assessment that the leaders of the Cuban Revolution themselves made of the policy of the Soviet government.

The Chinese government, however, in a Statement not made public until

23. About mass demonstrations in Peking, Gittings, p. 176; also Jen Ku-ping "The Tito Group's Shameful Role" (PR, Nov. 16, 1962, pp. 7-9).

24. Pravda, Dec. 13, 1962.

25. "On the Statement of the CP of the USA," People's Daily, March 8, 1963 (PR, March 15, 1963); also Open Letter of the CC of CPSU to the Party Organizations, July 1963, Pravda, July 14, 1963.

the Sino-Soviet dispute reached its climax, September 1, 1963, responded with the countercharge that "during the Caribbean crisis the Soviet leaders committed the error of adventurism and the error of capitulationism." Instead of criticizing themselves, these leaders had prided themselves on the "slap in their face," boasted of their genuine proletarian internationalism, and proclaimed what they called a "major victory of the policy of reason, of the forces of peace and socialism." It was "thoroughly disgusting" to hear them wantonly attacking the CPC, alleging that China had hoped for a head-on clash between the United States of America and the USSR.[26]

According to Peking, there was no threat of nuclear war in the Caribbean until, "as a result of the rash action of Soviet leaders," nuclear weapons were introduced there. Peking raised the question whether the Soviet government, before the transport of rockets to Cuba, had ever consulted the Soviet people or the other socialist countries or the working class in capitalist countries. "Without consulting anybody, you wilfully embarked on a reckless course and irresponsibly played with the lives of millions upon millions of people." The Chinese were patently furious and their merciless accusation and outright mockery of the Soviets reached the high-water mark.

After the event, because the Soviet leaders asserted that hurling rockets from the Soviet Union at enemy territory instead of from advanced bases would take "slightly longer" but their accuracy would not be impaired, Peking found it incomprehensible that missiles had been sent to Cuba in the first place. Furthermore, "anyone with common sense will ask: since the rockets were introduced, why did they have to be withdrawn afterwards?" If one were to believe the Soviets, there was "a great deal of finesse in first putting them in and then taking them out. In recklessly introducing the rockets into Cuba and then humiliatingly withdrawing them, the Soviet leaders moved from adventurism to capitulationism. . . . They have inflicted unprecedented shame and humiliation on the international proletariat. All this has been unalterably written into history. No matter how the Soviet leaders lie or what sleight-of-hand they perform, they can never wash away their shame."

Khrushchev on Two Crises

In his address to the Supreme Soviet on December 12, 1962, only a few weeks after the Cuban crisis, Khrushchev acknowledged that there were various ideological roads to Communism and underlined once again that

26. Statement by the Spokesman of the Chinese Government—a Comment on the Soviet Government's Statement of Aug. 21, *People's Daily*, Sept. 1, 1963 (*PR*, Sept. 6, 1963).

Soviet and Yugoslav views on European and international affairs were basically identical. Also, "dogmatists" rather than, as claimed earlier,
"revisionists"—in other words, China rather than Yugoslavia—presented
the "main danger" to Marxism-Leninism. He still criticized only indirectly
China's attitude toward the Caribbean confrontation. Referring to the
Sino-Indian conflict, Khrushchev expressed his pleasure that, after the
frontier dispute between a socialist and a nonaligned country had regretta-
bly erupted into fighting, China had finally announced that she had unilaterally ceased fire and withdrawn her troops. But he still made critical reference to "lives lost and bloodshed" and also pointed to unknown critics
of Peking's policy who denounced its "retreat."[27] Stung by Chinese criticism that the USSR had retreated in the Caribbean, he flung this very
charge against the CPR.

Communist China had left Macao and Hong Kong undisturbed. This
Khrushchev   contended—seemingly   graciously,   though   not
convincingly—was by no means an indication that the Chinese did not
hate colonialism or had retreated from Marxism-Leninism. He pretended to
have full understanding of what was clearly a soft policy on China's part:
"Everyone proceeds from their own conditions." Yet Peking had not applied this maxim in its own judgment of Soviet policy toward Cuba.
Khrushchev, though claiming to criticize merely the Albanian leaders, castigated the promptings of all "ultrarevolutionary loudmouths" during the
recent Cuban crisis. "Some dogmatists," having taken Trotskyite positions, were seeking to push the Soviet Union onto the path of unleashing a
world war. The Albanian leadership was clearly disappointed that the
Caribbean crisis had been peaceably settled. And in the same speech
Khrushchev solemnly promised that Soviet policy would be directed toward reaching agreement on general and complete disarmament.

In his review of the Sino-Indian conflict, Khrushchev took special care
again to maintain a neutral position such as the USSR had adopted during
the hostilities. Expressing "great regret" over the "bloodstained border
conflict," he noted the absence of military conflicts along the Sino-Indian
border over "many centuries." "Some" were saying that China ceased
hostilities because India began to receive support from the American and
British imperialists. "Evidently the Chinese friends took account of the
situation," and this rather spoke for their wisdom. They also had probably
taken account of the recent mass arrest of Communists and other progressive figures in India. Khrushchev discounted the idea that China had ever
set for herself the aim of invading India—a mere "slander"—but also rejected the notion that India had wanted to start a war with China. Clearly,

27. *Pravda*, Dec. 13, 1963.

this line was not to endear the Soviet leader and his government with the Chinese fraternal Communist Party.

Gromyko's Analysis

In the discussion following Khrushchev's address to the Supreme Soviet, the speech of Foreign Minister A. A. Gromyko was one of the most revealing regarding the new international situation. It was marked by a remarkably conciliatory tone and spirit in regard to the United States. According to Gromyko, mankind had indeed come very close to the "abyss" of war, "only one step, or perhaps only half a step remained."[28] The leaders of the United States had displayed "circumspection." History had so developed that "without mutual understanding between the USSR and the United States of America not a single serious international conflict can be settled, agreement cannot be reached on a single international problem." If the USSR and the United States of America would unite their efforts to settle the conflicts and complications that arise, the emerging flames of war would subside and tension would abate. The Soviet foreign minister drew from the cataclysmic events the conclusion that agreement and understanding between the two superpowers represented the key to peace in the world. Communist China did not seem to figure at all in Gromyko's calculations.

Following Khrushchev's indirect but quite apparent criticism of China, Gromyko's speech must have displeased Peking to the utmost. The prospect of the two superpowers deciding important world issues, one of these in the very backyard of China (Gromyko pointed especially to Laos as an "example" of an accord between Khrushchev and Kennedy reached at the Vienna Conference) without consulting the latter, must have been highly irritating to Peking. Talks like the foregoing one by Gromyko laid the basis for the open charges Peking was soon to raise against Moscow about her alleged "collusion" with the United States of America.

Differences at Party Congresses

The differences between Peking and Moscow, which rapidly deepened after the Cuban crisis, were discussed at the Congress of the Hungarian Socialist Workers' Party held on November 20-24, 1962, at the Czechoslovak Party Congress that met between December 4 and 8 and, in regard to Peking in most critical terms, at the Italian Party Congress held between December 2 and 8. All this was climaxed by the East German Party Con-

28. *Pravda*, Dec. 14, 1962, pp. 5-6 (*CDSP* 15, no. 1 [1963]: 11-12).

gress in mid-January.[29] The General Secretary of the Italian Communist Party, Palmiro Togliatti, while coming out in support of recent Soviet policy which, in his view, had successfully defended Cuban independence and averted nuclear war, criticized sharply the commencement of Chinese hostilities against India as "absurd," thought China's solidarity with the Albanian leaders "unacceptable," and ridiculed the Chinese claim that capitalism had been restored in Yugoslavia.[30]

The European Party Congresses in December 1962, which accentuated the Sino-Soviet dispute, were followed closely both in Peking and Moscow. On December 10 *Pravda* promptly reprinted the criticism of Peking made at the Italian and the Czechoslovakian congresses by Togliatti and Novotny respectively. Directing their fire at Peking, the Congresses had focused on the political sins and alleged organizational transgressions of the CPC.[31] Polemics on theoretical issues were broadly dealt with in direct exchanges between Peking and Moscow during the months of December and January. These months after the Cuban conflagration and the eruption of war in the Himalayas saw no relaxation; on the contrary, they witnessed a distinct escalation of the conflict.

The last of the European Party Congresses in the wake of the October crisis was held in East Berlin on January 15, and it was a most carefully Soviet-staged gathering.[32] In spite of some earlier signs of East German sympathy for the CPC, Walter Ulbricht's criticism of Communist China was one of the sharpest. Gomulka on this occasion praised Khrushchev, while the Cuban representative made it clear that his country leaned toward neutrality between the two Communist giants. In spite of Moscow's recent help and Cuba's continued dependence on the USSR, Fidel Castro clearly disliked Moscow's theme of peaceful coexistence. But the great majority of delegations took the Soviet line. The Chinese delegate was booed and humiliated in Berlin, and delegates of three pro-Peking Asian Communist parties were virtually denied the right to address the Congress. Such happenings were bound to further aggravate the Sino-Soviet rift.

Soviet-American Rapprochement

Early in 1963 Khrushchev and Kennedy exchanged messages on nuclear-test-ban inspection that were to bear fruit later in the year. It was hardly an accident that this exchange closely followed the acute missile

29. *Neues Deutschland,* Jan. 15-22, 1963.
30. *Pravda,* Dec. 4, 1962, about Togliatti; about the Tenth Congress of the Italian Communist Party, see Griffith, *The Sino-Soviet Rift,* p. 79.
31. *Pravda,* Dec. 10, 1962.
32. See Griffith, pp. 97-103; about Wu's speech in East Berlin, *People's Daily,* Jan. 19, 1963 (*PR*, Jan. 25, 1963, pp. 7-9).

crisis in October 1962, which had raised the specter of atomic war. Quite in accord with the major propositions contained in Gromyko's foregoing speech and with his general tone, Khrushchev, on January 21, 1963, sent an open message to President Kennedy. "The period of the greatest acuteness and tension in the Caribbean basin is past," he began.[33] Neither the Soviet Union nor the United States wanted war. In order to avoid a thermonuclear catastrophe, which would inflict enormous sacrifices and sufferings on all peoples of the world, "we must. . .resolve all disputes by means of negotiations and mutual concessions." Following the Caribbean crisis, the Soviet leadership, in a kind of anticlimax, was in a mood for negotiating directly with the United States of America.

Communist China could only look with suspicion, fear, and hostility upon negotiations and "mutual concessions" between the two superpowers. Comrade Wu Hsiu-chuan, the chief delegate of the CPC to the sixth congress of the Socialist Unity Party of Germany, denounced imperialism, which aimed at "breaking up the socialist camp."[34] He furthermore criticized some fraternal parties that had attacked Albania and had also assailed the CPC "by name." He gave credit to the Cuban people for having in the recent crisis defended the independence and revolutionary accomplishments of Cuba against American imperialism, and also extended recognition to the peoples of Latin America and the whole world for their sympathy and support; but he had not a single word of appreciation for the USSR. At the very same time the Soviet press showered congratulations upon its own government for having saved socialist Cuba and the peace of the world. Khrushchev then claimed that the USSR, "together with Cuba," had forced the United States of America to renounce the armed invasion of the Caribbean island.[35]

Khrushchev Defends His Policy

Much of Khrushchev's talk at the Congress of the SED in January 1963 was simply an indirect rebuff of the Chinese criticism of Soviet Russian policies. "Some persons," he remarked, who considered themselves Marxists, denied that the struggle against imperialism consisted primarily in building up the economic might of the socialist countries and, like witch doctors, flung interminable curses at imperialism.

Not one problem of the revolutionary movement of the working class and of the national liberation movement, Khrushchev asserted, could be considered apart from the struggle for peace, for preventing world ther-

---

33. *New York Times*, Jan. 21, 1963.
34. *People's Daily*, Jan. 19, 1963 (*PR*, Jan. 25, 1963, pp. 7-9).
35. *Izvestiia*, Jan. 17, 1963, pp. 1-4.

monuclear war. In the history of the workers' movement there had been previous instances in which the "struggle for peace became the chief requirement of the struggle for socialism." True, the Russian proletariat had scored revolutionary victory during World War I, and a number of new socialist states had arisen after World War II. This did not mean in the least that the Bolsheviks under Lenin had unleashed war between states in order to achieve the victory of the revolution. On the contrary, Lenin and the Bolsheviks had done everything they could to keep the war from breaking out, but since they could not prevent war, they posed the task of turning the imperialist war into a civil war.

Yet contemporary "fledgling theoreticians" were attempting to devise a theory to the effect that the path to the victory of socialism lay through war between states, through destruction, bloodshed, and the death of millions of people. Such a theory was bound to repel the masses, not attract them to the Communist Parties. "If all the nuclear weapons would burst over people's heads, 700-800 million people, according to calculations by scientists, would die in the first strike alone. Not only the large cities of the two leading nuclear powers—the United States of America and the USSR—but also the cities of France, Britain, Germany, Italy, China, Japan and many other countries would be wiped from the face of the earth and destroyed." A nuclear war would lower the life expectancy of many generations of people, would produce disease and death, and lead to the monstrous development of mankind. Though the capitalist system that gave rise to such a war would perish in it, the socialist countries and the cause of the struggle for socialism would not gain from a "thermonuclear catastrophe."[36]

Khrushchev, anxious to defend his Cuban policy, wished to wipe out the impression of having retreated in face of danger. He claimed to have saved world peace, while denying that this policy was a renunciation of world revolution and of the goals of the national liberation movement.

The Soviets on War and Revolution

Khrushchev and Pravda *about Albania and Yugoslavia*

Finally, Khrushchev ridiculed the Albanian leaders who "chattered away" about a nuclear-missile war—leaving no doubt as to the ultimate target of his criticism, namely Peking. He added contemptuously that this "bothered" no one, since chatter was "all they [the Albanians] have";

36. *Pravda*, Jan. 17, 1963.

they had no real possibilities. The advocates of the so-called victory of socialism through war were also, according to Khrushchev, those who denied that it was possible to take a peaceful path toward the victory of socialism, and they were also devotees of the Stalin cult.

Peking's aggressive thrusts against Albania's neighbor, Yugoslavia, were likewise blunted by Khrushchev. Though new difficulties had in the meantime arisen between Moscow and Belgrade, Khrushchev was unwilling to let Communist China dictate Soviet Russian policy toward Yugoslavia. Differences between Soviet Russia and Yugoslavia were nothing more than temporary episodes, while relations between the peoples of socialist countries are "now being established for the ages." It was not proper for Communists to imitate churchmen who excommunicated persons for failure to observe vows and rituals and to practice " 'excommunication' from socialism." While the CPSU disagreed with the Yugoslav leaders on certain ideological questions, it could not assert that Yugoslavia was not socialist, since "objective indications" clearly proved the contrary. The CPSU, in spite of "profound" differences of opinion with the leadership of the Albanian Party of Labor, which it combated on account of its "incorrect and subjective approach," similarly considered Albania also a socialist country.

At the very time Khrushchev shunted aside what was actually Chinese criticism, *Pravda* turned to the most serious aspect of Communist China's activities, which went to the very heart of Communist organizational policy. Early in January 1963 *Pravda* had already denounced "splitters" in world Communism.[37] While officially directing its guns only against the Albanian Communist leadership, the criticism was an unmistakable warning aimed at Peking, since the paper openly alluded to the defense of the Albanian Communist leaders by Chinese Communism. The top leaders of the Albanian Party of Labor, *Pravda* asserted, were the "most outspoken proponents" of "dogmatic and divisive views" in international Communism. Repeatedly, most recently from the rostrum of the Twenty-Second Congress of the CPSU, delegations of the CPC, in spite of "irrefutable facts," had tried to shield the Albanian leaders from the criticism of fraternal Parties and placed the blame for the differences that had arisen on the latter. Yet Albanian leaders had attacked the line of the Twentieth Congress of the CPSU and the propositions of the Declaration of 1957 and the Statement of the eighty-one Communist Parties of November 1960. Even at that time they had voiced their disagreement with the policy of peaceful coexistence of states with different social systems, with the struggle in the cause of disarmament and of peaceful settlement of issues

37. *Ibid.*, Jan. 7, 1963, pp. 1-3 (*CDSP* 15, no. 1 [Jan. 30, 1963]: 1-10, 28).

through negotiations, and with the proposition that there were a variety of forms of transition to socialism. *Pravda* did not have to add that the Albanian leaders were only the mouthpieces of Peking and that Chinese Communist leaders had their reservations about significant parts of the 1957 Declaration and the 1960 Statement.

Though "rebuffed" by the 1960 conference, the Albanian leaders would not listen to reason and thereafter came out repeatedly against basic propositions of the 1960 Statement. The leaders of the Albanian Party were "openly breaking" with the Communist movement, were "sinking deeper and deeper into the morass of dogmatism, sectarianism, and virulent nationalism and resorting ever more extensively to the methods of the cult of the individual," all of which was alien to Marxism. In the question of peaceful coexistence and the threat of a devastating war—"there is no other alternative"—they had taken a position not different from the point of view of the adventuristic circles of imperialism. The position of Tirana, according to *Pravda*, thus hardly differed from that of the imperialist arch-enemy, the United States. Yesterday's "fraternal" Party had adopted a line hardly distinguishable from the imperialist devil himself!

The Albanian leaders dared to libel the USSR, the main force of peace and socialism. In the most critical hours during the Caribbean crisis, the "loudmouths" in Tirana had not supported the Soviet Union, but had actually helped the imperialist circles to "push the world into the abyss of war." While the whole world recognized that credit for saving the peace belonged to the Soviet Union, "the dogmatists" and "leftist phrasemongers" were slanderously trying to make it appear that the Soviet Union had capitulated to imperialism, had acceded to a "second Munich."[38]

The Albanian charges, more specifically the Peking-Tirana accusations, clearly hurt Moscow; also, the CPSU no longer entertained any illusions as to the real wirepullers behind the vituperative charges. The extent and length to which Khrushchev went in attacking the Albanian leaders would be incomprehensible unless it was understood that he was actually aiming his shots at the CPR. At the moment Albania was still the convenient whipping boy for the USSR, just as Yugoslavia then fulfilled the very same function for the CPR. *Pravda's* blows were aimed at Mao Tse-tung and the Chinese leadership, not at Enver Hoxha and his entourage. It was characteristic of this stage of the Sino-Soviet dispute that the major contestants fought against straw men, Moscow against distant Tirana and Peking against even farther-away Belgrade. In due time the two Communist giants were to come to direct verbal and even physical blows with each other.

38. *Ibid. (CDSP*, p. 6).

Peaceful Coexistence

After attempting to show that the settlement in the Caribbean allegedly had been reached on the basis of mutual concessions and exemplified peaceful coexistence in action, *Pravda* continued to try to prove that such coexistence did not prevent the progress of the national-liberation movement and of the class struggle in capitalist countries. The paper seemed especially sensitive in regard to the accusation that Soviet Communism was prepared to sacrifice revolution for the sake of "bourgeois" comfort and convenience. There followed a sharp attack on those who gave no thought to the consequences of modern war, who underestimated or simply discounted nuclear weapons. Vast destruction of productive forces in a nuclear war would make it extraordinarily difficult to build a new society on the ruins left by a world nuclear war. Yet the socialist revolution has no need to have the way paved for it by atomic and hydrogen war, "for the final goal of the working class is not to die 'gallantly' but to build a happy life for all mankind."[39]

To eliminate any doubt, *Pravda* then recalled that while the Statement of 1960 had considered "revisionism"—then crystallized in the Yugoslav deviation—the "principal danger" to Communism, it had already warned that "dogmatism and sectarianism" could at some stage also become the main peril. In Moscow's eyes, Communist China was the leftist bugaboo, representing the heresy of "sectarianism and dogmatism," just as in Peking's view Moscow, in addition to Belgrade, had become the very incarnation of "revisionism." Moscow, of course, as always, claimed to follow the correct Marxist-Leninist course, avoiding the pitfalls of both right and left deviation, of revisionism and dogmatism. *Pravda* claimed that it was "more complicated" to expose left opportunism than, for instance, revisionism, since the former hid behind "ultrarevolutionary phraseology" that played on the feeling of the masses. The paper stressed the need for waging an uncompromising struggle against any distortions of Marxism-Leninism. Thus Moscow cleared the deck for the battle with Peking.

The Chinese Rejoinder

During the early months of 1963, the Chinese began to retaliate. The *People's Daily* of Peking made a point of publishing excerpts from the worst anti-Chinese outbursts of Soviet journals and pamphlets, and also reported the maltreatment of the Chinese delegate to the Party Congress of

39. *Ibid.* (*CDSP*, p. 7).

the SED held in East Berlin.[40] The Chinese journal went so far as publicly to demand Khrushchev's removal from his party and government posts. While Peking tried to corner Moscow over the question of Yugoslav revisionism, pointing especially to anti-Yugoslav Soviet statements made between 1957 and 1959, Moscow replied by quoting favorable, pro-Yugoslav Chinese policy statements uttered in 1957.[41]

Between December 15, 1962, and March 8, 1963, the leading Chinese papers, The *People's Daily* and *Red Flag,* published seven major articles on the Sino-Soviet dispute. Some of these polemics were directed against prominent French and Italian Communist leaders like Maurice Thorez and Palmiro Togliatti, then noted foreign exponents of the Moscow point of view. Peking apparently was stung not only by Moscow's increasing criticism of its stand and general policies, but also by the growing anti-Chinese chorus among Communists everywhere, especially the prestigious and influential Italian and French Communist Parties. On December 31, 1962, *People's Daily* published the long article "Differences between Comrade Togliatti and Us," referring to the recent Tenth Congress of the Italian Communist Party at which Togliatti had "rudely attacked" the CPC and "very firmly rejected" the opposing views of the representative of the CPC. The leading Chinese paper unleashed a bristling attack on Togliatti and the CPI. The Italian Party's stand "boiled down to this—the people of capitalist countries should not make revolutions, the oppressed nations should not wage struggles to win liberation, and the people of the world should not fight against imperialism." The CPI actually prettified imperialism, American imperialism in particular, while it "slanderously" distorted the position of the CPC as a warlike one. Those who attacked the CPC wanted people to believe in the "sensibleness," the "good intentions" of imperialism, and to place their hopes for world peace on "mutual conciliation," "mutual accommodations," and "sensible compromises." "To beg imperialism for peace, these persons do not scruple to impair the fundamental interests of the people of various countries, throw overboard the revolutionary principles and even demand that others also sacrifice the revolutionary principles."

Six days later, in the article "Leninism and Modern Revisionism," *Red Flag* claimed that Leninism was being distorted and adulterated by modern revisionists more viciously than ever before. The Soviet doctrine of "democracy of the whole people" was branded as an attempt to make a mere fetish of bourgeois democracy, that is, of bourgeois dictatorship. Re-

---

40. "Whence the differences. . . ?" *People's Daily,* Feb. 27, 1963 (*PR*, March 1, 1963, p. 14).

41. *People's Daily,* March 9, 1963 (*PR*, "For Marxist-Leninist Unity. . . ," March 15, 1963, p. 8).

visionists actually were attacking Leninism under the pretext of opposing dogmatism. The purpose of modern revisionists was to prevent the oppressed people and oppressed nations from rising in revolution and fighting for their emancipation. What they called the "logic of survival" was nothing but the "logic of slaves, a logic that would paralyze the revolutionary will of the people of all countries, bind them hand and foot and make them submissive slaves of imperialism and of reactionaries of various countries."

Pressing its attack against revisionism, *People's Daily,* on January 27, in the editorial "Let us unite on the basis of the Moscow Declaration and the Moscow Statement," directed its main criticism against Yugoslav revisionism, warning that one's attitude toward Belgrade was not a minor, but a major question. What was at stake was the correctness of the Moscow Declaration and the Moscow Statement, which had condemned Titoist revisionism. And these two international documents were binding on all fraternal parties! Yet, when the thirteenth anniversary of the signing of the Sino-Soviet Treaty of Friendship, Alliance, and Mutual Assistance on February 14 came around, meetings were held in several Chinese cities in honor of the occasion. Acting Secretary-General of the Sino-Soviet Friendship Association, Chang Chih-hsiang, assured the Peking gathering that, "whatever storms may arise," the great friendship and unity between the people of China and the Soviet Union could not be destroyed by anybody.

Replies to Thorez and Togliatti

On February 27, *People's Daily,* in the article "Whence the Differences?—a reply to Thorez and other Comrades," unleashed a full attack against Thorez and the Moscow-oriented CPF. It pointed to Thorez and other French comrades who, since the latter part of November 1962, had in quick succession made numerous statements attacking the CPC, the main content of which had already been published by the paper on February 24. In the swelling anti-Chinese chorus, Thorez and friends had outdone the others in assailing the CPC. Contrary to Thorez, however, it was not the CPC's publication of the pamphlet *Long Live Leninism* in the summer of 1960 that brought the Sino-Soviet differences into the open. *People's Daily* rejected the charges that China had bared the dispute to the enemy, but rather held that the indirect Soviet criticism of China in September 1959 on the occasion of incidents along the Sino-Indian border had been the turning point in the disclosure of the latent Sino-Soviet rift to the world at large.

Similarly, according to *People's Daily,* it was the USSR that was responsible for the deterioration of Soviet-Albanian relations. China had offered her advice to the Soviet comrades "many times," holding that the larger of the two immediately concerned Parties and the larger country should take the initiative in improving Soviet-Albanian relations and settle the differences through inter-Party consultation on an equal footing. Yet no consideration had been given to Peking. There had followed the withdrawal of the fleet from the naval base of Vlore, the recall of experts from Tirana, and the cessation of aid to Albania, and interference in her internal affairs. The Soviets had refused to publish the replies of the Albanian comrades to their accusations.

While rejecting Thorez's accusation that China on the occasion of the Caribbean crisis had wanted to bring on war between the Soviet Union and the United States and to plunge the world into thermonuclear war, the Chinese journal rather pointed out what it considered Thorez's and the CPF's "mistakes" in connection with this crisis and their "primary concern" of fighting the CPC rather than the United States. Prior to 1959 the CPF and Thorez had correctly pointed to United States imperialism as the leader of the forces of aggression and had also denounced the Yugoslav Tito clique, but then had produced a complete turnabout "in response to the baton" of Moscow. How unbending Peking's attitude was could be seen not only by its suggestion that attacks on the CPC and against the Albanian Party of Labor cease immediately, but also by its insistence that it was "absolutely impermissible to use the pretext of stopping polemics in order to forbid the exposure and condemnation of Yugoslav revisionism," as demanded by the Moscow statement.

As this article revealed, Peking was "disgusted" by the large-scale and systematic public attacks to which it was subjected at the congresses of several European parties held between November 1962 and January 1963. It was thus hardly surprising that it hit back forcefully, giving tit for tat. On March 4, the editorial department of *Red Flag* published an article, "More on the Differences between Comrade Togliatti and Us." In the present great debate among Communists, what was at issue was, in the last analysis, the struggle between revolutionary Marxism-Leninism and bourgeois ideology, which had infiltrated into the ranks of workers, meaning "an anti-Marxist-Leninist ideology."

Since Marxism had become predominant in the working-class movement, *Red Flag* asserted, a number of struggles had taken place between Marxists on the one hand and revisionists and opportunists on the other. The first had been the debate that Lenin had with Karl Kautsky and Eduard Bernstein. The second was the great debate that Communists of the USSR and other countries, "headed by Stalin," conducted against Trotsky, Bukharin, and other Left adventurists and Right opportunists. "Side by side with this dispute" had been the fierce and fairly protracted debate inside the CPC that Comrade Mao carried on against the Left adventurists and Right opportunists. The current great debate was first provoked by the Tito clique, which had taken the road of revisionism long ago, in the winter of 1956.

Red Flag subjected Comrade Togliatti's "new ideas" to sharp criticism. Despite the fact that he and others employed some Marxist-Leninist phraseology as a camouflage, they actually attempted to substitute class collaboration for class struggle, "structural reform" for proletarian revolution, and "joint intervention" for the national liberation movement. The paper gave due emphasis to the Asian, African, and Latin American continents in which two-thirds of the total population of the capitalist world lived. These areas were the "weakest link in the imperialist chain and the storm center of world revolution." The proletarian parties of the metropolitan imperialist countries were duty-bound to heed the voice of the revolutionary people in these regions. "They have no right whatsoever to flaunt their seniority before these people, to put on lordly airs, to carp and cavil, like Comrade Thorez of France who so arrogantly and disdainfully speaks of them as being 'young and unexperienced.' "

Red Flag vehemently disputed the views of modern revisionists and of Togliatti, according to whom the fundamental Marxist-Leninist theory concerning war and peace was outmoded. Mao had taken the destructiveness of atomic weapons into full account when he had called the atom bomb a "weapon of mass slaughter." But at the same time the paper quoted approvingly Stalin who, in September 1946, had minimized the significance of the atom bomb and had warned that it was a means "intended for intimidating the weak-nerved." *Red Flag* especially resented Togliatti's implication that some socialist countries wanted to export world revolution. No one could impose a revolution from without. Togliatti also distorted the Chinese point of view in regard to the parliamentary struggle. Peking did not deny that such struggle may have its temporary uses. However, Togliatti and other comrades exaggerated the role of the bourgeois parliament and saw it as "the only road for achieving socialism in Italy."[42]

In the earlier article Togliatti "and certain other comrades" had already been taken to task for strongly opposing the Marxist-Leninist proposition that "imperialism and all reactionaries are paper tigers." In the second article, "More on the Differences between Togliatti and Us," the latter was reminded that Mao's views on the weakness of imperialism had always been "crystal clear." As Mao had once told Anna Louise Strong, from a long-term point of view, from a strategic point of view, imperialism and

42. "More on the differences between Comrade Togliatti and us. . . ," *Red Flag*, March 4, 1963; Editorial Departments of *People's Daily and Red Flag*, no. 3-4 (*PR*, March 15, 1963, pp. 10-11, also pp. 8-58).

all reactionaries were "paper tigers." "On the other hand, they are also living tigers, iron tigers, and real tigers which can eat people. On this we should build our tactical thinking." "Strategially, the enemy can be despised," because imperialism and all reactionaries were decaying, had no future, and could be overthrown. "Failure to see this results in lack of courage to wage revolutionary struggle, loss of confidence in the revolution." The article ended by underlining the doctrine, expressed in the Moscow Declaration and the Moscow Statement, that modern revisionism was the main danger in the international working-class movement. The common denominator of all these articles in the Chinese journals could easily be discerned: it was fight against revisionism—against Moscow!

Pravda *on Unity*

While Peking attacked Moscow as a diluter of revolutionary Marxism-Leninism, Moscow saw in Peking merely the upstart and rival who, while spouting revolutionary phraseology, actually aimed at splitting the international Communist movement to gratify its own ambitions. Nevertheless, about five weeks after denouncing the "splitters" in world communism, *Pravda* on February 6 had issued a call for unity of the Communist Parties.[43] While so far Chinese Communism, though the unquestionable target, had not been directly assailed, the new Soviet article directed broadside charges against Peking itself—a clear indication of the sharpening of the dispute between the two Communist giants. Admitting the existence of "polemics. . .on a number of important problems" that had lately arisen in the Communist movement, *Pravda* castigated the baseless and harsh criticism by Chinese Communist leaders of the speeches of representatives of Communist Parties at the Sixth Congress of the German Socialist Unity Party, the CPC's "one-sided interpretation" of the 1957 Declaration and the 1960 Statement of the two Moscow Conferences, and their groundless attacks on Yugoslavia. Moscow considered these views anti-Marxist, erroneous, and harmful.

Moscow Calls for an International Communist Conference

If the Chinese comrades agreed with the CPSU about the validity of the principles of the Declaration and the Statement, then, according to *Pravda,* the necessary conditions for settling current differences existed. But the Chinese were taken to task since, pursuing their one-sided way, they saw only the danger of revisionism. Differences between Communists on a few ideological and tactical questions must not be used to inflame nationalistic

43. *Pravda*, Feb. 6, 1963, pp. 2-3.

feelings and prejudices, mistrust, and dissension among socialist peoples. The *Pravda* editorial recalled that the CPSU, the "initiator" of both Moscow conferences in 1957 and 1960, was now in favor of calling a new conference if the fraternal parties considered this desirable. Part of the proper preparation for it would be to halt open polemics among the fraternal parties.

But the editorial made clear that the purpose of the conference would not be arranging a half-way compromise between the Soviet and Peking point of view, but rather on reaching a decision on "who is right and who is in error." It was not enough to cease open polemics and thus to freeze the existing differences and remain in the previous positions. The CPSU rather aimed at actively "overcoming" the differences that had arisen and at promoting unity on the basis of the principles of Marxism-Leninism. It was evident that the trumpet call for a conference was to serve Moscow's purposes. If Peking was to be received with open arms, the ensuing embrace was likely to crush it. Moscow seemed to be confident that the conference would turn its way and that the CPC would be completely isolated, suffer a resounding defeat, and be forced to surrender.

A call from Moscow to settle the differences that had arisen around the conference table had actually been extended in a letter to the Chinese Central Executive Committee as early as May 31, 1962.[44] In an editorial of February 10, 1963, addressed to the Central Committee. of the CPC, *Pravda* asked again for a joint meeting of representatives of the two parties to set the stage for a conference of Marxist-Leninist parties.[45] The CPC had invariably asserted that it was firmly committed to the Declaration and the Statement and their conclusions and propositions, and had also stressed its support for the policy of peaceful coexistence. Though the Soviets doubted the Chinese commitment to these documents, they took advantage of the Chinese claims of allegiance to the principles that were embedded in them. "It depends on us, on our Parties," stated the letter, "whether we march from here together, in the same formation, or let ourselves be drawn into a painful and needless struggle," which could only lead to mutual alienation and to undermining the unity of world Communism. Only a few days later, on February 21, 1963, the Central Committee of the CPSU, following *Pravda*'s appeal, sent a formal letter to its Chinese counterpart, suggesting a conference for the purpose of settling the outstanding differences separating the two great fraternal parties.[46]

---

44. Moscow to Central Exec, Comm., CPC, May 31. 1962, quoted in D. Floyd, *Mao against Khrushchev*, (New York, 1964), p. 323.

45. Open Letter to CC of CPC, *Pravda*, Feb. 10, 1963.

46. CC, CPSU to CC, CPC, Feb. 21, 1963 (*PR*, March 22, 1963, pp. 8-10).

The Soviet letter was answered by the Central Committee of the CPC on March 9 and in turn published by *Izvestiia* in mid-March.[47] Peking welcomed the Soviet suggestion; actually, Mao Tse-tung had earlier approved it in a talk with Chervonenko, Soviet ambassador to China.[48] The latter even claimed that as early as April 7, 1962, the CPC Central Committee, in a letter to the Central Committee of the CPSU, had made a conference proposal. The Chinese reply, however, while superficially conciliatory and in seeming agreement with the Soviets about basic purposes, clearly poured cold water on any hopes for reconciliation that Moscow might have entertained: it made plain that the Peking and Moscow interpretations of Marxism-Leninism and of the recent basic documents of international Communism were at hopeless variance with each other. The Peking letter also expressed its opposition to the airing of disagreements between fraternal Parties "in the face of enemies." Actually, neither side had displayed any aversion to washing dirty linen in public.

The Soviet answer in turn came in a letter of March 30, 1963. Preferring to ignore the ironic undertone of the Chinese communication, it welcomed the "positive response" to the Russian overture from the Central Committee of the CPC and expressed the hope that as a result of the planned meeting a number of constructive measures would be taken to overcome the existing difficulties.[49] In reply to the Chinese suggestion that Khrushchev, while on his trip to Cambodia, might stop off in Peking, the Soviets pointed out that no such journey had been scheduled—also that Khrushchev had already made three visits to the Chinese People's Republic. Mao, on the other hand, while in Moscow in 1957, had expressed his desire to spend some more time in the Soviet Union "so that he could get to know our country better." Mao had been invited again in 1960, but, as the Soviet letter states, had been unable to come. A new invitation was now extended to him. Should, however, such a visit not seem feasible at the present time, a high-level meeting of representatives of the two Parties could be prepared in Moscow around May 15, 1963, if that date would be acceptable to the Chinese representatives. The forthcoming bilateral meeting should set the stage for a general conference that would in turn strengthen the unity of the international Communist movement.

The Soviets, while inviting Communist China for bilateral discussion, underlined the "preliminary nature" of such talks; at the same time they pointed to the more definite character of a general meeting that could be

47. CC, CPC to CC, CPSU, March 9, 1963, *Izvestiia*, March 14, also *PR*, March 27, 1963, pp. 6-8.

48. *Izvestiia*, Feb. 23, 1963.

49. Soviet letter, March 30, 1963, in *Pravda*, Apr. 30, 1963, pp. 3-9, also *PR*, July 26, 1963, pp. 10-26.

held later on. In "collective discussion" the Chinese, in view of the pro-Soviet orientation of most of the Communist Parties, were outnumbered and could easily be cornered. Also, the Soviets had in mind the issuance of a major statement by such a conference, comparable to the Declaration of 1957 and the Statement of 1960. Both of these conferences, the Soviet letter stressed, had been linked with serious changes in the international situation and the necessity for devising appropriate tactics for the Communist movement. It was the current Soviet view that in preparing for a conference the fraternal Parties could thoroughly and comprehensively analyze new developments in international affairs and translate the collective decisions of the Communist movement into action.

The Soviets were probably anxious to get the *ex post facto* approval of international Communism on their policy in the Cuban missile crisis in the Caribbean confrontation. A vindication, possibly even a ringing endorsement of their recent course and of the policy of peaceful coexistence as against the more reckless Chinese policy, would strengthen their hand vis-à-vis China. Yet, while aiming at a new conference and a new formulation of strategy and tactics, the Soviets made it clear that they expected the new proclamation not to differ from the main lines of the Declaration and the Statement, but rather to reenforce them.

The Soviets gave no indication that they were going to compromise for the mere sake of reaching a consensus at the conference. To the contrary, they expressed, for instance, their unbending opposition to the Stalin cult. Its elimination, they asserted, had played an enormously beneficial role in strengthening the unity of the entire socialist commonwealth and had brought about "the growth of our friendship on the basis of equality"—a not-so-subtle allusion to the fact that Stalin, though esteemed in Communist China, had actually denied genuine equality to the fraternal Party in Peking. And in a kind of frontal attack on the Chinese Communist leadership, the Moscow letter proclaimed "left opportunism [is] today no less dangerous than revisionism, right opportunism." The Soviets promised to spare no effort to clean up, through patient, comradely discussion, questions on which a difference of views had become apparent, in order to remove all the superficial obstacles to unity among Communists. They were resisting, their letter concluded, the passions of polemic strife and were trying to arrest the dangerous slide toward a new round of debates. However, as a reiteration of their well-known stand on the "fundamental" problems indicated, these happened to be just those problems which sharply divided Moscow and Peking.

The written exchanges between the CPC and the CPSU during February and March 1963 aside, the general relations between the two rival parties worsened during the first two months of the year. At the Afro-Asian Solidarity Conference in Moshi, Tanganyika, tensions rose high, and remained acute at the Afro-Asian Journalists' Conference in Djakarta, Indonesia, and at a meeting of the World Federation of Trade Unions in January in Prague and at another one in March in Brussels. At the first-named meetings the racial issue was unabashedly introduced by Peking, and with apparent success; the Russians were compelled to take a back seat. In 1962 elements of the Communist Party of Brazil, expelled as an "anti-party" group after the Twenty-second Party Congress of the CPSU, had formed a pro-Chinese Communist Party; a delegation of theirs arrived in Peking on April 19. About two months earlier a delegation representing the pro-Soviet Communist Party in Brazil had gone to Moscow. The two Communist Parties of Brazil were at sword's point. Moscow must have seen in the reception of the delegation of a hostile splinter-party group in Peking an insulting and dangerous gesture. Also, following a visit of Chinese Chief of State Liu Shao-chi to North Vietnam, Ho Chi Minh effected a definite shift of the party line in the direction toward Peking. Moscow had reason to show concern, even alarm, about these developments.

This situation was hardly altered by Castro's visit to Moscow.[50] The October crisis of 1962 had imposed a severe strain upon the relations between the Soviet Union and Cuba. Castro's visit produced a number of mutual concessions—especially the Soviet recognition of the Cuban party as a Marxist-Leninist Party, acknowledgment of the significance of the Cuban example for Latin America's national liberation movement, and in return the public endorsement of Soviet policy in the recent Cuban crisis and praise for Khrushchev. But the final communiqué remained silent on China and the closely related issues of Albania and Yugoslavia. It thus revealed a neutrality on the Sino-Soviet rift that could not be to Moscow's liking.

For an International Conference in 1964

The question of holding an international Communist conference to deal with the Sino-Soviet dispute had repeatedly cropped up in 1963. During the year 1964, it became a major issue in that rift.

Both Moscow and Peking then reversed themselves on the matter of an international conference. Moscow, which earlier had displayed an obsessive fear of an international Communist gathering, now hoped to improve her position by coming out in behalf of a conference. Peking, in an aggressive mood and driven by a messianic fervor, had first held it tactically advantageous to press that attack and insist on a conference. By 1964, however, it apparently dawned upon the leaders of the CPC that they had garnered all possible benefits and that the minority status of the CPR

50. *Pravda*, May 25, 1963.

within the Communist world was not likely to change in the foreseeable future. An international Communist conference would only reveal Peking's political isolation.

On November 29, 1963, the Central Committee of the CPSU made a seemingly generous proposal. It held out the possibility of a conference that might lead to the resumption of Sino-Soviet trade and technical cooperation, to the return of Soviet experts to China, and to the restoration of unity. The Chinese leaders, though delaying their formal reply, continued with their critical comments on the Soviet Open Letter of July 14, 1963. To the six Comments already published in 1963, they added on February 4, 1964, a seventh Comment. Hurling back Soviet accusations, the CPC branded the CPSU as the "greatest splitter of our times." The CPC Central Committee, addressing its Soviet counterpart, charged it with "distortion and slander" and criticized its "self-important and domineering attitude."

Finally, on February 29, 1964, Chinese leaders responded to the Soviet letter of November 29, 1963. They accepted the idea of a conference, though they suggested holding also various bilateral talks for the purpose of halting public polemics; the conference could convene in Peking, but not before October 1964. Obviously Peking thought it advantageous to procrastinate in order to gain time for making converts. The Soviets, puzzled about the late date, expressed their fear of exacerbating the conflict. They suggested first holding a bilateral meeting as a forerunner of a preparatory gathering, and second an international meeting, to be held in May 1964.

After a failure, in the meantime, of a Rumanian mediation attempt, a new round of polemical debate began on March 31 with Peking's eighth Comment on the Soviet Open Letter of July 14, 1963, and the Soviet publication on April 3 of a very critical report by M. S. Suslov about Sino-Soviet affairs, made on February 14, 1964, to the Central Committee Plenum.

Suslov's Report and Peking's Reaction

In this report to the CPSU Central Committee, Suslov had branded the Chinese Communist leaders for their "nationalistic arrogance." The CPC, he said, inculcated in the Chinese population "a spirit of hostility" against the USSR and the CPSU and was responsible for the distribution throughout the world of slanderous articles and broadcasts in foreign languages. Suslov indignantly rejected these as "filthy attacks."

According to Suslov, the Chinese leaders had previously confined themselves to assailing the foreign policy of the CPSU, but more recently they had begun also to subject Soviet internal policy to open attacks. They particularly criticized the struggle against the Stalin cult as a mistake and cast aspersions on the 1961 program of the CPSU. They attempted to place the Soviet people in opposition to the leadership of the party.

After Suslov's foregoing report on February 14, 1964, the CPSU Central Committee adopted a resolution expressing its profound concern over the splitting activities of the leadership of the CPC. Under cover of verbal assurances of fidelity to Marxism-Leninism, the leaders of the CPC had launched an attack on the basic theoretical and political principles by which the Communist movement was guided at the present stage. Having rejected all the proposals of the CC of the CPSU for normalizing Soviet-Chinese relations, they had intensified anti-Soviet propaganda inside the CPR and were grossly interfering in the internal affairs of the Soviet Union. The Chinese political and ideological course was branded a mixture of petty-bourgeois adventurism and great-power chauvinism. The resolution concluded with a call for an ideological exposure of the anti-Leninist position of the CPC leadership.

On April 27, 1964, *People's Daily* published the full text of what it called the anti-Chinese report delivered by M. Suslov on February 14 and the anti-China decision adopted the following day. *People's Daily* also revealed that Khrushchev had in rapid succession made twelve anti-Chinese speeches and statements in the sixteen days between April 3 and April 18. It held that these speeches revealed nothing new "besides his greater vulgarity." The Soviet documents that the paper produced disclosed "the most vicious language" and showed that Mao himself and his thought were the main target of Soviet attacks. The Chinese daily challenged the Soviet press to publish Peking's statements.

On May 8 *People's Daily* devoted three pages to so-called anti-Chinese statements made recently by leading personalities of the CPSU and the USSR. These utterances were grouped under three headings, "Anti-China Meetings held by CPSU Organizations at All Levels," "Soviet Press Prints one Article after another attacking China," and "Anti-China Speech by Y. P. Andropov at the Moscow Meeting Commemorating the Anniversary of Lenin's Birth."

The first group included ten round-up reports about diverse types of anti-Peking meetings held throughout the USSR, as reported by *Tass* and *Pravda*. According to *People's Daily*, following the "anti-China" resolution at the February Plenum of the CC of the CPSU in early April, the Soviet leadership mobilized central committees of the Party everywhere to stage meetings for the purpose of denouncing Peking's stand. Leading Party members attended these meetings and, in the Chinese view, whipped up anti-Chinese sentiments.

The second group of anti-Peking statements carried in *People's Daily* quoted excerpts of criticisms of the CPC contained in nineteen editorials and articles published by *Pravda, Izvestiia,* and the journals *Communist* and *Party Life*.

The Chinese press followed up these reports with bitter denunciation of the "unscrupulous tactics" used by Soviet delegates and their followers to dominate the proceedings of the Second International Trade Union Conference on Questions Concerning Women Workers in Bucharest. On September 4, *Peking Review* reported that *Shijie Zhishi* (World Culture) Press had published a fifth volume of Anti-China Material From the Soviet Press. This volume included, it revealed, 117 anti-Chinese items carried in Soviet newspapers and periodicals. It disclosed that the publication of such material would continue. In August 1964 there appeared the first volume of *Statements by Khrushchev* published in Chinese by *Shijie Zhishi* Press, the second volume to follow in October. The first volume was comprised of statements made by Khrushchev from 1932 to 1941, while the second volume included those made by him from 1942 to September 1953. The "Publisher's Note" called Khrushchev "the biggest revisionist of contemporary times, the biggest teacher by negative example in the history of the international communist movement." The publisher dwelled on the contradictions between Khrushchev's statements past and present, drawing attention to the "ugly features of this big intrigant, careerist, and double-dealer."

The very summer months had witnessed a further escalation of the Sino-Soviet dispute. On July 30, 1964, the CC of the CPSU addressed a letter to the CC of the CPC in which it pointed out that the differences that had sprung up in Communist ranks four years ago had become more and more serious. The "open conflict" threatened to lead to a definite split in the international Communist movement. The CPSU therefore invited the fraternal Parties to come to Moscow by December 15, 1964, to start preparation for an international meeting. In its reply dated August 30, 1964, the CPC Central Committee claimed that the Soviet letter actually slammed the door tight against consultations on the question of convening an international meeting. It reiterated its stand, as stated in an earlier letter dated July 28, 1964, expressing opposition to "your schismatic meeting" and warned again that calling such a conference was equivalent to "stepping into your grave." If this was Peking's language to "friends," what did Peking say to its enemies?

The Rift in International Organizations and Communist Parties

Even before the Sino-Soviet dispute erupted into the open, the sessions of the World Peace Council in Stockholm and in 1963 in Moscow already reflected serious disagreements on national liberation and disarmament. During the year 1963 the Sino-Soviet rift soon enveloped other international organizations and Communist Parties everywhere. Sharply different points of view by the partisans of the Moscow and Peking positions were voiced at the meeting of the Presidium of the World Peace Council in Malmö" in March 1963 and at another one at Warsaw, which was held between November 28 and December 3, 1963. At the latter meeting the Chinese motion opposing the Test Ban Treaty was defeated and the Chinese objection to the homage rendered to the late President Kennedy was ignored.

Another dynamic organization whose work was adversely influenced by the Russo-Chinese dispute was the Afro-Asian People's Solidarity Organization. At its third conference at Moshi, Tanganyika, in February 1963, and at the meeting of its Executive Committee in Nicosia in September 1963, the lobbying by the Chinese and Russian delegates and dubious Soviet practices at the latter meeting led to an open break, with the Chinese declaring that the resolutions at Nicosia were not binding upon them. At the 1960 Moscow conference the issue of "fractionalism," which dealt with the relationship between Communist parties of different countries, though much debated, had not been resolved. From the beginning it was indissolubly tied up with the even greater crime of "factionalism," that is the attempt to undermine the unity of the fraternal party by secret lobbying among its rank and file. It was a fact that both Russian and Chinese parties engaged in these practices. The issue of factionalism came to the forefront when the Sino-Soviet dispute grew more menacing in 1963. Peking, being in a definite minority position and also the aggressive challenger, seemed to be the more vulnerable party on this issue.

Partiinaya Zhizn, recalling Lenin's definition of faction and factionalism, pointed out that a factionalist group usually had a special platform, group discipline, and a special press organ. On the basis of these criteria the CPC leadership, in its opinion, was clearly guilty of factionalism.

Actually, the CPC acknowledged the facts of the accusation, though it turned the argument against the Soviet attackers. Peking rejected the "slanderous" charge that the CPC leadership organized and supported splinter groups or larger parties in the United States, Brazil, Italy, Belgium, Australia, and India. The splits that had occurred in certain Communist Parties in recent years were "largely due to the forcible application by the leaders of the CPSU of their revisionist and divisive line." These people had led the revolutionary movement of their own countries "astray." They had illegitimately ostracized, attacked, and expelled Communists who adhered to principle. Communists were "makers of revolution." If they ceased to be that and became revisionists, they deserved repudiation. The CPC had never concealed its position. "We support all revolutionary comrades who adhere to Marxism-Leninism." The Chinese

Communists had contacts with revisionists; "why then can we not have contacts with Marxist-Leninists?" This was not a divisive act, but simply a proletarian, internationalist obligation that it was their duty to discharge.

The Chinese paper, rather than hiding its "factionalist" support to adherents of Peking's point of view in other Parties, proudly acknowledged it, and even offered theoretical justification for it. The Sino-Soviet struggle, by affecting the organization of the Communist party, the very instrument of the class struggle and of the fight for socialism, had reached the point of no return. In the political life-and-death struggle with Moscow, Peking contemptuously discarded established Communist rules relating to the type of in-fighting and political maneuvering that was permissible and that was prohibited. In the struggle for political survival and against political heresy, everything was allowed.

There existed, of course, before the rise of Sino-Soviet differences, disagreements within most Communist Parties on a number of grounds. That the CPC offered some of these minority groups financial and other support in return for endorsement of its particular views, can hardly be doubted. By no means, however, were the various pro-Peking-oriented Communist splinter groups the result merely of Chinese propaganda and intercession. In 1963 and 1964 a number of rival parties were set up in different parts of the world, as, for instance, in Australia, India, Ceylon, Nepal, Lebanon, Belgium, Colombia, and Paraguay. In Peru a pro-Peking party virtually replaced the pro-Moscow party. One pro-China party had already been established in Brazil in 1962.

In a number of European countries pro-Chinese publications multiplied, with *Révolution* in Paris becoming the best known and most widely read. In New Zealand the Communist Party was unquestionably pro-Peking. The ruling Communist Parties of North Vietnam and North Korea took the Chinese side in 1963, as did the large and influential parties of Japan and Indonesia, though all of them were stressing their organizational and ideological freedom and independence. Of the European parties only the Albanian Party clung to the Chinese line, and that with a vengeance; Rumania occasionally dissented from Moscow on the Chinese issue. A rival pro-Chinese group under the leadership of Jacques Grippa operated in Belgium.

Escalation of the Polemics

Peking's Letter, June 1963

In the spring of 1963 Peking battered Moscow with the dispatch of three letters of protest against the Soviet agreement to sign a test ban treaty with the West; the last of these letters bore the date of June 6. But the USSR remained unmoved. Peking's failure to dislodge the Soviets from their entrenched position on the test ban treaty then triggered an outburst by Peking, which in turn was to produce an abrupt and equally violent Soviet rejoinder. This eruption occurred in the course of the exchange of the vitriolic letters between the CPC and the CPSU in June and July 1963. It represents the very climax of the Sino-Soviet dispute in 1963.

The Soviets delayed publication of the June letter of the Central Committee of the CPC until they were ready to return the fire. The Chinese letter and the reply of the Central Committee of the CPSU were thus published simultaneously in *Pravda* on July 14.[51] The long-smoldering conflict now flared into the open. The publication bared to an unsuspecting and stunned world the chasm that separated the two Communist giants. It raised questions about the unity of the world Communist movement and of its future, and even augured a change in the balance of power in the world.

In first withholding the publication of the letter the Central Committee of the CPC, the CPSU had voiced the fear that it might exacerbate the polemics between the two Parties. In particular, it might defeat the purposes of the impending talks between representatives of the CPSU and the CPC that were to begin in Moscow on July 5, 1963. But Chinese Embassy officials and other citizens of the CPR had begun to distribute the letter from Peking in the USSR, in public buildings, airports, and railway stations. The Soviet authorities promptly responded by denouncing these activities as "illegal" and declaring that the Chinese citizens involved therein were "unwelcome." They were ordered to leave the Soviet Union without further delay. Yet, in Peking the expelled Chinese received a hero's welcome. A mass rally was staged in their behalf at which public officials made an appearance and delivered speeches that sharply attacked the USSR.

The letter of the Central Committee of the CPC was finally distributed by the Soviets themselves among the delegates of the Central Committee of the CPSU at its June plenary session. On this occasion M. A. Suslov, B. N. Ponomarev, and Y. V. Andropov explained the Sino-Soviet disagreements to the assembled delegates, but their speeches were not made available to the public at large. At the same time the CPSU Central Committee formally protested the distribution of the Russian version of the Chinese letter in the USSR, promising an answer in "due time." This reply was finally delivered on July 14. Moscow did not send its answer to Peking, but turned it over to its own Party units. It thus retaliated for the

51. *Pravda*, July 14, 1963, pp. 1-4 (*CDSP* 15, no. 28 [Aug. 7, 1963]: 16f).

impropriety of addressing the Russian people without permission of the Soviet government.

The Chinese letter, in the intensity and breadth of its attack, surpassed anything that Peking had so far unleashed against Moscow. The former esoteric criticism was replaced by direct brutal attack. While previously "certain comrades"—including, of course, Khrushchev—were considered at fault, now "comradeship," without an eye's blinking, was dropped, and "certain persons," rather than "certain comrades," took the burden of blame. Common party ties were suddenly as good as forgotten.[52]

The Chinese letter began as usual with a reference to the two conferences of the international Communist movement, both held in Moscow in 1957 and 1960, and the conclusions subscribed to by the participants, including the CPC and the CPSU. Both Peking and Moscow still claimed in 1963 that these documents expressed their guiding principles and determined their policy.

According to the Chinese letter, the cardinal difference between Moscow and Peking was "whether or not to accept the fact that the people still living under the imperialist and capitalist system who comprise ⅔ of the world's population, need to make revolution and whether or not to accept the fact that the people already on the socialist road, who comprise ⅓ of the world's population, need to carry their revolution forward to the end." The CPSU was accused of paying only lip-service to revolution in capitalist countries and of not moving ahead with the socialist revolution in the USSR.

Moscow Accused of Betraying the Revolution

The Chinese document warned that a "one-sided" reduction of the general line of the international Communist movement to "peaceful coexistence," "peaceful competition," and "peaceful transition to socialism" violated the revolutionary principles of the 1957 Declaration and the 1960 Statement. "Certain persons" went so far as to deny the great international significance of the anti-imperialist revolutionary struggles of the Asian, African, and Latin American peoples and had developed a new "theory" designed to preserve the domination of the allegedly superior nations over oppressed ones. The Soviets were accused of taking "a passive or scornful or negative attitude" toward the struggles of the oppressed nations for liberation. Also, though the Chinese letter did not deny the usefulness of the proletariat of all forms of struggle, it asserted that for a Marxist-Leninist party to "fall into legalism or parliamentary cretinism" would inevitably

52. Letter of the CPC, June 14, 1963 (PR, July 26, 1963, pp. 10-26).

lead to the renunciation of the proletarian revolution. These blunt charges were a measure of the extent of the revulsion of the CPC against the Moscow line.

The Soviet leaders were accused of turning the CPSU into a "reformist party," of sliding down the path of "opportunism" and "degenerating into bourgeois nationalists." While they slandered China, claiming that the CPC wanted to extend socialism by wars between states, they were in fact opposed to revolutions by oppressed peoples and nations of the world. They confined the foreign policy line of the socialist countries to peaceful coexistence. No one could ever demand in the name of peaceful coexistence that the oppressed peoples and nations give up their revolutionary struggles.

Then followed an attack against the Soviet concept of "the state of the entire people" and the Communist Party as the "party of the entire people," concepts that were declared to be the very epitome of Khrushchevism and of the 1961 new Soviet Party programme. Such theories, the Chinese Statement warned, were likely to disarm the proletariat and the working people organizationally and ideologically and were tantamount to helping restore capitalism. "Certain persons"—the name of Khrushchev himself, following the general pattern of the dispute, was still avoided—engaged in "great-power chauvinism," "sectarianism," "splittism," and subversion. The very charges leveled by Moscow against Peking were thus returned by the latter. Peking even repeated Moscow's assurance that relations between socialist countries were "international relations of a new type." Here was one judgment on which there was concurrence, and justified it was!

Every socialist country, Peking asserted, "must rely mainly on itself." Defending itself against the charges of "going it alone" and being "nationalistic," Peking hurled the countercharge of national egotism against all socialist countries that unilaterally demanded that other fraternal countries submit to their needs and that put economic pressure on others. It was impermissible for any party "to place itself above others, to interfere in their internal affairs and to adopt patriarchal ways in relations with them." It was likewise impermissible to impose the program, resolutions, and line of one's own party on other fraternal parties as the "common program" of the international Communist movement. Instead of emphasizing " 'who is in the majority' or 'who is in the minority' and bank on a so-called majority to force through one's own erroneous line" and carry out sectarian and splitting policies, one should follow the principle of reaching unanimity through consultation.*

*Clearly, Communist China was in the uncomfortable position of the perennial minority in the socialist camp—comparable to a position held by the USSR for a considerable length of time in the United Nations. Angry and frustrated, it insisted on "unanimity," on a virtual

The Chinese letter of June 14 was a clarion call to independence from Moscow and an outright challenge to the ideological eminence and practical leadership of the CPSU in international Communism. Peking actually went so far as to defend the formation of new Communist Parties, thus raising the banner of revolt and "revolution" against a mere "pretender." Only a revolutionary Party can lead the proletariat and the broad masses of people in defeating imperialism and bringing about the Socialist Revolution.

The Chinese statement then went on to criticize the "preposterous attacks" that, in disregard of facts, were leveled against the CPC.[53] The letter from Peking ended with an appeal to workers and oppressed peoples and nations of the world to unite and to oppose the common enemy —American imperialism. The increasingly virulent rift between the two Communist superpowers was still officially minimized as a temporary misunderstanding between the two fraternal parties, which were bound by common ideology and common goals.

The Soviet Reply: The Open Letter, July 1963

On July 14 *Pravda* finally published Moscow's reply to the letter of the CC of the CPC. Because of both its content and tone, it cast serious doubts on the possibility of an early resolution of their deep-seated conflict.

In its answer the CC of the CPSU stated that it considered it necessary to address an Open Letter to the Chinese comrades.[54] The Soviet and Chinese peoples, it conceded, were united by the same hopes and desires. While for many years good relations had existed between their parties, the CC of the CPSU was becoming increasingly concerned over the words and actions of the leadership of the CPC, which were "undermining the unity of our parties and friendship of our peoples." The recent letter of the CC

veto within the fraternal socialist community comparable again to the Soviet veto in the United Nations. How unyielding Communist China was, was shown by its refusal to treat Yugoslav and Albanian questions on the same level—"they must on no account be placed on a par": Yugoslav leaders were a "revisionist clique of traitors." Peking sharply attacked the Soviet view of Yugoslavia, as it also criticized the view of those who were now saying that dogmatism, not revisionism was the main danger.

53. Of the many major articles that appeared then in China, see especially "Let us unite on the basis of the Moscow Declaration and the Moscow Statement," *People's Daily*, Jan. 27, 1972 (*PR*, March 15, 1963, pp. 6-9); "Whence the Differences?—A reply to Thorez and other Comrades," *People's Daily*, Feb. 27, 1963. (*PR*, March 1, 1963, pp. 7-16); *Red Flag*, March 4, 1963, "More on the Differences between Comrade Togliatti and us. Some important problems of Leninism in the Contemporary World," Editorial Departments of *People's Daily* and *Red Flag*, nos. 3-4, March 4, 1963 (*PR*, March 15, 1963, pp. 8-58).

54. *Pravda*, July 14, 1963, pp. 1-4, CC of CPSU to CC, CPC (*CDSP* 15, no. 28 [Aug. 7, 1963]: 16-30, also *People's Daily*, Editor's Note, July 22, 1963, pp. 27-28 (*PR*, July 26, 1963, pp. 27-46).

of the CPC distorted the most important clauses of "historic documents" of international Communism, such as the 1957 Declaration and the 1960 Statement of the two Moscow conferences, and contained "baseless, slanderous attacks on our party," on other Communist parties, on the decisions of the Twentieth, the Twenty-first and Twenty-second Congresses and on the CPSU Program.

The Soviet letter claimed that the CPSU had shown remarkable restraint when it refused, in order to avoid aggravation of the dispute, to publish the Chinese leaders' charges. This, however, had been distorted by the Chinese comrades as an attempt to "conceal" the views of the Chinese leaders from the members of the CPSU and from the Soviet people. The openly unfriendly actions of the CPC leaders and their persistent efforts to intensify polemics in the international Communist movement, as well as their "intentional distortion" of the position and the motives of the CPSU, had finally forced the latter to make the Chinese letter of June 14 public. Its authors had resorted to insults by accusing the Soviets of "betraying" the interests of the proletariat, of "departing" from Marxism, Leninism, and internationalism, of showing "cowardice before the imperialists," of "disarming the proletariat," and of "helping to restore capitalism." Such accusations were leveled against the "party of the great Lenin, about the motherland of socialism," about the people who were "performing miracles of heroism and selflessness in the struggle for the construction of communism. . . ." The Soviet people had generously shared with their Chinese brothers the whole of their many years' experience in social construction and their achievements in the fields of science and technology. The USSR had helped China in numerous ways in the development of their economy and the training of Chinese specialists and workers in the Soviet Union.

The Peking letter, however, pinpointed the major differences in theory and practice between the CPC and the CPSU. At the center of the dispute, in Moscow's opinion, were questions involving the vital interests of the peoples, namely, questions of war and peace, the question of the role and development of the world socialist system, problems of the struggle against the ideology and practice of the "cult of the individual," questions of the strategy and tactics of the world workers' movement and the national-liberation struggle.

Peking's "Lip Service" to Peaceful Coexistence

When the CPC leaders were speaking of "peace and peaceful coexistence," they were, according to the Soviets, merely paying lip-service to concepts that they well understood to be widely popular. "To come out openly against the struggle of the peoples for peace, for the peaceful coexistence of states with different social systems, against disarmament, etc., would mean to expose their positions before the eyes of Communism throughout the world and of peace-loving peoples and alienating them.'' Therefore the Chinese Communist leaders resorted to concealing their real views.

Regarding the problem of war and peace, which involved the fate of entire peoples and the future of mankind, there could be, according to the Soviets, no vagueness or reservations. There had arisen over this question fundamental differences of principle between the world Communist movement and the CPC leaders. The Soviets had placed before Communists, ''as a first-priority task,'' the struggle for peace and the averting of a world thermonuclear catastrophe. In the Soviet view, under modern conditions ''the forces of peace'' could, through united efforts, avert a new world war. Though the nature of imperialism had admittedly not changed and the danger of the outbreak of war not been eliminated, a new balance of forces had emerged in the world, among them the ''chief bulwark'' of peace, the ''mighty commonwealth'' of socialist states.

Also, the Soviets appraised ''soberly'' ''the radical qualitative change in the means of waging war and consequently its possible consequences.'' The detonation of only one powerful thermonuclear bomb exceeded the explosive force of all the munitions used in all preceding wars, including World War I and World War II. There were many thousands of such bombs in stockpiles. Communists had no right to ignore this danger. The Chinese leaders, however, asserted that telling people ''the whole truth'' about it would have a ''paralyzing'' effect on the masses.

It was the historic task of the Communists to organize and lead the struggle of the peoples to avert thermonuclear war. This was held to be a fully realistic and feasible task. The Statement had given expression to these views when it asserted that ''world war can be prevented'' and ''the real possibility of excluding world war from the life of society will arise even before the complete victory of socialism, with capitalism still existing in part of the world.'' Though the Statement had also been subscribed to by the CPC, now its leadership maintained that peaceful coexistence was an ''illusion'' and that war could not be eliminated while imperialism still existed and that the principle of peaceful coexistence impeded the revolutionary struggle.

The Chinese comrades, the Soviet letter continued in its accusations, did not believe in the possibility of averting a new world war. They actually underestimated the forces of peace and socialism and overestimated the forces of imperialism. Behind the ''ringing revolutionary phrases'' of the CPC lay essentially lack of faith in the forces of the working class, in its victory in the class struggle. All peace-loving forces, whatever their class background and class interests, were united in the struggle to avert war. They all feared the destructive power of the atomic bomb. To enter upon the path proposed by the Chinese comrades would mean to "alienate" the popular masses from the Communist parties. The latter had won the sympathies of the peoples through their persistent struggle for peace. And in the mind of the broad masses peace and socialism were now "inseparable."

The Atomic Bomb a "Paper Tiger"?

The leaders of the CPC also clearly underestimated the full danger of thermonuclear war. They held the atomic bomb to be a mere "paper tiger," not a terrible weapon. "The chief thing, they say, is to do away with imperialism as rapidly as possible, but how this is to be done and the losses involved are, it would seem, questions of secondary importance." The Soviet letter raised the question whether this would indeed be of secondary importance for the hundreds of millions of people who would be doomed to die if a thermonuclear war broke out, and for the states that would be wiped from the face of the earth in the first hours of such a war. "No one, including the big states, has a right to play with the fates of millions of people." Those who made no effort to avert mass annihilation of people and the destruction of the values of human civilization merited condemnation.

The letter of the CPC Central Committee, according to the Soviets, spoke of "inevitable sacrifices," allegedly in the name of the Revolution, and referred to the anthology "Long Live Leninism," where it was promised that the victorious people would create rapidly, "on the ruins of dead imperialism, a civilization a thousand times higher than that under the capitalist system." Yet the CPSU and the Soviet people could not share the views of the Chinese leadership about the creation of "a civilization a thousand times higher" on the corpses of hundreds of millions of people.

Of course, the Soviets supported the destruction of imperialism and capitalism. Yet, under modern conditions a world war would be a thermonuclear war, since the imperialists would never agree to leave the stage voluntarily. The Soviets, well aware of the destructive power of thermonuclear weapons would never use them first, and would only resort to these "terrible weapons" for defensive purposes.

The Soviet letter finally raised the question whether the Chinese comrades who proposed to build a beautiful future on the ruins of the old world had "consulted" with the working class in those countries where imperialism reigned. "The working class in the capitalist countries would certainly answer them: Are we asking you to unleash a war and, in eliminating imperialism, to destroy our countries also?" The monopolists and imperialists were after all only a small handful, while the majority of the population of the capitalist countries consisted of the working class, the peasantry, and the intelligentsia. "And the atomic bomb makes no distinction between where the imperialists are and where the working class is." The revolutionary working class wanted to win socialism through the class struggle and not by unleashing world thermonuclear war, which would bury both the exploiters and the exploited. The leadership of the CPC was thus accused of making, for other peoples and for the broad segment of working masses of the world, the momentous decision on the very question of their physical survival.

The "profound difference" between the views of the CPSU and the CPC concerning the questions of peace and peaceful coexistence was, according to the Soviets, clearly manifested during the 1962 crisis in the Caribbean. Never before had mankind come so close to the brink of thermonuclear war as in October 1962.

The Soviet letter claimed that the agreement to remove the missiles in response to a pledge by the U.S. government not to undertake an invasion of Cuba, and support of Cuba by the peace-loving peoples, "had frustrated the schemes of the adventurist circles of American imperialism." Were the Chinese leaders "perhaps dissatisfied with the fact that it was possible to avert an invasion of Cuba and the outbreak of a world war?" During the Caribbean crisis they had concentrated the fire of their criticism less on the aggressive imperialism of the USA than on the CPSU and the government of the Soviet Union. At the most difficult moment the CPC leadership had played the role of a critic instead of acting as a militant ally and comrade, and had made no meaningful pledge in defense of the Cuban revolution. Instead, they had openly tried to aggravate the already tense situation in the Caribbean, "throwing tinder on the smouldering fire of the conflict."

The true position of the CPC leadership on questions of war and peace revealed itself in their complete underestimation, indeed their deliberate ignoring, of the struggle for disarmament. The imperialists can and must be forced to undertake disarmament. Recently the balance of forces had changed rapidly in favor of the forces of socialism and peace, and disarmament had thus become quite practical. To stand now for the inevitability of war meant to demonstrate a lack of faith in the forces of socialism and to surrender to a mood of hopelessness and defeatism. The Soviet struggle for disarmament was not a "tactical method. We sincerely want disarmament.—An absolute majority of mankind is on the side of the socialist camp in this struggle."

The Chinese comrades had put forward the slogan of "blade against blade," counterposing their policy to that of the other socialist countries, which aimed toward easing the international situation. One had the impression that the leaders of the CPC thought it advantageous to maintain and intensify international tension, especially in the relations between the USSR and USA. In their view the Soviet Union should answer provocations with provocations. But to accept the challenge of the imperialists to enter a competition in "adventurism and aggressiveness" would not ensure peace but unleash war.

A struggle must be waged "to curb the aggressor in good time;" yet, as is evident from the context, this struggle is a political one, designed to force the imperialists to make concessions, to compel them not to resort to war. The struggle to be waged is one for peaceful coexistence. Far from sacrificing revolutionary goals, this fight assists, it is claimed, "the revolutionary struggle of the working class and the national-liberation struggle of the peoples." To separate the struggle for coexistence from the revolutionary struggle against imperialism and colonialism and to "counterpose" them, as the Chinese comrades were doing, meant to "emasculate it of real content." The leaders of the CPC were distorting the concept of peaceful coexistence of states with different social systems, applying it to the relations between the exploiters and the exploited, between the oppressed and oppressing classes, between the toiling masses and the imperialists. They ignored the fact that the Communist parties always supported the revolutionary struggle and just wars of liberation against imperialism, in spite of absurd assertions of the CPC to the contrary. "When we speak of peaceful coexistence, we mean by this the state relations of the socialist countries with the countries of capitalism. The principle of peaceful coexistence, naturally, cannot in the slightest degree extend to relations between antagonistic classes within the capitalist states."

Peking Perpetuates the "Stalin Cult"

Furthermore, serious differences existed between the CPC and CPSU on the question of "struggle against the consequences of the Stalin cult." The Chinese leaders were accused of having assumed the role of defenders of the cult of the individual, of being disseminators of the mistaken ideas of Stalin. The CPSU had come out against the cult of the individual "to cleanse the ideals of socialism" of the abuses of personal power and of the arbitrariness that had besmirched the ideals. Back in 1956 even Chinese leaders, including Mao Tse-tung, had praised the work of the Twentieth Party Congress, but since then they had made a 180-degree turn in their appraisal of that Congress. The Soviet declaration attributed a great deal of progress to the new course of struggle against the cult of the individual, of de-Stalinization. The "atmosphere of fear, suspicion and uncertainty" that had poisoned the life of the people during the period of the cult of the individual "has gone forever."

It was impossible to deny the fact that Soviet people found it also "strange and outrageous" that the Chinese comrades were trying to belittle the CPSU Program, "the majestic plan" for creating a Communist society. The CPC leaders appeared to deprecate the Soviet struggle for a better life for the people and hinted at some sort of "bourgeoisification" and "degeneration" of Soviet society; "according to their logic, if people walk about in bast sandals and drink their cabbage soup from a common bowl, this is communism, but if a working person lives well today and wants to live better still tomorrow, this is all but a restoration of capitalism!"

The Chinese criticized allegedly mistaken tenets of the CPSU Program, especially its concepts of the state of the entire people and of the party of all the people. The Chinese insisted that "hostile classes" still remained in Soviet society and therefore the dictatorship of the proletariat was still needed. The Chinese comrades pointed to "bourgeois hangers-on, parasites, speculators, swindlers, idlers, hooligans, and embezzlers of state funds" in Soviet society. The Soviet letter, ridiculing the Chinese conception of Soviet society, pointed out that the survival of misfits signified only survival of capitalism and that no proletarian dictatorship was needed against such people. Soviet society today was composed of two basic classes, the "workers and peasants, and also the intelligentsia," and no one class was in a position to exploit other classes. Dictatorship, however, was a "class concept." After the victory of socialism only friendly classes would be left and the need for dictatorship of the proletariat would disappear. It was characteristic of the Chinese position that they did not "even mention the development of democracy in conditions of socialism, in conditions of the construction of communism." This very argument, notwithstanding the Russian Communists' apparent disinterest in the development of democracy, bandied about so long by Mensheviks and other democratic socialists against the Bolsheviks, was now turned by them, in an ironic twist, against their ultraleftist critics from Peking.

Differences on Methods of the Revolutionary Struggle

Another major issue separating the CPC and the CPSU was the question of the ways and methods of the revolutionary struggle of the working class in the countries of capitalism and of the national-liberation struggle, the question of the ways of the transition of all mankind to socialism. According to Chinese Communist leaders, the CPC stood for world revolution, while the CPSU had forgotten revolution, even feared it, "and instead of revolutionary struggle, was concerned about matters held 'unworthy' of the attention" of a true revolutionary. Such matters were peace, economic development of the socialist countries and the improvement of the living standards of all peoples, and the struggle for democratic rights and vital interests of the working people of the capitalist countries.

The leaders of the CPC liked to parade "revolutionary" phrases on every occasion. In actuality, however, the Communists of the USSR and of other countries, in coming out for peaceful coexistence, "were not thinking only of themselves" and had not forgotten their class brothers in the countries of capitalism. Under present conditions socialism was conquering the hearts and minds of people not just through books, but by its living example—Soviet Russia.

The Chinese Communist leaders displayed a lack of faith in the abilities of the countries of socialism to defeat capitalism in economic competition. Also, their position may be that of people who, having encountered difficulties in building socialism, have become disenchanted and "want to reach the moon sooner, by other, what seem to them shorter, routes." "But a victorious revolution can consolidate and develop its successes, can prove the superiority of socialism over capitalism by the labor and only by the labor of the people."

The Soviet letter stressed that it was conditions of peace and peaceful coexistence, rather than conditions of international tension and cold war that were "advantageous" for the revolutionary struggle of the working class of the capitalist countries. The Communist struggle for peace strengthened their ties with the masses and created the political army of the revolution. Such struggle did not delay, on the contrary it provided, the opportunity for achieving the ultimate goals of the international working class. The Chinese comrades, "arrogantly and insultingly," accused the Communist Parties of France, Italy, and the USA and other countries of nothing less than opportunism and reformism, of "parliamentary cretinism," merely because they did not call for an immediate proletarian revolution; they did not understand that this was impossible without the existence of a revolutionary situation.

The CPSU and other Marxist-Leninist parties proceeded from the possibility of a peaceful and a nonpeaceful transition to socialism. Yet the Chinese comrades persistently ascribed to the CPSU endorsement of the peaceful path alone. The Soviet letter countered that the CPC actually denied the possibility of employing peaceful forms of struggle and recognized only violent ones.

Differences on National Liberation and Economic Integration

Another important question separating Peking from Moscow was, in the latter's view, that of the relation between the struggle of the international working class and the national-liberation movement of the peoples of Asia, Africa, and Latin America. The correct relationship between them was one of the chief conditions of victory over imperialism. According to the theories of the Chinese comrades, "the basic contradiction of our time" was the contradiction not between socialism and imperialism, but between the national-liberation movement and imperialism. According to this "theory," the Soviets maintained, it was not the industrial working class but the national-liberation movement that was the "decisive force" in the struggle against imperialism. The leaders of the CPC apparently hoped to win popularity with this thesis among the peoples of Asia, Africa, and Latin-America. Yet this theory tended to isolate the national-liberation movement from the international proletariat.

The many peoples of Asia, "despite all their heroism and selflessness," could never have triumphed if the October Revolution had not shaken the very foundations of imperialism. Though Marxist—Leninists had always emphasized the world-historic importance of the national-liberation movement and its great future, they considered one of the chief conditions for its future victories a firm alliance with the workers' movement of the capitalist countries. The slogan "Proletarians of all countries, unite" had been and remained the chief slogan of the struggle for victory of the world revolution. Under the new conditions the substance of this slogan had to be broadened and oppressed peoples included. But the leading role of the working class—under existing conditions, the ruling Communist Parties and the CPSU in particular—must be maintained.

While the "Chinese comrades" acknowledged in theory that unity was the mainstay of the whole socialist commonwealth, they were in fact "undermining the ties with our party and with our country in all directions." They had recently advanced the theory of "relying on one's own forces." The Soviet Union, the first country of socialism, had had no choice but to depend on her own forces, using exclusively internal resources. Now, of course, there was an entirely different situation in the world, since new revolutionary movements could count on the support of the USSR. Behind the new Chinese formula was actually concealed the concept of creating self-sufficient national economies. The Chinese comrades wanted to restrict economic links to other, even socialist, countries to trade alone. Such a policy had nothing in common with the principles of socialist internationalism. The CPC leadership was also "organizing and supporting var-

ious anti-Party groups of renegades'' in many countries. Especially listed
were the U.S., Brazil, Belgium, Australia, and India. Chinese comrades
were trying to subject other fraternal parties to their influence and control,
as for instance the Albanian Labor Party. It was now known that the CPC
had pushed the Albanian Party onto the road of open warfare against the
Soviet Union.

Finally, the Soviet statement, raising the question as to the reasons for
the "false tenets" of the CPC leadership on vital problems of our time,
attributed Peking's errors to the "complete estrangement of the Chinese
comrades from actual reality," their "dogmatic, bookish approach." The
Soviet letter denounced the Chinese letter of June 14 as an attempt to impose upon the world Communist and workers' movement a new line, as
"groundless and harmful." This policy constituted a deviation from the
Statement of 1960, which had been adopted by eighty-one Communist parties! But the CPSU, the Soviets claimed, still stood for close friendship
with the CPC.

During the next few months the polemics between Peking and Moscow
continued unabated. Each side elaborated its own position and renewed its
criticism of the opponent. Neither was above board in ascribing to the opponent views that he officially disclaimed or at least found embarrassing to
admit as being part of his ideological baggage. In this polemical battle
some additional light was cast upon various aspects of the foremost issues
that divided the two Communist giants. But in the heat of battle reckless
and exaggerated charges often blurred the real differences. By wrapping
around themselves the cloak of Marxist-Leninist theory and language, the
opponents made comprehension of the issues more difficult, at least for the
unsophisticated by-standers, the great majority. Finally, the arguments used
by both sides were at times comparable only to the small visible portion of
the iceberg, while its bulk remained hidden to the human eye. Some important matters remained unsaid, while some issues were overly exposed
and debated. But the questions for the first time raised openly, and with
brutal frankness, during the hot summer of 1963, continued to grip and to
divide the Communist rivals.

Dispute about the Test Ban Treaty

Of all the issues dividing Moscow and Peking, none perhaps was more
serious than the military one, the Soviet insistence on remaining the dominant military power in the socialist bloc. Peking could never forgive
Moscow for reneging on the promised aid to help develop China's atomic
capacity. At the same time Peking was painfully aware of Moscow's rap-

prochement with the West: it considered the partial test ban treaty between the USSR and the Western Powers an agreement made at her own expense. On July 19, 1963, *People's Daily* quoted Averill Harriman to the effect that the American purpose in signing the partial test ban treaty was to prevent China from getting a nuclear capacity.[55]

During the month of July 1963, Moscow was host both to a CPC delegation and to a Western delegation. The meeting with the Chinese representatives was to reduce the Sino-Soviet dispute to a more rational and dispassionate level and that with the Western delegates had the purpose of concluding a test ban treaty and preventing the proliferation of atomic weapons. The Sino-Soviet meeting opened on July 5, the Soviet negotiations with Britain and the United States on July 15.[56] The latter negotiations were brought to a successful conclusion ten days later. Some in the Soviet capital, and perhaps even in Peking, must have recalled the double negotiations carried on in Moscow in August 1939. Those had been carried on, also simultaneously, between the Soviets and the Nazis on the one hand, and the Soviets and the Western Powers on the other. The negotiations in July 1963 may not have had the same far-reaching implications and they were also not carried on secretly. But to the participants their outcome may well have been a corroboration that Moscow had chosen the West and given a rebuff to Peking—just as in 1939 Germany had been chosen as partner and the West had been spurned.

Perhaps the Sino-Soviet conference of July 5 never had a real chance. As its final communiqué indicated, the Chinese delegation had moved for a virtually indefinite adjournment—"until some time later."[57] Indeed, after the Soviet-British-American test ban treaty there seemed little purpose in meeting again in the foreseeable future.

On July 25 the representatives of the USA, Great Britain, and the USSR signed in Moscow a treaty on partial cessation of nuclear weapons tests.[58] Four days later *Pravda* commentator Yuri Zhukov came out scoring the Chinese attitude on the treaty banning nuclear weapons tests in the atmosphere, underwater, and in space. He particularly criticized *People's Daily* for allegedly using the same arguments as the French bourgeoisie. Zhukov castigated Peking for the false slogan "all or nothing" and for pursuing the tactics of sabotage. The leaders of Chinese Communism were in strange company, that of some American and German militaristic "madmen" who also sharply opposed the Moscow treaty.[59]

55. *People's Daily*, July 19, 1963 (*PR*, July 26, 1963).
56. *Pravda,* CC, CPSU, July 14, 1963, pp. 1-4 (CDSP 15, no. 28 [Aug. 7, 1963]: 16f.
57. *Ibid.*
58. *People's Daily*, July 19, 1963 (*PR*, July 26, 1963, p. 47).
59. "Who is for, who is against?" *Pravda,* July 29, 1963.

Actually, Peking issued its authoritative comment on the test ban treaty only after July 31, when it published an official government statement bearing the somewhat pretentious title "A proposal on the general, complete, final and unconditional banning and destruction of nuclear weapons and on calling the conference of the Heads of Government of all countries of the world." On August 4 *Pravda* and *Izvestiia* branded the Chinese comment unadulterated "slander" against the USSR and the CPSU and a maze of "jugglings and distortions."[60] Though this "shameful document" was unworthy to occupy space in the pages of the press of the first socialist state in the world, the Soviets were nevertheless publishing it, to show the Soviet people "how far the Chinese leaders have gone."

The Chinese official Statement asserted that the Moscow treaty had the purpose of "consolidating the nuclear monopoly [of the USSR] and of binding hand and foot all peace-loving countries that are subjected to the nuclear threat.[61] The Statement was a violent blast at Moscow, removing once and for all the pretense of fraternalism that theoretically still linked the two socialist countries. The treaty was denounced as a "fraud," which the Chinese government as a secret duty must "completely expose," a "filthy fraud," and again, the "greatest fraud" possible. The treaty would not hamper the USA in the slightest. Its "fundamental goal" consisted in depriving all peace-loving countries, including China, of the opportunity of strengthening their defensive might. In signing the treaty the Soviet government had actually reversed its earlier stand by a sharp, 180-degree turn and was willingly reconciling itself to American imperialism's gaining military superiority. It had thus "betrayed" the interests of the Soviet people, of the peoples of the socialist camp, including China, and the interests of the peace-loving peoples of the whole world. This Soviet policy was not a victory for the policy of peaceful coexistence, but "capitulation" to American imperialism. The Chinese government favored universal disarmament and firmly supported the complete banning and destruction of nuclear weapons. But the nuclear problem should be discussed and solved by all countries of the world. "It is intolerable that a few nuclear powers should have in their hands the fates of more than a hundred non-nuclear states."

In its rejoinder, the statement of the Soviet Government pointed out that almost everywhere the news of the signing of the test ban treaty had been joyfully received.[62] The treaty had been warmly supported by the govern-

60. Statement, Chinese Government advocating. . . .prohibition and destruction of nuclear weapons," *People's Daily,* July 31, 1963 (*PR*, Aug. 2, 1963, pp. 7-8), and *Pravda* and *Izvestiia,* Aug. 4, 1963.

61. See n 54 above, Statement of Chinese Government.

62. Soviet Government answers Statement by the Chinese Government on nuclear weapons test ban, Aug. 3, 1963, *Pravda* and *Izvestiia,* Aug. 4, 1963, pp. 1-2.

ments and peoples of the socialist countries and by all progressive people in the world. Contrary to the Chinese Government's denunciation of the agreement, it testified to the viability and correctness of the policy of peaceful coexistence. People everywhere saw in the treaty a real possibility of easing international tension and the possibility of curtailing the arms race. The treaty also raised hopes that unsolved international problems were capable of settlement.

One could count on one's fingers those who dared to oppose the test ban treaty. These people, whatever "verbal devices" they might resort to, exposed themselves as opponents of peaceful coexistence. It was no surprise that the so-called madmen in the U.S.A., extremists of the West German militarist and revanchist camp, and French ruling circles opposed the treaty. "But when Communists—and, what is more, Communists who head a socialist country—oppose the treaty banning nuclear tests, then this cannot but provoke justified astonishment." Nothing was more absurd than to speak in this connection of "surrender" to American imperialism; the treaty was rather a measure of safeguarding humanity against the dangerous consequences arising from the contamination of the atmosphere, water, and outer space with radioactive substances.

The treaty, of course, did not solve all problems. But the Soviets considered it "better to make a pact than to do nothing." "One must have completely lost all sense of reality to propose the alternative 'all or nothing' in matters involving the fate of the world, the lives of millions of people."

The treaty, *Pravda* asserted, did not alter the basic correlation of forces in the world. In any case, the Soviets ought to be better judges than the Chinese leaders of whether or not the test ban treaty was advantageous to the USSR. Also, the new program now expounded by the CPR government had actually been earlier proposed by the Soviet Union and the other socialist countries. The whole world knew that the Soviet Union and the other socialist countries had waged and were continuing to wage an active struggle for the realization of general and complete disarmament, which included the complete abolition of nuclear weapons. The USSR and the other socialist countries—the Soviets always claimed to be spokesmen for the latter, taking advantage of their having taken their side as against Peking's—considered the statement of the government of the CPR to be an "unprecedented, profoundly regrettable act."[63]

The Chinese leaders dared to speak in the name of the Soviet people and on their behalf and on behalf of the peoples of the other socialist countries. Who had empowered them to do so? They were clearly disregarding

63. *Ibid.*

the elementary norms of international conduct between states, "let alone the norms of relations between fraternal socialist countries." They attempted to set the Soviet people against the Soviet government and to "smear" the peace-loving policy of the Soviet Union. Such attempts of the imperialists had failed during the Civil War and the Second World War, and were failing again at present. The Soviet people supported the peace-loving policy of the CPSU.

Through wide publicity given to the Soviet reply to Peking, the Soviet public gained an insight into the scope and depth of the rift with Peking as never before. The very circumstance that the government had decided to take the Soviet public into its confidence was sufficient proof that in its view the conflict was not soluble in the immediate future. It thus felt the need of enlisting the support of its own people during the continuing confrontation with Communist China. While appealing to plain nationalism, underlining Soviet primacy in Communist affairs, and stressing its desire for peace and peaceful coexistence, the Soviets seemed assured that strong popular support would be forthcoming.

After the Signing of the Test Ban Treaty

Chinese attacks on Soviet Russia multiplied after the signing of the test ban treaty. The editorial staffs of both *People's Daily* and *Red Flag* unleashed in the following months a flood of critical articles dealing with Sino-Soviet relations, Stalin, and Yugoslavia; the underlying theme of all of them was Soviet sins and errors. The authors disputed Moscow's right to leadership of the Communist bloc and criticized Khrushchev in particular. They assailed Yugoslavia where capitalism had allegedly been restored and a bureaucratic capitalist class was supposedly holding the reins of power. Thus aspersion was cast upon the Soviet leadership, which was seeking rapprochement with revisionist Belgrade.

Soviet counterattacks were as numerous, swift, and devastating. The Chinese leaders charged that between July 15 and October 27 the Soviet press published more than 700 anti-Peking articles, and 430 of them after September 1.[64] Yet the Soviets, according to their own account, were compelled to defend themselves against mounting Chinese criticism, which was no longer confined to foreign affairs but also bore down heavily on the Soviet domestic scene and the ordinary day-to-day life of Soviet citizenry. V. Ulyanov in *Pravda* denounced the "methods of falsification, the juggling of facts and the deliberate distortion of the true state of affairs" that were resorted to frequently in the anti-Soviet campaign of the Chinese press. Until recently only arch-reactionary hostile newspapers had

64. *People's Daily,* Oct. 31, 1963 (*PR*, Nov. 4, 1963).

engaged in falsification of life in the USSR. Therefore nothing but bewilderment and indignation could be aroused by the fact that now newspapers of the CPR had adopted such questionable methods.[65]

On August 14 *Izvestiia,* under the heading "Dark Glasses of Peking Newspapers" again castigated the Chinese press for applying the "bankrupt technique of the big lie," which had long been a weapon of the capitalist press of the West. The purpose of the Chinese editors was to smear Soviet life. *Izvestiia* raised the question why the Chinese Communists displayed "such furious malignancy" toward the Soviet Union—a country that was helping the Chinese people so generously and considered their cause to be its own. Why, to use the words of a Chinese proverb, "did they bring down the heavens" on the Soviet Union?[66] On August 15 *Pravda* followed up the counterattack against Peking with another article, "Against Falsification," and on August 16 with one by V. Korionov entitled "Bereft of Common Sense."[67]

China's Official Criticism

On August 21 *Pravda* printed a declaration of the CPR, dated August 15, which was a reply to the Statement of the Soviet Government of August 3 on the Chinese Government's Statement on the complete banning of nuclear weapons. In a prefatory note the Russian daily asserted that it was merely publishing the Statement so that the Soviet people could see "once again what methods the Chinese leaders are resorting to" and how far they had gone in their actions. According to the Chinese, the USA had first advanced a proposal on cessation of nuclear tests on April 13, 1959, which, because of its unilateral military advantages to America, was soon rejected by Khrushchev. Between June 15 and July 25, 1963, however, the Soviet leaders had made a complete turnabout. Their reversal constituted a "betrayal" of the Soviet people, of the countries of the socialist camp, and of the peoples of the whole world.[68]

The Chinese statement made the following further points: the course of American imperialism had not changed, only the Soviet leaders had changed their position.[69] The three-power treaty created an illusion of

65. V. Ulyanov, "Unworthy methods," *Pravda,* Aug. 9, 1963, p. 4.

66. *Izvestiia,* Aug. 14, 1963, p. 2.

67. *Pravda,* Aug. 15 and Aug. 16, 1963.

68. *Pravda,* Aug. 21, 1963, and *Izvestiia,* Aug. 22, 1963; *PR,* Aug. 16, 1963, pp. 7-15, and Statement of Soviet Government, Aug. 3, 1963, *ibid.,* pp. 16-19.

69. CPC Statement, *PR,* Aug. 15, 1963; see also *People's Daily,* Aug. 3, 1963, "A Betrayal of the Soviet People," *PR,* Aug. 9, 1963, pp. 10-11; see also Statement by Spokesman of the Chinese Government—A Comment on the Soviet Government's Statement of Aug. 21, 1963 (*PR,* Sept. 6, 1963, pp. 7-16).

peace by lulling the vigilance of the peoples of the world. It only met the global strategic interests of American imperialism, but did not prevent the USA from distributing nuclear weapons and from building the forces of the imperialist camp. The CPR rejected the charge that it opposed the easing of international tension. She merely declined to pay the high price of the détente between the USA and the USSR, namely, sacrificing the interests of the socialist camp and the interests of the peoples of the whole world.

The Soviet leaders, the Chinese statement continued in its charges, cared only for their own well-being and not about the fate of others. "They tirelessly affirm that only if they exist and develop will the peoples of the whole world be saved." In actuality, to secure themselves a moment of quiet, they had abandoned the vital interests of the peoples of the whole world. If the Soviet Union should grant American imperialism the freedom to suppress the revolutionary struggle of the peoples of the world, if she "unites [!] with it" in the struggle against the fraternal countries, she will ultimately lose ground.

Long ago the Soviet leaders had begun to "enter deals with American imperialism, trying to bind China hand and foot." As long ago as June 20, 1959, the Soviet government had unilaterally broken the agreement on new defense technology that had been concluded with the CPR on October 15, 1957. It had refused to give China models of an atomic bomb and technological information for its production. The Chinese statement charged that this was a present to President Eisenhower on the occasion of the forthcoming trip of the Soviet leader to the USA in September 1959.

On August 25, 1962, the Soviet government, the Chinese Statement continued, informed the Chinese government of the proposal by American Secretary of State Dean Rusk concerning the nonproliferation of nuclear weapons. The Chinese government in several notes sent to the Soviet government on September 3 and October 20, 1962, and June 6, 1963, had warned the latter not to assume a pledge for China, in violation of the sovereignty of the CPR, not to produce nuclear weapons. It was obvious that the Chinese government considered the Soviet-American agreement on partial cessation of nuclear tests both a violation of earlier promises of Moscow and a means to "exert pressure on China" to make the pledge too.

Clearly, it had been the test ban treaty that had raised Peking's anger and frustration to a fever pitch. The outburst of the CPC leadership was an accurate measure of Peking's fear of being left out due to the rapprochement, possibly even collusion, between Moscow and Washington, and fear of her growing encirclement. What was at stake here for Peking were not seemingly abstruse theories, but practical decisions of immediate and long-range political and military significance.

The Soviet Defense of the Treaty

Simultaneously with the foregoing statement from Peking appeared the official Soviet statement on the test ban treaty. It read: "For the first time after long years darkened by the Cold War," East and West had reached an agreement on a pressing international question. The peoples of the world had come out firmly in support of the treaty; even Chancellor Adenauer, under pressure of world opinion, had decided to halt open obstruction. Yet, the leaders of the CPR, hiding behind pseudo-revolutionary phrases, were not merely refusing to sign the treaty but also tried to impose on others "their adventuristic platform" on the questions of war and peace.[70] Like their preceding statement of July 31, the new Chinese statement, it was charged, was only verbally in agreement with the line of peaceful coexistence, while actually sabotaging its translation into reality.

The Soviets recognized that the Chinese leaders were "extremely resentful," since Moscow had not given atomic bombs to the Peking government. A feeling of vexation over the Soviet refusal to aid them in the development of nuclear weapons had, in their view, prompted their attacks on the USSR. Yet, if a few socialist states should become nuclear powers, the socialist camp in its entirety was not likely to gain in military posture. Also, the USSR could not well pursue "one policy in the West and another one in the East." She could not on the one hand wage a struggle against arming West Germany with nuclear weapons and oppose the spread of nuclear weapons in the world and on the other hand supply such weapons to China.

Even if China could produce two or three bombs, it would, without enhancing her military stature, be a drain on her economy. And the CPR could rely on being protected by the USSR! While the Chinese leaders were "abusing" the Soviet Union in all possible ways for having nuclear weapons while the CPR had none, in actuality they could afford the luxury of coming out against the nuclear test ban treaty only because the external security of China was protected by the might of the Soviet Union and the whole socialist commonwealth. Without this assurance China could not peacefully engage in solving her internal problems of economic and state construction.

The Soviet statement went on criticizing the government of the CPR for publicizing secret documents bearing on the defense of the socialist commonwealth. It castigated the Chinese tendency to speak in the name of practically all the peoples of the world—those of the Soviet Union, the peoples in the other socialist countries, and those in the young national

70. Soviet Statement, *Pravda*, Aug. 21, 1963, *Izvestiia*, Aug. 22, 1963, pp. 1-3 (*CDSP* 15, no. 34 [Sept. 18, 1963]: 8-13; also *PR*, Sept. 6, 1963, pp. 16-23).

states of Asia, Africa, and Latin America. "But Soviet people ask indignantly: Who gave the Chinese leaders the right to decide for us, for the Soviet government and for our Communist Party, what serves and what does not serve our interests?" The Soviet statement went even farther, questioning in fact whether the CPR leaders had actually consulted their own people when they came out in opposition to the treaty banning nuclear tests. As far as the Soviets were concerned, they had not heard the Chinese people approve of the continuation of the tests and, with it, of continued radioactive fallout, which would poison their blood.

No Communist-Leninist could fail to experience feelings of "natural repulsion" to the posture of the CPC leaders "with regard to thermonuclear war: Even if one half of mankind perishes, even if 300,000 Chinese are killed, this matters not, because imperialism will be wiped from the face of the earth, and upon its ruins the survivors, we are told, will build a higher civilization one thousand times higher." The Soviets excoriated this "anti-Marxist, anti-Leninist, inhuman position." The Chinese people had not given the CPR leadership the authority to write "advance death warrants for them."

In this context the Soviets posed a further question. "If in a thermonuclear war, according to the prognoses of Chinese leaders, about one-half of the population of a large country is killed, how many people will die in a country whose population is measured not in hundreds of millions but in tens of millions or only millions of people?" Obviously, many countries and peoples would disappear altogether. Who had given the Chinese leaders the right to decide the fate of these peoples and to speak in their behalf? "The demagogy and adventurism of the Chinese leaders' slogans can be smelled a mile away."

And to link the fate of the national liberation struggle with an exacerbation of international tension and with pressing mankind toward world thermonuclear war was "tantamount to promising the peoples freedom after death." The new peoples in Asia, Africa, and Latin America did not achieve independence only to face destruction. They had subscribed to the pact banning nuclear tests. They wanted to live, to strengthen their states, to develop their economies and to create the material foundations for true independence.

The Chinese statement of September 1, 1963, had disavowed as inaccurate the quotation from the magazine *Red Flag* to the effect that manpower and other losses would be outweighed because of an infinitely higher new civilization to be built. Yet the Soviets held that the denial was an opportunistic one and that the foregoing view that one-half of mankind would be "wiped from the face of the earth in the event of atomic war and that the entire world would then become socialist" expressed their real opinion.

The Soviet statement referred to a Chinese anthology, "Imperialism and all Reactionaries are Paper Tigers," according to which the struggle of the revolutionary forces will grow with the number of people killed by reactionaries.[71]

The Soviet statement proclaimed the "lofty humanism" of Soviet foreign policy, which held dear the fate of all peoples. If Communists, the fighters for peace, permit atom bombs to begin falling, the question of human losses will be decided no longer by governments, but by military technology and by the number of countries exposed to nuclear weapons. At the Bucharest Conference Khrushchev had told the Chinese comrades that their experience of war was limited, being chiefly that of "guerrilla war," "while we the Soviet people have waged a more serious, so to say, classic, war against Hitler Germany."

Actually, countries with the densest population would suffer most in a thermonuclear war and might lose more than half of their people. Chinese officials had indicated the likelihood that all of the 13 million people of Czechoslovakia and the entire population of Italy might be destroyed in the event of a nuclear war, yet insisted that small countries in the socialist camp had to subordinate their interests to those of the camp as a whole. "This was the true viewpoint of the Chinese leaders who in essence were preaching the permissibility of thermonuclear war."

Though the Chinese leaders spoke of an atomic war as a necessity only if the imperialists unleashed it, the Soviets considered this more moderate interpretation as a mere attempt to deceive the world. To them the Chinese leaders considered war "inevitable" and "even more desirable" than the peaceful road. Every time in recent years when a relaxation of tension seemed noticeable, the CPC leadership had made all possible efforts to frustrate this relaxation. The Chinese leaders had ignored the Soviet leaders' "frank" declaration and warning about the outbreak of hostilities between China and Japan. China had fought India, but had gained nothing. The actions of the Chinese leaders had only undermined the policy of neutralism and had helped the imperialist powers to increase their influence in the liberated countries, especially India. The CPR government at the same time was accused of inconsistency, since it "flirted" in every way with patently reactionary regimes in Asia and Africa, including those having joined imperialist military blocs. And starting in 1960, Chinese military and civilian personnel had systematically violated the Soviet border. There had been 5,000 violations of the Soviet border by the Chinese in 1962 alone. They had made secret attempts to attach border strips to the CPR.

71. Statement answering China on Test Ban, *Pravda*, Sept. 21, 1963, pp. 1-2, and Sept. 22, 1963, pp. 1-2 (*CDSP* 15, no. 38 [Oct. 16, 1963]: 3-15).

6

The "Cold War" Continues, 1963-1964

Kommunist Restates the Case against Peking

Among the most comprehensive and hard-hitting anti-Peking articles that appeared in the Soviet press in the autumn of 1963 were two essays published in the Party magazine *Kommunist*. The author, retaliating for the personal attacks against Khrushchev, criticized Mao Tse-tung with a vengeance. For the first time, a leading Soviet journal accused Peking of substituting "Mao Tsetungism" for "Leninism." But in the end the author, in a surprising volte-face, concluded rather meekly that the Chinese deviation from Marxism was "no less a danger" than "revisionism."[1] Still, this formulation was a far cry from the 1957 Moscow Declaration.

Peking, *Kommunist* asserted, followed an anti-Marxist line both in theory and in practice. It pursued so-called "Sinification" of Marxism-Leninism, its actual distortion under the pretext of adapting its principles to national conditions. Under the guise of aiming at equality, the Chinese leaders favored enclosed national economies. Only a few years ago a version of "equality" directly opposite to the present one had been intensively disseminated from Peking. It was then asserted that the obligation of economically advanced socialist countries "allegedly consisted in waiting for" the lagging ones, giving them everything that had been created by the forward-moving countries. This "parasitical understanding of the principles of proletarian internationalism" with regard to the relations between socialist countries was in radical contradiction to Leninism, in particular to

1. "For Triumph of Creative Marxism-Leninism, against revising Course of World Communist Movement," *Kommunist*, no. 15, Oct. 1963, pp. 13-47 and *ibid.*, no. 11, July 1963, pp. 3-36; also *PR*, Oct. 25, 1963, p. 12.

Lenin's principle of material interest, and could do no less harm to the cause of socialism than the present emasculation of these principles, reducing them to a formal, bourgeois, and, in essence, nationalistic understanding of equality.

Unable to make headway with their views and postulates among the international working class, the CPC, *Kommunist* continued, was striving to assume the position of leader of the national-liberation movement. Thus they adopted various demagogic theories about the "zone of revolutionary storms," and definitely racist notes cropped up in their propaganda. In making their plans the Chinese leaders apparently aimed at tearing down the international Communist movement and creating a new one under their own aegis. Therefore, they made the CPSU itself the prime target of their attacks.

Turning to the national-liberation movement, the Chinese propagandists, according to *Kommunist,* had invented the theory about a certain "special" community of interests of the peoples of Asia, Africa, and Latin America. This theory completely contradicted Marxism-Leninism. By reducing the matter at hand to "a certain historical and geopolitical community" of the destinies of the peoples of these continents alone, the Afro-Asian solidarity served less as a weapon for the struggle against imperialism than as "a means for isolating the peoples of these continents from the socialist states."

The Chinese leaders were also striving wherever possible to isolate the democratic public organizations of the above-mentioned three continents to create separate confederations, opposing them to the international confederations of the working people. At the Jakarta conference, for instance, they had attempted to create a separate organization for journalists of the Afro-Asian countries. At the Tanganyika conference the Chinese representatives went as far as to resort to outspoken racist attacks. Referring to the Soviet delegation and delegations of other socialist states, as well as to the representatives of the European Communist parties, they had told the representatives of the Afro-Asian countries: "These are whites; it is impossible to come to agreement with them on the struggle against imperialism."

Peking was also accused of Trotskyism, the worst of all possible heresies. The Chinese leaders' concept of world revolution closely corresponded to what was propounded as far back as the 1920s by Trotsky and his sympathizers. Like the Trotskyites, the Chinese leaders were taking up arms, questioning the possibility of the working class ever peacefully winning power. Also, the Fourth or Trotskyite International had expressed its delight over the Chinese leaders' departure from the line of the international Communist movement. There followed a detailed account of the schismatic activity of the Chinese Communists in the ranks of the Interna-

tional Communist movement. At the same time, the Chinese press and
radio propaganda were accused of not striking against the common enemy,
imperialism, and of having turned against the socialist countries and
against the international Communist movement.

Kommunist concluded with a section entitled "For the Purity of Revolutionary Theory." The cause of socialism could not successfully move
forward without a decisive struggle for the purity of Marxism-Leninism; of
course, Moscow was to be the guardian, the high priest of doctrinal purity.
The Chinese leaders were guilty of doctrinairism, which Lenin in his time
had called an "infantile disorder." Chinese theoreticians combated
Marxism-Leninism under the pretext of struggling against revisionism.
They raised a hysterical campaign, trying to distract attention from the
danger of left opportunism. "The Chinese leaders' statements against the
method of collective leadership are an appeal to support the idolization of
Mao Tse-tung in which Chinese propaganda is intensively engaged." This
preaching of the Mao cult had been actively conducted within the ranks of
the Chinese Communist Party for a number of years. It could be said with
complete certainty that the Communist movement was confronted with an
attempt to replace Leninism with Mao-Tse-tungism.

While the Chinese leaders shouted "loudest of all about fidelity to
Marxism-Leninism," they were actually trying to replace internationalism
with chauvinism and introducing a "nationalized," "sinified" version of
Marxism-Leninism. In 1960, soon after the Moscow Conference, Chinese
propaganda had begun to circulate throughout the world an interview that
Liu Shao-chi had at one time given to Anna Louise Strong, in which he
declared: "Marx and Lenin were Europeans: They wrote about European
history and problems, rarely touching upon Asia or China. . . .
Mao. . .created the Chinese or Asiatic form of Marxism." The magazine
Sinkiang Hungchi wrote similarly: "Mao's. . .ideas are the creative development of Marxism-Leninism in a new historical period. . .the
Marxism-Leninism of the epoch of socialist revolutions and socialist construction."

The two articles in *Kommunist* were a wide-ranging and hard-hitting attack on Peking. The author accused the CPC of being chauvinistic, hero-
worshiping, aspiring to leadership of the Communist bloc and of the national liberation movement, and wishing to sinify Marxism-Leninism. All
this could hardly be exceeded, either in polite or impolite Marxist-Leninist
company.

Still, *Kommunist* stopped short of making any final recommendation,
displaying either restraint or weakness, or both. The Communist movement
was already so deeply split and the USSR had lost so much ground that
any attempt by the Soviets to lead a movement for the excommunication of

China was no longer likely to succeed. Strangely enough, it was apparently the "rightist" Italian Communist party that opposed calling an international congress for the apparent purpose of striking the deadly blow of expulsion against the CPC. The Polish and Rumanian Communist Parties quickly followed suit. Khrushchev sensed the possibility of defeat if he should press his campaign against Peking. None of these European Communist Parties was ideologically pro-Chinese. But all had come to understand that the Sino-Soviet dispute had terminated Moscow's undisputed hegemonic position in world Communism and enhanced their own importance and prestige. As long as China challenged Moscow, Moscow was compelled to woo her fraternal parties, both those which ruled and the others that were still battling and aspiring to power.

Peking Counter-Attacks

There was some indication in mid-October of a lessening of the controversy; in a long interview with Reuter's, Chou En-lai dismissed the possibility that either party or state relations might be broken off between Moscow and Peking, but the publication of three more major articles in the Chinese press, all highly critical of Moscow, told a different story. First, on October 21, appeared an article entitled "Apologists of Neocolonialism" by the Editorial Departments of *People's Daily* and *Red Flag*.[2] The USSR was accused of having devised prescriptions for abolishing the revolution of the oppressed nations, for putting up with imperialist plunder and enslavement forever, and for not rising up in revolution. The policy and purpose of the leaders of the CPSU in their aid to newly independent countries in recent years were open to suspicion. They had often adopted an attitude of great-power chauvinism and national egoism. They had aided India to encourage the Nehru government in its anti-Communist policies. Contrary to lip-service paid to the support of wars for national liberation, they had actually tried everything to make the people of Asia, Africa, and Latin America abandon their revolutionary struggle, because they themselves were "sorely afraid of the revolutionary storm." Fearing a world conflagration, they were anxious to put out the sparks of revolution everywhere. A case in point was the Soviet policy toward Algeria and the Congo. Turning the table against the Soviets who had accused the Peking leadership of racism, the Peking editorial charged the Soviets with peddling the theory of racism and aiming at inciting racial hatred among the white people in Europe and North America. Khrushchev in particular had "stepped into the shoes of William II" to propagate the "theory of the

2. *People's Daily and Red Flag* (*PR*, Oct. 25, 1963, pp. 6-15).

Yellow Peril.'' The author urged the national liberation movement to shake off Soviet influence and to align itself with Peking, its true friend.

On November 2, *People's Daily* singled out Soviet policy toward India for attack.[3] In reply to an article in *Pravda* on September 19 on the Sino-Indian boundary question, entitled ''A Serious Hotbed of Tension in Asia,'' *People's Daily*, reprinting it on September 25, commented that Soviet leaders, having discarded all camouflage, had long allied themselves with the Indian reactionaries to oppose socialist China. According to this paper, the Sino-Indian boundary question involved 125,000 square kilometres of Chinese territory and was therefore, contrary to Soviet estimates, a major issue. The Soviet leaders' assertion that Communism need not bother about where the frontier line ran was only ''clever talk.'' Should socialist countries forgo all right to defend their own frontiers? How about the Oder-Neisse boundary between Germany and Poland? The position of Soviet leaders on the Sino-Indian boundary question was a ''betrayal'' of proletarian internationalism and could not even be called neutral.

Finally, on November 19, Peking printed the fifth in the series of long letters in reply to the Soviet July 14 Open Letter entitled ''Two Different Lines on the Question of War and Peace,''[4] Khrushchev and others vigorously propagated the view that all wars can be prevented and ''a world without weapons, without armed forces and without wars'' can be brought into being while imperialism still existed. Their purpose was all too clear. It was to make people believe that permanent peace can be realized under imperialism and thereby to make superfluous revolution and national liberation wars. Reversing the charges, the paper accused Khrushchev rather than Mao of being the real danger to world peace. Khrushchev's military ideas, ''based on nuclear fetishism and nuclear blackmail,'' were entirely wrong. As a result the Soviet air force and navy had ''lost their former importance.''

Here was a little disguised appeal to Soviet military leaders to rid the USSR of Khrushchev. The Soviets were reminded of Mao's often-quoted 1938 statement that ''political power grows out of the barrel of a gun'' and his saying that ''the army is the chief component of state power.'' The military leaders were also reminded of Khrushchev's ''retreats before the imperialists'' and that in his relations with the West he appeared as ''an unrequited lover and too often a laughing stock.'' The goal of the article was both to humiliate Khrushchev and to enlist Soviet national pride and military prowess in behalf of the forces aiming at his removal.

In their sixth article commenting on the Soviet Open Letter, the Editorial

3. ''The Truth about how the leaders of the CPSU had allied themselves with India against China,'' *People's Daily*, Nov. 2, 1963 (*PR*, Nov. 8, 1963, pp. 18-27).

4. *People's Daily* and *Red Flag*, Nov. 19, 1963 (*PR*, Nov. 22, 1963, pp. 6-16).

Departments of *People's Daily* and *Red Flag* asserted that Lenin and Stalin had adhered to a policy of peaceful coexistence. But it was the CPSU that in fact was violating this policy of Lenin. Lenin's policy of peaceful coexistence was directed against the imperialist policies of aggression and war, whereas Khrushchev's peaceful coexistence catered to imperialism. Khrushchev had changed the policy of peaceful coexistence into one of class capitulation. The heart and soul of the CPSU leaders' general line of peaceful coexistence was Soviet-American collaboration. Lenin and Stalin had never knelt before the enemy, but now the USSR was "bullied" by United States imperialism and the socialist camp was "disgraced" by the leaders of the CPSU.

In the course of 1963 the Sino-Soviet dispute had run the gamut from indirect and esoteric criticism to all-out and overt struggle along political, organizational, and ideological lines, and even actual confrontation along the border. On both sides few illusions were left by the end of the year about their mutual relationship, but Moscow, which seemed all set to banish Peking from the ranks of the true believers, apparently ran into unexpected opposition from some East European Communist Parties, though on other issues they firmly sided with Moscow. The unrelenting escalation of the conflict can best be seen in the mounting fury of the exchanges, the ever-widening scope of the accusations, and the type of charges leveled at the opponent. The Soviet accusations focused on chauvinism, imperialism, racism, leadership-cult, and the like, charges virtually indistinguishable from the period of struggle against Nazism during World War II, and against Western imperialism. At times they even exceeded the accusations against the latter. The Chinese accusations in turn centered on Soviet hegemonism and great-power ambitions, collusion with imperialism, abandonment of Marxism-Leninism, alleged restoration of capitalism, and betrayal of the world socialist revolutionary movement and the national-liberation movement. Not only were the forces of Communism weakened and split by the Sino-Soviet rift, but two Communist giants were at sword's point, ready to give battle along all but military lines.

Territorial Questions, 1962-1964

During 1962-64 territorial questions played a prominent role in the polemics between Moscow and Peking. It all began when in March 1963 the government of the CPR stated for the first time publicly that the Russo-Chinese treaties of Aigun (1858), Peking (1860), and Ili (1881) were "unequal treaties."[5] Thus Peking compared these treaties with other

5. *People's Daily* editorial, March 8, 1963 (*PR*, March 15, 1963).

"unequal" treaties that Western imperialism had wrested at bayonet's point from China in the course of the nineteenth century. The Peking government thus suggested that these treaties would have to be abrogated, as had been those which had been concluded with the Western powers. The fraternal CPSU was subtly reminded to fulfill its long overdue internationalist and socialist obligations in the field of Russo-Chinese relations.

The CPC expressed its irritation that of all neighbors of China only the Soviet Union and India, led by "reactionary nationalists," had deliberately created border disputes.[6] The Soviets were also accused of having flagrantly carried out large-scale subversive activities in Chinese frontier areas. They were trying to sow discord among China's minority nationalities by means of the press and wireless, to incite China's minorities to break away from their motherland, and to inveigle and coerce tens of thousands of Chinese citizens into going to the Soviet Union. But Peking made it clear that it was prepared to respect the territorial status quo and to consider the old unequal treaties as a basis for a reasonable settlement of the Sino-Soviet boundary question.

The Soviet position, of course, was a quite different one. While Peking deplored alleged Soviet border transgressions, Moscow, in an official statement dated September 21, 1963, turned the table, complaining of Chinese border violations. On November 29, 1963, the Central Committee of the CPSU proposed to define accurately the boundary in individual sections of the Soviet-Chinese border, but made clear its opposition to redrawing the Sino-Soviet boundaries in their entirety.[7] While not wishing to defend the tsars' expansionist policies, it remarked: "We are convinced that you, too, do not intend to defend the Chinese Emperors who by force of arms seized not a few territories belonging to others." Also, the Central Committee could not disregard that there existed now "historically formed [!] boundaries" and that "our common aim is communism under which state borders will gradually lose their former significance."[8] The two fraternal parties had an opportunity of demonstrating the existence of truly friendly relations between two socialist states. Actually, frontier questions were taken up by them with the arrival of a Soviet delegation in Peking on February 25, 1964, but the negotiations failed to reach a fruitful conclusion.

During the years 1962-64, those territorial issues which centered on Sinkiang and Outer Mongolia figured most prominently in the Sino-Soviet dispute. Soviet interest in Sinkiang had been strongly asserted during the

6. Letter of CC, CPC to CC, CPSU, Feb. 29, 1964, *People's Daily*, May 9, 1964 (*PR*, May 8, 1964).
    7. Letter of Nov. 29, 1963, *People's Daily*, May 9, 1964 (*PR*, May 8, 1964).
    8. Soviet Government Statement, Sept. 21, 1963, *Pravda*, Sept. 21 and 23, 1963.

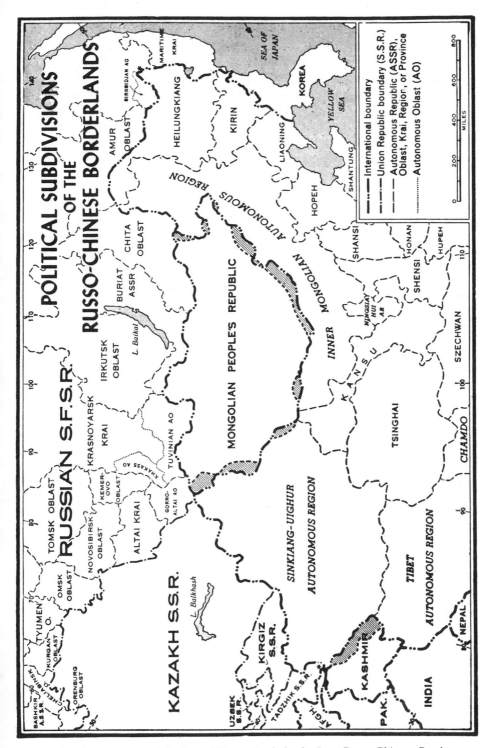

2 Political Subdivisions of the Russo-Chinese Borderlands. From *Russo-Chinese Border-lands* by W. A. Douglas Jackson. Von Nostrand Searchlight Book #5, Princeton, N.J., 1962. Used with permission of D. Van Nostrand Co., Inc.

governorship of Sheng Shih-ts'ai between 1937 and 1942 and continued until 1949 when the CPR was proclaimed. Since 1949 the CPC had reasserted its control in Sinkiang and attempts had been made to sinify the numerous ethnic groups such as Kazakhs, Uighurs, and others. Communist China had aimed at the fulfillment of this policy by various means: colonizations with army veterans and civilian Han immigrants from China proper, the resettlement of nomadic tribes, and through the encouragement of Chinese administration and Chinese language and civilization. Frontier incidents increased, however, when many among the indigenous population, reacting with violence to the enforced assimilation and increasingly repressive foreign rule, fled across the Chinese border, only to be received with open arms by their kinsfolk on the other side of the frontier. They were often pursued by Chinese troops, and serious frontier clashes ensued. Incidents in the Ili region in April and May 1963 gave rise to mutual recriminations. Another incident took place at the Soviet Siberian railway border station at Naushki in Mongolia on September 12, about which contradictory evidence was produced by both sides. According to Peking, Soviet customs officials forcibly seized Chinese literature, in particular the Peking September Statement in the Russian language, while, according to Moscow, the Chinese locked up Soviet officials, refused to permit the train to continue, and violated publicly, like vagabonds, the most elementary sanitary and hygienic practices in the railway station by urinating in public.[9]

Though Outer Mongolia, long a Soviet satellite, separated from China formally in 1945—a separation acknowledged by the CPC in the Sino-Soviet treaty of 1950—Mao revealed later that in 1954, when Khrushchev and Bulganin visited Peking, he had attempted to reopen the issue, but that they had "refused to talk to us." In 1964 Mao told a delegation of the Japanese Socialist party, which was then visiting Peking, that there were "too many places occupied by the Soviet Union" and that the Kuriles should be returned to Japan, and Outer Mongolia, "which is considerably greater than the Kuriles," to the CPR.[10]

Khrushchev disputed Mao's views, appropriately enough, in a talk also with a Japanese parliamentary delegation on September 15, 1964.[11] According to him, the territory of the Soviet Union had "evolved historically" and the USSR was a multinational state. The same was true of China. But the independent Mongolian People's Republic had developed as a result of a national-liberation struggle; Khrushchev reminded Mao, not

9. *Pravda*, Sept. 10, 1963, p. 2 (*CDSP* 15, no. 36 [1963]: 20-21).

10. *Sekai Shuno*, Tokyo, Aug. 11, 1965, quoted in Doolin, *Territorial Claims in the Sino-Soviet Conflict* (Stanford, 1965), pp. 43-44.

11. Khrushchev, Sept. 15, 1964 (*CDSP* 15, Oct. 14, 1964).

especially tactfully, that "another part of the territory inhabited by Mongols is still [!] part of the Chinese state." He also pointed out that the majority of the Kazakh people lived in the USSR and that some Kazakhs and Kirghizs resided in China. Soviet Russia was in favor of self-determination and wanted disputed issues to be settled on this basis. This was an ominous threat to China's integrity, though of course it was China that had raised the question of territorial revision in the first place. Khrushchev furthermore stressed that the Chinese had not lived in Sinkiang "since time immemorial," and that the region was rather made up of Uighurs, Kazakhs, Kirghizs, and other minorities. The Chinese Emperors had waged wars of conquest just as had the Tsars of Russia, and had brought under their control Korea, Mongolia, Tibet, and Sinkiang. All this could not have been too reassuring to the Peking government. It was obvious that the USSR, feeling threatened by Chinese claims, resorted to counterthreats of her own and reminded China of her own vulnerability, on both ethnic and historic grounds.

Mao's Interview. The "Intermediate Zone"

On September 2, *Pravda* also took issue with Mao's aforementioned talk with Japanese Socialist deputies headed by Kozo Sasaki. With it the Sino-Soviet dispute reached fever heat. By criticizing Mao himself, Soviet authorities were well aware that they were not likely to improve matters. But the territorial sovereignty of the USSR was at stake.

Pravda started out by saying that it was difficult to believe that Mao's talk was "authentic," yet Peking had confirmed its authenticity. Also, by August 1 the Japanese newspaper *Asahi* had already published a statement by Chou En-lai that had contained "essentially the same ideas." As the interview revealed, the Chinese leaders, according to *Pravda,* had large expansionist aspirations, which they no longer tried to disguise. While back in 1960 the leaders of the CPC had developed a polemic about seemingly purely ideological questions—the possibility of preventing world war, peaceful and nonpeaceful transition to socialism, and the like—now Mao did not even touch upon these kinds of problems. There was no word about Marxism-Leninism, no class-analysis of the present-day world, no class approach to the choice of friends and allies in the fight against imperialism. Mao seemed to be concerned only about "whipping up anti-Soviet feeling" and playing on nationalist sentiments of the most reactionary forces; and he was plainly agitated by territorial greed.[12]

12. "Concerning Mao Tse-tung's talk with a group of Japanese Socialists," *Pravda,* Sept. 2, 1964, p. 2 (*CDSP* 16, no. 34 [Sept. 16, 1964]: 3-7).

In his interview Mao had stressed the concept that Japan and China should "act in unity, cooperate with each other." He had flattered his guests when he said that Japan was a "great nation which during World War II had fought many great powers and conquered many lands." Japan and China, he suggested, should support each other not only economically but also politically. As a result of the war Japan had come under the domination of American imperialism, which also dominated South Korea, the Philippines, Thailand, and more. Though now dependent upon the United States of America, Japanese monopoly capital, according to Mao, would ultimately cast off the American yoke.

According to *Pravda,* Mao had developed the theory of the zones as early as 1946. He had distinguished between a) the zone of American imperialism, b) the zone comprising the territories of the USSR and the other socialist countries, and c), territory lying between these zones, therefore "intermediate," chiefly the countries of Asia, Africa, and Latin America.

Now, however, Mao had revised his "theory," "slanderously declaring" that the USSR had entered into "collusion" with the United States for a struggle for world domination. This left only two zones, the Soviet-American and the so-called intermediate one which, of course, included China. According to Chinese theoreticians, the intermediate zone represented revolution and progress. The peoples of this zone, the Chinese communist leaders concluded, were to struggle against American imperialism and at the same time against the Soviet Union.

Pravda blasted the theory of the intermediate zone as having nothing in common with Marxism; on the contrary, "it is a militantly anti-Marxist, anti-Leninist concept." The present-day world was not divided into geographical zones but into opposing social systems, the socialist and capitalist one. Yet Mao's intermediate zone "mixed" exploiters and exploited, oppressors and oppressed. Mao's theory not only ignored the class approach but substituted for it a strictly nationalistic approach, dictated by the purposes of the great-power policy of the CPC leaders. Chinese Communist leaders, instead of pursuing a policy of revolutionary and proletarian internationalism, were only interested in "great-power policy"!

Although in the interview Mao had tried to minimize the struggle against the USSR as a mere "war on paper" in which no one would be killed, he had admitted that the polemic with the CPSU was "a kind of war." He thus had shown disregard for the interests of the unity of the world Communist movement. While *Pravda* did not equate the Sino-Soviet dispute with the one between the USSR and Western imperialism headed by the United States, Mao's mere comparison of this struggle with the "cold war" of the West against the socialist camp in many of its aspects—not the least in its "fierceness," the methods employed, and the scope it had assumed—spoke volumes.

Geography, History, and Chinese Claims

Pravda continued: "How far the Chinese leaders have gone in the 'cold war' against the USSR, becomes graphically clear from Mao's pronouncements on the territorial questions." Mao did not simply claim this or that Soviet territory, but spoke of "the general territorial question" and developed an openly expansionist program, making far-reaching claims. This program did not originate today or yesterday. In 1954 a textbook on modern history had already been published in the Chinese People's Republic with a map of China showing that country as it was in the opinion of the authors before the Opium War. This map included the following countries as being part of China: Burma, Vietnam, Korea, Thailand, Malaya, Nepal, Bhutan, and Sikkim. In the north, the border ran along the Stanovoi mountain range, cutting the Far Eastern territory off from the USSR. In the west, a part of Kirghizia, of Tadzhikistan, and of Kazakhistan (up to Lake Balkash) was also included in China. Sakhalin too was shown as belonging to China. This apparently had shocked the Soviets back in 1954, but it was only now, after an entire decade, that they let their people share their irritation and anger.

Subsequent events refuted the conjecture that the publication of such a textbook was perhaps the result of an oversight or the mere provocations of nationalistic elements. Only recently Chinese representatives had referred with increasing frequency to "hundreds of square kilometers of Soviet territory allegedly belonging by right to China."

Mao had declared in his recent interview: "The region east of the Baikal became the territory of Russia approximately 100 years ago, and since then Vladivostok, Khabarovsk, Kamchatka, and other points have been the territory of the Soviet Union. We have not yet presented the bill for this roll call." In support of their claims, the Chinese leaders cited the fact that many hundreds of years ago the Chinese Emperor once used to collect tribute from these inhabitants. If the question involved were not so serious, such historical arguments could only be called childish. With the help of such arguments one could also prove that the boundary of the CPR passed along the line of the Great Wall of China, less than 100 kilometers away from Peking, since once the boundary of China ran there. *Pravda* referred specifically to the boundary along the Amur river fixed more than 100 years ago in the treaties of Aigun and Peking. True, the tsarist government had carried out a "predatory policy," but so had the Chinese Emperors.

The Soviet Position

   Pravda continued: "Do those who question whether an area of more than one and a half million square kilometers belongs to the Soviet Union think of how these claims will be regarded by the Soviet people who have lived and worked on this land for several generations and consider it their homeland, the land of their ancestors?" The Soviet-Chinese boundary, *Pravda* asserted, had been "historically formed." (This argument, of course, appeared out of place after the foregoing criticism of alleged "historical rights.") The boundary had "been fixed by life itself"—another favorite Soviet phrase, but actually nothing more than a redundancy. *Pravda's* justification of the territorial status quo was based on treaty rights: "The boundary treaties of Aigun and Peking, 1858 and 1860 respectively, are a basis that cannot be disregarded." Actually, the Soviet Union has regarded such rights rather lightly in disputes between other countries when her own interests were not at stake.

   Pravda followed up with an account of alleged Soviet generosity toward China after the October Revolution, of the Soviet renunciation of all unequal treaties with China—the very point that China disputed—and a reminder that after 1945 the Soviets had renounced the use of the naval base at Port Arthur and had turned over to the CPR, "free of charge," all its rights in the joint management of the Chinese-Changchun Railroad.[13] (Of course, if the Soviets were to be credited for these noble postwar deeds, how should one evaluate their wresting these concessions from China in the first place, in the summer of 1945?) Lenin, who was quoted as having condemned the tsarist seizure of Port Arthur and the tsarist penetration of Manchuria, was significantly cited again: "Vladivostok is far away, but this city is nevertheless ours." The CPC was lectured about the difference between Imperial and Soviet Russia: "The boundaries of Tsarist Russia had been determined by the policy of imperialist usurpers, but the boundaries of the Soviet Union were formed through the voluntary declaration of the will of the peoples on the basis of free self-determination of nations. The peoples who joined the Soviet Union will never allow encroachment on this right to settle their destiny themselves." In other words, Russia's boundaries after the October Revolution had received a "democratic" baptism; their Tsarist illegitimacy was thus miraculously wiped away.

   The demands of the CPR were of course insulting to the USSR, since Peking ignored the power and the prestige of the Soviet Union and dared question the territorial integrity of a fraternal nation, of the leading socialist state. They were also a demonstration of base "ingratitude" on

13. *Ibid.*

the part of the CPR and an intolerable challenge to Soviet leadership in the socialist camp. Peking's demands were to the Soviets the insolent proclamation of an upstart rival who still lagged behind in regard to economic achievement and military accomplishment. All this aside, the CPR expressed doubts regarding the claim of the USSR that it represented a voluntary federation of equal nationalities, a new type of multinational state which, for the first time in history, had solved the age-old and thorny nationality problem. The Chinese territorial claim, painful to Soviet Russia on numerous grounds, embarrassed and hurt especially because in the eyes of the fraternal CPC the USSR was a colonialist power that held Asiatic peoples against their will, by force, within her confines; it thus punctured one of the most cherished Soviet myths, the myth of the USSR's granting freedom and equality to all its nationalities. (Actually, Communist China's nationality theory, closely patterned after that of the USSR, is, like its model, generous only in theory, being oppressive, assimilatory, and imperialist in practice.) To cap matters, the Chinese accusation, by strange coincidence, reiterated the charges made earlier in the West against Soviet nationality policy.

In his interview Mao bemoaned the fate of Mongolia which, he charged, the Soviet Union, had "placed. . .under its domination." *Pravda,* pointing to the sovereign status of the Mongolian People's Republic for more than four decades, burst with "indignation" about "such obviously wild statements." Mao would like to deprive Outer Mongolia of her independence in order to make it a Chinese province. The paper revealed that the leaders of the CPR had made this very proposition to Khrushchev and other eminent Soviet personalities during their visit to Peking in 1954. Khrushchev had retorted that the destiny of the Mongolian people was decided neither in Peking nor in Moscow, but in Ulan-Bator.

Let us consider whether the Soviet point of view was a consistent one. It was Soviet Russia's position that her own territorial status quo, her boundaries in Europe and Asia and those of her East European friends and allies were sacrosanct and their defense imperative; yet the support for the territorial status quo elsewhere in the world was an act of injustice and demanded only by the forces of dark reaction. The USSR encouraged the "just wars" of so-called national liberation which aimed at totally upsetting the territorial status quo, aside from changing the social and political complexion of the new nations. The USSR, while not inclined to negotiate what was hers, was quite disposed to enter into negotiations regarding territories belonging to her opponents—the latter, of course, being conveniently reactionaries and imperialists, or their tools.

The problem for the Soviets was thus how to reconcile their often contrary positions. As *Pravda* wrote, "One must distinguish the nature of the territorial issues. It is one thing when the matter is a question of the just striving of peoples to eliminate the survivals of the shameful colonial system, to get back old territories populated by the nation concerned and held by the imperialists.'' The return, for instance, of Goa to India was, and the reunification of Taiwan and Hongkong with China would be, fully justified. Yet territorial claims stemming from attempts ''to revise historically formed boundaries between states, to force in any form a revision of treaties and agreements concluded after World War II as a result of Hitler's fascism and Japanese militarism, are quite another matter.''[14] The people who won victory at the cost of millions upon millions of lives would never agree to it! Soviet great-power nationalism and imperialism—as real as Chinese Communist chauvinism and expansionism—has its own peculiar rationalization; it was unable to put forth an inherently consistent and convincing explanation of why the boundaries of other states ought to be changed while her own boundaries remain sacrosanct.

In his interview Mao had further declared: ''The places occupied by the Soviet Union are too numerous.'' *Pravda* accused Mao of pouring fuel to inflame nationalist passions. He could not have been unaware of the very dangerous consequences that would arise from any attempt to recarve the map of the world under present conditions. While Mao pretended to be threatening the interests of only the USSR, such ''provocational appeal'' to revise borders, if taken seriously, would generate numerous demands, claims, and insoluble conflicts. Not only was Mao presenting unreasonable claims to the Soviet Union, but he was trying to fabricate so-called territorial issues between a number of socialist countries. Soviet Russia, however, cleverly tried to align the socialist nations and other beneficiaries of the last war that had a material stake in upholding the status quo.

The transfer of the Kurile Islands in particular to the full possession of the Soviet Union, *Pravda* asserted, was not at all the result of Soviet expansion, as Mao claimed. This act was dictated by the need to stop the aggressive policy of Japanese imperialism, which since 1918 had harbored plans of seizing Soviet territory in the Far East. Of course, now that there were United States military bases in Japan, it was imperative to hold onto the Kuriles. Besides, the CPR, on August 15, 1951, had specifically approved the Kuriles being handed over to the USSR and Southern Sachalin and adjacent inslands being returned to the Soviet Union. Japan had no claim to the Kurile Islands. However, in accordance with earlier Soviet statements, *Pravda* reasserted its position that this did not mean that in changed circumstances searches for solution of the problem would be excluded.

14. *Ibid.*

Suggesting territorial changes, Mao had appealed not only to history but also to "justice," pointing out that the population of the globe was unevenly distributed and hence justice demanded a redistribution of territory. *Pravda* blasted the "evident demagoguery of this thesis." Communists fought precisely to ensure all peoples a better life. In a completely socialist world, state boundaries would lose their significance. But it was harmful to raise the question now when opposing social systems still existed. "History knows many instances in which the most reactionary wars were undertaken for the purpose of enlarging 'Lebensraum.' " Mao had predecessors of whom he could hardly be proud. His compliments about the "greatness of Japan" were quite surprising, coming from a Communist. He obviously admired the factor of brute force in international relations, spoke with "extraordinary enthusiasm of the crimes of the Japanese military," and declared the aggressive actions of the Japanese samurai to be Japan's national greatness—that is, actions the Japanese people themselves regarded as a national disgrace. All who cherished the interests of socialism and wished to preserve peace could not but denounce the expansionist views of the CPR leaders. Their designs were "permeated through and through with great-power chauvinism and hegemonism." *Pravda's* article thus ended by comparing Mao Tse-tung with Adolf Hitler. The circle was complete.

A New Round of Debate

Izvestiia on "Coordination" of National and International Interests

Between May and August 1964, *Izvestiia* published several articles on the Sino-Soviet dispute, restating once more the case against the CPC. The articles stressed the need for coordinating efforts against the imperialist enemy along political, economic, and military lines; the need for unity; and the danger of schism. While seemingly tolerant, the authors demanded the end of Peking's schismatic and divisive activities and the termination of the anti-Soviet campaign everywhere, including the Third World. Peking, it was suggested, should see the error of its ways, return to the socialist camp and, of course, accept Moscow's version of Marxist-Leninist theory and policy.

On June 4 *Izvestiia* published the article "On the Nature of Relations between Socialist Countries: Combine National and International Interests." The writer urged socialist countries to agree upon actions and to coordinate policy, which involved the "skillful combination" of national and international interests. Each socialist country has, vis-à-vis capitalist

countries, "its own complex of primary problems." For China, this was
Taiwan and the final emergence from foreign-policy isolation. For Poland,
it was the western boundary and relations with the Federal Republic of
Germany. For Vietnam and Korea, it was unification of the country. Of
primary significance for Cuba was the struggle against attempts at imperialist intervention by the United States of America. "The objective solution of each of these problems accords with the long-range interests of the
entire socialist commonwealth." But daily political practice posed certain
problems: "When this or that aspect of international life is perceived
through the prism of 'one's own' No. 1 problem (and this is inevitable to
some degree), different approaches and opinions, a lack of coincidence of
concrete interests and tasks may arise."[15] Coordination of policy meant
working out a joint line of conduct and planning activities that coordinate
the interests of each socialist country with the interests of the entire
socialist system. In the Soviet view, coordination of tactics and strategy
was absolutely essential. The Soviet Union was concerned about maintaining unity of direction and policy in the face of different priorities vigorously promoted by the individual communist parties.

Majority of Unanimity in the "Socialist Commonwealth"

The USSR, facing the Chinese challenge, was confident of majority
support within the "socialist commonwealth." While the Soviet Union
frequently deprecated the majority vote in the U.N., especially in the early
years of the organization, it considered majority approval and majority rec-
ommendations in the socialist commonwealth sacrosanct. The Soviet
Union wanted Communist China to accept and follow the policy adopted
by the socialist commonwealth, a policy that of course bore largely a
Soviet imprint. The leaders of the USSR wanted to avoid a situation in
which Chinese Communist hotheads or any of their North Korean and
North Vietnamese followers could pull the Soviet Union into an Asiatic
conflict against her wishes, vital interests, and better judgment. The Soviet
Union wished to remain master of her own destiny, and of that of the
socialist commonwealth, rather than be at the mercy of some fanatic and
reckless Asiatic comrades determined to spread revolution even at the risk
of a global war.

The Chinese Communist leaders, on the other hand, feared that coordination of policy would be equivalent to submerging Chinese revolutionary
goals, shelving Marxism-Leninism, and abandoning Chinese national
interests—in their view always identical with the true interests of pro-

15. *Izvestiia,* June 4, 1964, p. 4 (*CDSP* 16, no. 23 [July 1, 1964]: 4-5).

letarian internationalism. As *Izvestiia* put it: "They interpret the policies [of the USSR and of international Communism] as the intention of one country to impose its will on others, an attempt to deprive them of their independence." They also looked suspiciously on the growing economic integration of the socialist commonwealth and regarded measures for extending and strengthening economic ties as an encroachment on the independence and wealth of the Chinese People's Republic. There could be, *Izvestiia* concluded, no coordination of policy, "and no cooperation in general," if one adhered to such logic.

According to the Soviets, the government of the CPR had not only ceased to coordinate its actions in the international field with the other countries of the socialist commonwealth, but was even waging "open warfare" against the line agreed on by the majority of the socialist countries. While the Warsaw Treaty countries held regular consultations on all major international problems, the CPR government was accused of having "repudiated" this kind of consultation and alliance. "Despite repeated invitations," the Chinese representatives had ceased to participate in the work of various conferences of leaders of the socialist countries. Not only did the CPR, in matters of foreign policy, not take counsel with the other socialist countries, but it also did not give them advance information on its moves.

In accordance with the Treaty of Friendship, Alliance and Mutual Aid between the USSR and the CPR, the governments of the two countries were to exchange information on international questions affecting their common interests. While the Soviets had strictly adhered to this agreement, China, Moscow charged, had, within the last years, sent few items of informational material, many of them being of only secondary importance, and recently had stopped sending such materials altogether. The Chinese leaders even expressed scorn for the treaties they had concluded. In December 1963, the Chinese Minister of Foreign Affairs, Chen Yi, alleged that Soviet assurances as to the defense of China in the event of imperialist aggression were of no value. The leaders of the CPR asserted, it is true, different things at various times; "apparently," *Izvestiia* sneered, this was one of the "peculiarities of 'Sinified Marxism.' "

The Chinese Communist leaders were also severing economic ties with the fraternal countries. By rejecting the advantages of the internal specialization of production, they deliberately placed a number of countries in less favorable and unequal conditions for building socialism, as compared with those socialist countries having a more capacious domestic market, a larger territory, and a more abundant supply of raw materials. The Soviets thus aimed not only at discrediting Communist China in the eyes of East European Communist countries, but also at underlining at the same time their own "generosity." Soviet Russia, by tying her economy to that of the smaller East European neighbors, was not exploiting them; on the contrary, she acted from pure unselfishness. By opening her doors to them—as well as by asking them to keep their gates open—she accelerated their building of "socialism"!

The Chinese Communist leaders instead were propagandizing the policy of "relying on one's own forces," and extolling their "noble revolutionary style." The Soviet daily rather ridiculed these claims and pointed to the increasing trade of the CPR with "imperialist" countries in strategic raw materials.

Two days later *Izvestiia* published a sequel to this article, "The Policy of Unity versus the Policy of Schism." Two political lines were struggling within the socialist commonwealth, the internationalist line of the CPSU and the majority of the fraternal parties, and the nationalist line of the leadership of the CPR and a few other parties that were following the CPC. The boundaries were thus clearly drawn between the "internationalist" course of the USSR and the "nationalist" policies of the leaders of Communist China. No doubt, nationalism would be defeated. Yet the victory of internationalism over nationalism, of the policy of unity over the policy of "schism," required a persistent and apparently prolonged struggle. Practice had shown that between socialist countries there can and do arise differences on essential problems of domestic and foreign policy.[16]

The Soviets did not minimize the gulf that separated Moscow and Peking. But debates with the Communist Chinese leaders were insisted upon in the interest of "unity," and so was the need for presenting a common front against "imperialism." There appeared to be at times some hope of isolating the Chinese Communists and of bringing them peaceably into line. But then again *Izvestiia* blasted "political adventurism and great-power chauvinism," "schism," and violations of Communist discipline —some of the most formidable charges to be leveled against Communists in and out of court.

The Soviets accused the leadership of the CPR of having "deviated from the principles of Marxism-Leninism" and embraced a "petty bourgeois ideology," not a proletarian one, and "nationalism" rather than "internationalism." The CPC's leadership had demonstrated that nationalism had become "the chief danger" for the socialist commonwealth.

On Ending the "Cold War" between Moscow and Peking

Debates under these circumstances might hardly be fruitful, but they ought at least to lead to calling off the hostile exchanges between the CPC

16. *Izvestiia*, June 6, 1964, p. 4 (*CDSP* 16, no. 23 [July 1, 1964]: 5-6).

and the CPSU. If unity of views could not be achieved since this or that Communist Party was not yet ready to renounce its incorrect views and mistaken appraisals, the task, in the Soviet view, lay in trying at least not to extend ideological differences to interstate relations. Regardless of existing ideological differences between socialist countries, interstate relations should be developed, and commitments made with respect to another socialist country should be strictly observed. "Economic, scientific, technological, and cultural cooperation" between socialist countries ought to be continued and expanded to strengthen the mutual defense against the imperialists and to operate in a united front in the international arena.

Izvestiia made several suggestions on how to restore the unity of the socialist commonwealth. In any case, the methods the leadership of the CPC was trying to impose, "namely, abuse, insults, falsification, blackmail, and so on," clearly undermined unity. What was required was "a comradely tone, respect for the other side, a careful, objective analysis of arguments and counterarguments"[17]—good practices to which Russian Communism itself in its intra-party struggles, not to mention others, had not always lived up to. Nor, in spite of preaching "comradeship," did the Soviets offer to Peking the other cheek!

No discussion could be fruitful, *Izvestiia* continued, if the participants were completely lacking in self-criticism. The Chinese leaders were resorting to all kinds of intrigues and hidden speculation in the area of foreign trade, in the work of international democratic organizations, in sports, and so on. What the USSR suggested was simply to end the "cold war"—the very word used—between Communist China and the Soviet Union, to establish a kind of "peaceful coexistence" based upon an end to namecalling, and also to end Chinese "splitting activities."

In view of these "splitting activities" of the leadership of the CPC, some people, *Izvestiia* continued, had voiced "pessimism and despair" and were ready to acknowledge the victory of nationalism over Communism. Yet *Izvestiia* preferred taking a long-term view. The temporary setbacks and failures were part of the historical process. While nationalist prejudices might temporarily overcome Communist ideology in this or that party, the time would come when the whole socialist camp would again consolidate on the foundation of Marxism-Leninism and proletarian internationalism. As the Soviets prophesied the ultimate victory of socialism over capitalism, they similarly anticipated the final victory of the policy of the CPSU over the policy of the CPR within the socialist camp. In either case, however, the Soviets were careful enough not to predict a definite date of that historic event.

17. *Ibid.*

Peking's "Racism" and the National-Liberation Movement

Control, leadership, or at least preeminence of the USSR among East European Communist countries could not, due to purely geographic and strategic reasons, be seriously challenged by Communist China. But in Asia, Africa, and Latin America this geographic advantage for the Soviet Union was virtually nonexistent, and racial considerations, at least in the eyes of the CPC, were likely to work against "white" Soviet Russia and to favor China. The very backwardness of these continents also established a closer bond with Communist China than with the relatively advanced USSR. Peking was resolved to take advantage of these circumstances in its struggle with Moscow for hegemony in the Communist world.

On June 7, Matveyev in *Izvestiia* sharply attacked the "Chinese leaders" who were attempting to drive wedges between the peoples of Asia, Africa, and Latin America on the one side, and the USSR on the other. Matveyev pointed out that today not only the USSR and more than fifty new independent states, but also "patriots" in the Caribbean, South Vietnam, South Africa, the Arabian peninsula and the Panama Canal zone were fighting the imperialists. Yet in the not-too-distant past, particularly in "moments of especially critical trials," as for instance in the Suez Canal crisis of 1956 or in the October 1962 Cuban crisis, "it has been our country that has had to take decisive steps in order to tip the scales of the anticolonialist, anti-imperialist struggle in favor of the forces of freedom." In past decades it had been primarily Britain that had tried to prevent even simple "physical" contact of the USSR with the peoples of the East.[18] But recently at the Jakarta meeting, preparatory to the convocation of the second conference of the countries of Asia and Africa, the Minister of Foreign Affairs of the CPR, Chen Yi, had fought against participation in the conference of the Soviet Union, which was not only the largest European, but also the largest Asian power!

A government statement of the CPR, published on May 30, 1964, made the assertion that the USSR was not an Asian power. Peking wrote "virtual treatises" to implant the idea that the Soviet Union was "only a European power." The writer ridiculed the arguments advanced by the Chinese against Soviet participation in the Conference, among them that the Soviet Union's "political center was in Europe and that Peking was the 'political center of Asia' "; all this ignored, of course, such capitals of the USSR's Asian republics as Tashkent, Alma-Ata, Ashkhabad, Dushaube, and Frunze. The "hegemonic claims" of the leaders of the CPR, their desire to speak "in the name and, most important, for the other countries of Asia,

18. *Izvestiia*, June 7, 1964, p. 4. V. Matveyev.

and not Asia alone," had emerged in recent statements with extreme clarity. The Chinese leaders' pretensions were "exorbitant," and their manifest purpose was to "estrange" the countries of Asia, Africa, and Latin America in general from the Soviet Union. Peking was dreaming up ways to erect some kind of "Chinese wall" between the Soviet Union and the Afro-Asian countries.

On August 2 there appeared another anti-Peking article in *Izvestiia*, "Into Whose Hands They Are Playing—National Egoism of CPC Leaders Merges with Neocolonialism," from the pen of V. Kudryavtsev. The article clearly showed that the dispute between the USSR and the CPR was to a large degree a struggle for hegemony over the young, independent, but economically still undeveloped nations, many of which, on account of their colonial past, had distinct anti-Western sentiments; on the other hand, they were greatly impressed with the quick rise to industrialism and military power of Russia and China. These latter states, in their eyes, had also the advantage of not being tainted with colonialism and expansion, at least not in their part of the world.

Asia, Africa, and Latin America were the beneficiaries of the new international situation, of the fact that the socialist countries had tipped the balance of forces in the world in their favor. But "a mortal danger" lay in ambush for the national-liberation movement of the economically backward peasant countries. The long domination of colonialism with its inherent racial chauvinism had "exacerbated" local nationalism in African countries. The leaders of the CPR had taken petty bourgeois nationalism as the basis for their views of the present-day national liberation movement. The Chinese leaders utilized the "unhealthy vanity" of some African leaders, whose national egoism was stronger than their internationalism. Peking gave itself and other national-liberation movements, rather than the USSR, credit for most of their accomplishments! The Chinese leaders tried to "divorce the national-liberation movement of the peoples of Asia and Africa from the Soviet Union—the mighty bulwark of victorious socialism."[19]

The attempt to bar the Soviet Union from participation in the national-liberation movement of the peoples of Asia and Africa was not a transitory matter caused by the Chinese leaders' dissatisfaction with certain specific actions of the USSR. The Peking statement of May 30 specifically emphasized, *Izvestiia* held, that even if relations between China and the USSR improved, the Chinese leaders still would not favor participation of the Soviet Union in the conference of Asian and African countries. The theory and practice of the Chinese leaders, *Izvestiia* charged, played into the hands of the neocolonialists who dreamt of "an Africa separated by a

19. *Ibid.*, Aug. 2, 1964, V. Kudryavtsev.

great Chinese wall from the world socialist system," an Africa which, under the cover of formal independence, would remain an object of plunder. Thus Communist China's leaders actually were helping colonialism and imperialism!

On Soviet "Aid"

Peking's leaders, *Izvestiia* charged, aimed also at "discrediting Soviet aid." The Soviet writer accused Chou and other Chinese Communist leaders of ingratitude toward the USSR, considering the help China had received from the latter. He voiced his indignation at the Chinese Premier's placing Soviet assistance "on a par" with American aid. This deeply hurt the Soviets, who had persistently denounced American and Western capitalist "aid" and at the same time had indefatigably boosted their own assistance, allegedly marked by conspicuous generosity and unstinting unselfishness.

The sharp accusations of the Chinese Communist leaders went to the very heart of Soviet policy among the uncommitted or unaligned nations. It was these nations who were, according to the Party program of 1961, the target of Soviet agitation and propaganda; their move from the stage of the noncapitalist path and nonalignment to socialism and alignment was supposed to change the political and economic complexion of the world.

And in was in this very area that the Chinese, in the Soviet view, aimed at the frustration of Moscow by building a "wall" against the USSR, compounded of a new racialism, suspicion of alien aid, and accusations of neocolonialism and imperialism—the very type of charges that in the past the Soviets had flung, and continued to fling, against the Western world. As the foregoing article showed, the CPSU, indignant of the CPC, finally retaliated with vituperation of its own against the "slander and falsification" originating in Peking. Still, the Soviet Union would be prepared, *Izvestiia* assured the Chinese Communist leaders, to let bygones be bygones in the interest of unity and to enter any time into comradely talks with them for the purpose of again presenting a united front against the "imperialists"; nevertheless, continued accusations against Soviet "imperialism" and outright "slander" could not be tolerated.

Ideological Combat

On "Proletarian Dictatorship" and the "State of the Entire People"

Izvestiia had earlier made clear that in its view Peking had also strayed from the right path in the field of Marxist-Leninist theory proper. On May

17, 1964, *Izvestiia,* in the article "Revolutionary Theory is Guide to Action: On the Dictatorship of the Proletariat," assailed the CPC in the seemingly abstruse realm of pure Marxist-Leninist theory, in particular in regard to the doctrine of the dictatorship of the proletariat. The fundamental substance of the dictatorship of the proletariat, the writer explained, consisted in guiding the creation of the new socialist society. The proletarian dictatorship, according to Marx, Engels, and Lenin, was not needed forever. The working class was the only class in history that did not set perpetuation of its rule as a goal.

The dictatorship of the proletariat, according to Moscow, was designed merely for the transition period from capitalism to socialism, the first phase, in Marx's terminology, of Communism. The proletarian dictatorship ended with the establishment of socialism. Of course, this stage belonged to the past, since the USSR was in the early process of constructing Communism. The Soviet doctrine proclaimed that "the state of the entire people" had replaced the dictatorship of the proletariat in the USSR.*[20]

According to *Izvestiia,* the CPSU program had taken "a forward step" in creatively elaborating Marxist-Leninist teaching about the dictatorship of the proletariat. It had for the first time in the history of Marxism concretely defined the conditions and the movement in history when the dictatorship of the proletariat, having fulfilled its historic tasks, was "no longer necessary or, as V. I. Lenin said 'ceases' and. . .[has] developed into the socialist state of the entire people." These conclusions, *Izvestiia* reminded its readers, had received universal recognition and support within the world Communist movement, except for Chinese theoreticians, who saw in the new theoretical postulates of the CPSU Program a departure from the class position of the proletariat and even a "service to the restoration of capitalism."

According to *Izvestiia,* the Chinese leaders saw the dictatorship of the proletariat exclusively as an instrument of violence, keeping silent about the most essential thing, the fact that it was "a socialist democracy." In the numerous Chinese articles and official documents there was not even a mention of democracy. "The practice of state construction in China conformed to this interpretation of the essence of the dictatorship of the pro-

---

*The pertinent part of the CPSU program reads as follows: "Having brought about the complete and final victory of socialism—the first phase of communism—and the transition of society to the full-scale construction of communism, the dictatorship of the proletariat has accomplished its historical mission and has ceased to be essential in the USSR from the point of view of the tasks of internal development. The state that arose as a state of the dictatorship of the proletariat has in the new present stage turned into a state of the entire people, an agency expressing the interests and the will of the people as a whole."

20. "Revolutionary Theory. . . . Guide to Action." *Ibid.,* May 17, 1964, On the Dictatorship of the Proletariat, p. 3 (*CDSP* [June 17, 1964]: 3-5).

letariat.'' The Chinese campaign against so-called right-wing elements and right-wing opportunists, their violation of socialist legality, their narrow concept of the role of the Party as a ''command force'' rather than as organizer and educator of the people, the absence of state and inner-party democracy, and the replacement of proletarian dictatorship by a ''dictatorship by a group of leaders''—all this testified to the absence of the concept of democracy in the CPR.

Neither in theory (the CPC leaders spoke of a ''democratic dictatorship of the people'' rather than of ''dictatorship by the proletariat'') nor in practice did the Chinese working class occupy the place in society and in the agencies of state administration that it should, according to Marxist-Leninist theory. The Chinese leaders pinned their hopes on the peasantry. If one were to believe Liu Shao-chi, the ''peasant lads'' were superior to any proletarian revolutionary. The CPC was thus criticized both for clinging to the idea of the ''dictatorship by the proletariat'' for a much longer period than Moscow considered objectively justified and for emaciating the concept of proletarian dictatorship by turning it into one based on increasing support by peasants and other nonproletarian elements.

In a subsequent article, ''The Socialist State of the Entire People,'' *Izvestiia* accused the Chinese leaders of having recently extended their polemics to questions of the internal development of the Soviet Union and other socialist countries. They had chosen the CPSU Program as the main target of their attack and had in particular taken up arms against the propositions dealing with the socialist state of the entire people. The transformation of the state of the dictatorship of the proletariat into a state of the entire people was a logical and natural process that began in the USSR in the mid-1930s. The 1936 constitution had abolished every limitation on democracy. Unfortunately, the process of evolution into a socialist democracy of the entire people had not made progress in subsequent years. The threat of war, the outbreak of the Great Patriotic War, and the Stalin cult signified as many limitations on democracy. With the restoration of Leninist norms and principles, however, progress was once more resumed toward the Soviet socialist state of the entire people.[21]

While Soviet society was not yet classless, the classes of workers and peasants were not engaged in any class struggle, but fraternal unity and a community of interests and goods prevailed. Contrary to Chinese theoreticians, speculators, swindlers, and other bearers of bourgeois survivals were, of course, not classes in the Marxist sense of the word. Aside from the ''wild and absurd'' statements of Chinese theoreticians that so-called

21. *Ibid.* ''Revolutionary Theory, Socialist State of the Entire People,'' May 23, 1964, p. 2, May 24, p. 3 (*CDSP* 15, no. 2 [1964]: 6-8).

new bourgeois elements constantly made their appearance in the Soviet Union, the Chinese leaders also seriously asserted that the dictatorship of the proletariat was needed in the conditions of full-scale construction of Communism.

The writer of the *Izvestiia* article attacked the Peking theoreticians for considering the idea of the state of the entire people "unscientific and absurd" and for ridiculing it. They were reminded that Mao himself, as early as 1949, on the eve of the final victory in China, had spoken of a "People's state." The writer concluded thus: "The comprehensive development and improvement of socialist democracy, the active participation of all citizens in managing their state, in the guidance of economic and cultural construction, the improvement in the work of the state apparatus and the intensification of public control over its activity constitute the chief direction in the development of the socialist state system during the period of communist construction. The socialist state of the entire people is the most important stage in the evolution of the socialist state system into communist public self-government."

What had aroused *Izvestiia* about the Chinese doctrine of the need of a continuing dictatorship of the proletariat? According to the Soviets, Peking's position contained some dangerous implications. Communist China seemed to express doubt that the USSR was in an advanced stage as compared to the other socialist countries, especially China, and thus that she was in a position of serving as model and leader of the world Communist movement.

On Democracy, the Building of Communism, and Preeminence

In practice there was little difference between the USSR and CPR in regard to democracy either in party or state; a Western observer would not find genuine democracy in either. But on the theoretical level, democracy was a point of separation for the two parties. The CPSU paid lavish lip service to it, while the CPC in its official doctrinal pronouncements kept rather silent about it. Moscow, on domestic and again international grounds, was extraordinarily proud of having allegedly moved, after Stalin's death, toward democratization in theory and practice. Its claim to preeminence and leadership in the socialist commonwealth was, in its view, tied up with it.

The Chinese theoreticians, however, as *Izvestiia* complained, ignored Soviet "democracy" and the circumstance that the USSR had left the stage of socialism behind, while China was still in that stage. The Soviets, with their greater experience in dealing with Communist parties and the world at large, understood the great propagandistic value of democracy at home and abroad. They resented that Peking was disputing their theoretical position on democracy, which was proving attractive to Communists and non-Communists throughout the world.

The Soviets claimed that the absence of class struggle in the USSR and general improvement of its internal conditions, the absence of terror and violence, and adherence to socialist legality in combination with combating the personality cult were characteristic of the advanced stage of building Communism and entitled the USSR to leadership in the socialist bloc. The Chinese, of course, were not interested in substantiating, but in destroying this claim. Besides, they saw in each of these claims, rightly or wrongly, a direct or indirect criticism of the CPR. They not only ridiculed Soviet pretensions but professed to see in the Soviet system alarming symptoms of bourgeoisification and indications that Moscow had abandoned the revolutionary credo.

The Soviet Union claimed to be building Communism, while relegating other socialist states like the CPR to the less advanced stage of building socialism. The Chinese leaders, on the other hand, were not only bent on bypassing certain stages and leaping into Communism, but went so far as to say that the USSR had "restored capitalism." These claims, in Communist eyes, put them far ahead of the Soviet Union. The apparently largely theoretical dispute had thus very practical aspects. While Marxist theology seemed to soar high above the clouds, it had its down-to-earth devotees, dedicated not to the salvation of deviationist souls but to the strangulation of their rather secular bodies. When Peking began raising questions even about matters of internal Soviet policy and the CPSU program, Moscow was clearly aroused and seemed as little squeamish about methods of fighting as the Chinese. It hit back hard at Chinese practices and the CPC's theoretic vagaries and deviations from Marxism-Leninism, in the present and also the past. The CPC was accused of extolling the peasant and his anti-Marxist and puzzling role in the revolutionary struggle, of spurning socialist legality, of ignoring democracy in party and state, and of clinging to an extremely narrow conception of the role of the party. It was no doubt vulnerable on these and other grounds.

The sharp battle of words between Moscow and Peking continued in 1964 unabatedly on several levels, including the theoretical one. While Peking considered the absence of the concept of proletarian dictatorship from the program of the CPSU a cause for alarm and a symptom of the decline of the revolutionary spirit and dedication, Moscow lashed out, castigating the CPC for the violations of its own fundamental rules, the absence of intra-party democracy, the Mao cult, and the adoption of "fantastic, unrealistic" goals.

Lack of "Intra-Party Democracy" in the CPC

On April 25 *Pravda* published an article "On Certain Aspects of Party Life in the CPC." The CPSU, *Pravda* wrote, had and still has to make "serious reproofs" about some aspects of the activities of the CPC but had so far refrained from making a public issue of them because it considered these matters the business of the CPC. But since Peking had recently "arrogated" to itself the right to interfere in Soviet internal affairs of state as well as into the Party, Moscow was compelled to set matters straight. If the CPC loudly hailed the Stalin cult, it interfered, of course, seriously in the affairs of the Soviet Party. Furthermore, the Chinese leaders had subjected the CPSU Program and Statutes to unscrupulous criticism and had pinned the "great-power label on us." Therefore, *Pravda* was forced to expose the violations of Leninist norms of Party life in the CPC, though it would "not imitate the Chinese manner of lies and falsifications, rude attacks, abuse and insults."[22]

The writer of the article pointed out that during the past 35 years the CPC had held only two congresses. The Sixth Congress of the CPC had convened in 1928, the Seventh in 1945, and the Eighth not until 11 years later, in 1956. The Chinese Party Statutes provided that delegates were to retain their rights for a term of five years, but the rules had been repeatedly violated since, contrary to Leninist principles of intra-party democracy. The leadership of the CPC did not even consider it necessary to explain to its own Party membership the reasons for not complying with the Statutes and for not convening congresses.

There had been a time when the CPC was on the right track. In 1958, at its Eight Congress, the Party had come out for "peaceful coexistence," had also approved the 1957 Moscow Declaration and the Peace Manifesto, and had favored economic cooperation between socialist countries. However, the CPC leadership had subsequently ignored these policies and her own Party Statutes and directives.

During the past few years the so-called line of the "Three Red Banners" had been proclaimed as the embodiment of domestic economic policy in China. The Peking leadership had charted this course without authorization by any Party congress. As a matter of fact, in the resolutions and directives of these congresses was to be found a different formulation of the general line of the party, together with serious warnings against imprudent "leaps." But the resolutions of the CPC had been disregarded in order to justify the setting of "fantastic, impracticable tasks" and of a new adventurist policy. There had followed the establishment of the communes.

22. *Pravda*, Apr. 28, 1964, pp. 5-6, also *ibid.*, Apr. 29, pp. 2-3 (*CDSP* 16, no. 17 [May 20, 1964]: 18-24).

In 1962 the slogan "Place the development of agriculture in the foreground" had been adopted. No economic data had been published for several years.

In 1949 the CPC was made up chiefly of the peasant population, representatives of which comprised about 90% of all party members. By June 1956 the percentage of workers was still only 14%. Also, the CPC operated in a most secretive manner. For instance, at the Party Congress in 1958 the fact that Mao addressed the congress was listed in the communiqué, but the speech itself was not published!* Yet the most serious "peculiarity" of the CPC, by will of its leaders, was the actual lack of a party program. The CPC itself did not consider the Manifesto, adopted at the Second Congress in 1922, its program. In contrast, of course, Lenin and the CPSU had always attached greatest importance to the Party's program. "The absence of a program breeds the conditions for the cult of the individual, since in such a case this cult is constrained by nothing." The writer finally drew a parallel between the cult of the individual in the USSR during Stalin's lifetime and the cult of the individual as still existing in China. In conclusion, *Izvestiia* accused Peking of having embarked on the road of revisionism.[23] The accusation, usually hurled by Peking against Moscow, was thus flung back at Peking.

Historical Sciences in the CPR and Chinese Chauvinism

The political and economic isolation and growing nationalism of the Chinese leadership was, according to the Soviets, also reflected in its cultural policies and the intellectual life of Communist China. Her cultural climate bore the mark of the great-power chauvinist tendencies and bourgeois national prejudices that were so rampant in the CPR. In an article "Some Questions of Historical Science in the Chinese People's Republic" in *Voprosy istorii*, authors R. V. Vyatkin and S. L. Tikhvinsky referred to the difficulty of obtaining an adequate picture of the development of Chinese historiography, since there had been a sharp reduction in the number of Chinese scholarly works recently sent to the Soviet Union. Also, the scholarly contacts between Chinese historians and Soviet scholars had decreased and the book exchange with China had become a very one-sided affair. Marxist-Leninist Chinese historiography, the foundations of which had been laid in the twenties and thirties, progressed satisfactorily during the first decade of the existence of the CPR. Yet, during the past four or five years, the process of growth had been retarded.[24]

---

*The writer omitted to mention that Khrushchev's speech denouncing Stalin at the Twentieth Congress of the CPSU has never been published in the USSR!

23. *Ibid.*

24. *Voprosy istorii*, Oct. 1963, pp. 3-20.

Familiarity with world history was only a relatively recent phenomenon in China. After 1949 textbooks on world history came into use, with more than 100 books by Soviet historians having been translated. But the majority of works by Chinese historians were still restricted to the history of their own country and to Chinese literature and sources. During the past four years, for instance, the journal *Lishih Yenchiu* had published about 250 scholarly articles, yet hardly more than ten were in the field of world history, not to mention the erroneous theses and views expressed in these few contributions. In one of these articles the Europocentric concept of bourgeois world history was criticized, without crediting Soviet historians who had exposed these concepts before. The Chinese author of the article in question was "by no means original," since Japanese bourgeois historians since the Meiji revolution had propagated the "Greater East Asia theories," theories that were endorsed by the ideologists of Japanese militarism. A Chinese writer, Chou Ku-cheng, delighted in the military successes of the Mongolian Empire, stressed the alleged "culture-bearing" role of the Mongolian campaigns and conquests, while remaining silent about the "calamities" that these conquests brought upon the world. This writer, shelving the Marxist-Leninist principle of historical analysis, substituted "a racial principle" for it. Actually, he replaced "Europocentrism" with an "undisguised 'Asia-centrism.' " The magazine's editors had apparently endorsed this writer's views.

According to another Chinese writer, the Soviet historians continued, virtually every great European thinker from Descartes to Hegel had been influenced by Chinese philosophy. The only evidence adduced was a few laudatory statements by European thinkers about Confucius. The replacement of Marxist principles of historical research by the great-Han sinocentrism was "a blatant concession to bourgeois nationalism whose traditions were rooted in the historical science of the old China." Similarly, a claim originally advanced in 1913 by the Chinese bourgeois nationalist press that Chinese explorers had discovered America, has in recent years been put forth again.

Of special interest to *Voprosy istorii* was the recent Chinese reevaluation of the Mongol and Manchu rule over China. While previously the bloody and destructive character of the Mongol yoke (which had also lain on Russia) had been emphasized, Chinese historical writing since about 1960 began to call the Mongol's dynastic supremacy a "period of great unification of the country," disregarding the terrible losses suffered by the Chinese people. Genghis Khan was depicted as the creator of a multinational state; the Manchu domination over the non-Manchurian nationalities of China was similarly pictured; and it was strongly implied, erroneously, that the Manchus too forged a polyglot empire.

Another Chinese historian was taken to task for ignoring the international significance of the 1905-07 Russian Revolution and for holding that the national liberation struggle of the Chinese people of that period was completely free from any sort of external ideological influences. Chinese historians were accused of ignoring revolutions other than their own and holding that conclusions drawn from the limited Chinese experience might be useful in making revolutions elsewhere. "The foisting of a purely 'Chinese way' of development upon the peoples of Asia, Africa and Latin America, regardless of the level of their economic development, their historical tradition, the existence of their own Communist parties, etc. (which is typical of the views of the leaders of the CPC) is taking place simultaneously with the defamation in every possible way of everything 'European!' "*

---

*If one replaced the words "Chinese way" with "Soviet" or "Russian way," the Soviets could have recalled frequently hearing these very accusations from socialists or even some Communist comrades abroad.

7
"Khrushchevism without Khrushchev," 1964-1965

The CPR, 1956-1965. Mao's Thought

Substantial differences between Peking and Moscow had gradually developed under Stalin, though they were hardly visible to outsiders due both to the geographical distance and to the ideological walls between the Communist camp and the major Western powers. But these differences grew in intensity and scope under Khrushchev and were to continue to do so under his successors. No wonder that Peking, which persisted in clinging to the carefully nurtured myth of both Stalin's greatness and his friendship for China, placed the blame for the worsening of the relations between the CPR and the USSR on Khrushchev's shoulders and welcomed his overthrow enthusiastically.

Yet, the roots of the disagreements lay rather in the increasing divergence of national interests and the different directions of the ideological routes along which Peking and Moscow traveled. In the post-Stalin era far-reaching changes took place both in the CPR and the Soviet Union. Ideologically, politically, and economically, not to mention in the broad field of international relations, Peking and Moscow simply grew apart. Let us turn to an overview of the developments in the CPR during the decade after 1956.

After victory on the mainland, Communist China had first followed a moderate policy. While in the cities the "national" capitalists continued to serve as salaried managers of their enterprises, in the countryside there was no drive toward collectivization. Individual ownership of land was retained and only the political influence of the rich peasants was curtailed. Lenin—and in China Communists following the lead of Liu

Shao-ch'i—always stressed that collectivization would have to wait for the development of the industrial foundation that alone would make mechanized farming possible. Mao, however, with his characteristic belief in the all-powerful revolutionary will as being able to move mountains and to shape the economic foundation, was ideologically and temperamentally inclined to challenge the Soviet model of rational economic planning and of economic management administered by the bureaucracy.

This tendency was strengthened by the strong nationalistic currents in Chinese Communism and by Mao's self-assurance and his adherents' belief in his infallibility. There were years during which Mao repressed these voluntaristic tendencies, but by 1955 he began to move rapidly toward the goal of a radical transmutation of the economic and social structure of China, and, last but not least, of the transformation of the mentality of its people. Communist China then turned toward agricultural collectivization, and at a frenzied pace. Having announced its first Five-Year Plan early in 1953, Peking also launched a campaign against "bourgeois" ideological influences. A speech of Mao in 1956 revealed his ambivalence between following the Soviet example—his realization that further modernization and mastery of technical competence were imperatives—and placing his emphasis on voluntarism and speed, the latter foreshadowing the utopian visions of the "Great Leap Forward" of 1958 and, later, of the "Cultural Revolution."

But in 1956 the tempo of the economic transformation of China was definitely slowed down. Similarly, the Eighth Congress of the CPC in September 1956, which minimized Mao's thought, was a decided setback for Mao: his thought had been extolled at the Seventh Congress in 1945. In the spring of 1956, Mao launched the "Hundred Flowers" campaign, which reached its height in 1957. The apparent liberalization of this phase, however, came to an abrupt halt when Mao and the Party came face to face with a flood of criticism directed not, as they perhaps anticipated, against minor features of the system, but against the very foundation upon which their socialist regime rested.

The criticism during the Hundred Flowers campaign, Mao had hoped, would have the salutary effect of letting off steam; it might prove useful in combating bureaucratism and in preventing the kind of popular explosion that had occurred in Hungary in 1956. When, however, the floodgates were lowered, an inundation of unexpected fury swept the country. There followed an abrupt change of policy by the government. The acceleration of the economic and cultural development of the country that had been Mao's and the CPC's goal was to be achieved no longer through the liberation of individual initiative, but by insistence on organization and discipline. In the field of production, this was to find expression in the policy of the "Great Leap Forward," and in the area of social organization it meant establishment of People's Communes. This new, radical policy was crystallized in the theory of the Permanent Revolution.

The doctrine of Permanent Revolution had been proclaimed by Trotsky. Trotsky, however, in spite of de-Stalinization, has remained the archvillain in the USSR as well as in China and thus could be given no credit for the doctrine. Liu Shao-ch'i, in a speech in May 1958 at the Party Congress, "rehabilitated" the doctrine of Permanent Revolution by unceremoniously ascribing it to Mao. This doctrine, officially proclaimed in December 1958, was apparently designed to calm some anxieties that Peking's competitive drives had aroused in Moscow. The Wuchang resolution of the CC of December 1958 seemed to assure Moscow that Peking was not thinking of bypassing the socialist stage and of being able to jump directly into Communism—a mere "utopian hope."[1] Thus the theory of Permanent Revolution was originally not developed for the purpose of challenging Moscow, rather the opposite. But its stress on organized turmoil rather than on political quietude could not please the Soviets.

The theory held that, even after the elimination of all class conflict, contradictions bound to arise in the field of production would generate contradictions in society. Thus, even after the establishment of Communism there would be, according to Mao, an infinite number of revolutions.[2] The theory of Permanent Revolution was designed to fit the needs of backward, colonial countries to attain Communism by bringing about numerous necessary "qualitative changes" on their long road to the ideal society.

The theory of Permanent Revolution, one author insists, is in profound harmony with Mao's personality, in particular his combativeness in regard to man and nature, his Promethean urge to fashion nature, and his passionate desire to transform man. This heaven-storming approach found its climax in 1958 in thoughts that characterized the beginning of a rupture with Leninism and foreshadowed the "Cultural Revolution."

According to Marx and Lenin, the future for Asiatic peasant societies with their technological and economic backwardness lay in the "Europeanization" of their countries. Though revolutionary movements might arise in these backward regions, they must be guided by the workers of advanced Western countries. The USSR still clings to this view. Having achieved the status of a great economic power and being the leading industrial state in the Communist camp, she has developed a definite stake in Marxist orthodoxy which, in a self-serving manner, assigns to her a preeminent role.

1. Stuart R. Schram, *Documents sur la théorie de la 'révolution permanente' en Chine* (Paris, 1963), pp. ix-x.
2. For the following, see Schram, *Political Thought of Mao,* pp. 100-110.

To Mao, however, activist, ambitious revolutionary and dedicated nationalist at the same time, the subordination of underdeveloped countries, such as China and other Asian and African nations, to the economically advanced West and in particular to the USSR, was evidently intolerable. Mao is a proud Asian (when Lenin spoke of Russia as a "semi-Asiatic" country, he was a shame-faced one). The relative wealth and comfort of the West, including Soviet Russia, was in Peking's eyes the very source of materialism, selfishness, and revisionism. The very backwardness of China, her "blankness," was not a mortal sin to Mao, but on the contrary the seed of virtue and also of opportunity.

Mao, as Li Ta-chao before him, preferred the more retarded countryside to the sophisticated city. With the establishment of communes in the villages, Communism was to score in the countryside and its victory was then to spread to the cities. Just as during the long civil war the Communist military conquest of China had started with the countryside, so the political victory, aiming at the building of Communism, would begin in the village.

As a student of Maoism put it, Mao made his "choice in favor of the peasant rather than the worker, the army man rather than the Party cadre, the politically zealous Red Guard rather than the able student," in other words in favor of "the man who wills rather than the man who knows." To a large degree, Mao's preferences were of course shaped by his own philosophy of activism and voluntarism, fortified as they were by the guerrilla experiences of the struggling CPC.

The years from late 1958 to the eve of the "Cultural Revolution" were years during which Mao held little power. When his radical policies had ushered in economic bankruptcy, the Party bureaucracy shoved Mao aside and replaced his "guerrilla methods" by practices that were less at variance with the Soviet experience. Mao then was confined to writing and fulminating against both modern revisionism and imperialism. In 1962 he was trying to steer China back toward the road of revolutionary struggle. Early in 1964 he attempted to revive the memory and heroic history of the Long March among the young and instill in the "successors" the revolutionary spirit of self-sacrifice.

In 1964 the General Political Department of the People's Liberation Army published the first edition of Quotations from Chairman Mao. This event became a turning point in China's internal history, signifying as it did the resurgence of Maoism as well as the replacement of the Communist Party and its associate, the Youth League, by the army as the rising power in the country. Since 1962 Mao had spoken of the need of a "socialist education movement." In January 1965 the movement was renamed "the four clean-ups" (political, economic, organizational, and ideological). Then, for the first time, Mao warned against "people within the Party who are in authority" and were taking the capitalist road. In November 1965 the Great Proletarian Cultural Revolution began in earnest. Though this revolution may be traced back to the "Great Leap" of 1958 and earlier phases, the revolution beginning now had so much more depth and scope as also to represent qualitatively a novel thing.[3]

In spite of the attacks against the Party, the latter was still looked upon as the key instrument that was to shape the course of events. Both Stalin and Mao were organization men, keenly conscious of the importance of the Communist Party as the indispensable instrument for achieving the goal, first of seizing power and then of steering the ship of revolution toward the ports of socialism and Communism. But for Mao the Party was never to become a purpose in itself. He had combated Party bureaucracy before through the means of frequent rectification campaigns. But now he treated the Party cadres "as enemies" to be terrorized by the Red Guards and publicly to be humiliated.

The main thrust was directed at the old Party apparatus and Liu Shao-ch'i. Effective control lay in the hands of the army. Early in 1967 came the seizure of power: "Revolutionary Committees" were set up in the cities and provinces involving the People's Liberation Army (PLA), new revolutionary activists, and old Party and state cadres, whose administrative know-how was considered essential. These bureaucrats, surrounded by army men and young Red Guard fanatics who were opposed to capitalism and revisionism, could be counted upon as being unable to be corrupted or to corrupt. While Stalin always claimed to be the servant of the Party even when he abused its power, Mao, during the "Cultural Revolution," clearly set himself above the Party, claiming that he represented the will of the proletariat. Mao thus negated Leninism, which always had extolled the Party.

Differently from in Soviet Russia—and closely linked with the lesser role of the Party in the CPR—there has emerged in China the concept of *chung,* or loyalty to the ruler. While Lenin was canonized after his death, Mao was raised to sainthood during his lifetime. Absolute devotion to Mao was made an article of faith itself. Every other issue of *Peking Review* produced for years a likeness of Mao with the caption "our great teacher, great leader, great supreme commander and great helmsman." The submissiveness to, and the unlimited hero worship of, Mao may be plainly nauseating to the critical Western mind and recall the adulation of Hitler and Stalin. Mao strides across the stage not as a demigod, but as savior or God himself. And Mao's thought and quotations from the Little Red Book allegedly offer guidelines to the simple collective farm worker, the factory

3. The authors of virtually all studies on the Cultural Revolution link it with the "Great Leap Forward" and earlier revolutionary visions of Chinese Communism.

worker, the miner, the artist, poet, scientist, the neurosurgeon, and everyone else.

Differently from in the USSR, equalitarian tendencies have asserted themselves strongly in China. During the "Cultural Revolution" the ignorant masses, the "poor and the blank," were extolled at the expense of the intellectuals. In December 1968 students and city-dwellers were sent to the countryside to be "reeducated" by the poor and the lower-middle-class peasants and to be given by them a "profound class education." The notion that class consciousness can be acquired in the villages rather than among workers in the factories represents a reversal—in the judgment of Moscow, a betrayal—of Leninist principles, and underlines the populist ideas embodied in Maoism.

While the differences that had emerged between the USSR and the CPR were varied, political, economic, and territorial, they were to a substantial extent also ideological, as indicated in the foregoing. Maoism extolled the doctrine of the Permanent Revolution and the eminent importance of China as model for the revolution of the undeveloped countries of the world, stressed the revolutionary role of the peasantry, and exalted Mao, Mao's Thought, and his voluntarism. It actually made the CPC an instrument of the personality cult and thus departed significantly from Leninism. Differently from the Soviet Union, Peking spurned rational economic planning, claimed that it had found a shortcut to Communism, laid stress on immediate equalitarianism in China, and challenged the Soviet Union's primacy in international Communism. It also questioned her domestic policies, going to the extreme of charging her with "restoration of capitalism" and accused her of abandoning her Marxist-Leninist creed.

After Khrushchev, 1964-1966

The coup that removed Khrushchev silenced the contending parties in Moscow and Peking. The personal antagonism between Khrushchev and Mao had been an important element in the dispute between the two sides. But to what extent its disappearance or the departure of one of the two contenders would affect the relationship between the CPR and the USSR could not be fully anticipated. Immediately after the coup both sides displayed cautious hope. Since under Khrushchev their relationship had reached bottom, some reasoned that now matters could only improve. But it soon became evident that most of the serious differences that had produced the rift in the first place, and a veritable explosion in 1963, were to continue and that Khrushchev's removal would not result in an abrupt change of course and in the sudden improvement of relations between the contesting parties. Khrushchev's successors, Kosygin and Brezhnev, displayed greater diplomatic circumspection and tactical restraint, but were unwilling to yield on the substance of policy.

The Central Committee of the CPSU moved quickly to set "unilaterally" an end to the public debate, which had deteriorated into a mudslinging match. The Chinese followed this example, though pro-Peking Communist Parties were apparently more difficult to restrain. The CPC also accepted the Soviet invitation to send to Moscow, on the occasion of the celebration of the forty-seventh anniversary of the October Revolution, a Chinese delegation, which was headed by Chou-En-lai, President of the Central Committee of the CPC and China's Premier.

The editorial of *People's Daily* on November 7, commemorating the forty-seventh anniversary of the October Socialist Revolution, was jubilant over the resignation of Khrushchev. It denounced him as "the chief representative" of modern revisionism, which in turn was pictured as the main danger to the international Communist movement. He had "betrayed" Leninism, proletarian internationalism, the legacy of the October Revolution, and the interests of the Soviet people. His removal from leading posts in the Party and the state was "a very good thing" and had the support of Marxist-Leninists and revolutionary people all over the world.[4] The Chinese people had always had the deepest respect for and confidence in the long-tested Soviet people and were convinced that the temporary difficulties that had arisen between China and the USSR and between the two Parties represented only a "historical episode" and would be "gradually resolved."

Soon thereafter an editorial in *Red Flag* similarly rejoiced that Khrushchev, the "archschemer who usurped the leadership of the Soviet Party and State," had finally been driven off the stage of history. This should prove beneficial to the revolutionary cause of the people all over the world. In opposing Stalin, Khrushchev had opposed Marxism-Leninism. There followed a long list of well-known "crimes" that he had committed: He had allegedly violated the 1957 Declaration and the 1960 Statement of the Moscow international conferences of Communist Parties, had catered to the nuclear blackmail of the United States, and had prevented socialist China from building up her own nuclear strength for self-defense. He had sponsored the doctrines of "peaceful" transition to socialism and "peaceful coexistence" with imperialism, which led him to adopt a hands-off policy in the Algerian struggle for national liberation and to stand aloof in the face of the American intervention in Vietnam. Khrushchev furthermore was castigated for his friendly attitude toward the Tito clique, his hostility against Albania, and his "hatred" for the CPC.

4. "Unite under the banner of the great October Revolution," *People's Daily*, Nov. 7, 1964 (*PR*, Nov. 13, 1964, pp. 14-17).

"He spread innumerable rumors and slanders against the CPC and Comrade Mao Tse-tung and resorted to every kind of baseness in his futile attempt to subvert socialist China. He perfidiously tore up several hundred agreements and contracts and arbitrarily withdrew more than one thousand Soviet experts working in China. He engineered border disputes between China and the Soviet Union and even conducted large-scale subversive activities in Sinkiang. He backed the reactionaries of India in their armed attacks on socialist China, and, together with the United States, incited and helped them to perpetuate armed provocations against China by giving them military aid."[5]

Charges against the Soviet Union, which the CPC in spite of everything had still refrained from making, were hurled against Khrushchev the moment he lost power. They revealed, of course, deep-seated anger not only against the dethroned leader, but also against the entire Soviet leadership. Peking escalated its accusations charging that Moscow engaged in subversive activities against Chinese territory itself and provoked Peking's enemies against the CPR.

Furthermore, Khrushchev had interfered in the internal affairs of other countries and Communist Parties, had encouraged subversive and disruptive activities among fraternal parties by bribing political "degenerates and renegades." He was made responsible for creating an open split in the international Communist movement. Khrushchev had endorsed revisionist policies leading the USSR even back to capitalism.

The catalogue of Khrushchev's "sins" was perhaps too long and the sins were of such terrifying magnitude as to stagger the imagination. Could one man alone, especially one who had "usurped" power, affect international relations and the mutual relationship between great Communist parties so adversely? Even *Red Flag* seemed to have its doubts. It prophesied—and thus belied its terrible indictment—that Khrushchev's removal would not favorably affect the course of history and of Russo-Chinese relations in particular. Even after Khrushchev, the road would be likely to continue to be a "tortuous" one.

Still, there was apparently a new spirit in Moscow, a few new hopes in Peking, and seemingly new opportunities rose on the horizon. Under such conditions the delegation of the CPC and of the CPR Government led by Chou En-lai journeyed to Moscow on the occasion of the forty-seventh anniversary of the October Socialist Revolution.

Chinese criticism of the new leadership was not long in coming. One week after the disappointing meeting with the Soviet leaders in Moscow in November 1964, *Red Flag* made it clear that it was up to the Soviet lead-

5. *Red Flag*, Nov. 27, 1964 (*PR*, Nov. 27, 1964, pp. 6f.).

ers to move toward conciliation—by abandoning their position.[6] At the same time the views of pro-Chinese Communist parties that had begun to renew their attacks against the Soviets were fully reprinted in the Chinese press.

The Chinese and the Soviet leadership were equally resolved to make not the slightest concession to the other side. Brezhnev's speech of November 6 gave no indication that Moscow, after having removed Khrushchev, intended to alter radically any portion of its domestic or foreign policy program.[7] On November 13, on the occasion of a formal meeting in Moscow between the Soviet leadership and the Chinese delegation, the latter was informed that no change in Soviet policy was contemplated. As *People's Daily* later reported, on November 19, 1964, the Chinese delegation was explicitly told "that there was not a shade of difference between themselves [the new leadership] and Khrushchev" on the question of the international Communist movement or of relations with China. Chou hurriedly returned to Peking.[8]

If the Chinese Communists had excoriated Khrushchev when he fell from power, Khrushchev later was to strike back at them with his memoirs. Against critics of his policy toward China who blamed him for the rise of differences with Mao and the CPC, Khrushchev argued persuasively that had Stalin lived only "a little longer," the conflict with Peking would have come out in the open earlier. Mao, he held, had never been able to reconcile himself to any other Communist Party being "in any way superior to his own" within the world Communist movement. Khrushchev was anxious to shift any responsibility for the worsening of Sino-Soviet relations from his own shoulders to others, especially to those of Soviet ambassador P. F. Yudin, who was originally asked by Mao to come to China to edit Mao's works, but who clashed with Mao on philosophical grounds.

In his memoirs, the authenticity of which has been questioned by some experts, Khrushchev devoted an entire chapter to the Sino-Soviet dispute. His account on this issue has the ring of truth and thus fortifies the case of those who are convinced of the basic authenticity of his work. According to Khrushchev, the Soviet government and he himself considered Mao a nationalist whose "chauvinism and arrogance sent a shiver" up his spine. (That Mao and the CPC might have felt similarly about the Soviets was apparently a thought that never occurred to Khrushchev.) He felt particu-

6. "Why Khrushchev fell?" *Red Flag*, Nov. 20, 1964, Nov. 21, 1964 (*PR*, Nov. 27, 1964, pp. 6-8).

7. *Pravda*, Nov. 7, 1964 (*CDSP* 16, no. 43 [Nov. 18, 1964]: 6-7, 9).

8. "The Anti-Chinese Statements by the New Leadership of the CPSU and their Followers," *People's Daily*, Nov. 10, 1965 (*PR*, Nov. 12, 1965).

larly repelled by Mao's discursions about the "distinctiveness" of the Chinese culture and language, and was of course especially shocked about the extensive territorial claims presented to the USSR, which included Vladivostok. Khrushchev felt it also "incredible" that Mao could dismiss American imperialism and the atomic bomb in particular as a "paper tiger" and found his military thinking, which dwelt on the number of Chinese divisions, "out of date." He also admitted being unable to penetrate the secret of Communist China's real views on peaceful coexistence. It is less comprehensible that he was unable to understand Mao's refusal to grant the Soviet Union a submarine base in the CPR when he points out: "We've had the British and other foreigners on our territory for years now, and we're not going to let anyone use our land for their own purposes again."

Khrushchev underscored the propagandistic need for distinguishing between Mao and the ruling clique on the one hand and the Chinese people on the other, leaving the question open whether it was not just tactics and opportunism that made him and the Soviets insist on this distinction. "If we started reviling the Chinese people, we would be stepping over the line that separates objective analysis from nationalistic prejudice" and the Soviet people would then be guilty of chauvinism. But Khrushchev also disclosed that it was fear of "Chinese" ideas spreading to the USSR that motivated the Soviet leadership. In 1962 Khrushchev "discovered" that the Soviet Ministry of Defense under Marshall Malinovsky, a usually intelligent man, was publishing the military works of Mao in Russian, and bawled him out for this "stupid waste of time": the Soviet army had crushed the crack forces of the German army, while Mao's men have spent "twenty-five years poking each other in the backsides with knives and bayonets!"

In this and other cases Khrushchev was plainly afraid that Chinese conceptions would be disseminated throughout the USSR and would adversely affect Soviet life. He revealed that China's egalitarian reforms "came across the border and started circulating widely in Soviet Siberia." Khrushchev, according to his account, thereupon told his comrades: "This must stop immediately. The slogans of the Chinese reforms are very alluring. You're mistaken if you don't think the seeds of these ideas will find fertile soil in our country." Clearly the Soviets were fearful not only of the spread of Western ideas into the USSR, but also of breezes coming from the East!

Khrushchev had now unceremoniously departed from power and for a short moment Peking rejoiced. But on the very same day on which Chou returned from Moscow in November 1964, there went on sale in the Soviet capital the November issue of the Russian edition of *Problems of Peace and Socialism,* edited by A. M. Rumyantsev, member of the CC of the CPSU. It contained a large number of articles in which the CPC was attacked by name. Y. P. Andropov, Secretary of the CC of the CPSU, therein levied against Peking the serious charge of promoting splitting activities in the international Communist movement. The publication of this issue, several weeks after the fall of Khrushchev, was an unmistakable sign that the new Moscow leadership was not prepared to abandon Khrushchev's China policy, but, rather, was determined to pursue it. Both sides remained convinced of the righteousness of their cause and of the deep-seated hostility of the opponent. Thus Khrushchev's fall was to give merely a short pause in the relentless war of words and hostile acts of both sides.[9]

People's Daily in Peking later accused the new leadership of the CPSU of having pursued "Khrushchevism without Khrushchev."[10] Since assuming office, the new leadership had persisted in the general line laid down at the Twentieth and Twenty-Second Party Congresses of the CPSU and in their revisionist program of so-called "peaceful coexistence," "peaceful competition," and "peaceful transition," which had also featured the doctrines of the "state of the whole people" and "the Party of the entire people." The new leaders had energetically pressed ahead with the policy of Russo-American collaboration for world domination and had gone further in undermining the unity of the socialist camp and the international Communist movement. While talking about Soviet-Chinese relations, they were engaged in anti-Chinese activities, in spreading rumors and slanders to malign the CPC.

In December 1964 the new Soviet leaders resumed their counteroffensive by proposing that a drafting committee of twenty-six parties convene in Moscow on March 1, 1965, to tackle the outstanding problems that caused the deep division in international Communism. The meeting, attended by only eighteen parties, urged that a new conference be called. While Moscow claimed that this meeting was a great success, Peking came closer to the truth when it described the convention as a "fragmented," "divisive," and "gloomy and forlorn affair."[11] It was hardly coincidental that while this meeting was taking place, demonstrations against the United States' Embassy in Moscow, apparently staged by Chinese and Vietnamese students, led to violent clashes and to suppression by the Soviet police.

9. *Khrushchev Remembers*, pp. 463-79. Also Andropov in "Problems of Peace and Socialism" (*CDSP* 16, no. 43 [Nov. 18, 1964]).
10. See n 6 above (*PR*, p. 8).
11. Editorial Departments of *People's Daily and Red Flag*, "A Comment on the March Moscow Meeting," *People's Daily*, March 22, 1965 (*PR*, March 26, 1965).

The Second Afro-Asian Conference, 1965

In the early sixties China and Indonesia suggested calling a second Afro-Asian conference. The first Afro-Asian conference had been held at Bandung in April 1955. Though the Soviet Union had not attended the Bandung Conference, Khrushchev's successors were anxious that a Soviet delegation attend the second Afro-Asian conference. At a preparatory meeting, held in Djakarta in April 1964, it had been decided to hold the conference in March 1965.

After the Djakarta meeting the Chinese delegate, Chen Yi, however, had bluntly asserted that the Soviet Union as an allegedly non-Asiatic power had no business at the forthcoming conference. The Soviet Union, as *Pravda* later restated the Soviet position, was certainly not only a European, but also an Asian country. This was known to every elementary school pupil. Chinese leaders themselves, less than six years ago, had also held to this view. It was "quite obvious" to *Pravda* that the Peking leaders would like to "cut off" the Soviets from the anti-imperialist front created at the 1955 Bandung conference, that they would like to isolate the peoples of Asia and Africa who were fighting for their consolidation and independence and for the liberation of those who were still suffering under the colonial yoke.[12] The CPC leaders wanted the new anti-imperialist bloc, once created, to follow "the Chinese line" in world politics and to claim for Peking "the role of a leading center which would issue instructions to the young developing countries as to what they should or should not do." *Pravda* however, reminded all concerned that the political support of the Soviet Union and the other socialist states for national liberation had proven to be of great importance. The Soviet veto in the Security Council of the United Nations had frequently been an obstacle to the imperialists in their attempts to harass various detachments of the national liberation movement.

The Chinese position was presented with brutal frankness by the *People's Daily Observer* on May 31, 1964. The paper went so far as to dispute as untenable the Soviet argument that the USSR, two-thirds of whose territory lay in Asia, was therefore also an Asiatic country. Each state was a single entity and could not be characterized as an Asian as well as a European state "simply because its territory extends over both continents."[13] The USSR was reminded that three-fourths of the Soviet population lived in Europe and that the political center of the Soviet Union

12. "Who profits by the isolation of the peoples of Asia and Africa?", *Pravda*, Apr. 26, 1964.
13. "What right have Soviet Leaders to issue orders to Asian and African countries?" *People's Daily* Observer, May 31, 1964 (*PR*, June 5, 1964).

had always been in Europe. Also, in 1955 she had abstained from participation in the Bandung Conference. In the United Nations the Soviet Union likewise had not been invited to join the Afro-Asian group. The Asian union republics of the Soviet Union were component parts of the Soviet Union and not states independent of her. Naturally, they could not take part in the summit conference of independent Asian-African states. Referring to the principle adopted at Djakarta of reaching unanimity through consultation—meaning, of course, giving each consultant the right to a veto—Peking expressed its opinion that the decision not to invite the USSR was irrevocable.

The Soviets, in support of their claim to the right to participate in Afro-Asian conferences, were shying away from obvious geographical, geopolitical, and also legal arguments, and rather stressed pragmatic considerations. They focused upon the tangible services that the USSR had rendered in the past and could offer to the national liberation movement in the future. A policy, wrote *Pravda,* aimed at weakening the bonds of friendship and solidarity between the peoples of the Soviet Union on the one hand and the other peoples of Asia and the peoples of Africa on the other, would benefit only imperialism and could inflict great harm on the national liberation movement. *Pravda* recalled the position of the USSR from 1956—at the time of "the triple aggression against Egypt"—on the West's intervention in Lebanon and Jordan in 1958, and Soviet reaction up to 1965, underlining the indebtedness of Asia and Africa to the Soviet Union's policies, aside from her invaluable assistance to the cause of economic development of the newly liberated countries of Asia, Africa, and Latin America.[14]

About a week leter, on June 18, 1965, *People's Daily* rejected the substance of the Soviet brief for participation in the planned conference. The planned Afro-Asian gathering was supposed to be a conference of the heads of states of Afro-Asian countries. Therefore its participants had to be Asian or African countries, or national liberation organizations of Asia or Africa. All the Asian and African countries, *People's Daily* asserted, had to a greater or lesser extent "suffered or were suffering" imperialist and colonial aggression and oppression. Soviet Russia was thus reminded of being in a different category. Also, with few exceptions, almost all of the Afro-Asian countries were economically backward.[15]

The Chinese paper brusquely rejected arguments in support of the Soviet plea for participation in the Conference as "absurd," as aimed "at making

14. "Strengthen the unity of forces. . . , *Pravda,* June 12, 1965 (*CDSP* 17, no. 24 [July 7, 1965]: 6-7).
15. "Soviet Union is not qualified to participate in African and Asian Conference," *People's Daily,* June 18, 1965 (*PR,* June 25, 1965).

trouble'' and unable to stand the least refutation. China's opposition, however, *People's Daily* in conclusion assured all concerned, had nothing to do with Sino-Soviet ideological controversies.

On the very eve of the second Afro-Asian Conference, which was to open its doors in Algiers, President Ben Bella of Algeria was overthrown and replaced by Defense Minister H. Boumedienne. This threw the conference into turmoil.[16] Against the opposition of a small group of states led by China, the conference was postponed until November, and later indefinitely. China had continued to insist on the exclusion of the USSR from the conference, but after encountering overwhelming opposition, had produced a *volte-face* and come out for the postponement of the conference. It was quite apparent that China had overreached herself. The extremes to which she had gone were also a clear indication of the abyss that had come to separate the two great Communist powers.

The Chinese setback at the conference was closely followed by the destruction of the Indonesian Communist Party, the strongest pro-Peking Communist Party in Asia and in the world, and thus by additional loss of face for Communist China.

The Indonesian Revolt, September-October, 1965

Politically Indonesia was virtually split into two camps: one was the Communist Party of Indonesia (Partai Kommunis Indonesia) under its leader, Aidit, the other was the rightist army, led by Defense Minister Nasution. Sukarno, the father of the Indonesian Revolution with its strange tricolor of nationalism, religion, and Communism, held the hostile forces apart, played them against each other, but inclined toward the PKI. To many in the West it appeared that Indonesia under the leadership of Sukarno, who was gravely ill, was plunging down the Communist precipice. But it was toward the CPR, not the USSR, that Indonesia was moving ideologically. When in 1964 Indonesia made the startling decision to withdraw from the U.N., the CPR alone had applauded this precipitate and reckless move. She also supported Indonesia's policy of confrontation with Malaysia. Sukarno in return granted new privileges to the pro-Chinese PKI. China appeared to Indonesia as a trusted ally. Though Soviet Russia had fully equipped Indonesia's armed forces and given the country generous economic assistance, her influence seemed to be dwindling rapidly.

On September 30, 1965, a Council of Generals suppressed an Indonesian uprising, in the course of which several military leaders had been

16. *Pravda*, Aug. 15, 1965 (*CDSP* 17, no. 33 [Sept. 8, 1965]).

assassinated. The aftermath of the rebellion, which the PKI had belatedly joined, was a slaughter of the Chinese minority in Indonesia; at the same time many of the leading cadres of the PKI, including Aidit himself, were killed. The generals were firmly in the saddle, Sukarno's position was reduced to that of a figurehead—he became a virtual prisoner, and the PKI was destroyed.[17] Communist China lost her closest ally. The USSR, which had already written off her investment in Indonesia as a bad debt, expressed no grief over the spectacle of a defeat for China. In the words of a leading student of Soviet foreign policy, the USSR did not see fit to administer to the Indonesian government "even a slap on the wrist," such as the temporary suspension of diplomatic relations.[18]

The reactions of Moscow and Peking to the adverse events in Indonesia, the destruction of the Communist Party, which had seemed so close to seizing power, varied according to their different interests. On October 8, *Pravda,* repeating the statement of the Politburo of the PKI that the Party had "nothing to do" with the September 30 movement and was innocent of the charges leveled against it by the victorious rightist generals, revealed not only the bankruptcy of Indonesian Communism but also the confusion reigning in Moscow.[19] Peking was even more perplexed than Moscow. It was not before October 18 that Djawoto, Indonesia's ambassador, was summoned to Peking's Ministry of Foreign Affairs and handed the first of what would become innumerable formal letters of protest. This protest, like those which followed it, was limited to such petty matters as the harassment of Chinese correspondents and diplomatic personnel and the raiding of the Chinese Embassy or of Chinese consular offices, rather than dealing with the brutal killing of either Indonesian Communists or of members of the local Chinese community in Indonesia.[20] Communist China seemed more engrossed with proper interstate relations and "bourgeois" proprieties of International Law than with fraternal help for Indonesian comrades and with ethnic and racial concern for its own Chinese kinfolk, a hapless and exposed minority whose very survival was threatened in the raging Indonesian storm.

In the midst of apparent atrocities, *Pravda* called for an end to vengeance and appealed to the military authorities not to commit rash acts.[21] But Soviet press reaction, while bitter and indignant at the excesses that were encouraged or condoned by the Indonesian military authorities, was

17. *New York Times,* Oct. 31, 1965; see also *PR,* Oct. 22, 1965, p. 5.

18. Ulam, *Expansion and Coexistence. The History of Soviet Russian Foreign Policy* (Washington, D.C., 1968), p. 718.

19. *Pravda,* Oct. 8, 1965.

20. "China lodges strong protest with Indonesian Government," *PR,* Oct. 22, 1965, p. 5.

21. *Pravda,* Oct. 18, 1965 (*CDSP* 17, no. 42 [Nov. 10, 1965]: 13); also *Izvestiia,* Nov. 19, 1965 (*CDSP* 17, no. 46 [Dec. 8, 1965]: 18).

not threatening. The USSR, just as did Communist China, seemed to have a realistic appreciation of the limits of her power.

The Soviet press never mentioned the close connection between the PKI and the CPC. Even after the virtual destruction of the former, it carefully refrained from informing its own reading public of the strong appeal that the CPC had exerted on the Communists of Indonesia. (Strangely enough, it also ignored the persecution of the overseas Chinese minority in Indonesia.) On the other hand, the CPSU could hardly gloat openly at the debacle of Peking and the inglorious end of a pro-Peking-oriented Communist Party. But in view of the deep rift with Peking, it must not have been displeased at the startling turn of events in Indonesia and the loss of prestige suffered by the CPC. By demonstrating restraint in its criticism of the new Indonesian rulers while they ruthlessly crushed the Chinese minority and eliminated every kind of Chinese influence, the USSR may have hoped to ride out the anti-Communist storm and stage a comeback in Indonesia in better times.

China, for obvious geographic, ethnic, and political reasons and because of the strength of the CPI, was incomparably more deeply involved in Indonesian affairs than the USSR, and her helplessness and loss of face were unquestionably shattering experiences. Peking had repeatedly hurled the insult of being a mere "paper tiger" at both the U.S.A. and the Soviet Union. Now she herself was revealed as utterly powerless and unable to stem the tide of events in a geographically adjoining region.

In the first days after the successful coup of the generals, the Chinese dailies, like the Soviet press, first denied and ridiculed the involvement of the PKI in the September 30 movement, allegedly designed to seize power by the extreme Left. Soon, however, Hsinshua went to great lengths to underscore the anti-Chinese sentiments of the military counter-revolution and denounced the hooligan demonstrators and the Council of Generals as both CIA-controlled.[22] Like the Russian press, perhaps with greater conviction, the Chinese press still praised Sukarno—whose permanent loss of power and prestige could not yet be fully ascertained—for representing sanity and moderation in the midst of atrocities and chaos. As the unspeakable excesses against the Chinese minority in Indonesia became more widely known, the Peking press belatedly denounced the outrageous persecution.

Within a period of two months the Peking-Djakarta axis had been broken. From being a close ally, Djakarta now moved into the opposite corner, becoming a rabid enemy. Peking overflowed with frustration, being unable to help either the CPI or its own people, the beleaguered Chinese minority in the Indonesian islands.

22. *PR*, Oct. 22, 1965, p. 9.

The Indonesian events represented no direct clash of interests between the two Communist superpowers. With the annihilation of Indonesian Communism, both Peking and Moscow were among the official mourners. Moscow, however, which had long lost its grip on Indonesia, had suffered little loss and, privately, shed few tears. In view of the hot dispute with Peking, the latter's loss must have caused some satisfaction in Moscow and, looked at from the narrow angle of Sino-Soviet differences, represented a gain for it.

The War in Vietnam

At the time of the Tonkin Gulf incident in August 1964, the United States of America proposed that the Security Council of the United Nations place this matter on its agenda. North Vietnam, which had reason to suspect the impartiality of the United Nations, sharply opposed this move. Communist China joined North Vietnam in protesting the Tonkin Gulf provocation, warning that aggression against the Vietnam Democratic Republic meant "aggression against China." Peking also warned that no socialist country could "sit idly by" while North Vietnam was attacked by the United States, thus raising the specter of a possible Chinese intervention and a repetition of the fighting on the Korean pattern. At the same time China, like North Vietnam and for many of the same reasons, opposed the United Nations' "poking a hand in the question of Indo-China."

At one time the Soviet government had seemed prepared to withdraw from Indo-China and leave North Vietnam in the Chinese camp. But in the summer of 1964 it began to reexamine its foreign policy in Southeast Asia. The USSR apparently desired to reestablish Soviet predominance in North Vietnam and defeat China in her own backyard, in North Vietnam and possibly also in North Korea. In November 1964 the Soviets issued a statement containing a firm promise of support for North Vietnam in the event of an attack by the United States. Soon thereafter the National Liberation Front of South Vietnam was permitted to set up headquarters in Moscow. But at the same time the USSR, according to a later Chinese account, transmitted an American warning to Hanoi to stop supporting its partisans in South Vietnam, especially to stop the attacks on South Vietnamese cities. The Chinese leaders were quick to criticize Soviet willingness to convey to Hanoi "these preposterous demands" that aimed at forcing the Vietnamese people into unconditional surrender.[23] They accused Moscow of running errands for the United States aggressors, who were anxious to find a way out of their predicament in Vietnam.

The American attack, on February 7, 1965, against various targets in

23. *People's Daily*, Nov. 11, 1965 (*PR*, Nov. 12, 1965 "Refutation of the new leaders of the CPSU . . .").

North Vietnam represented a turning point in the history of the war in Vietnam. The attack was depicted as a retaliatory move against the attack on the American base at Pleiku in South Vietnam by the forces of the National Liberation Front.

It appeared that at that very moment the USSR was ready to take the diplomatic initiative in Indo-China. On the morning of February 7 (in the evening of the same day occurred the American bombing raids against the North Vietnamese targets) Kosygin, visiting Hanoi at the invitation of North Vietnam, condemned the United States, but came out in favor of peaceful coexistence and of a negotiated settlement in Indo-China. For the first time he committed the USSR to the support of a Geneva conference on Indo-China.

While journeying to and returning from Hanoi, Kosygin stopped each time in Peking; he also visited North Korea. According to the Chinese account, Kosygin, while exchanging views with the Chinese leaders, stressed the need to help the United States find a way out of Vietnam. But Peking expressed the hope that the new leaders of the CPSU would support the struggle of the Vietnamese people and "not make a deal" with the United States on Vietnam. Kosygin then voiced agreement with the views of the leaders of the CPC, but thereafter, according to Peking, the new leaders of the CPSU reneged on their promises.[24]

Pursuing this line of criticism and harking back to President Johnson's "fraudulent game of 'unconditional discussions,' " Peking accused the Soviet government of having, after Kosygin's return to Moscow, placed before Vietnam and China a proposal that was in fact identical with Johnson's demands. In a nutshell, the Soviet purpose was to help the United States bring about peace talks "by deception, peace talks which would allow the United States to hang on in South Vietnam indefinitely."[25] Whatever the motives Peking ascribed to Moscow, the latter was then genuinely interested in arranging an international conference, but its plans, and France's and Britain's parallel projects, came to naught due to the resistance of the United States to carrying on negotiations at that time.

At the same time, the Soviet initiative for a meeting of the representatives of three Parties, those of North Vietnam, the USSR, and China, for the purpose of rendering assistance to Hanoi and discussing measures of joint cooperation, ran into Chinese opposition. The Soviets underlined the need for "unity of action" to bring effective assistance to North Vietnam. According to the Chinese, Soviet proposals involved sending via China a regular army formation of 4,000 men to be stationed in Vietnam, all this allegedly without first obtaining the consent of the Hanoi government. As

24. *Ibid.*
25. *Ibid.*

the letter of the CC of the CPC of July 14, 1965, to its counterpart of the CPSU further specified: "Under the pretext of defending the territorial air of Vietnam you wanted to occupy and use one or two airfields in Southwest China and to station a Soviet armed force of 500 men there. You also wanted to open an air corridor in China and obtain for Soviet aeroplanes the privilege of free traffic in her air space."[26]

It was quite apparent that Communist China rejected Soviet proposals because of plain mistrust of the "ulterior motives" of the USSR. Peking was keenly conscious of the need of protecting her own sovereignty regarding territory and air space and that of her North Vietnamese neighbor against the Soviet Union, even in the face of the American threat. Peking, charging Moscow with "collusion" with United States imperialism, was also fearful that Moscow, especially in view of what it called "Khrushchev's evil practice of control under cover of aid," was determined to gain control in North Vietnam and China under the guise of rendering assistance to hard-pressed Hanoi.

The CPC's attitude toward the war in Vietnam, the U.S., and the USSR found expression in a long address of Lin Piao and in the declaration of the army general staff Lo Jui-ch'ing. Lin Piao's speech had the effect of a bombshell in some circles of the West, though its basic ideas were by no means novel and had been articulated by Peking before. Its major significance, despite superficial bellicose appearances to the contrary, lay probably in the advice apparently tendered to Hanoi to base its continued struggle against the American "aggressor" on Mao's guerrilla strategy, to stress self-reliance—just as the CPC had done in its own Civil War and in the war of resistance against Japan, and, in spite of the absence of outright Chinese and Soviet military intervention, refuse to take a "gloomy view" of the war.

To give at least verbal encouragement to Hanoi, Lin Piao stressed once again the thesis that imperialism and all reactionaries were only "paper tigers."[27] This was also in accordance with Mao's advice that "one must depise the enemy strategically" (though tactically he should be taken seriously). Lin recalled China's revolutionary precept to gain control of the countryside first and only then to spread revolution to the encircled cities, and based his analysis of the world situation and prognosis of future global developments on the Chinese experience. His comparing North

26. CC, CPC, to CC, CPSU, July 14, 1965, quoted by Crankshaw, in *Observer*, Nov. 14, 1965.

27. Lin Piao, "Long Live the Victory of People's War," *People's Daily*, Sept. 2, 1965 (*PR*, Sept. 3, 1965, pp. 9-30); Lo Jui-ch'ing, "People defeated Japanese fascism and they can certainly defeat US imperialism too," *People's Daily*, Sept. 2, 1965 (*PR*, Sept. 3, 1965, pp. 31-39); see also W. E. Griffith, *Sino-Soviet Relations, 1964-65*, pp. 110-14.

America and Western Europe, "the cities of the world," to China's cities and Asia, Africa, and Latin America to the revolutionary Chinese countryside may have intimidated some people in the West, but nothing seemed further from Lin Piao's mind or that of the Chinese Communist leadership at that moment than actively to engage in armed intervention in Vietnam. Perhaps the Peking leadership might have feared an American invasion of China and in apparent boldness defied the United States to send troops into their country: it warned that a few million American "aggressor troops" would be submerged in "the vast ocean" of several hundred million Chinese people. At the same time Lin Piao assailed the Khrushchev revisionists as "betrayers" of the "people's war" who had no faith in the masses and were afraid of American imperialism. Communist China was not "bellicose," but resolved to use revolutionary bellicosity to cope with counterrevolutionary belligerence. Though war brought destruction and suffering, it could also "push history forward. In this sense war is a great school."

Though Lin Piao assured Hanoi that the determination of the Chinese people to support and aid the Vietnamese in their struggle against U.S. aggression and for "national salvation"—meaning unification with South Vietnam—was "unshakable," he refrained from making definite pledges to Hanoi. Instead, he recommended to Hanoi the most important of Communist China's "methods" of fighting American "aggression," namely, "mobilizing the people, reliance on the people, making everyone a soldier and waging a people's war." He further advised not to "lean wholly on foreign aid, even though this be aid from socialist countries which persist in revolution"—meaning, of course, China. The main thrust of the article was unmistakable; so also were the side-blows against the U.S. and the USSR.

Actually, the position of Lin and the Chinese leadership in the fall of 1965 in regard to the war in Vietnam and the great powers involved in it turned out to be an accurate anticipation of the CPC's policies in regard to Vietnam.

At the tri-continental conference in Havana in January 1966, the Soviet delegation, apparently to blunt Chinese criticism, came out in behalf of creating an international aid organization to help North Vietnam. But the Chinese were by no means mollified by the new Soviet suggestion. They apparently feared that even an international organization would be subject to Soviet maneuvering and wanted North Vietnam to receive aid directly from other countries. They especially criticized the Soviet delegation for "saying nothing" about the contributions made by the Vietnamese people's anti-imperialist patriotic struggle toward the revolutionary struggles of the people of the whole world, but "keeping on boasting about

Soviet 'aid' " in terms of aircraft, rockets, and other modern weapons to Vietnam.[28] The Chinese delegation supported the position of the Indonesian delegation that the Vietnamese people's "victory" in the fight against United States aggression was primarily a result of their own struggle and that, besides, it was not only a matter of the socialist countries helping Vietnam but of the Vietnamese people, by their courageous struggle, supporting all other peoples of the world.

Further, the Chinese delegate pointed out that, in seeking to mislead the world, the Soviet delegates had "played up" the question of transport for Soviet aid supplies to Vietnam. It was a lie that China had obstructed the transit of material for Vietnam. The Soviets merely wanted to "use aid" as a means to intervene in Vietnam, to obtain capital with which to bargain with the United States, and to stir up anti-Chinese sentiments at the conference and bring about a split in the name of "united action."

The Chinese must have been aware that their position on help to Vietnam was unpopular among Communists and was also likely to subject them to sharp criticism throughout the "third world." Their stand obviously harmed the struggle against imperialism in Vietnam by undercutting every possibility of united action. But their fear that the USSR might gain increased influence in Hanoi and with the National Liberation Front and obtain even a minor foothold in China apparently outweighed all other considerations. In a letter to the CC of the CPSU the CPC Central Committee, on July 14, 1965, accused Moscow in regard to Vietnam of practicing great-power chauvinism toward fraternal countries and of attempting to gain military control over them and "hitch them to the chariot of Soviet-United States collaboration for the domination of the world." It charged Moscow with only talking about "united action" but in practice undermining it and carrying on "incessantly. . .anti-Chinese propaganda, . . .constantly spreading lies about China," and aiming at the role of the "father Party" among the "fraternal Parties."[29] The mistakes that the CPSU had committed in regard to Vietnam were the "inevitable result" of its obdurate pursuit of the revisionist line, as laid down by the Twentieth and Twenty-Second Congresses and in the programme of the Soviet Communist Party.

Parts of the foregoing letter were incorporated into the *Red Flag* and the *People's Daily* article "Refutation of the new leaders of the CPSU on 'United Action,' " published in November 1965. While the Chinese accused the Soviets of helping the American aggressor, the Soviets in *Pravda* made their countercharge, leveling this very accusation against the CPR.

28. Hsinshua, "The First Afro-Asian-Latin American People's Solidarity Conference (*PR*, Jan. 21 1966).
29. See n 26 above.

The Soviets repeatedly accused Communist China of obstructing Soviet aid to Vietnam, accusations that were regularly and vehemently denied by the CPC. But the Chinese indirectly conceded that Soviet aid by air was prohibited by Peking when they claimed that Communist China did her utmost to speed to Vietnam all military matériel "in overland transit." According to the Soviets, even in regard to overland transit the Chinese engaged in obstruction.[30] The Chinese also wanted to make permission for the transit of military goods contingent on a declaration by Hanoi that it would accept them. This would have necessitated advance approval by Hanoi for every single Soviet shipment. Communist China was apparently unwilling to have a growing number of Soviet troops and Soviet experts on North Vietnamese soil.

Dispute over aid to North Vietnam appears to have developed first during the summer of 1965, though it was not yet publicized at that time. The Chinese also accused the Soviets of their aid's being neither in quality nor quantity commensurate with their country's strength. In reply the Soviets often quoted North Vietnamese sources that had expressed gratitude and appreciation for Soviet help rendered. These North Vietnamese utterances, however, could hardly be taken at face value. In view of her dependence, North Vietnam could not engage in public polemics with the powerful Chinese neighbor about obstacles raised by Peking to the speedy transit of badly needed Soviet military supplies to Hanoi. Hanoi, threatened by the United States, could not afford to make remonstrations and throw down challenges to either Moscow or Peking.

In 1966 and 1967 the Soviet campaign against Chinese obstructionism in the matter of overland transit of Soviet military equipment destined for North Vietnam grew in intensity. The Soviet press went so far as to repeat Western stories about China's having allegedly sold steel to the United States to be used in North Vietnam. The United States, Moscow also asserted, would not have dared to bomb North Vietnam if Soviet missiles and anti-aircraft batteries had not been held up in China.[31] The *People's Daily,* on the other hand, disavowed stories according to which Red Guards had removed Russian trade marks from the military shipments on the way to North Vietnam and replaced them with Chinese characters. The *People's Daily* denounced these accusations as being patently designed to drive a wedge between the Chinese and Vietnamese peoples.[32]

On May 3, 1966, the Chinese Foreign Ministry rejected the charges made by the Soviet Minister of National Defense, Malinovsky in a speech in Budapest on April 21, that Communist China obstructed Soviet aid to

30. Letter of CPSU, CC of Jan. 1966 in *Die Welt,* March 21, 1966.
31. Moscow Radio station, quoted by Gittings, p. 258.
32. "New Disciples of Goebbels," *People's Daily,* March 1, 1967 (*PR*, March 10, 1967).

Vietnam and charged the Soviet marshal with plainly "lying" about these matters.[33] Marshal Malinovsky ought to know that, besides ground and air communications, there were sea routes to link various countries in the world. It was quite wrong to say that aid could not be rendered in the absence of a common boundary. The Soviet Union had no common boundary with far-away Cuba, yet she could ship rocket weapons to and from Cuba. Since Vietnam was closer, "why can't she ship even conventional weapons there?" Also, the USSR had no common boundary with India, yet it had shipped large quantities of military matériel there to help Indian reactionaries attack China. "The heart of the matter was that the Soviet revisionist clique had already degenerated into an accomplice of United States imperialism. Its so-called aid to Vietnam is a sham. Its real aim is to oppose China, Vietnam, and all people persevering in revolution. What it hankers after is world domination through United States-Soviet collaboration."

The Chinese apparently were hoping that Soviet aid carried over sea routes to Vietnam might involve the USSR in a showdown with the United States of America. Their negative attitude toward all American moves aimed at bringing the conflict in Vietnam to a peaceful solution in turn aroused Soviet suspicion. The Soviets accused Peking of needing "a long conflict in Vietnam" in order to keep up the international tension and to picture China as a "besieged fortress." The CPSU Central Committee charged that one of the political objectives of the Chinese leaders in the Vietnam affair was to provoke a military conflict between the USSR and the United States of America. They wished the USSR to clash with the United States "in order to be able, as they themselves say, 'to sit on the mountain and to watch the battle of the tigers.' "

On December 14, 1966, *Pravda* denounced the "duplicity of the Chinese leaders' policy," which was growing more and more evident in the international arena. On the one hand they were trying to impose on the fraternal parties the kind of course that would lead to continual deterioration of the international situation and ultimately to war, allegedly for the sake of world revolution. On the other hand, the Peking leaders themselves were pursuing a line calculated to leave them outside the struggle against imperialism. They never missed a chance to develop relations with capitalist countries, including the United States of America. It was revealing that the Western press constantly emphasized that the escalation in Peking's noisy campaign against the United States was purely verbal.[34]

Communist China's position on the war in Vietnam did hurt her prestige

33. Statement of Foreign Ministry's Spokesman, May 3, "Malinovsky is a liar," *PR*, May 6, 1966.
34. *Pravda*, Dec. 14, 1966.

and image in the Communist and non-Communist world. Her verbal bravadoes were of course in striking contrast to her cautious passivity, faced with what she did not cease to denounce as a United States imperialist adventure next door. Her "Cultural Revolution" underlined her preoccupation with domestic rather than international affairs. Her growing isolation in the world and in world Communism laid her open to Soviet attacks. The Soviets, themselves a target of the continued Chinese charges of collusion with the United States, angrily countercharged that since the beginning of the "Cultural Revolution" Chinese pledges to Vietnam had gradually eroded. They accused China of being prepared for military action only in the event of a direct American attack upon China. They thus raised the specter of a "tacit agreement" between America and Communist China, of a collusion of their own, as they tried to turn the table on Peking.

8

From the "Cultural Revolution" to Military Conflict, 1965-1969

The "Cultural Revolution." Charges and Countercharges

Moscow's deep concerns about the most recent developments in the CPR were soon reflected in the Soviet press. On September 27, 1966, *Izvestiia* criticized the Great Proletarian "Cultural Revolution" in China by contrasting it with the Leninist cultural revolution, with its allegedly characteristic respect for true culture, appreciation of knowledge and books, and its esteem for the world of learning and scholarship.[1] The Party of the Bolsheviks, the vanguard of the working class, *Izvestiia* continued, had formed its first government from among people who had written more books than some European professors. Lenin himself had been a "true luminary of culture." *Izvestiia* raised the question how a proletarian "Cultural Revolution" could ever reject knowledge. In view of the widely known outrages then committed in China under the name of the "Cultural Revolution," it left the contrasting of the genuine thing with mere sham, of the USSR with the CPR, to the reader.

A few months later *Pravda* wrote as follows: "What is being done in China under the guise of cultural revolution in fact has nothing to do with it."[2] Several years later the Hungarian Communist Party chief Janos Kadar commented similarly that the "cultural revolution" in China was nothing but the evil spirit of nationalism, anarchy, and devastation that had broken loose in the CPR.[3] By giving conspicuous display to Kadar's utterances,

1. *Izvestiia*, Sept. 27, 1966.
2. *Pravda*, Nov. 27, 1966 (*CDSP* 18, no. 47 [Dec. 14, 1966]).
3. *Pravda*, and *Izvestiia*, July 4, 1968, pp. 2-3 (*CDSP* 20, no. 27 [July 24, 1968]: 8).

Pravda and *Izvestiia* obviously endorsed this view. And L. Lvov in *Pravda* pointed to the political character of the alleged "Cultural Revolution," which was recently admitted by its organizers. Under the flag of the "Cultural Revolution," Mao and his entourage were actually pursuing a course aimed at establishing their absolute dictatorship in the country. Mao's group, realizing that it would be unable by ordinary methods to transform the Chinese working people into "docile cogs" and "obedient buffaloes," had decided to resort to outright coercion of the Party and the people.[4]

By May of 1968, when the tumultous waves of the Great Proletarian Cultural Revolution had already made deep inroads, and when its character, while still baffling people in China and beyond it, had emerged in sharper outlines, *Kommunist,* focusing on "The Nature of the 'Cultural Revolution' in China," described how by 1966 China's grave economic situation and patent failures in the foreign policy field—her loss of international prestige and growing isolation—had exacerbated discontent in the Party and among the people. Mao had seen in this mood and attitude a direct threat to his autocracy and his political doctrine. To perpetuate his name and become the symbol of the faith of the Chinese people "for tens of thousands of years," he had unleashed the "Cultural Revolution." Its goals were to suppress oppositionist attitudes, to assert Mao's absolute dictatorship, and to excise from the people's consciousness the correct conception of Marxism and Leninism.[5]

Mao and his group, exploiting the nation's illiteracy—more than 300 million remained completely illiterate in China—were, according to *Kommunist,* attempting to rally the people, especially the younger generation, on the basis of reactionary ideas and the concepts of nationalism and alleged racial superiority of the Chinese over other peoples. The cult of Mao, which had been raised to the level of idolatry, was supported by resort to violence and outright reprisals against everyone who was dissatisfied or merely doubtful. "Storm detachments" of young people and the army, "indoctrinated in the spirit of fanaticism," became the chief tools of this violence. Mao had trained an organization of pogromists and its first target became the creative intelligentsia, in particular its Party stratum.

Mao could not strike directly at the leading Party and state cadres. Thus his political campaign had to be camouflaged as having cultural connotations and was passed off as a movement of the popular masses against "bourgeois culture." But thereafter the attack was shifted against the Party and state cadres. Under the guise of wresting power from those who allegedly followed a capitalist path, Mao was able to disclaim responsibility

4. *Pravda*, Jan. 11, 1969, pp. 4-5 (*CDSP* 21, no. 2 [1969]: 3).
5. *Kommunist,* No. 7, May 1968, pp. 103-14.

for past setbacks and place it on the shoulders of real or potential rivals. As a result of the internecine struggle, Chinese society had polarized into two camps. The anti-Mao camp was highly heterogeneous; it included genuine Marxists, but also those who, while opposed to Mao's methods and the "Cultural Revolution," were in agreement with its great-power aspirations. But there was no real unity among the supporters of the Mao group. The army and the *hung weiping* and *tsao fan* detachments were split and struggled against each other, and the center was no longer capable of controlling events in the localities.

China's "Cultural Revolution," according to *Kommunist,* was leading to the destruction of the political system of the CPR. The CPC was currently paralyzed. More than two-thirds of its members and candidate members, elected by the Eighth Party Congress in 1956, had been publicly humiliated, declared "black bandits," "scum," and "enemies of Mao." In conformity with Mao's call to "open fire on headquarters," almost all provincial, city, and country Party committees had been broken up or were unable to function normally. In attacking the Communist Party, Maoists might possibly preserve the party's outward characteristics, but they had radically changed its nature and class character. According to a scheme announced in the autumn of 1967, the army, *hung weiping,* and *tsao fan* were to be the backbone of the party, of a new party, the Mao Party. The electoral bodies of people's rule in the localities had been broken up. They had been replaced by the "revolutionary committees," created on the basis of "an alliance of the three"—the army, the cadre officials who had gone over to Mao, and the "revolutionary masses" (the *hung weiping* and *tsao fan*).

Contrary to Peking's propaganda that the Great Proletarian Cultural Revolution aimed at strengthening the dictatorship of the proletariat, the "Cultural Revolution" discredited this very idea. In China, the working class, peasantry, and intelligentsia were prevented from participating in the administration of the country, and the Party itself had been crushed. Far from freeing the initiative of the popular masses, "big democracy" Mao-style was persecution organized from above.

"Cultural Revolution" meant seizure of power by Mao and his group, supported by army and security agencies. The army not only was performing police duties, but it also supervised industry and agriculture. With the Party and administrative bodies having been destroyed, the army in fact became the sole prop of the regime. During the "Cultural Revolution" the political superstructure of the CPC was destroyed, and was replaced by a military-bureaucratic dictatorship.

In Soviet eyes China's national economy, which had begun to be stabilized after the "great leap," was again in a grave situation during the "Cultural Revolution." Production had been sharply curtailed and the entire system of production management was disorganized. The links between economic regions had been cut or disrupted and serious difficulties had arisen in the supply of food to the population. Industrialization, which should be the chief means of overcoming China's backwardness, had been virtually halted and scientific and technological progress was being retarded. The Mao group had no constructive program of economic development.

Posters called upon the Chinese "to prepare for disaster, famine and war." The Maoists were trying to frighten the people into submission and to justify the brutality of the Red Guards and the comprehensive military control over all aspects of life.[6] As reported to *Pravda* in June 1968, the axe of the "Cultural Revolution" for the third consecutive year had been chopping off the heads of Communists and those who had resisted the anti-popular Mao group.[7] Shootings had been organized by the Maoists in the presence of tens of thousands of *hung weiping, tsao fan,* and military men. The Mao group had widely publicized these abominable scenes of monstrous violence and even broadcast them on radio and television in order to implant fear among the population. Most of the intelligentsia rejected the "Cultural Revolution," but this segment of the population had become the first of its victims. Only a small number of scientific and technical specialists, primarily those connected with carrying out the nuclear missile program, remained untouched by the revolution. The national bourgeoisie, which was not a target of persecution and harassment, had adopted the tactics of passive endurance with respect to the "Cultural Revolution."

During the "Cultural Revolution," the government had also attempted to introduce militarized forms of production organization and to establish low levels of consumption. The notion of raising living standards had been denounced as a "bourgeois" desire for "satiation." The sayings of Mao, including "Poverty is good" and "It is terrible to think of a time when all people will be rich," had been widely disseminated.

The majority of China's working people had not yet reached a complete understanding of the true goals of the political struggle going on in China. But the opposing camps acted under the guise of "defense of Mao." The situation was thus far from stable. The propaganda of ascetic socialism, the decline in living standards, the outrages committed by irresponsible

6. A. Zhelokhovstev, "A Policy alien to Socialism," *Novy Mir,* no. 10, Oct. 1969, *Current Abstracts of the Soviet Press* 1, no. 9 (Feb. 1969): 3.
7. V. Pasenchuk and V. Viktorov, *"The Anti-Popular Policy of the Peking Rulers," Pravda,* June 22, 1968, pp. 4-5 (*CDSP* 20, no. 23 [1968]: 12-13).

youths—all this had caused increasing dissatisfaction among the masses. The Mao group was waging an offensive against the economic and political rights of the Chinese workers. The principle of payment for labor had been violated and the workers' rights to social insurance and a working day with a definite number of hours, won during the revolution, had been voided.

The "Cultural Revolution," in Soviet eyes, had an especially deleterious effect on China's spiritual and cultural life. A genuine cultural revolution had been stopped. During the past two years instruction in schools and higher educational institutions had come to a virtual halt: no engineers, physicians, teachers, or specialists in other fields were being trained. During the so-called Cultural Revolution, the Chinese had actually closed themselves off from world culture. Even humanistic works of Chinese social thought, literature, and the arts had been withdrawn from circulation. Many books had been burned. Practically everything that constitutes the treasure house of world civilization had been denounced as "bourgeois" or "counterrevolutionary." The latest Chinese novel appeared in 1965. No new plays or films were being produced and the theaters were run by the military. Mao's wife, Chiang Ching, had been placed in charge of all cultural activities.[8]

The "Cultural Revolution," in Moscow's judgment, exposed the methods of political struggle typical of Mao and his group: intrigue, playing certain groups of the population off against others, demagoguery, the humiliating practice of public confession, the use of religious cult forms such as mystical incantations and burning adversaries in effigy, and so on.

The deification of Mao differed very little from the cult of the emperors in ancient China. Mao's statements were to determine the behavior, life, and existence of every person in the CPR. Any Communist who had ever disagreed with Mao on some question was denounced as a "national traitor" or "agent of counterrevolution."

Maoism had exploited young people. The student movement inspired by Mao was designed to create the illusion of support from below. This reliance on politically immature young people was deeply regretted by *Kommunist*. Affiliated with the *hung weiping* were detachments of *tsao fan*, recruited for the most part from among young people who had just entered industry and the state apparatus.

Communist China was of course sensitive to the charges the Soviets leveled against the Great Proletarian Cultural Revolution. *People's Daily* wrote as early as June 4, 1967, that throughout the past year "scarcely a day has passed without the Soviet revisionist clique headed by Brezhnev

8. *Literaturnaya gazeta*, no. 16, Apr. 15, 1970, *Current Abstracts. . .* , May 1970, p. 5.

and Kosygin viciously slandering, attacking, and vilifying China's Great Proletarian Cultural Revolution." The Soviet leaders, in an "outpouring of venomous abuse," had charged that China's great Cultural Revolution was a "great tragedy." Such great tragedy as had taken place in the international Communist movement of our time, however, had occurred in the Soviet Union, not in China. In the Soviet Union the dictatorship of the proletariat, Peking asserted in all seriousness, had "today become the dictatorship of the bourgeoisie; capitalism had been restored."[9] The Red Star over the Kremlin had lost its radiance completely.

In spite of the sharp Soviet criticism, Peking pretended to be undisturbed and remained self-assured and even anticipated a whole series of new Cultural Revolutions in China in the more or less distant future. No member of the CPC nor anyone in China should think that "everything will be all right after one or two great Cultural Revolutions, or even three or four." China must be very much on the alert and never lose her vigilance. Maoism was "a great leap forward" in the revolutionary theory of Marxism-Leninism. The Great Proletarian Cultural Revolution had not only prevented in China a repetition of the Soviet Union's tragedy and "smashed the dream of imperialism and revisionism to restore capitalism in China," but it had also opened up a new epoch in the international Communist movement, a new era of proletarian socialist world revolution. According to Peking's own assessment, the Cultural Revolution, in spite of its name, had large political, social, and foreign policy objectives. Among the latter the most characteristic was unfurling the flag of the CPR's great-power nationalism and challenging the primacy of Moscow.

When the "Cultural Revolution" began to unfold in 1966, the anti-Soviet course of Peking intensified. In August 1966, at the eleventh plenary session of the CC of the CPC, the Maoists scored heavily when their anti-Soviet aims and campaign were recognized as "absolutely correct and necessary." There followed a vigorous, unrelenting campaign against the USSR and noisy demonstrations before the walls of the Soviet Embassy in Peking. Numerous memorials previously erected to Sino-Soviet friendship throughout China were desecrated or destroyed.[10] Anti-Sovietism became a highly important component of the policies of Mao's group. In some documents approved in October 1968 by the so-called twelfth plenary session of the CC of the CPC, the Party openly proclaimed it its task to "fight for the overthrow" of the Soviet system in the USSR.

Day after day Chinese propaganda bombarded the CPSU and the USSR

9. "China's great revolution and the Soviet Union's great tragedy" *People's Daily*, June 4, 1967 (*PR*, June 9, 1967).

10. Soviet Government Statement, *Pravda*, Feb. 5, 1966, p. 5 (*CDSP* 18, no. 5 [1966]: 1-2).

with what in the Soviet view were filthy streams of slander. According to Moscow, Peking seemed resolved to transfer the "Cultural Revolution" to the USSR and to establish Mao's military-bureaucratic dictatorship in the Soviet Union. The volume of Russian-language broadcasts by Radio Peking, Moscow charged, had increased enormously and the broadcasts were transmitted over 40 different frequencies. No demonstration, no rally, no matter on what subject, went by without anti-Soviet slogans and appeals. During the "Cultural Revolution" period, Moscow accused Peking of committing more than 200 provocatory acts against Soviet institutions and representatives. But Maoism actually was "in a de facto state of war" with all Communist Parties. Back in 1967 Peking had openly called the major Communist Parties irreconcilable enemies and "cliques."

On August 22, 1966, *Pravda* reported from China the anti-Soviet campaign that began immediately after the armed provocations committed by the Maoists on the Soviet border on August 13. This campaign was continuing on an unprecedented scale. Everywhere, on city squares, at plants, and in institutions and schools, the Maoist orators presented their own version of the latest border incident, accusing the USSR of "aggression" and "imperialism."[11] This type of anti-Soviet propaganda, alternating with military marches and anti-Soviet songs, was ceaselessly broadcast over the radio. The Maoists, the Soviets concluded, were apparently hoping to solve their complicated internal problems by arousing an anti-Soviet hysteria. They raised a false hue and cry about a "Soviet threat" to justify the further militarization of China. They justified the shortages of foodstuffs and other goods by pointing to the alleged danger from Moscow. Even school children were being indoctrinated to the effect that a large part of the territory of the USSR in the Far East and Central Asia was once Chinese territory and ought to be so again. The other day, *Pravda* reported, the Hsinshua wire service had circulated a bulletin in the capitals of several African states asserting that the peoples of the Soviet Central Asian republics were seized with a common desire to "enter into a close union with China." According to Moscow, there was thus a Chinese "threat" to the integrity of the USSR rather than vice versa.

The "Cultural Revolution": Mao and Maoism

The "Cultural Revolution" was more closely interwoven with personality cult, the idolization of Mao, and the extolling of Mao's thought than any other phase of the recent history of the CPC and the CPR. After their own shattering experience with the personality cult of Stalin, Soviet

---

11. *Pravda*, Aug. 22, 1967, p. 5; *Izvestiia*, p. 2.

Russia's leadership could look upon the Mao cult only with growing concern. In view of the undisguised hostility of Mao both to de-Stalinization and Stalin's "unworthy" successors as well as the growing rivalry in the world Communist movement, the Soviet government was bound to cross swords with Mao. Still, the Soviet leadership had traveled far since the days of Khrushchev's denunciation of Stalin: Khrushchev himself had been forced to backtrack and had become more cautious. Though innovating at home, he spurned radical departures in domestic policy. But in his relationship with Mao himself, Khrushchev had come reluctantly to play the role of an iconoclast.

At the Seventh Party Congress in April 1945, Liu Shao-ch'i had hailed Mao's thought as the key to the future transformation of Asia. According to Liu, it had been Mao's great accomplishment to change Marxism from a European to an Asiatic form. "Marx and Lenin were Europeans; they wrote in European languages about European histories and problems, seldom discussing Asia or China. Mao was Chinese and used Marxist-Leninist principles to explain Chinese history and the practical problems of China." He had created a "Chinese or Asiatic form of Marxism."[12] Conditions in Southeast Asia were similar to those in China. The course chosen by China would influence people everywhere. At a Congress of the World Federation of Trade Unions in November 1949, Liu, to the discomfiture of Soviet Russia, strongly reasserted the notion that China's road to power was of general relevance. There was, of course, an inherent contradiction between the claim that Mao had "sinified" Marxism and that Mao's version of Marxism-Leninism was of general significance.

Since 1958 Mao had openly laid claim to theoretical leadership of the entire world Communist movement. The apologists of the personality cult of Mao had proclaimed him "the greatest Marxist-Leninist of our time." In December 1960 Lin Piao called Mao's thought the Marxism-Leninism of "the epoch of the fall of imperialism and the triumph of socialism." In March 1967 the newspaper *People's Daily,* and *Red Flag,* the theoretical journal of the CC of the CPC, speaking about contributions of Marx, Engels, Lenin, and Stalin respectively, asserted that Mao had developed Marxism-Leninism, solving a number of problems of the proletarian revolution in the contemporary era and representing thus the third great stage in the history of the development of Marxism. A Chinese leaflet, issued in June 1967, entitled, in accordance with this view, "Three Great Stages in the History of Marxism," opened with the words: "We acclaim the entry of the world into the new era of Mao."

The Soviet views on the "Cultural Revolution" and Maoism found

12. Quoted by Schram, *Political Thought of Mao. . . ,* p. 111.

clearest expression in an article in *Kommunist* by the academician R. Rumyantsev. He accused Maoism of completely ignoring the dialectical law of the negation of negation, according to which the rise of the new presupposes the retention and preservation of everything valuable accumulated in the preceding stages of social development. In the so-called Cultural Revolution the Maoists proclaimed that they were building a new Communist culture on the basis of destroying the entire old culture. Mao's thought clashed sharply with the national and all-human pillars of Chinese culture. Maoism encouraged the desecration of the graves of China's progressive leaders and trampling upon the memory of democratic fighters who perished in the revolution, beloved writers and prominent scientists and artists. This was all deeply alien to the feelings of the Chinese people.[13]

The Cultural Revolution had actually created a new party, Chairman Mao's party, and had replaced the principles of Marxism-Leninism with "Mao's ideas."[14] Mao was portrayed as the heir of Marx and Lenin and he was credited with "great discoveries" in the realm of theory. The CPC lacked, however, any positive program for economic and cultural construction; this failure gave Mao a free hand for the further subordination of China's resources to chauvinistic ends. In Maoism the masses submitted in the most servile manner to the "leader," in the spirit of reactionary traditions of feudalism and monarchism. Maoism was an unscientific system of ideas alien to Marxism-Leninism and elevated, in effect, to the rank of religious dogma, poisoning the minds of millions of Chinese.[15]

The phenomenon of Maoism produced a veritable flood of books and pamphlets in the Soviet Union. After the scarcity in the 60s of news from China, beginning in 1967 Soviet publishing houses put out a large number of books and monographs on China, as distinguished from the mere newspaper articles that had earlier reached the Soviet public. Some of their titles were *The Roots of the Present Events in China,* Moscow 1968; *Where is Mao Tse Tung's group leading China?* by J. Vital (translated from French), Moscow 1967; *The Cultural Revolution in China* by L. P. Delyusin, Moscow 1967; *Screaming Battalions: A Close Look at China's so-called Great Proletarian Cultural Revolution,* by G. Yeliseyev, A. Krushinsky, and V. Milyutenko, Moscow 1967; and *Where Mao's Policy is Going,* by Vl. Khukov, Moscow 1967. Needless to point out, the reaction of the Soviet printed word to Mao Tse-tungism was entirely negative, as can be seen by the critical titles of most of the Soviet writings. The main attempt of the authors of these and other polemical tracts was to il-

13. A. Rumyanstev in *Kommunist,* Jan. 1969, pp. 91-106.
14. *Za Rubeshom*, May 29-June 4, 1970, pp. 20-22; "Maochuhsitang—Tool of the Renegades," M. Medvedev and V. Pasenchuk, *Current Abstracts* . . . 2, no. 6 (June 1970): 8-9.
15. *Kommunist,* no. 2, Jan. 1969, pp. 91-106.

luminate the causes of the "deformation" of the sociopolitical structure of the CPR and of the claimed deviation from Marxism-Leninism. M. S. Kapitsa, in his book *Left of Sense,* focused on the CPR's sharp turn in foreign policy, its impact upon its world position, and the CPR's link-up with the most violent enemies of international Communism. Other writings on Maoism were F. Burlatsky's pamphlet *Maoism-Threat to Socialism in China,* which criticized the new trends in China from the point of view of Marxist-Leninist theory, and the book by Altaisky and V. Georgiyev, *The Anti-Marxist Essence of the Philosophical Views of Mao-Tse-tung.* This study, however, did not confine itself to an exposition of the distortion of Marxism-Leninism by Mao, but also stressed that many who embraced Marxism in China used it as a mere vehicle to restore China's former greatness. Nationalist excesses in Mao's China were critically dealt with in V. Sidekhemenov's book *Classes and Class Struggle in a Crooked Mirror,* and in a pamphlet authored by L. S. Kyuzadzhan.

The exploitation of the national liberation movement by Peking and how it was sacrificed to China's selfish ambitions in the era of the "Cultural Revolution" was treated in a pamphlet by Yu. Bogush entitled *Maoism and the Policy of Splitting the National Liberation Movement.* The control of literature and art, and the persecution of Chinese writers and poets were analyzed in a book by M. Nadeyev, issued by the main editorial board of Oriental Literature of the Science Publishing House in Moscow. As A. Dymkov in his review in *Izvestiia* of some of these tracts pointed out: "These books lifted the veil on much that the Maoists assiduously kept hidden until recently and help provide a better understanding of Peking's chauvinist practices."[16] In Moscow's eyes all this underlined the danger that Maoism posed to the Communist and national liberation movements.

The "Cultural Revolution," a creation of Mao, in turn raised Mao to a higher level than that of most Chinese Emperors in the past. But the new exaltation of Mao and the excesses of the Mao worship came only a decade after Khrushchev's denunciation of Stalin and of the "cult of personality." To Moscow it must have appeared as if Peking deliberately opted for a course diametrically opposed to that which the Soviets had carefully chosen earlier. That the new trend and developments in the CPR associated with the "Cultural Revolution" only deepened the abyss between Moscow and Peking could cause little surprise.

The Six-Day War, June 1967

On May 24, 1967, about two weeks before the eruption of war in the

---

16. *Izvestiia,* Aug. 8, 1969, p. 2; *Current Abstracts. . . ,* Feb. 1969.

Mid-East, *Pravda* took issue with the growing tension in that region.[17] Referring to a retaliatory strike of the Israeli forces against Syria on April 7, it heartily approved the resolve taken by eight Arab states to aid Syria in a future emergency. *Pravda* criticized Israel for following what it claimed was an imperialist course and warned that the Soviet government would keep a close watch on developments in the Near East. The preservation of peace and security in this region, one "directly adjacent to the Soviet Union," corresponded to the vital interests of the peoples of the USSR. A few days later *Pravda* took to task some of the reactionary regimes of Saudi Arabia and Jordan for having split the ranks of the Arab countries and having entered into open collusion with the imperialists against the revolution of the Arab people in Aden and the occupied South of the Arabian peninsula.[18] Imperialism, Zionism, and reaction in the Arab world were contraposed to the Arab peoples and their patriotic, progressive, and revolutionary forces; the latter were allegedly supported by the forces of liberation, progress, and socialism the world over, "first of all the Soviet Union."[19]

On June 6, one day after the outbreak of war in the Middle East, *Pravda* published a Soviet Government statement accusing Israel of having commenced military operations and committed aggression against the United Arab Republic. "Because of the adventurism of the rulers of one country—Israel, which has been encouraged by covert and overt actions of certain imperialist circles—a military conflict has flared up in the Near East." The statement climaxed in a clear warning that recklessness and adventurism might undermine the very existence of the Israeli state—a threat far in excess of usual threats made by the USSR.[20] On June 10 the Soviets handed *Pravda* the copy of a note to Israel's ambassador in Moscow, warning that the USSR, with other peaceloving states, might impose sanctions against Israel.[21] At the same time they announced the severance of their relations with the Israeli government.

In his analysis and comment on the Mid-East War and the Arab defeat, which deeply embarassed the USSR, Jury Zhukov in *Pravda,* while denouncing alleged Israeli aggression, was anxious to implicate the U.S. in the conflict and to shift the burden of guilt to her shoulders. He pointed out that imperialism more than once, especially in 1956 and in 1958, had attempted to impede the strengthening of the national independence of the Near Eastern countries. The USA was inclined to turn Israel's temporary

17. *Pravda*, May 24, 1967, p. 1 (*CDSP* 19 no. 21 [1967]: 29).
18. *Ibid.,* June 2, p. 14 (*CDSP* 19, no. 22 [1967]: 22-23).
19. *Ibid.,* May 29, p. 5; Mayevsky (*CDSP,* June 1, p. 3, June 4, p. 5).
20. *Pravda,* June 6, 1967, p. 1.
21. *Ibid.,* June 11, 1967, p. 1.

advantage into a lasting one, as a cover for making a fresh attempt to restore the colonial order in the Arab East. Against this backdrop Zhukov praised the "truly noble role" that the USSR and other socialist states were playing in the Near East. He especially recalled the "enormous assistance" the USSR had given to the Arabs to strengthen their economy and defense, somehow ignoring the circumstance that apparently all these efforts had borne no fruit. Washington's role, in contrast, had been to stop the national liberation movements. The attempt, however, by Western imperialism to restore colonialism was doomed to failure.*

But Moscow apparently was even more concerned about Peking's objections to the Soviets' Mid-East policy and met Peking's criticism with scathing countercriticism. The CPR was listed among "various types of provocateurs" who had become active in connection with the situation in the Near East. Zhukov poured bitter irony on the CPC. In Peking, official assurances had been heard that the CPR was allegedly prepared to send all 700,000,000 of its people to give military assistance to the Arabs. Anyone could see that a reference to 700 million was "utter nonsense, that for geographic, transportational, and military reasons cannot be taken seriously." Peking's appeals were either a provocation or a wail of despair by people frightened to death.

On the eve of the outbreak of hostilities in the Middle East, on May 27, Peking had pointed out that the Arab people's struggle against United States imperialism and Zionism was an important component of the world-wide struggle against imperialism.[22] Facts showed once again that the United States, which had sent its Sixth Fleet to the Eastern Mediterranean, was the archcriminal supporting Israeli aggression against the Arab states, and that it was the most ferocious enemy of the Arab people. U.S. imperialism had suffered ignominious defeat in its aggression against Vietnam and it would certainly come to no better end in its aggression against the Arab states. The Chinese papers attempted to demonstrate that U.S. aggressive imperialism, whether operating against Vietnam or the Arabs, was basically one and the same phenomenon. They were anxious to present the Chinese as natural allies of the Arab people and vice-versa. In accusing the U.S. as the power ultimately responsible for the outbreak of hostilities in the Middle East, there was little difference between Peking and Moscow.

But then Peking parted ways with the Soviets in the analysis of the

---

*Sympathies in the USSR and Eastern Europe must at least have been divided between Israel and the Arab states, since Zhukov felt it necessary to stress that the obligations of revolutionaries was "to be on the Arab side." He who took Israel's side, was, "willy nilly, an accomplice of imperialism, colonialism, and reaction."

22. *PR*, June 2, p. 29.

Mid-East political scene. In Peking's eyes the Soviet revisionist clique was the "No. 1 accomplice" of U.S. imperialism. Everywhere, according to Peking, it rendered service to the U.S. imperialist policies of aggression and war. Now, once again, Soviet revisionism was colluding with U.S. and British imperialism in a vain attempt to sabotage the just cause of the Arab people against imperialism.

On June 6 Premier Chou sent messages of support to the Presidents of the UAR and of the Syrian Arab Republic and to the President of the Palestine Liberation Organization.[23] At the same time Peking in a government statement denounced the Israeli attack on several Arab states as "another towering crime" against the Arab people. It also castigated U.S. imperialism for this aggression, which was also a grave provocation against the people of Asia, Africa, and the world. Facts fully proved that U.S. imperialism was the backstage manager of Zionism and the main enemy of the Arab people. The statement also denounced the Soviet revisionist clique for conniving at the aggression committed by Israel. The Chinese government concluded with the solemn declaration: "Armed with Mao Tse-Tung's thought, the 700 million Chinese people who are victoriously carrying on the Great Proletarian Cultural Revolution absolutely will not allow the U.S. imperialists and their collaborators to ride roughshod and commit aggression everywhere."

For three days beginning June 7, masses in Peking and other cities poured into the streets to demonstrate support for the Arab people's struggle against "aggression" by U.S. imperialism and Israel.[24] In Peking alone more than 1.2 million people took part in demonstrations expressing "staunch support" for the 100 million Arabs fighting "Israeli aggression." Foreigners from more than 20 countries working in Peking marched shoulder to shoulder with the angry demonstrators to the Office of the British Chargé d'Affaires. The ruling Soviet revisionist clique, it was charged, had been ganging up with the U.S. imperialists to betray the Arab people. The Soviet government was condemned in similar terms for its vile deceit. Though Peking did not hold back its vituperative criticism, castigating Moscow's policy of big words in combination with small deeds, Peking itself pursued a rather cautious course. As *Peking Review* wrote: "The great thought of Mao is the sharpest weapon [!] with which Peking's proletarian revolutionaries support the Arab people in their struggle against U.S.-Israeli banditry." While Moscow offered real weapons, advice, and diplomatic assistance—though refusing military intervention—Peking offered intermittently the help of 700 million Chinese and the Little Red Book containing Mao's thoughts.

23. *PR*, June 9, 1967, pp. 8-10.
24. "We firmly stand by the Arab people," *PR*, June 16, pp. 12-14.

On June 13, *People's Daily* denounced the "joint statement" of "the Soviet Revisionist Renegades' clique" because it did not contain a single word of condemnation of U.S. imperialism. Their pledge to render all necessary help to the Arab countries to rebuff the aggressor was "worthless, empty talk" and "simply sickening."[25] Though the Soviet revisionists in their statement of March 23 had given warning to potential aggressors in the Middle East that the Soviet Union would oppose them with "resolute action," actually the USSR, after Israel had launched her aggression, had simply looked on "with folded arms." The Soviets had, it was charged, fully cooperated with U.S. imperialism, shielded Israel, and brought pressure to bear on Arab countries. They also had protected the U.S. and British Embassies in Moscow by obstructing the protest demonstrations of Arab, Asian, and African students. They had not cut off relations with Israel at the time of the surprise attack on the Arab couhntries, but had done so only later, and on the ground that Israel had ignored the Security Council resolution cooked up by them in partnership with U.S. imperialism. This move was designed to uphold the power of the U.S., a tool jointly manipulated by Soviet revisionism and U.S. imperialism, but not to protect the Arab countries.

The Soviets had thus betrayed the Arab people, just as they had been engaged in betrayals and had acted as accomplices of U.S. imperialism wherever there was revolution or struggle against aggression.

At the time of Kosygin's journey to the United States following the Six-Day War, and his meeting with President Johnson at Glassboro, *People's Daily* pointed to the Soviet policy of speaking soothing words to the Arab countries, but Kosygin's omitting, while in America, any reference to U.S. imperialism, "the chief culprit" in the aggression against Arab countries. Though Kosygin had a mouthful of fine words for the Arabs, he was "a devil at heart." His dialogues with the American president provided further proof that the Soviet revisionist ruling clique was a "pack of rotten renegades" betraying the people of the world and that they were "the heinous accomplices" of U.S. imperialism in trying to put out the flames of world revolution.[26] The charge of collusion between U.S.-British imperialism and Soviet revisionism was repeated by *Red Flag* on September 8. The Six-Day War had clearly shown that they had openly joined forces. The activities of the Soviet clique during the Middle East crisis had been an "utterly shameless renegade performance."[27]

Red Flag was still puzzled how the Arab countries with more than 100

25. *People's Daily* June 13, 1967 (*PR*, June 16, pp. 17-18).
26. *People's Daily,* June 22, 1967 (*PR*, June 30).
27. Chou Tien-Chih, "Lessons of the Arab War against Aggression," *Red Flag,* no. 13, 1967 (*PR*, Sept. 8, 1967).

million people could have suffered a setback in the war. Oppressed nations, *Red Flag* warned in conclusion, should not rely on modern weapons, still less have blind faith in them. It also will not do for them to adopt the strategy of a war of quick decision, a Blitzkrieg, such as Israel adopted "after the Hitlerite fashion."[28] The Arabs should neither employ the military methods of the imperialists nor copy the methods of the Soviet revisionists. Only the strategy and tactics of a people's war would provide them with the key to victory. In other words, by following Mao's military concepts and adopting the Chinese example, they would march toward victory. Peking was not averse to exploiting to the hilt the Arab disillusionments in the brief but disastrous war and reaping political advantages at the expense of the USSR. But what it offered, Mao's military precepts, "a magic weapon," must have been a disappointment to the Arabs still smarting from defeat.

In its analysis of the Six-Day War, Peking resorted to obvious half-truths, if not plain lies. It not only reversed the actual situation by making beleaguered little Israel one of the main culprits, while acquitting the Arabs—in spite of their threatening preparations for imminent war and ignoring their openly proclaimed genocidal intentions, but also made it appear that Israel was a mere stooge of the U.S. and that the latter allegedly pushed Israel into the war. It also distorted Soviet Russia's vast material and advisory support of the Arabs into an abandonment of the Arab cause, merely because the USSR retreated from the risk of a war with America over the Middle East for the sake of Arab "liberation." Once again a major crisis in international affairs, which threatened for a brief moment to bring about a confrontation of the two superpowers, the U.S.A. and the USSR, and to engulf them in war, resulted also in violent and abusive propagandistic warfare between the Soviet Union and Communist China.

Soviet Intervention in Czechoslovakia, 1968. "Limited Sovereignty."

According to a Tass statement, published in *Pravda* and *Izvestiia* on August 21, party and state leaders of the Czechoslovak Socialist Republic (CSR) had "requested" the Soviet Union and other allied states to give the fraternal Czechoslovak people immediate aid, "including assistance with armed forces." The reason for the appeal, according to Tass, was the threat posed to the socialist system existing in Czechoslovakia by counter-revolutionary forces that had entered into collusion with external forces that were hostile to socialism. The exacerbation of the tense situation in Czechoslovakia, the statement continued, also affected the vital interests of

28. *Pravda* and *Izvestiia,* Aug. 21, 1968.

the Soviet Union and the security interests of all states in the socialist commonwealth. The decision of the socialist countries to dispatch troops to Czechoslovakia, it was also claimed, was in complete accord with the right of states to individual and collective self-defense.

The following day a Tass communiqué asserted that the troops of the allied socialist countries were advancing in Czechoslovakia without hindrance and that many Czechoslovaks had expressed their gratitude for giving them support against the forces of reaction. The communiqué disclaimed any intention of restoring former President A. Novotny to a position of leadership and confined the goal of the allied socialist countries to the consolidation and development of socialism in the CSR and to the strengthening of the leadership role of the working class and its vanguard—the Communist Party.[29]

On the same day *Pravda,* attempting editorially to justify the use of Soviet troops and those of the allied socialist countries in the CSR, referred to the "centuries-old traditions of the Slavic community," which had been deepened by the past joint struggle for freedom, independence, and social progress of their peoples. More than 20 million Soviet people had given their lives in mortal combat with fascism for Russia and for the liberation of other enslaved peoples; 100,000 Soviet soldiers were buried in Czechoslovak territory. *Pravda* pointed to the treaties of Friendship, Mutual Aid, and Postwar Cooperation, signed in 1943 and renewed in 1963, and the Warsaw Pact, which united a number of socialist countries in Europe.[30] The developments in Czechoslovakia since January 1968 had alarmed the CPSU and other allied parties in Eastern Europe, since allegedly anti-socialist elements and right-wing forces had consolidated themselves in the Czechoslovak television, press, and radio installations.

On August 23 V. Kudryavtsev in *Izvestiia* took account of reproaches by "some of our friends" directed against the Soviet Union and her socialist allies for bringing troops into Czechoslovakia, but pointed to the threatened restoration of a multi-party system in Czechoslovakia as proof of an alleged retreat from socialism backward toward a bourgeois-democratic system.[31]

Three days later *Izvestiia* reprinted the attack of the Polish newspaper *Tribuna Ludu* against Chou En-lai for castigating the Soviet move against Prague.[32] Mao too had joined in the anti-Communist and anti-Soviet chorus, raised by the imperialists of the capitalist countries.

29. "Defense of Socialism is the highest international duty," *Pravda*, Aug. 22, 1968 (*CDSP* 20, no. 34 [Sept. 11, 1968]: 5-14, esp. p. 5).
30. *Ibid.*
31. V. Kudryavtsev, "Counterrevolution disguised as Regeneration," *Izvestiia,* Aug. 25, 1968 (*CDSP* no. 35 [Sept. 18, 1968]: 7-8).
32. "Peking without Camouflage," *Izvestiia*, Aug. 30, 1964 (*CDSP* 20, no. 35 [Sept. 18, 1968]: 21); also *PR*, Aug. 23, 1968.

The Soviets were keenly sensitive to foreign criticism, especially to that by Communist China and other Communist Parties. In view of the tense relations between Peking and Moscow, the perhaps unexpected show of Soviet determination, strength, or recklessness in Czechoslovakia, and its apparent implications for Soviet relations with "fraternal" parties, the Chinese reaction was sharp and swift.

The first and most authoritative position on the Soviet invasion of Czechoslovakia was Premier Chou En-lai's speech in the Rumanian Embassy in Peking on August 23.[33] According to Chou, the Soviet revisionist clique and its followers had brazenly dispatched large numbers of armed forces to launch a savage attack on Czechoslovakia and had perpetrated towering crimes against the Czechoslovak people. The Soviet aim was to prevent the Czechoslovak revisionist clique from directly hiring itself out to the Western countries, headed by U.S. imperialism. According to Peking, both the perpetrator and the victim of the crime were "revisionist." The Soviet move was the "inevitable result of great-power chauvinism and national egoism, practiced by the Soviet revisionist leading clique." Discarding all its fig leaves, its so-called Marxism-Leninism and internationalism, the Soviet leadership was trying to create puppets with the help of guns. Chou compared the Soviet invasion with Hitler's past aggression against Czechoslovakia and U.S. imperialism's aggression against Vietnam. The Chinese denunciation of the Soviet move against Czechoslovakia could not have taken any sharper form.

Chou voiced his conviction that the Czechoslovak people, with its glorious revolutionary traditions, would never submit to Soviet revisionist military occupation. Now Rumania was facing the danger of foreign intervention and aggression. Chou pledged the support of the Chinese people to the Rumanian party and state, without, however, specifying what form such aid might take.

At about the same time *People's Daily* denounced Moscow's "naked armed intervention," which had brought to the fore the grisly fascist features and acute contradictions of Soviet policy. The *Hsinshua Report,* on the other hand, criticized the Czechoslovak ruling clique for having advised its people "not to offer any resistance."[34] It also ridiculed the Soviet justification of their invasion of Czechoslovakia, the alleged need for "defending socialist gains," since actually capitalism had been restored under Khrushchev, Kosygin, Brezhnev, and Novotny in their respective countries. The invasion of Czechoslovakia was denounced as a "monstrous crime" and "barbarous aggression."

When on August 27 the Soviets published the Communiqué on Soviet-Czechoslovak talks, held in the aftermath of the invasion, *People's Daily*

33. *PR*, Aug. 23, 1968.
34. *People's Daily* (*PR*, Aug. 23, 1968, p. vi).

castigated them as a prime example of outright pressure. The Communiqué was branded as a typical imperialist document.[35] It was the height of shamelessness to talk of "territorial integrity," "friendship," and "noninterference in internal affairs," after dispatching hundreds of thousands of troops to occupy Czechoslovakia, whisking Czechoslovak Party and government officials off to Moscow, and permitting Russian tanks to run amuck in Prague. Hsinshua News Commentary finally denounced the Soviet and Czechoslovak treaty that the Soviets, after the occupation of Czechoslovakia, had forced upon the ruling clique in Prague. The treaty trampled unscrupulously on Czechoslovak sovereignty, while preposterously claiming not to violate the country's independence. While the Soviets were the main target of Peking's criticism, and "revisionism" appeared as the main culprit of the aggression, the Czechoslovak leadership was also continually denounced on account of its revisionist errors.* There was a definite implication that correct Leninist and Maoist conceptions on the part of the Czechoslovak Communist Party might have produced different results, though this was not stated explicitly.

Soviet-Czechoslovak relations were patently of considerable interest to the CPR. Under normal circumstances, if Sino-Soviet relations had not already reached fever heat, the establishment of full Soviet control over a small East European satellite would not have aroused Communist China, especially not if it seemed likely to worsen Soviet-Western relations and deflect Soviet pressure from the Chinese border. But given the explosive nature of the Sino-Soviet relationship, the bold and reckless Soviet thrust against a satellite at the moment the latter asserted a more independent attitude deepened Chinese concerns and made Peking assume a more resolute stand and—fearing worse things to come, aggression against Rumania —adopt a defiant posture against Moscow and sharply denounce the Soviet government. Peking was especially interested in establishing a common base with European and other Communist satellites of the USSR against the arbitrary rule and selfish domination of international Communism by the revisionist leadership of the CPSU.

A short while after the occupation of Czechoslovakia, Brezhnev and the Soviet leadership produced the so-called Brezhnev doctrine, which aimed at the justification of Soviet intervention anywhere in Eastern Europe, for

---

35. *People's Daily* Commentator (*PR*, Aug. 23, 1968, pp. iv-vi).

*Peking's ideological position was as often identical with that of Tirana or vice-versa. Four weeks before the invasion of Czechoslovakia, *Peking Review* reprinted an article from the Albanian newspaper *Zeri i Popullit,* "Soviet Revisionism and Czechoslovakia," published originally on July 24. According to the paper, Czechoslovakia, "a revisionist satellite of the Soviet revisionists," was striving to detach herself from the Khrushchevites and to ally herself with American and Western capitalism. Both Novotny and Dubcek had pursued a wrong policy and the latter was surrounded by "revisionists and extremists released from jail."

the alleged purpose of defending socialism against foreign and domestic attempts to overthrow it and to restore capitalism and bourgeois democracy. The Soviets, according to Brezhnev in November 1968, were entitled to adopt "military measures" against a given member of the socialist "community" and carry out armed intervention. Peking promptly denounced the Brezhnev doctrine as an "outright doctrine of hegemony."[36] The *Peking Review* castigated the Soviet revisionist press for endorsing the view that the interests of the socialist "community" must be put "in the first place," while the sovereignty of its individual members were "limited." The doctrine of "limited sovereignty," a corollary of the Brezhnev doctrine, also alleged that the "community" had the right to determine the destiny of the individual community members, "the destiny of their sovereignty." Also, in November 1968, K. T. Mazurov clamored for the transformation of the proletarian dictatorship "from a national into an international" one, thus transcending national boundaries, and urged the "further perfection" of the Warsaw Treaty Organization and the CMEA.[37]

Peking refused to see any difference between the Soviet invasion of Czechoslovakia by the USSR and her satellites, and the invasion of China by the allied forces of eight powers in 1900, or the fourteen-nation armed intervention in the Soviet Union in 1919-1922 or the sixteen-nation aggression organized by United States imperialism against Korea. The invasion of Czechoslovakia merely demonstrated that the new tsars in the Kremlin had taken over the old tsars' expansionist tradition and, like them, dreamed of a vast empire. On February 7, 1969, referring to demonstrations by the Czechoslovakian people against the military occupation by the "Soviet revisionist renegade clique," *Peking Review* assured the Czechoslovakian people that they were "not alone," that the Chinese people and the revolutionary people the world over stood on their side.[38]

Of all the doctrines propagated by Moscow, none, for obvious reasons, infuriated Peking more than the one of limited sovereignty. In denouncing this doctrine used by the USSR and her satellites against Czechoslovakia—a doctrine that could be used again against any other socialist country, perhaps even Communist China, Peking of course understood that it was fighting for its own survival.

In an article in the *Peking Review*, "Theories of 'Limited Sovereignty' and 'International Dictatorship' are Soviet Revisionist Social-Imperialist Gangster Theories," the paper charged that it was the ruling Soviet clique that had fabricated these "fascist" theories.[39] These fallacies once again

36. *PR*, Apr. 24, 1970, p. 10, Editorial Departments of *People's Daily*, *Red Flag*, and *Jiefangjun Bao*.
37. *Ibid.*, pp. 10, 15.
38. *PR*, Feb. 7, 1969, pp. 15-16.
39. *PR*, March 28, 1969, pp. 23-25.

demonstrated that, like the United States imperialists, the Soviet revisionist social-imperialists were a "bunch of out-and-out fascist gangsters" who were aggressive by nature. These "theories" served only the "criminal" aim of the Soviet leaders to dominate the world. According to their logic, other countries could exercise only "limited sovereignty," while Soviet revisionism itself assumed unlimited sovereignty. The new Soviet theories were merely "shopworn junk," picked up from the ideological arsenal of Russian tsars and fascists and imperialists of all description. The only difference was that Soviet leaders gave it a "socialist," "international" fig leaf.

Soviet Domination of Eastern Europe. New Soviet Expansionism on Land and Sea

Peking accused the "new tsars" of "riding roughshod" not only over Czechoslovakia, but over all of Eastern Europe. For years the Soviet revisionist clique had been pursuing a "social-imperialist policy towards some East European countries, a policy of tight political control, ruthless economic plunder, and arrogant militaristic intervention and aggression. Its fond dream is to build a colonial empire with itself as the overlord and to realize its aggressive designs to redivide the world in collaboration with US imperialism. The biggest colonial ruler and the biggest exploiter of East European peoples, the Soviet revisionist clique is a gang of new tsars riding on their backs."[40] The USSR thus was indistinguishable from any capitalist and imperialist power. After its usurpation of the Party and government leadership in the USSR, the Soviet leadership had actually betrayed the Soviet people and was restoring capitalism at home.

The Soviet clique had also begun to "expand" tsarist foreign policy and even to surpass the Tsars. "Its aggressive ambition is even bigger and more rapacious than that of the tsarist imperialists and the methods of aggression it resorts to are even more treacherous and vicious."

The East European countries were victims of Soviet imperialism. The Soviet revisionist renegade clique had said the most pleasant things, but done everything evil in order to establish its colonial empire in Eastern Europe. For years it had treated the East European countries as its colonies and dependencies. "Politically, it wantonly tramples underfoot their independence and sovereignty and crudely interferes with their internal and external policies; economically, it plunders the wealth created by the working people of these countries and even sends its troops to engage in mili-

40. "Wanton aggression abroad by the Soviet Revisionist Social-Imperialism" *PR*, May 30, 1969, p. 16.

tary occupation." However, the new tsars in the Kremlin described their out-and-out acts of social imperialism as "proletarian internationalism." They blustered about "mutual assistance and cooperation" with the East European countries for the purpose of building a "socialist commonwealth" in common prosperity. But what they really practiced was "social-imperialism and big-nation chauvinism. . .oppression and plunder. . . . Under the signboard of socialism, they are going about their imperialist villainies."

The Warsaw Treaty organization was an important tool used by the Soviet clique in pursuit of their ambitions, in "pushing neo-colonialism" in East European countries. The Warsaw Treaty provided for the Command of Joint Armed Forces and for a General Staff, but its main organs were located in Moscow. Thus Moscow had established control over the armed forces of several countries. Soviet troops stationed abroad were an important military force for the direct control of the East European peoples. Prior to August 1968, when Czechoslovakia was invaded, she was one of the few East European countries without Soviet troops. After the occupation of Czechoslovakia, the Soviets have taken advantage of the new situation to dispatch troops to Bulgaria. They also deployed troops along the borders of some other East European countries to blackmail them.

To further neocolonialism in Eastern Europe, the Soviet clique also used the Council of Mutual Economic Aid (CMEA) as another important instrument. In the name of "international division of labor" and "economic cooperation," the Soviet government had set up in some East European countries a number of "supra-state" organizations, by means of which they controlled many vital branches of the economy of the member states of the CMEA and their financial and economic planning, "grossly trampling under foot the sovereignty of these countries." Soviet revisionism had taken advantage of its monopoly position in the foreign trade of Eastern Europe to rake fabulous profits through the exchange of unequal values. To the Chinese, but also to many less biased observers, the Soviet insistence on economic integration between the Soviet Union and the European communist satellites, whatever its high-sounding internationalist and Marxist phraseology, was nothing but a camouflage for economic exploitation, indistinguishable from that by any imperialism of the past.

According to *Peking Review,* economic integration in essence meant further colonization of all the East European socialist nations linked by the CMEA. The first step, according to the Soviet new tsars' scheme, was to "coordinate" the national economic plans of some East European countries, while the final goal was to create an "organ of unified planning" for all the member states of the CMEA.

"Coordination" of economic plans meant that the national economic plans drawn up by the CMEA states be based on the principle of "international division of labor," actually in accordance with the needs of the Soviet social-imperialists. Everything was to be geared to the "predatory" demands of the Soviets. Once a supra-state organ for unified planning was accepted, all the countries would be completely deprived of what little independence remained and would be turned into regions or union republics of the USSR.

In accordance with Soviet ambitions, Khrushchev already had "howled for abolition of state boundaries," stressing that economic organization in a single country was too narrow a concept for the socialist community of nations. The Soviet clique directly controlled the CMEA countries through the "organizations for economic cooperation." Through these instruments it controlled the industrial planning, production and sales, power resources, finance and banking, and the scientific and technological development of all of Eastern Europe. In accordance with the program of international division of labor, CMEA countries were allowed only to produce industrial, agricultural, and mineral products of certain types and specifications. This had deprived these countries of their right to independent development of their economies, had aggravated their lopsided economic growth, and turned them into dependencies of Soviet revisionism.

Both the Soviets' domination in Eastern Europe and their thrust into the Mediterranean are geographically and ideologically closely linked with each other, though Soviet interests in the former are of a proprietary nature, in the latter of a competitive and expansive kind. According to *Peking Review,* Soviet revisionist social-imperialism had vigorously expanded its navy and engaged in large-scale expansion in the Mediterranean over the last few years to intensify its contention with U.S. imperialism over the Middle East, Europe, and Africa, and for maritime supremacy.[41] It was after Israel's June 5 "war of aggression" against the Arab countries that Soviet Black Sea Fleet vessels swarmed into the Mediterranean, at one time exceeding 60 naval units. Soviet revisionists made no secret of their desire to dominate the Mediterranean and the chiefs of their navy boasted that a century-old dream of a southward thrust had become a reality. But the Mediterranean belonged by right to Mediterranean countries, and France, Italy, Malta, Yugoslavia, Algeria, Libya, Morocco, Tunisia, and other countries opposed the scramble of the superpowers for hegemony in the Mediterranean Sea. The Chinese people resolutely supported them in their endeavor to make the Mediterranean a sea of the littoral countries only, and to exclude both the Soviet and American naval powers. The

41. "Superpowers' Contention for Hegemony in the Mediterranean," *PR*, no. 15, Apr. 14, 1972, pp. 15-16.

CPR here played upon anti-Russian sentiments among Mediterranean peoples and even the Arab states.

Not only in Eastern Europe and the Mediterranean, but the world over, the USSR carried out policies indistinguishable from past and present Western imperialism. Soviet revisionism, as Peking described it in another context, was following the beaten track of aggression of British imperialism in Asia and Africa in former days.[42] It was trying to build a vast network of naval bases, extending from the Mediterranean to the Indian Ocean. In 1968 and 1969, during numerous visits to India, Soviet leaders had promised New Delhi massive aid; at the same time they had grabbed two Indian naval bases and acquired the right to use naval bases on the Andaman and Nicobar islands, which were of great military importance in controlling the Stait of Malacca and the Bay of Bengal. They increasingly collaborated with the reactionary regimes of Malaysia, Singapore, the Philippines, and Thailand. The new Soviet tsars entertained hopes of filling the "vacuum" in the Indian Ocean left by the British imperialists' projected withdrawal of their forces from east of Suez, to build up Soviet sea supremacy from the Black Sea to the Far East via the Suez canal and the Indian Ocean. The Soviet leaders' attempt to open up such an arc-shaped maritime route, extending from the Black Sea through the Mediterranean, the Red Sea, the Indian Ocean, and the western Pacific to the Sea of Japan, strikingly revealed the aggressive nature of Soviet social-imperialism.[43]

As early as 1965, according to *Peking Review,* the Soviet Union's Pacific Fleet and Black Sea Fleet had begun to "visit" ports in almost every city on the Red Sea, the Arabian Gulf, and the Indian Ocean. Soviet naval vessels, disguised as fishing boats, and electronic spy ships were sent into the Indian Ocean to engage in "criminal activities."[44]

The Soviets worked from two directions: from the Sea of Japan and, in the west, from the Black Sea via the Mediterranean to the Indian Ocean. The Kremlin's "criminal design" was to build the eastern sector of this maritime arc by sending its Pacific Fleet, based at Haishen-wei, to prowl the seas and thrust its way into the Indian Ocean through the Sea of Japan, the western Pacific, and the Strait of Malacca between Malaya and Indonesia. The present-day "maneuvering ground" of the Soviet Pacific fleet extended from the Sea of Japan and the Kurile Islands to east of Taiwan. This display of sea power was blackmail aimed at the Pacific countries.

42. See n 40 above.

43. "Soviet Revisionist 'Gunboat Policy': Attempt to Build Up Naval Supremacy," *PR,* June 27, 1969, pp. 16-18.

44. "U.S.-Soviet Scramble for Hegemony in the South Asian Subcontinent and Indian Ocean," *PR,* Jan. 14, 1972, pp. 16-17.

For some time Chinese Communist propaganda against Japan and the alleged resurgence of Japanese militarism had been sharply mounted and had reached new heights. On the occasion of American Vice-President Spiro Agnew's visit to Japan, *People's Daily* referred to Agnew and Prime Minister Sato as "sneaking" into South Korea for "sinister activities" in the name of attending the presidential inauguration of the "U.S. imperialist lackey" Pak Jung Hi.[45] This represented an act of aggression by both U.S. imperialism and Japanese imperialism. American imperialism, the Japanese reactionaries, and the Pak puppet clique in South Korea were colluding through bilateral military agreements to establish a "triangular military alliance." America's so-called new Asia policy gave Japanese militarism the active role as a pawn for its aggression in Asia. Ambitious Japanese militarism was eager to carry out military expansion by all means in South Korea. But this would be a mere step in its reembarkation on the old path of launching aggression in Asia. Japanese militarism had recently carried out a series of frantic activities. It had flagrantly announced the inclusion of Korean and Chinese territories in Japan's "sphere of defense." One could easily see that the reviving Japanese expansionism had definitely become a very dangerous aggressive force in Asia. Just like American imperialism, Japanese militarism, attempting now to play the role of shock force for American aggression in Asia while rebuilding its own sphere of influence, would simply dig its own grave in the event it should dare to unleash a new war.[46]

Communist China was not only concerned with the Soviet-American rapprochement and the military and diplomatic link-up between the U.S.A. and Japan but also increasingly with the tightening of Russo-Japanese relations. The Soviets, *Peking Review* asserted, had decided to collaborate with the Japanese reactionaries for the joint development of Siberia, and all for the purpose of rigging up a U.S.A.-Soviet Union-Japan military alliance, though running thus the risk of selling out Soviet Russia's sovereign rights.

On the occasion of the fortieth anniversary of the "September 18 incident" in 1931, which signaled the beginning of the Japanese aggression against Manchuria and China, *People's Daily* warned of the revival of Japanese militarism. It had become "so rampant" because it was backed not only by U.S. imperialism but also because it was "abetted by social-imperialism," the USSR.[47]

While collaborating and struggling with each other, the Soviet revisionists and U.S. imperialists tried to redivide the world. In regard to

45. *Ibid.*, pp. 20-21.
46. *PR*, May 30, 1969, p. 16.
47. *People's Daily*, Sept. 18, 1971 (*PR*, Sept. 24, 1971).

Czechoslovakia and Vietnam, Peking claimed to know they had reached a "tacit" understanding. Working hand in glove with U.S. imperialism, the Soviet revisionists did their utmost, Peking claimed, perhaps again taxing the gullibility of its readers, to peddle the "political solution fraud" on the Middle East issue in an attempt to strangle the Arab people's struggle against imperialism and aggression. Prompted by their common needs to oppose China and revolution, the Soviet leadership in 1968 had made one despicable deal after another with U.S. imperialism—on the "nuclear non-proliferation treaty," on the provision of "nuclear protection," and on many other problems to strengthen the bilateral Soviet-U.S. "cooperation" and collaboration for world domination. Collaborating with the reactionaries in Japan, India, Indonesia, and other countries, the Soviet revisionist clique was trying to rig up a "ring of encirclement" against China.[48]

Fears of Encirclement

Just as the CPC was fearful of the specter of encirclement by the USSR, America, and Japan, the Soviet Union similarly claimed to fear encirclement by China and the U.S.A. in combination with other European powers, especially West Germany.

In an article in *Literaturnaya Gazeta,* "Notes on the History of our Times: Bonn-Peking?—The Attraction of Opposites," Ernst Henry warned that it was precisely their seeming oppositeness that could bring Bonn and Peking together under certain conditions. The CPR and West Germany were beginning to gravitate toward each other.[49] In the event that NATO should collapse, West Germany would be isolated. But the same kind of isolation had already been encountered by Maoist China in Asia. In Peking they were thinking that it might be possible to compensate for the failure of the great-power Maoist policy in Asia by collusion with Bonn.

The Maoist attempt to establish China's hegemony in Eastern and Southeast Asia had miscarried. The attempt to "maoize" Indonesia and break through to the Indian Ocean at one leap had not succeeded. The armed conflict with India and China's intrigues in the Arab countries had all failed to produce the hoped-for results. Nor had Peking been able, it was claimed, to create alliances with Karachi and Tokyo. Therefore, as seen from Communist China, a Peking-Bonn axis would be especially useful.

48. *PR*, Jan. 10, 1969, pp. 23-24, 31.
49. Henry, in *Literaturnaya gazeta,* no. 15, Apr. 14, 1968, p. 14, and no. 16, Apr. 17, p. 15 (*CDSP* 20, no. 21 [June 12, 1968]: 7-10).

During World War II Hitler was ready to strike an alliance with Japan, despite all racial principles. Similarly, Minister Strauss was quoted to the effect that Peking could help in the reunification of Germany. As far as Peking was concerned, politicians of Mao's type have never shunned deals with the "devil" himself. In August 1967 the French journalist Geneviève Tabouis had reported on a top-secret circular from Peking to leaders of pro-Chinese organizations in Europe, dealing with how to answer the questions of alarmed followers of Mao regarding the Chinese "flirtation with Bonn." The circular pointed out that Marxist-Leninists must not ignore reactionary regimes if these regimes were enemies of their enemies. Both Communist China and the FRG were natural allies in the struggle against a plot such as the treaty on nonproliferation of nuclear weapons. Peking had repeatedly oriented itself toward extreme rightists.

Peking, according to *Literaturnaya Gazeta,* was anxious to create a big anti-Soviet bloc in Asia and to strengthen its western flank. No doubts of an ideological nature, no pangs of remorse, would seize Peking. The Chinese leadership had already concocted a special pseudo-Marxist theory for the justification of collusion with the West German revanchists, the so-called theory of the intermediate zones. According to this theory, China must strengthen her ties not only with the revolutionary peoples of Asia, Africa, and Latin America, but also with the capitalist countries over which the U.S.A. was trying to establish its dominion. West Germany was among these countries. Economic contacts between Bonn and Peking had rapidly increased and the Federal Republic of Germany had become China's largest West European supplier. In the contemporary age it was not so far from the Rhine to the Yangtze.

The same journal, *Literaturnaya Gazeta,* in a follow-up article six weeks later, "William II, Gerstenmaier and Mao," pointed to the sharp denunciation of its previous article "Bonn-Peking" in both West Germany and Japan as sure proof that the accusation had touched a raw nerve. The Chinese were reminded of William II's calling for merciless struggle against the "yellow peril." It was not Russia, they were now told, that had invented the "yellow peril" myth.[50]

Peking's Foreign Policy in the Russian Mirror

While Peking castigated Moscow's foreign policies, Moscow had no good word to say about Peking's foreign course; each country charged the opponent with deviation from and betrayal of Marxism-Leninism both in its domestic and foreign policy.

50. *Literaturnaya gazeta*, no. 21, May 22, 1968, p. 9 (*CDSP* 20, no. 21 [1968]: 10).

A scathing criticism of Peking's foreign policy appeared in March in *Kommunist*.[51] According to it, Peking had long calculated on turning Albania into China's beachhead on the European continent. Tirana was used for intensive pro-Chinese propaganda beamed at the socialist countries. The visit to Albania of a delegation headed by the chief of the Chinese Army General Staff in late 1968 had led to wide speculation centering on the installation of Chinese missiles on Albanian territory. The Maoists, Moscow charged, sought in the Balkans a clash between the USSR and socialist countries on one hand and the forces of imperialism on the other.

The Peking leadership, according to *Kommunist*, in line with its general policy of aggravating international tensions, had long promoted a deepening of the Vietnam conflict.[52] It hoped that the DRV would wage a "protracted war" and draw the USSR and other socialist countries deeper into the conflict. On the other hand, practically every stage in the escalation of the aggression in Vietnam had been accompanied by mutual assurances between the U.S.A. and the CPR that they would not attack each other. Mao had not only rejected unity of action in the struggle against American aggression. He still placed obstacles in the way of shipping armaments and strategic material through Chinese territory from the socialist countries to Vietnam.

The central component of Mao's struggle in his fight against the socialist system and the world Communist movement was, according to *Kommunist*, his anti-Soviet course. In September 1968 Mao declared in a telegram to Albania's leaders that he was initiating a "new historical period in the struggle" against the CPSU. An anti-Soviet policy had been made the basis of the CPR's long-range domestic and foreign political program. The Maoists were trying to obliterate from the Chinese people's minds the image of the Soviet Union as the prototype of China's future—an image long held high—and to let loose against her a filthy stream of slander and misinformation. During 1968 *People's Daily* alone had published more than 600 extensive anti-Soviet pieces. Since Mao's ideas had replaced Marxism-Leninism, the Peking leaders deemed it unnecessary in 1968 to mark the 51st anniversary of the October Revolution.

Mao and his group attempted to prepare the Chinese for the possibility of armed conflicts between the USSR and the CPR. Chinese leaders were taking a direct part in whipping up an anti-Soviet psychosis. On the eve of the 19th anniversary of the CPR, Premier Chou remarked at a state reception that "anything can be expected" of the Soviet Union, including an "attack on China."[53]

Bloody provocations along the Soviet-Chinese border, such as occurred

51. *Kommunist,* no. 5, March 1969, pp. 104-16.
52. *Ibid.*
53. *People's Daily,* Oct. 1, 1968.

on March 2, 14, and 15, 1969, highlighted the growing bellicosity of Peking. The CPC would like ultimately to foist its ideological-political program on the peoples of the USSR and turn the USSR and the CPSU into
instruments of Peking's policies.

The Maoists' anti-Soviet activities had had their effect on Soviet-Chinese
relations along both party and state lines. According to *Kommunist,* the
Maoists' actions and statements violated all the articles and principles of
the Treaty of Friendship, Alliance and Mutual Assistance concluded between the CPR and the USSR on February 14, 1950.[54] The small number
of still-operating channels and remaining interstate ties was constantly subjected to all kinds of attacks by the Chinese side. An atmosphere of tension around the Soviet Embassy and other Soviet establishments in Peking,
and provocative incidents nearby-by, impeded their normal functioning.

The CPSU was rebuffing the anti-socialist policy and schismatic activities of Mao's group, but assured the Chinese people that it did not iden-
tify it with the ruling clique. The CPSU had reared the Soviet people in a
spirit of respect for the Chinese people, its culture, customs, and revolutionary history. Memorable dates in the revolutionary struggle waged
by China's working class have been celebrated widely in the Soviet Union,
as have been the 100th anniversary of the birth of Sun Yat-sen; the 80th
anniversary of the birth of Li Ta-chao, one of the founders of the CPC;
the seventieth anniversary of the birth of the Chinese Communist Chu
Chiu-pai; the anniversary of the birth of Lu Hsun, the founder of modern
Chinese literature; and the anniversaries of the. births of the eminent
Chinese writers Chou Li-po, Lao She, and others.

Peking, however, bent on struggle against the socialist countries, was
seeking rapprochement with the leading powers of the capitalist world. In
1968 the CPR had expressed readiness to conclude an agreement on the
five principles of peaceful coexistence and in February 1969 proposed resumption of Sino-American talks in Warsaw.

Peking calculated that American imperialism, after proper reduction of
American commitments in Asia, would aim its aggressive ambitions at
Europe. Some circles in the U.S.A. wanted America to establish "close
ties" with China and, with the help of the CPR in Asia and the Federal
Republic of Germany in Europe, to create a kind of vise to "contain" the
socialist countries. West German Foreign Minister Willy Brandt had indicated that Bonn wished to expand trade ties with China. F. Strauss, the
leader of West Germany's reactionary forces, had suggested that West
Germany link plans for strengthening her stance in fighting the status quo

54. See n 51 p. 257.

in Europe to Mao's policy. The Maoist position coincided with the stand of West German ruling circles in favor of the struggle against the socialist camp, the hostile line toward the German Democratic Republic, the desire for nuclear weapons, the exacerbation of tension in Europe, and the revision of state boundaries.

As far as foreign economic ties were concerned, the Chinese trade had been radically reoriented. Between 1961 and 1967 the trade of the CPR with the socialist countries had dropped by almost two-thirds, the share of the socialist countries in China's foreign trade having declined from 64 percent to 23 percent. But in the same period the volume of the CPR's trade with the developed capitalist countries had tripled. And China was accepting Western capitalist loans, and the West's technical assistance and help in training cadres. At the same time Mao's group had virtually withdrawn from the anti-imperialist struggle except for routine and meaningless anti-American statements.

The Maoists were making efforts to strengthen their influence in the countries of the Third World. They tried to exploit differences among Asian countries by playing on the racial communality and promising aid to some, while practicing nuclear blackmail on others. The Mao clique was concentrating its efforts—undertaking economic aid and exerting political pressure—on specific countries that were viewed as beachheads for the propagation of Chinese influence and Maoist concepts. In Asia these countries were Laos, Cambodia, Burma, Yemen, and Pakistan. In Africa, they were Guinea, Tanzania, the Congo (Brazzaville), and Zambia.

Mao's group was using its impact upon Third World countries to discredit the influence of the socialist states. The Maoists were advancing the idea of creating a special Afro-Asian community to oppose the socialist countries. In practice they were thus clearing the way for the forces of reaction and neo-colonialism and for military-bureaucratic regimes. Chinese policies in Indonesia, Ghana, and other countries were among the causes of anti-democratic coups.

Actually, the Maoists were doing greatest harm to parties and groups that followed Maoist policy closely. The Maoists did not hesitate to encourage actions that led to the destruction of entire Communist Parties, as was the case in Indonesia. A typical example for the CPR's inciting physical violence against the representatives of progressive forces that try to escape their influence was the Communist Party of Burma. Peking prodded this party into conducting a "cultural revolution" in 1968 that turned into a bloody massacre of Communists. Maoist policy of stirring up conflicts and encouraging extremist, nationalist circles had been clearly manifested in Arab countries. The Mao group was trying to strengthen its influence on the Palestinian organizations that opposed a political settlement of the conflict in the Near East. There existed in the CPR several centers for military and political training of insurgents from developing countries.

Yet, the Peking leaders had recently failed to win over a single Communist Party. On the contrary, some parties that previously shared Peking's point of view became increasingly critical of Mao's political course. That was true of the Communist Party of Japan and the Communist Party of India. Numerous pro-Peking groups were in a state of crisis. This also applied to Grippe's group in Belgium, which had collapsed, and to the pro-Chinese "Communist Party" of Italy, which had split. Still, Maoists had retained their grip over the Albanian Workers Party, the Communist Parties of New Zealand, Burma, Thailand, and a part of the Communist underground in Indonesia. In January 1968 the creation of a Maoist "Communist Party" of France was announced. In December 1968 was proclaimed the formation of a pro-Chinese Communist Party of Germany and then of a Maoist party in Sweden.

Peking was keeping close watch on the stormy developments of movements of young people and students in West Europe. At the height of the student activities in France, pro-Chinese sympathies deepened. Peking played on young people's revolutionary impatience in every possible way. Chinese propaganda was trying to prove the thesis that Moscow-oriented Communist Parties have lost their vanguard role.

Peking was also employing the new tactics with respect to international democratic organizations (the World Federation of Trade Unions, the World Federation of Democratic Youth, the World Peace Council, and others). Peking apparently wished to strike at these organizations "from below" by intensifying the schismatic activities of its agents in trade unions and in youth, women's, and other organizations. On the other hand, Peking also wanted to take advantage of its formal membership in these organizations to continue its former campaign of sabotage and slander. Mao and his entourage were also trying to call an international conference of pro-Maoist parties to oppose an international conference of Communists called to Moscow. Peking's objective was to establish an international political current "directed from a single center," China's capital, and the spearhead of its struggle was directed against the socialist states and the world Communist movement.

A comparative analysis of the accusations leveled at Moscow by Peking and vice-versa is instructive in several respects. Both sides were deeply convinced of the implacable hostility of the other. Each side suspected the moves by the other side and its attempt to improve its relations with the imperialist arch-enemy, the U.S. Yet, in the emerging war of words, the "socialist" opponent was frequently denounced in more vituperative terms than the imperialist foe. The denunciation of the latter became almost a religious ritual, while the denunciation of the former was both an affair of the heart and a matter of deepest conviction. Each side feared the attempt of the other at "collusion" with capitalism and imperialism, at military encirclement. Both sides were convinced that they were involved in a struggle that might last for decades and end in war. The Soviet Union had no doubts that the opponent wanted to spread its "cultural revolution" into the USSR and the CPR feared that the Soviets wished to transplant "capitalism" to China, which had been "restored" in the USSR. Both seemed certain that the other side was prepared to assist in the overthrow of its government. Each party of course, charged the other with having strayed from the path of Marxism-Leninism, of staging bloody provocations along the border, of bearing responsibility for the deterioration of their mutual relations, for the weakening of economic and cultural ties linking the two countries, and for carrying on a ruthless diplomatic and political warfare against the other side in the countries of the Third World. The charges of great-power ambitions, chauvinism, social-imperialism, colonialism, and economic exploitation were freely hurled against each other, as were accusations of interventionism and violation of national sovereignty. Comparisons to fascist aggression and Hitler in particular were frequent. It can hardly be assumed that the war of words could be further escalated without becoming physical.

Judging by historical precedent, many a war has broken out with less acrimonious exchange preceding it. In the atomic age, however, the tolerance of even the greatest and most powerful states for absorbing insults and vituperation has apparently increased manifold. With its onset the diplomacy of courteous disagreement has become a thing of the past.

Nationality Problems and Policy

The territorial dispute between the two Communist giants was closely tied up with nationality problems on both sides of the extended Sino-Soviet boundary, the longest on earth between two states. While some of the national minorities in both the CPR and the USSR live in the interior, the bulk in both states inhabit the border areas. Both states are multinational and both have adopted the Leninist nationality policy and boast of their successes in this field. While the nationality question is of significance for the CPR, where minorities make up about six percent of the entire population, it is a problem of transcending importance for the USSR, where the Great Russians, contrary to Soviet official statistics, probably do not amount to more than 50 percent of the population.

Frequently the same ethnic groups, Mongols, Uighurs, Kazakhs, and others, live on both sides of the Sino-Soviet border. They had been sub-jected to Russification from Moscow and Sinification from Peking, in spite of high-sounding fraternal phrases of internationalism, and rejection of great-power chauvinism, and of forcible assimilation by both the CPSU and the CPC. The deeds never matched the professions. The practice has rather contradicted the concept of national equality, which has been ex-tolled in the USSR, allegedly crystallized in Lenin's and Stalin's nationality policy, and has been religiously copied in the CPR. But while accusing each other, both the CPR and the Soviet Union have extolled the exem-plary manner in which each has solved the nationality question in her own country.

Peking and Moscow have hurled at each other the most abusive charges with regard to nationality policy. They have accused each other of having violated the comradely Leninist concept of national equality and of having, under the thin camouflage of internationalism, established the domination of the Russians and of the Han nationality in their respective countries. Communists throughout the world tended to ignore charges of this kind, as long as they originated in "capitalist" and imperialist" circles, but they have been unable to continue belittling or even ignoring these accusations once they were leveled by another Communist-ruled nation.

China has never been inhabited only by the Chinese, or Han as they were called, but by numerous peoples such as the Chuang, Uighurs, Dun-gans, Yi, Tibetans, Miao, Manchurians, Bui, Koreans, and many others. Altogether, more than one hundred different nationalities and national groups live today in the CPR. According to Chinese figures, considered by many scholars untrustworthy, the total of all these peoples was between 42 and 43 million. Mao, in 1957, even put them at only over 30 million. But recently Russian experts have held that there are almost twice as many and that the lands of non-Chinese peoples account for about 60 percent of the present territory of China.

While the Chinese nationality policy was painted in dark colors by the Soviet comrades, it shone brightly when illuminated in Peking's own light. On March 3, 1972, for instance, *Peking Review* asserted that people of all nationalities in China were united as never before; large numbers of cadres of minority nationalities were maturing. Their industrial and agricultural production and living standards were rising steadily and their cultural and educational undertakings were advancing rapidly.[55]

Due to the institution of regional autonomy, democratic reform, and socialist transformation, Peking claimed, the people of all nationalities in China have established and developed a new relationship of equality, close

55. "Flourishing Minority Nationality Areas," *PR*, March 3, 1972.

unity, and common progress. Especially since the Great Proletarian Cultural Revolution, tremendous change has taken place in the country's border regions where the minority peoples live.

According to the CPR, striking industrial and agricultural progress has been made in nationality areas such as the Inner Mongolian Autonomous Region, the Tibetan Autonomous Region, the Sinkiang Uighur Autonomous Region, and others. The health and culture of the peoples concerned had also made tremendous strides and large numbers of minority nationality cadres had come to the fore. Continuous feuds among various nationalities before liberation, over land, mountain forests, and water resources in many parts of China, had been replaced by "unity among the people of all nationalities in their common struggle under the guidance of Marxism-Leninism-Mao Tsetung Thought."

In a speech in February 1957, "On the correct handling of contradictions among the people," Mao himself had directed attention to the nationality question in China and to the imperative need of fostering good relations between the Han people and the minority nationalities. "The key to this question" lay "in overcoming Han Chauvinism." But at the same time local nationalism, "wherever it exists among the minority nationalities, mustl also be overcome." Both kinds of nationalism were harmful to the unity of nationalities.[56] Still, according to this speech by Mao, it was Han chauvinism that appeared as the somewhat greater danger of the two.

In this analysis Mao followed the pattern of Soviet nationality theory that has always underlined the dangers of both kinds of nationalism, that of the dominant nationality and that of the minority nationalities. In practice, the dominant nationality in the USSR and the CPR was seldom treated as the sinner; but the minority nationalities were regularly accused of indulging in national excesses, harmful to the Party and the state and to the cause of socialism.

According to Mao in 1957, there had already been a "big improvement" in the relations among the nationalities of China, though a number of problems remained unsolved. In some areas both Han and local nationalism, he conceded, still existed "to a serious degree."

Mao was somewhat more willing to admit the continuance of problems in the field of nationality relations and nationality policy than the Soviets were. The latter have, for decades, unrelentingly claimed that the nationality question in the USSR has been completely solved.

In 1964, on the occasion of an Amateur Art Festival of the National Minorities, Lu Ting-Yi, Alternate Member of the Political Bureau of the

---

56. Eleventh Session of the Supreme State Conference, Feb. 27, 1957, *People's Daily*, June 15, 1967.

CC of the CPC and Vice-Premier of the State Council, presenting an authoritative talk on "The Cultural Revolution of China's National Minorities," claimed the most extensive progress in the field of nationality policy and national relations.[57]

Since the liberation of 1949, he said, the national minorities in China have developed national regional autonomy and the full rights of national equality and self-government. With only a few exceptions, Lu asserted, socialist transformation has been completed by most national minorities and people's communes have been set up throughout the areas they inhabited. The struggle, Lu indicated, to carry the democratic revolution further was especially sharp and complicated in the frontier regions. The latter were "at the outposts" of the struggle against imperialism, the Chiang gang, reactionaries of all countries, and modern revisionism. There was a pointed reference to the strategic significance of the ethnic border regions, their special importance in the context of the Sino-Soviet rift.[58]

In the Soviet judgment, Chinese claims in regard to positive achievements of their nationality policy were vastly exaggerated; actually, Han chauvinism, comparable to Imperial China's maltreatment of and arrogance toward China's national minorities, reigned supreme. The Soviets displayed conspicuously the denunciation of the CPR's nationality policy by the Party boss of the allied Outer Mongolian People's Republic, Tsedenbal, when on the occasion of the July 1969 Moscow Conference he referred to the "oppression and humiliation meted out to Mongolians, Kazakhs, Tibetans, Uighurs, and other national minorities in China, and the gross violations of these groups' rights and freedoms."[59]

A full-blast attack on Peking's nationality policy by T. Rakhimov, "The Great Power Policy of Mao. . .and his Group on the Nationalities," appeared in Kommunist in 1967. After detailing how the Tibetans, the Chuangs, and the Mongols of Inner Mongolia and other ethnic units, though living compactly, had been deliberately divided up into numerous administrative units, the author concluded that the so-called autonomy in China was nothing but "splintering of nationalities and the forcible and artificial breaking up of their historically evolved ethnic boundaries."[60] As a result of these administrative measures, the Mongolians were transformed into a minority in their own autonomous region and constituted no more than 8 to 10 percent of its population.

The master recognizes, of course, the ways of his disciples. The Soviets

57. Lu Ting-Yi, "Cultural Revolution of China's National Minorities," Dec. 4, 1964, pp. 22-24.

58. Ibid.; see also "Yunnan's Minority Peoples on Socialist Road" (PR, June 4, 1965, pp. 22-25).

59. CDSP 21, no. 23 [July 2, 1969]: 3-17.

60. Kommunist, no. 7, May 1967, pp. 114-15.

themselves have pursued the same policy in their own republics, settled Great Russians and Ukrainians in large numbers in the border republics; they have smothered, if not removed, the natives, redrawn administrative lines to weaken the will and the power of the national minorities, and forcibly speeded up assimilation.

In his article Rakhimov also charged Peking with having set forth quite frankly a policy of accelerated assimilation of China's minority peoples. Quoting the magazine *Sinkiang Hung Chi* in 1960, he underlined its views as to the superiority of the Chinese element, asking for "amalgamation" because it was the "inevitable trend" and was Marxist and "Communist assimilation." Rakhimov recalled that Marxism and Leninism of course rejected forcible assimilation on principle. Marxism held that the stage of amalgamation of nations, "a long and complicated process," developed only in the highest phase of Communism.

Kommunist accused the Chinese Communists also of having resettled Chinese in masses in the border regions; the Chinese had grown in Sinkiang from a mere 3 percent in 1949 to 45 percent in 1966, in Tibet from virtually zero to one-third of the population. The CPC had justified this on the basis of an alleged threat from the direction of the Soviet Union, the Mongolian People's Republic, and India. The author of the article in *Kommunist* underlined further the Sinification of the areas inhabited by the small border nations and the repression of their intelligentsia, all under the banner of fighting "revisionism." He stressed the artificial infusion of the Chinese language into the languages of small nations, the fight against schooling, and the teaching of national history, especially during the so-called Cultural Revolution. The Mao group was particularly concerned about eradicating love of the Soviet Union from the minds of the Uighurs, Kazakhs, Mongolians, and many other peoples of China who had kinsfolk on the Soviet side of the border.

Peking's nationality policy was repeatedly criticized in the Soviet press.[61] Chinese intellectuals had previously pointed with pride to the impact of the slogan "Let a Hundred Flowers Bloom" upon the culture of the small nationalities; later, however, books were burned, especially in the border regions, teachers were removed, and national minority writers and poets placed under "special surveillance." Peking apparently suspected and particularly resisted secessionist movements. A "ridiculous charge" was made, *Literaturnaya Gazeta* pointed out, against representatives of the Kazakh national intelligentsia, that they had tried to create a Kazakh Khanate and to unite all the Kazakhs in China, Mongolia, and the Soviet Union under its aegis. Another time representatives from Peking

61. "Exiles from Sinkiang on the 'Hundred Flowers,' " *Literaturnaya gazeta*, no. 4, Jan. 25, 1967, p. 14 (*CDSP*, 17, no. 4 [1967]: 9-10).

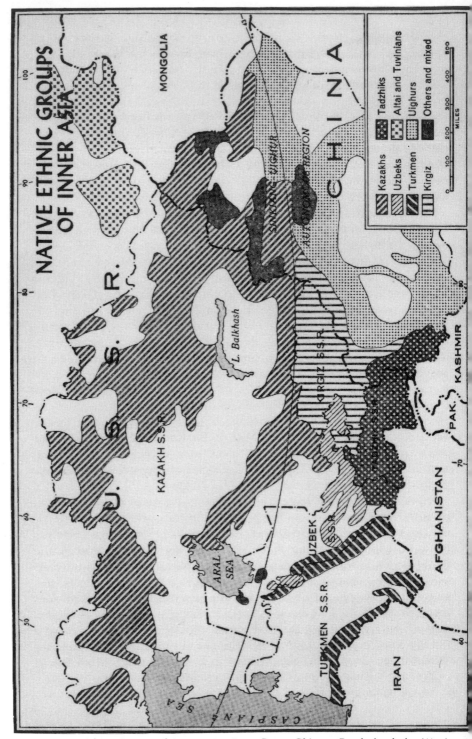

3 Native Ethnic Groups of Inner Asia. From *Russo-Chinese Borderlands* by W. A. Douglas Jackson. Van Nostrand Searchlight Book #2, Princeton, N. J., 1962. Used with permission of D. Van Nostrand Co., Inc.

had declared that the people of Sinkiang had two hearts, a yellow one, which was Russian, and a red one, which was Chinese, and they threatened: "We shall trample the yellow heart."

According to the Soviets, the victory of the Chinese Revolution in 1949 was received with great expectations by the minority nationalities. But they were soon to grow disillusioned. The non-Chinese peoples had hoped for the creation of their own states within People's China and for the elimination of economic and cultural backwardness. But after 1949, the Maoists, according to the Russians, had soon discarded their Marxist-Leninist nationality policy and had rather pursued a great-power policy, resting on the pillars of forcible assimilation and Sinification.

The Chinese had resorted to the most devious methods for the purpose of establishing and retaining their domination over the various ethnic groups in the CPR. A single people like the Tibetans, for instance, was deliberately split up into numerous administrative units by the dominant Chinese. The Tibetan Autonomous Region comprised only some Tibetans. The bulk of the Tibetans were forced to live separately in nine autonomous districts, though these were all contiguous to each other. Similarly politically motivated was Chinese policy toward the Inner Mongolian Autonomous Region, which had been created in 1947. Using the pretext of extending fraternal aid to the Mongol people, Chinese from two neighboring provinces were added to the Mongolian region. Furthermore, Chinese settlers in Inner Mongolia were plowing up the pasture land of the Mongolian livestock raisers, which resulted in a sharp decline of this industry.

In Sinkiang the Chinese had vigorously pursued a policy of colonization, giving resettled Chinese the richest and best-developed lands. In Sinkiang, Inner Mongolia, and Tibet, the Maoists, the Russians charged, were even resorting to compulsory marriages between local residents and Chinese settlers.

According to Moscow, the small nationalities of China and their cultures had been made the subject of intensive Sinification. Under the pretext of "developing" the languages of small ethnic groups, the Chinese vocabulary was deliberately introduced. Mongolian writing and language thus had no future. While the number of secondary and higher schools was increasing, most of the students were Chinese, and lectures at higher schools were delivered exclusively in Chinese. History was falsified. To attach the numerous minorities closer to China, it was claimed that Mongols, Uighurs, and Tibetans had lived on territory belonging to China virtually from the Stone Age. Actually, Inner Mongolia was conquered by the Manchurians in the seventeenth century, Tibet in 1792, and Sinkiang in 1759.

Since the beginning of the Cultural Revolution, Moscow has charged, the lot of minority peoples in the CPR has worsened; the autonomy of peoples, guaranteed by the CPC constitution, was practically eliminated. During the Cultural Revolution Moslem mosques and Buddhist temples and monasteries in the national regions were pillaged and religious sentiments of the non-Chinese peoples outraged. National cadres in the outlying regions of China were persecuted and even exterminated. In some areas outright uprisings and military clashes had taken place, as in Tibet in June and August 1968, and in Sinkiang in January 1969.

Russians have charged that the Maoist leadership's policy toward the Mongolian People's Republic was to a very great extent a "continuation" of the old anti-Mongolian policy of the Manchu-Chinese oppressors. The Peking leadership tried to reconcile Mongolians to Chinese rule by pointing out that sometimes they had ruled the Chinese "and sometimes history has charged [!] us with the task of ruling."[62] The Maoist propaganda, aimed at Outer Mongolia, had been stepped up in 1962 and had become even more aggressive in 1968-69. In Inner Mongolia, Mongolians and Kazakhs now had to speak the Chinese language exclusively and dress only in the Chinese manner; they were forbidden to celebrate their own nationality holidays, to perform religious ceremonies, and to wear articles of clothing with national ornaments. The policy of assimilation was pressed by various means.

The Soviets, while disputing the achievements of the CPR in the field of nationality policy, were magnifying their own accomplishments in this area. The new program of the CPSU, adopted in 1961 and hailed by Khrushchev as the "Communist Manifesto of the present epoch," made the most extensive claims also in regard to nationality policy. Allegedly, this policy has led to the full economic and cultural development of all Soviet nationalities, and has finally brought about the "solution" of the nationality question, "one of the greatest achievements of Socialism." "With reciprocal fraternal assistance, primarily from the Great Russian people, all the Soviet non-Russian republics have set up their own modern industries, trained their own national working class and intelligentsia and developed a culture that is national in form and socialist in content."[63]

Yet the CPSU itself continues to be controlled by the Russian element. National equality to this very day is a claim rather than reality, and national discrimination has not yet vanished from the USSR. The Russian culture and language enjoy a privileged position in the Soviet multinational state and the Great Russian nationality continues to play the dominant role. The cultural development of the non-Russian peoples lacks genuine freedom, not only in regard to content, but even in regard to form.

62. *Ibid.*
63. *Pravda,* Oct. 17, 1961; also A. D. Low, "Soviet Nationality Policy and the New Program of the CPSU," *The Russian Review* (Jan. 1963), pp. 3-29; *Pravda,* Nov. 16, 1967, p. 1 (*CDSP*, 19, no. 46 [1967]: 22-23); Podgorny on nationalities, *Pravda,* May 22, 1965, pp. 1-2 (*CDSP*, 17, no. 21 [1965]: 3-5).

The absence of genuine national self-determination and equality is the basic source of weakness of Soviet nationality policy, and as a matter of fact, equally so of Chinese nationality policy. National inequality and discrimination affect both the individuals of the various ethnic groups in the USSR and the nationalities of the border regions and of the interior region in their entirety. What appears to cause great concern to many a minor nationality in both the USSR and the CPR is that its territory, due to constant influx and colonization by Russians and Chinese on their respective sides of the border, may lose its national character and that the numerically dominant border nationality may cease to be a majority or plurality. Many a national minority in the Soviet Union or in China, anxious, like any biological species, to preserve its character, its cultural and linguistic identity, fears submergence and opposes assimilation, whether it is creeping or sweeping, "voluntary" or enforced.

Just as the USSR belittled and doubted the true Leninist character of the nationality policy of the CPR and the existence of genuine national equality in Communist China, so did the latter deny that the Soviet Union had solved the nationality question within her boundaries. Peking has questioned outright whether the USSR was a voluntary federation of equal nationalities, and has in addition accused her of imperialism and neocolonialism and the desire to extend the existing inequality beyond her borders and her East European satellite Empire.

Other Domestic Policies under Criticism

In the course of the increasingly acrimonious exchange between Moscow and Peking, the domestic policies and situations of the two Communist powers have become more and more the target of vituperative accusations by the other. Even "dictatorship," "capitalism," and "fascism" have become some of the common charges hurled by each of the two Communist powers against the other. Again, just as in the case of foreign policy, it is difficult to conceive of any accusations leveled against the capitalist West that were not directed with equal vehemence, if not with greater bitterness, against the other Communist superpower.

In the article "New Tsars' Social-Fascist Tyranny," *Peking Review* focused attention on the domestic scene of the Soviet Union and denounced the fascistlike repression of the Soviet people by the Mosvow "revisionist clique."[64] The masses of the Soviet working people were cruelly repressed and the ruling clique was doing its ulmost to strengthen the state machinery, its troops, police, prisons and courts, and suppress the

64. *PR*, Apr. 4, 1969, pp. 22-23.

people's revolutionary struggles at home. To reinforce their police apparatus, the Soviets in July 1966 had established a social security ministry and set up motorized police units and had resorted increasingly to "people's guardsmen" to suppress the populace. They had created a host of tricks to give legal grounds for their fascist outrages. Numerous decrees and regulations were designed to fetter the Soviet people through "legality, law, order" and "the iron discipline of the party." Early in 1969 a new regulation under the label "control by the whole people" had entrusted tremendous power to Soviet control organs set up throughout the entire country in all enterprises, collective farms, government institutions, army units, all departments of production, management, and service trades. Thus, under the signboard of "democracy for the whole people," the Soviet clique was actually practicing a fascist dictatorship, establishing concentration camps, jails and "lunatic asylums" all over the USSR. It is difficult to find in the *Peking Review* worse, even similar, descriptions of the political situation in Western countries!

No wonder that the Chinese press holds out to its readers the prospect and promise of an "overthrow" of such a vile reactionary government. In the article "Revolutionary Soviet People will rise up to overthrow reactionary rule of Kremlin's New Tsars," it is claimed that the Soviet revisionist ruling clique had turned the world's first socialist state created by the great Lenin into a "capitalist state" and "enforced fascist dictatorship of the bourgeoisie" over the Soviet working people. Using the camouflage of "culture for the whole people," it had allowed "bourgeois ideology to rule supreme" in the cultural sphere.[65]

For years the Kremlin's new tsars had shouted themselves hoarse that the Soviet Union was continually "perfecting socialist democracy." However, the myths and lies had been shattered by the Soviet people themselves. Many in the Soviet Union now realized that there was "absolutely no democracy and freedom of the working people, who are completely oppressed and enslaved by the bourgeois privileged stratum represented by the Soviet revisionist ruling clique." Many had poured out their bitter grievances against soaring prices, intensified class differentiation, and the economic exploitation of the broad masses of the working people under the rule of the revisionist ruling clique.

China's Great Proletarian Cultural Revolution had "opened a bright path for the consolidation of the dictatorship of the proletariat, for the prevention of capitalist restoration and for transition to communism." The Brezhnev-Kosygin renegade clique were "mortally afraid" of this unprecedented Cultural Revolution and took great pains to sling mud at it.

65. *PR*, Feb. 9, 1968, p. 21.

The Chinese press particularly underlined that the mere example of the Great Proletarian Cultural Revolution would have a strong revolutionary impact upon the Soviet people. One writer asserted: "Today more and more Soviet people are drawing inspiration and encouragement from China's great proletarian cultural revolution. They have not only come to realize that a second revolution is necessary to overthrow revisionist rule and reestablish the dictatorship of the proletariat in their country. They are already struggling in various ways against the Soviet revisionist clique. It can safely be predicted that a revolutionary storm still more violent [!] than the October Revolution will sweep the Soviet land."[66]

The same author, referring especially to Soviet agriculture as built up by Lenin and Stalin lamented that it allegedly had been completely destroyed by the "Soviet revisionist scabs." Collective and state farms had been converted into capitalist estates for the new Kulaks, where land was redivided among "teams" and the renting of land, hiring of labor, speculation, and profiteering were widely practiced. The polarization of the peasantry had brought about an appalling gap between the rich and the poor, and the great majority of the peasants were subjected to merciless exploitation and squeezed dry.

All this pointed to the capitalist restoration in the Soviet Union. This is the major theme of numerous articles, among them the following fairly representative one entitled "Capitalist Restoration in the Soviet Union: The True Picture of so-called 'Welfare for the Whole People.' "[67] The so-called welfare for the whole people, just like the formula "State of the entire people" was simply "demagogical nonsense." The Soviets advertised wage increases in the USSR. In reality, however, the incomes of the masses of the Soviet laboring people are very low, while the bourgeois elements such as academicians, factory directors, and managers provided themselves with high salaries. The salaries of some academicians were as high as 6,500 roubles a month, while many workers can earn only 60-70 roubles. Wage advances for Soviet workers and employees lagged far behind increases in commodity prices.

The all-round capitalist restoration had landed the country in economic chaos. Market supplies were in serious trouble; there were acute shortages of commodities in state shops and prices on the free market were extremely high. Long queues for consumer goods were the usual sight in Moscow, and elsewhere food prices were prohibitive. Though the Soviet ruling clique had made a big fanfare about "shortening" working hours and, on the occasion of the 50th anniversary of the October Revolution a big to-do about the "five-day week," allegedly marking the transition to

66. "The New Tsars Cover Their Hideous Features," *ibid.*, pp. 23-25.
67. "Capitalist Restoration in the Soviet Union," *PR*, Feb. 16, 1968, pp. 36-37.

Communism, it had actually insisted that the originally stipulated work be completed in the new work week; it had also cut down on lunch time. The interests of the Soviet ruling clique were the interests of the "privileged bourgeois stratum." "This stratum leads the luxurious, corrupt and rotten life of a bourgeois lord, while the broad masses of the Soviet laboring people have once again been oppressed, enslaved and exploited."

The Soviet revisionists' "New System" was a new means to exploit the working people. The "new system" placed capitalist material incentive in a leading position. While the ruling clique bragged that bonuses and other such material incentives can raise the labor remuneration of the workers, this actually was "pure eyewash." The larger part of the bonus payments went into the pockets of the managers and engineers, the high-salaried strata. Some heads of enterprises behaved exactly like capitalists. Under the pretext of "streamlining the staff" and "retrenchment," they had dismissed large numbers of workers and caused a sharp increase in unemployment.[68]

But Peking was not only concerned with the economic, social, and political aspects of the Soviet regime, its deline and bourgeoisification, but also with the alleged deterioration of Soviet culture in the broadest sense of the word.[69] The Komsomol for instance, it charged, had degenerated into a club for the pampered sons and daughters of the privileged stratum. Feasting and reveling had become the main aspect of its activities and testified to the corruption of Soviet youth with the bourgeois way of life. In Moscow, according to Tass, ancient wedding traditions were being revived: "Now the bride and groom can hire a Russian-type troika by telephone and ride to the wedding place." The *Moscow Evening News* had begun issuing a special advertisement supplement. Films were made that corrupted children. As *Peking Review* reported: "Not long ago a Moscow film studio trotted out a movie entitled "I Love You.' The Theme: love affair of teenage students." If one is to believe Peking, Moscow allegedly has totally abandoned its austere and ascetic character and socialist propriety and has opened wide the doors to bourgeois lascivity and capitalist promiscuousness![70]

All this deterioration and decline is, in Peking's eyes, of course, rooted in false anti-Leninist conceptions of the revolutionary proletarian Party and the abandonment of the correct Marxist-Leninist principles.[71] The Soviet ruling clique, it is seriously asserted, has turned the CPSU into a bourgeois

68. *PR*, March 22, 1968, p. 34.

69. "Soviet Revisionists' New System. . . ," *PR*, May 10, 1968, p. 28.

70. "Liberalization and Westernization in Culture," *PR*, Nov. 3, 1967, pp. 23-24.

71. "The CPSU reduced to instrument of bourgeois dictatorship. . . ," *PR*, Dec. 11, 1967, pp. 32-34.

political party and an instrument of the privileged stratum to exercise the "dictatorship of the bourgeoisie." The purpose of one big-scale purge after the other was to leave the leadership of the Party "from top down to the grassroots level" in the hands of the privileged bourgeois stratum. Seventy percent of the members of the CC who had been elected at the 19th Congress of the CPSU in 1952 had been purged by the time of the 22nd Congress in 1961 and nearly 60 percent of the CC members elected at the 20th Congress in 1956 were purged by the time of the 23rd Congress in 1966. In 1963, over 96 percent of the secretaries of regional committees were college men, the majority of whom were bourgeois "experts." "As far as the membership of the Party was concerned, bourgeois elements made up an even larger percentage of the entire membership, while the percentage of members of worker and peasant origin kept shrinking steadily. From 1961 to 1966 the percentage of members of worker and peasant background dropped by 9.3 percent, while the percentage of those members classified as "office employees and others" rose by the same percentage. The leading Soviet clique employed every possible means to indoctrinate the broad masses of Party members. It tried to "corrupt and poison" their minds with bourgeois ideology. The Soviet leaders were "particularly frightened" by the example of the great proletarian cultural revolution. They had made "anti-Chinese circuits" in various parts of the country. To this have been added repeated anti-Chinese resolutions in the name of the CC of the CPSU and the voluminous anti-Chinese articles which appeared in the daily press and other publications. At numerous meetings held throughout the country in January 1967 the revisionist clique tried "to incite anti-Chinese feelings" in a vain attempt to offset the tremendous influence of the thought of Mao on Party members and Soviet people.

The ruling clique exercised "a despotic rule within the CPSU"; a white terror reigned in the Party. Whoever expressed dissatisfaction with the Party leadership was subject to persecution. A mighty storm of proletarian revolution would some day overthrow the Soviet revisionist renegades.

There can be little surprise that the Soviet leadership took the bitter denunciations of their regime by the Chinese "comrades" most seriously. Surely, they exceeded by far the usual attacks by the capitalist and imperialist press; but these criticisms were the more dangerous because they were based on elements of real insight and perception—the knowledge of one totalitarianism about the other, and because, given the Communist mentality, they were more likely to strike a dangerous spark than criticism emanating from a capitalist country. Characteristically, the denunciation always climaxed in the prophecy that the Soviet government would be overthrown or even in a direct appeal to bring this prophecy to life.

If Peking at times appealed over the head of the CPSU to the Soviet people to stage an overthrow of the "Soviet revisionist renegade clique," the CPSU had in turn made little secret of its own wishes to see a change of government brought about in Peking by the long-suffering and betrayed Chinese people. It had pointed earlier to the lack of proletarian character and consciousness, the absence of a party program, and its unrestrained cult of the individual. It had criticized its lack of thorough planning and its adventurism.[72]

Chinese culture, politics, and economics were, according to the Soviets, all in a state of utter chaos. Peking's dominant economic concepts were in complete confusion and thus their basis of criticism of Soviet economic life was not Marxist-Leninist but was based on pseudo-revolutionary voluntarism. Soviet economic development, on the contrary, Moscow asserted, was making tremendous progress.

In the field of economic policy, as in most other fields, the USSR both defended its course against violent Chinese attacks and assailed China for her own "zig-zag" policy. In an article in 1966 *Pravda,* referring to deliberately slanderous statements of the ideologists of the bourgeoisie that Soviet policy was allegedly leading to the restoration of capitalist relationships, expressed the amazement of the Soviet people that the CPC, the newspaper *People's Daily,* and *Red Flag* had similarly spoken of the "restoration of capitalism" in the USSR. The working people in the Soviet Union resented this accusation. In *Pravda's* view, the Chinese statements were nothing but "provocational fabrications."[73]

According to *Pravda,* the development of the economy of the Soviet Union and the other socialist countries was "the best contribution" to the growth of the entire world socialist commonwealth as well as to the strengthening of its military might and to the support of the national liberation movement. *Pravda* came out in behalf of planned management of the economy instead of letting things drift. The present economic reforms in the USSR aimed at the strengthening of centralized planning in combination with giving enterprises broad scope for displaying initiative. At the highest stage of Communism there would be no room for commodity-money relations, but in the process of socialist construction it was necessary to make use of these relations. Also, the socialist principle of effective management had nothing in common with the capitalist principle of private profit and with personal enrichment. Under socialism profit went to

72. "Economic Policy and the Struggle of Communism," *Pravda,* Jan. 14, 1966, pp. 2-3 (*CDSP* 18, no. 2 [1966]: 21-23).
73. *Pravda,* Jan. 14, 1966, pp. 2-3, "Economic Policy and the Struggle of Communism" (*CDSP* 18, no. 2 [1966]: 21-23).

the working people and only to them, contrary to what "slanderers" might assert.

Similarly, aimed directly against Peking was *Pravda's* denunciation of poverty as a "blessing." Nothing was more a distortion of socialist construction than the assertion that poverty was an inevitable phenomenon throughout this entire phase. It was a misconception to concede the progress of material culture "altogether to capitalism. Communists are not fighting to make future generations happy through the ascetic self-denial of those living now." (Soviet people, of course, will probably heartily approve these lines, but be far from convinced that Soviet practice accords with this view of *Pravda*.) *Pravda* in conclusion came out also in support of differentiated payment of labor. Distribution, Lenin was quoted, was a means for increasing production until such a time when an economy of abundance was attained.

In an article on April 18 in *Pravda,* "Zigzags in Peking's Economic Policy," Yu. Kornilov took note that Peking, for the first time in the past ten years, had published some data on national production and had announced that as a result of her "enormous victories" the conditions for "a new leap" have been created.[74] But foreign observers and economists noted that these claims were obviously exaggerated and pointed out that only those branches of Chinese economy that facilitated the further build-up of the country's military potential had been greatly developed. It was obvious that Chinese steel production was not exceeding the Chinese potential of the early 60s and that her grain production was lower than in 1958. China's economy had not fully overcome the deep and serious economic difficulties that were a consequence of the adventurist policies of the "Great Leap" and the "People's Communes," and later the "Cultural Revolution."

The Maoists, according to *Pravda,* were still attempting to find solutions to economic problems by pinning their hopes on military-administrative and compulsory methods. The country's extensive labor resources continue to be regarded as the decisive factor in the development of the economy during the Fourth Five-Year Plan (1971-75). Yet there were some Chinese executive cadres who were realizing that voluntarist attempts to step up the rates of economic development by the extreme exertion of all working people's efforts, by relying not on objective economic laws and real possibilities but only on "Mao's ideas," could not bring the desired results. Life itself had forced the work of the industrial ministries and the CPR State Planning Committee, which were paralyzed in the period of the "Cultural

74. *Pravda*, Apr. 18, 1972, p. 5 (*CDSP*, 24, no. 16 [May 17, 1972]).

Revolution,'' to be resumed. While the latter is given credit in Peking for having given ''supreme impetus'' to the development of the Chinese economy, the Chinese newspapers criticized those who in that period fell ''under the influence of anarchism and ultraleftist views'' and denied the need for the planned development of the national economy.

According to reports from China, there was now, the *Pravda* article asserted, a growing tendency to restore the principle of distribution according to labor, though during the years of the Cultural Revolution this principle, like material incentives in general, was deprecated. But ''the wage-leveling dogma'' had finally been abandoned and productivity was stimulated once again by introducing differentiated pay. On the whole the writer concluded that the contradictory and sometimes diametrically opposite phenomena and processes taking place in China were still retarding the growth of China's economy. The ''zig-zags'' in Peking's economic policy were thus unfavorably contrasted with the rational planning and the steady progress of Soviet economic development.

9

Peking's Reversal of Isolationism. The Soviet Response. 1969 to the Present

Sino-Soviet Border Clashes. The Ninth National Congress of the CPC, April 1969

The long-seething issue between the two Communist super-powers came to a head when Soviet and Chinese frontier troops clashed over Damansky (Chenpao) island in the Ussuri river on March 2, 1969. The heavy Soviet casualties—31 dead and 14 wounded—and the circumstance that the Soviet troops involved were frontier guards[1] strongly suggested that the initial clash might have been a Chinese ambush.[2] The bloody occurrences resulted in massive demonstrations in both Moscow and Peking. On March 15 the island was regained by the Soviets, who used regular troops and at the same time shelled Chinese positions on the Manchurian bank of the Ussuri river.[3] This time the losses were incomparably heavier, especially for the Chinese, who lost about 800 men as against 60 Soviet casualties.

The Soviet communiqué denouncing the "provocations" along the border strongly "warned" the government of the CPR that it would be held responsible for the consequences of its adventurist policy.[4] A leading Chinese editorial in turn warned the "Soviet revisionist renegade clique" that Peking would never allow anyone to encroach upon China's territorial integrity and sovereignty, and threatened in unmistakable terms: "No mat-

1. E. D. Clubb, *Twentieth-Century China* (New York, 1964), pp. 500-501.
2. *Pravda*, March 8, 1969 (*CDSP* 21, no. 10 [1969]: 5).
3. China's Foreign Minister's March 13 Protest Note, *PR*, March 7, 1969, p. 6.
4. *CDSP* 21, no. 9 [1969]: 17.

ter in what strength and with whom you come, we will wipe you out thoroughly, wholly and completely.''[5] It was quite apparent that the bloody border incidents by far transcended in importance the actual strategic value of Damansky island. The tiny island had obviously become a symbol, revealing the deep and continuing general rift between the two Communist giants and their specific and extensive territorial differences.

Each side hurled the most violent vituperations against the other for being responsible for the eruption of the fighting, for staging demonstrations, and for vilifying the leadership of the opposing party. *Krasnaya Zvezda* on March 9 seemed also concerned about the American reaction to the border dispute, noting that Washington and Bonn were making use of Maoism "for their own ends."[6] Moscow and Peking each charged the other with pursuing imperialist-chauvinist objectives, but in spite of mounting hostility refrained from blaming the entire people beyond the border for the shameless provocations and limitless hostility demonstrated by its leadership, apparently hoping for, if not working toward, its overthrow.

The renewed outbreak of hostilities on Damansky island on March 15 almost erased the island from the map. When Chinese forces again attacked the Soviet position on the island, the Soviet troops apparently effected a sham withdrawal, only suddenly to open up upon the enemy along a front of several kilometers with artillery, missiles, tanks, and air power. Later in March, the border struggle erupted at Sui-Fen-Ho, several hundred miles south of Damansky Island. And in April hostilities broke out along the Sinkiang-Soviet frontier, about 2,500 miles to the west of the Ussuri river.

The frontier clashes in 1969 between the two Communist countries moved the specter of war into the realm of possibility, unbelievable as such a contingency might have appeared only a decade earlier. Under the title "Down with the new Tsars!" *People's Daily* and *The Liberation Army Daily* (Jiefangjun Bao) in a joint editorial of March 2, 1969, referring to the clashes on Chenpao Islanpd, wrote thus: "This grave border incident of armed provocation was completely premeditated and deliberately engineered by the Soviet revisionist renegade clique,''[7] "but the Soviet clique had the audacity to make false counter-charges and send China a so-called note of protest!" While the Soviets were ruthlessly plundering and brutally oppressing the people of some East European countries at will and setting up a new tsarist-type colonial empire, they were simultaneously pushing the same line in Asia. Not only had they turned the

5. *People's Daily* and *Liberation Army Daily* (*PR*, March 7, 1969, p. 6).

6. *Krasnaya Zvezda*, March 9, 1969 (*CDSP* 21, no. 10 [1969]: 5).

7. *People's Daily* and *Liberation Army Daily,* joint editorial, *PR*, March 2, 1969, pp. 6-7.

Mongolian People's Republic into a colony; they regarded those areas the tsars had occupied as theirs and were stretching their hands even into areas beyond those occupied before 1917. "They are even more voracious than the tsars. What is the difference between the gangsterism of the Soviet revisionist renegade clique and U.S. imperialism which occupies other countries' territory and encroaches upon their sovereignty at will and rides roughshod everywhere?" In 1900 Lenin, in the essay "The War in China," had condemned the policy of the tsars who had invaded China as "criminal." These words applied in their entirety today and portrayed "the shameless features" of the Soviet clique that had taken over the mantle of the tsars.

Shortly thereafter, on March 14, 1969, *Peking Review* repeated that Chenpao (Damansky) Island had always been Chinese territory. The difference that had recently arisen was traced back to the circumstance that, in spite of the Soviet pledge of 1920 to relinquish all seized Chinese territory, the "great testament of Lenin's" had failed to come true because China was then ruled by a reactionary government.[8] The paper thus somehow acquitted Lenin of the charge of double-dealing, but attempted to pin the blame on his unworthy recent successors.

China, according to *Peking Review,* had settled her boundary questions with neighboring countries such as Burma, Nepal, Pakistan, the People's Republic of Mongolia, and Afghanistan. Only the boundary questions between China on the one hand and India and the USSR on the other have remained unsettled. The negotiations carried on with the Soviets in 1964 had failed because of their adamant stand, their refusal to recognize the treaties relating to the present Sino-Soviet boundary as unequal treaties and to return territories seized from China in violation of even these unequal treaties. If the Soviets insisted on holding to their views "and inexorably refuse to mend their ways, the Chinese side will have to reconsider its position as regards the Sino-Soviet boundary question as a whole." It was with this threat that the Chinese article ended.

But threats leaped both ways across the border. Addressing the Supreme Soviet on July 10, 1969, Gromyko warned that the nineteenth-century treaties of Aigun, Tientsin, and Peking were still operative and were "the law that both sides are obliged to respect." The Soviet Union herself had no territorial claims on any of its neighbors.[9] Deputy A. P. Shitikov of the Khabarovsk territory similarly branded China as "a serious new hotbed of growing tension in the Far East."[10]

The Soviets, of course, offered a different version of the causes of the

8. Chinese Foreign Ministry statement, *PR*, March 14, 1969, pp. 14-15.
9. *Pravda*, July 11, 1969, pp. 2-4 (*CDSP* 21, no. 28 [1969]: 4-11).
10. *Izvestiia,* July 13, 1969, p. 3.

clashes that had occurred along the frontier in March and July 1969. They denied aggressive intentions and, turning the table, accused the Chinese of having planned and initiated the hostilities. On September 11, 1969, *Pravda* and *Isvestiia* referred to armed clashes along the Sino-Soviet border and also to captured documents. The incidents had included incursions into Soviet territory and treacherous armed attacks on Soviet border guards in the area of Damansky Island on March 15, 1969, the armed raid on the Soviet island of Kirkinsky in the Ussuri river on July 20, the raid on the Soviet river transport workers on the Amur river (Goldinsky Island) on July 8, and a number of other armed raids between May and August.[11] The Soviet papers charged that the captured documents revealed a definite plan behind all these provocations and attacks.

The Ninth National Congress of the CPC met under the shadow of the bloody encounters with the Soviet armed forces on Damansky Island. Vice-Chairman Lin Piao, then still "close comrade-in-arms" of Mao and his apparent heir, pointed in his report to the Congress the accusing finger at "revisionism," the set of false ideas ultimately responsible for raising the war threat. Quoting Mao, Lin Piao treated U.S. imperialism contemptuously, but held that the Soviet revisionist renegade clique represented no less a danger. People all over the world had, due to Mao's resolute struggles in the ideological, theoretical, and political spheres, learned to distinguish between genuine Marxism-Leninism and sham Leninism. By pointing in this context at Mao's sharp criticism of Liu Shao-chi's "revisionist line" in general, and to the destruction of Liu's counterrevolutionary revisionist clique, he likened Liu's position to that of the leadership of the Soviet Union. This leadership had been "usurped" by revisionists and had recently brought about the armed encroachment on the Chinese Chenpao Island. It was revisionism that was at the heart of the trouble.[12]

Since Brezhnev had come to power, the Soviet revisionist clique, with its baton becoming less and less effective, had been practicing "social imperialism and social fascism" more frantically than ever. This clique had intensified its suppression of the Soviet people and speeded up the all-round restoration of capitalism. Its dispatch of hundreds of thousands of troops to occupy Czechoslovakia and its armed provocations against China on Chenpao Island were "two foul performances" of the same Soviet revisionist phenomenon. The theory of "limited sovereignty" served the purposes of the new tsars, turned free countries into colonies of social-imperialism, just as the "New Order of Europe of Hitler" and the "Greater East Asia Co-Prosperity Sphere" of Japanese militarism had done and the "Free World Community" of the U.S. was still doing.

11. *Pravda,* and *Izvestiia,* Sept. 11, 1969.
12. Lin Piao report, *PR,* Apr. 28, 1969, special issue; also *PR,* Apr. 30 and Apr. 14, 1969.

Then Lin Piao turned to the analysis of the historic implications of the Sino-Soviet rift. The Sino-Soviet boundary question was the product of Tsarist Russia's imperialist aggression against China. On September 27, 1920, the Soviet government led by the great Lenin, however, had declared null and void all the treaties concluded with China by the former governments of Russia and had promised to restore to China without any compensation and forever all that had been predatorily seized from her by the Tsar's government and the Russian bourgeoisie. "Owing to historical conditions of the time, this proletarian policy of Lenin's was not realized." Lenin was thus acquitted of any wrong-doing in spite of the nonfulfillment of the pledge, which rather mysteriously was ascribed to "historical conditions." The Chinese government in 1960 had twice taken the initiative toward negotiations to "settle" the boundary question and in 1964 had started negotiations in Peking. But the Soviet clique had refused to recognize the nineteenth-century treaties as unequal and had insisted on retaining as legitimate property all Chinese territory even occupied in violation of these treaties. This great-power chauvinist and social-imperialist stand of the Soviet government had led to the disruption of the negotiations.

U.S. imperialism and Soviet revisionism were always trying to isolate China, but their rabid opposition to China did not do her the slightest harm. China had drawn a clear line between herself on the one hand and U.S. imperialism and Soviet revisionism on the other. Lin Piao quoted Mao to the effect that "a new historical period of opposing U.S. imperialism and Soviet revisionism has begun." It was quite clear that Communist China had not just one but two deadly enemies, Soviet revisionism being not the lesser evil, but one of two equal evils.

In the heat of battle Lin Piao shed all ideological ballast. The USSR was as much the foe as the leading capitalist and imperialist power, the arch-enemy itself, the U.S.A. He concluded with the words of Mao, "Working hand in glove, Soviet revisionism and U.S. imperialism have done so many foul and evil things that the revolutionary people the world over will not let them go unpunished."

Since 1960, Lin Piao charged, the Soviet government had gone farther and farther down the road of betraying Marxism-Leninism. The Soviets had incessantly violated the status quo of the boundary and had thus aggravated the situation. They had directed their troops to push their patrol routes into Chinese territory, to assault and kidnap Chinese border inhabitants, to sabotage their production, and to carry out all sorts of provocative and subversive activities. In 1962 the Soviet government coerced more than 60,000 Chinese citizens in the Ili and Tahcheng areas of Sinkiang into going into the Soviet Union and has up to now refused to send them back.

From October 15, 1964, to March 15, 1969, the Soviet side, the Chinese authorities charged, had provoked as many as 4,189 border incidents, two and one-half times the number of those it provoked from 1960 to 1964. Soviet troops had "intruded into Chinese territory, indulging in murder and arson, killing barehanded Chinese fishermen and peasants by beating and running armored cars over them and even throwing them alive into the river."[13] Lenin in his time had denounced the Russian government for atrocities against Chinese, of behaving "like savage beasts." There was no difference between past and present-day atrocities.

Soviet Russia's aggressive designs were even more ambitious and her "claws have stretched out even farther than those of tsarist Russia." Under Lenin and Stalin Soviet Russia had lent assistance to the Chinese people. But in the past decade the Soviet government had committed "towering crimes" against the Chinese people. It was not qualified at all to talk about assistance rendered to the Chinese in the eras of Lenin and Stalin. Still, Peking stood for peaceful negotiation and against resorting to the use of force.

The Moscow Conference, July 1969

The July 1969 Moscow Conference of Communist Parties followed on the heel of the Ninth Congress of the CPC and, in view of the Sino-Soviet border clashes, which continued into the month of July, stood also under the shadow of the perennial Sino-Soviet rift.[14] According to Brezhnev, the disagreements that existed within Communism were caused in large part by the penetration into the Communist movement of "revisionist influences" of both the "right-wing" and "left-wing" varieties. Thus Brezhnev turned the table on Peking, which only recently, at the Ninth Party Congress of the CPC, had once again accused Moscow of revisionism and had charged revisionist wrong-thinking with the ultimate responsibility for the border conflict. He slung back the very same charge at Peking, merely broadening the indictment so as to include "left-wing" revisionism also. By blaming both right-wing and left-wing revisionism, he also adopted the comfortable and safe centrist position of avoiding extremes. These revisionist influences, Brezhnev charged, made themselves felt not only in the sphere of "pure theory." Revisionism in theory paved the way for opportunistic practice. "Right-wing" opportunism means slipping into liquidationist positions, denying the leadership role of the Marxist-Leninist parties, while "left-wing" opportunism pushes the masses into adventurist actions. A striking example of the damage that could be done to the Communists'

13. *PR*, Apr. 28, 1969.
14. *CDSP* 21, no. 23 [July 2, 1969]: 3-7.

common cause by a departure from Marxism-Leninism and a break with internationalism could be seen, according to Brezhnev, in the position of the leadership of the CPC.

According to Brezhnev, the Ninth CPC Congress had decided to fight what it called "present-day revisionism," which actually, however, included the overwhelming majority of the socialist countries and Communist Parties, which were "by no means revisionists" in the true sense of the word. Peking's leaders leveled accusations against every party that did not share their views. Peking's schismatic activity, pushing the working people onto an adventurist path, was doing great harm to the proletarian struggle.

The struggle for hegemony in the Communist movement, Brezhnev went on, was inextricably bound up with the great-power aspirations of the present Peking leadership and with its claims on the territory of other countries. "The idea of China's Messianic role is being instilled in Chinese workers and peasants." What was under way in China was a mass indoctrination in the spirit of chauvinism and vicious anti-Sovietism. The Chinese people and its youth were taught: "Go hungry and prepare for war." Only two days ago the Peking newspaper *Kuangming Jihpao* had made an appeal to prepare for waging both a conventional and a large-scale nuclear war against Soviet revisionism. The direction of Chinese propaganda was unmistakable and under these circumstances the policy and militarization of China and the overall approach of her leaders to the problems of war and peace were taking on a special meaning.

According to Brezhnev, many of the comrades still remembered Mao's speech in this very hall, as he put it, at the 1957 conference. Mao had spoken with startling lightness and cynicism about the possible destruction of half of mankind in the event of an atomic war. Mao did not call for a struggle against war, "but, on the contrary, for war itself," which he regarded as a positive historical phenomenon.

China's foreign policy consisted of attacking the Soviet Union on all lines. She used a propaganda based on lies and slander against the USSR and the CPSU, fanned hatred against both, and was now even using arms. She resorted to intimidation and blackmail with respect to the other socialist states and the developing countries, and flirted with the major capitalist powers, including the Federal Republic of Germany.

Referring to the frontier clashes between the CPR and the USSR, the Soviet government in March 1969 had proposed to resume in the immediate future the bilateral consultations on border questions that were begun in 1964; but it also warned that force would be firmly rebuffed. The Chinese had recently issued a government statement which, though not rejecting the idea of talks, was judged not to be constructive. Filled with falsifications of history and contemporary events, it reiterated groundless claims of a territorial nature. The Chinese provocations along the border were still continuing.

Though Brezhnev declared ''imperialism'' to be the main enemy of the Communist movement, his real target was China. Taken in conjunction with Foreign Minister Gromyko's desire, as expressed in his address to the Supreme Soviet on July 10, for friendly relations with the U.S., and Brezhnev's own emphasis on familiar Soviet themes such as peaceful coexistence, the necessity of preventing nuclear war, and the continued build-up of Soviet economic strength as the major contribution to world revolution, it must have appeared obvious to the participants at the Conference that in the Soviet view the greatest obstacle to Moscow's policy lay in Peking rather than in Washington, D.C. Both Peking and Moscow had come a long way since each had declared U.S. imperialism the arch-enemy. Theoretically they had come to see in their former comrade-in-arms their heretical foe, a menace of at least equal proportion, and actually the greater and more dangerous enemy.

But the conference, convoked at the insistence of the CPSU, revealed once again that the Soviet party was unable either to excommunicate Communist China or to have its own leadership acknowledged without reservations. Of the fourteen ruling parties, five did not attend. The Chinese and Albanian Parties, a likely target at the conference, remained absent, as did also the North Korean and North Vietnamese Parties. The latter, while dependent on the USSR, were anxious to avoid arousing the ire of their populous and formidable Chinese neighbor and hoped to ride out the impending storm, at the same time remaining wary of taking the least risk. Yugoslavia too was absent; her leaders had raised their voice of protest against the occupation of Czechoslovakia and could not yet be certain that their criticism had been forgiven and forgotten. Cuba sent only an observer, demonstrating her aloofness from both Moscow and Peking and underlining her own independence.

The criticism of the CPSU, as heard at the Congress and even published by the Soviet press—in apparent fulfillment of conditions insisted upon by dissident parties as the price for their participation—demonstrated their growing self-assurance and the enhanced importance given to every Communist Party by the widening rift between Moscow and Peking.

The Czechoslovak question and the interrelated Soviet doctrine of ''socialist sovereignty''—actually ''limited sovereignty,'' as it was called in the West and, revealingly, also in China—figured large at the Conference. Husak, the new Czechoslovak Party chief, attempted both to defend the Soviet policy of intervention in his country in 1968 and to accuse Peking: ''Such facts as the Mao group's efforts to undermine the relations among socialist countries, to support and spread separatist nationalistic tendencies and anti-Soviet sentiments and disrupt the friendly ties of alliance between the Soviet Union and other socialist countries cannot be regarded as an internal affair of the CPC.''[15] Yet the policy of this ''collective'' intervention was explicitly or implicitly criticized by the Italian, Australian, Spanish, Austrian, Swiss, British, and Dominican delegates.

On the other hand, the CPC, as expected, came in for criticism by the leaders of East European Communist Parties, including Gomulka of Poland and Kadar of Hungary, and also by Waldeck Rochet of France. Ulbricht, Party boss of the German Democratic Republic, voiced his shock over the military raids staged by the Chinese leadership on the Sino-Soviet border: ''These acts of military aggression signify direct support of the global strategy of the U.S.A. and the expansionist policy of West German imperialism. When a country like the CPR, which calls itself socialist, tries to bring about changes in the boundaries of the world's first socialist state—the Soviet Union—it is playing with fire and at the same time is politically undermining the anti-imperialist struggle.''

In a similarly hostile vein were the remarks by Tsedenbal, chief of the Mongolian People's Revolutionary Party.[16] The Chinese leaders' hostile forays against the USSR represented ''an act of aggression'' committed against all socialist countries. It was a ''gross mistake'' to ignore or underestimate the danger that the Mao group might start a war. The setbacks in the Chinese leaders' domestic and foreign policies increasingly intensified their adventurism. Underlying the anti-Mongolian policy and actions of the Mao group were ''its great power-chauvinist claims to our country, inherited from the Chinese militarists and Chiang Kai-shekites.'' Tsedenbal recalled especially Mao's latest statement in 1964, expressing his intention to incorporate Mongolia into China. It was not difficult to imagine the plight that would have befallen the working people of Mongolia if these great-power schemes of Mao had actually been realized.

Communist China, however, was warmly defended by Ceausescu, Rumania's Party leader; he recalled, of course, China's strong stand in behalf of Rumania's independence when, after the invasion of Czechoslovakia, both Bucharest and the world at large feared a repeat performance of Moscow's aggression. In his view, the Moscow Conference should not have been held, since conditions were inauspicious. He also warned against moving against a nation that was fully determined to defend its freedom, its national independence, and the ''sacred right to decide for itself what its fate should be.''[17] Berlinguer, delegate from Italy, criticized the ''serious mistakes'' of the Chinese Communists, who put the USSR

15. *Pravda,* June 13, 1969, pp. 3-4.
16. Proceedings of International Communist Conference, July 30, 1969; *Pravda,* June 13, 1969, pp. 1-4 (*CDSP* 21, no. 27 [1969]).
17. *Pravda,* June 16, 1969.

and American imperialism on the same plane. They were, he charged, conducting splitting activities and intended to impose their own position and Mao's thoughts upon all parties. At the same time, Berlinguer warned that the problem of relations with China must not be resolved by excommunication or collective condemnation. It was necessary to try to understand the objective basis of the erroneous course that had taken the upper hand in China and at the same time to discover the mistakes and "shortcomings of our own policy" toward China. It was also necessary to exert all efforts to restore harmony and unity with Peking, since the struggle for peace and against imperialism needed China's contribution. The Italian Communist Party was aiming at "lessening the tension existing today." Berlinguer also criticized talk about doctrinal purity; no Party could claim the right of being the guardian of that purity. Similarly, the Spanish and Austrian delegates denied that there was a single leading center within the Communist movement or a single model that all Communist Parties were obliged to emulate.

The final document was signed by a large majority of delegates, by some only after voicing reservations; three refused to attach their signatures. The document expressed support for the Chinese claim for Taiwan and for the representation of the CPR in the U.N. The statements, which said that "the socialist countries must not infringe upon the unity of the anti-imperialist front" and that each Communist Party was responsible not only to its own working class and nation, but also to the international proletariat, could be interpreted by the CPSU as a victory. But it was surely a limited one, since apparently they lent themselves to different interpretations. Both China and Albania were included among the "14 socialist states" listed in the document; in spite of all the hostility against the CPR, this was more than Communist China conceded to the USSR, since she repeatedly expressed her view that capitalism in that country had been restored. On the other hand, the Congress denounced in unmistakable terms the leadership of the CPC and of the Albanian Party of Labor as petty bourgeois betrayers of Marxism-Leninism.

The Soviet Collective Security Pact for Asia and the Soviet Plan for an All-European Conference

China had not abandoned the isolationism characteristic of the Cultural Revolution, when in 1969 Brezhnev advanced the idea of creating a collective security system in Asia. Did Soviet Russia anticipate China's new foreign policy turn? Did she foresee the possibility of an improvement of Sino-American relations in view of the announced withdrawal of American forces from Indochina and gird herself against new dangers? Or was the Soviet move a quick riposte to China's new aggressiveness, as demonstrated in the border clashes in 1969, and to her new diplomatic thrusts?

Since the Soviet collective security pact for Asia held out the promise of freezing the territorial status quo and had apparently self-serving purposes, Peking opposed it as strongly as the USSR favored it. Ironically enough, had the pact been concluded in 1969 when it was proposed, Soviet Russia could not later have played the role of midwife when Bangladesh was born.

The implementation of the idea of a collective security system in Asia was, in view of aggressions in different parts of Asia, still imperative in the Soviet view.[18] There was, according to it, the imperialist aggression in Indochina, the continuing Israeli aggression in the Near East, and finally, there persisted "contradictions" between various Asian states. These "contradictions," apparently minimized in comparison with the foregoing conflicts, were not spelled out in the *Pravda* article, though the Sino-Soviet and the India-Pakistan differences come to mind. The idea of creating a collective security system in Asia was making headway, in spite of "opposition by major reactionary forces," the imperialist circles of the U.S.A. and Britain, and "chauvinist and militarist circles in certain Asian countries."

Some newspapers in the West and in Asian countries were writing, according to *Pravda*, that the Soviet idea of collective security was only an attempt by the Soviet Union to "fill the vacuum" that would form after the "withdrawal" of the U.S., Great Britain, and other imperialist powers from Asia. This was an attempt to put the Soviet Union, which invariably supports the national-liberation, anti-imperialist struggle of the Asian peoples, on the same level as the imperialist powers that oppressed the Asian peoples in the past, and was also an attempt to intimidate those peoples by unfounded theories about the "Soviet superpower." (Though Mayevski did not specifically mention Communist China, it is the latter that continually referred to the USSR as a "superpower.") In advancing the idea of collective security in Asia, the Soviet Union did not claim any privileges and was not seeking any advantages for herself; "she was prepared to act together with all Asian states on an equal basis, as a country whose interests are geographically, economically and politically connected not only with Europe but with Asia as well."

Some Japanese, Pakistani, and other newspapers, according to *Pravda*, alleged that the Soviet proposal was aimed "against China," at her "encirclement." The Japanese ambassador to the U.S.A., Ushiba, had, it was

18. "Collective Security in Asia is an urgent problem" *Pravda*, June 21, 1972, p. 4 (*CDSP* 24, no. 25 [July 17, 1972]).

reported, asserted that Japan objected to the collective security system proposed by the USSR because "its aim is to contain China." The Soviet Union, however, had stated several times that the idea it proposed was not directed against any state and that it presupposed the collective participation of Asian countries.

The essence of a security pact is, of course, the preservation of the status quo. Communist China, anxious to rid herself of the legacy of unequal treaties also vis-à-vis the USSR, and to reclaim territories and influence lost under the Manchu Emperors and in the early days of the Republic, has long opposed a collective security pact.

Mayevsky, while disputing that the idea of this pact had always been alien to Communist China, admitted that objections to it were voiced in countries that had territorial claims against other states. In view of this attempt to revise the post-war borders in Asia, Mayevsky recalled, referring to recent treaties between the USSR, and FRG, and Poland, that in Europe the border problem had found a realistic solution that was registered in well-known international treaties and that this was of paramount importance in strengthening European security.

Long before the USSR officially proposed a collective security pact for Asia, she had suggested one for Europe. In both cases the USSR expected to exclude non-Asiatic and non-European states respectively, primarily the U.S., and to be left confronting states that even in the aggregate would not be able to equal her own power, her own formidable concentration of power embracing both Asia and Europe. Thus, through two collective security pacts, one exclusively Asiatic, the other exclusively European, the Soviet Union would attain the long-sought-after superiority.

According to V. Pavlov's "Europe in Peking's Plans, " the Chinese leadership was seeking to maintain in Europe, as in other parts of the world, an atmosphere of tension.[19] In contrast to the peaceable policy of the USSR and other socialist countries which aim at establishing a collective security system on the European continent on the basis of recognition of the territorial and political realities that have taken shape as a result of the Second World War, the Chinese leadership was attempting to establish positions for extending its own influence and was pursuing this goal by the most diverse political and diplomatic combinations.

In a joint Sino-Soviet statement on January 18, 1957, the two powers had expressed their views that "all closed military groupings must give way to a system of collective peace and collective security" and referred to the Warsaw Treaty as a defensive military alliance that the socialist countries had been forced to set up after the conclusion of the aggressive

19. V. Pavlov, "Europe in Peking's Plans," *International Affairs,* March 1971.

military North Atlantic Pact. Later on the Warsaw Treaty countries had consistently stood for the elimination of both the NATO and the Warsaw Pact and their replacement by a treaty on collective security in Europe.

In the early sixties, however, the Chinese leadership abandoned this attitude. On February 4, 1960, an observer of the CPR, attending a conference of the Political Consultative Committee of the Warsaw Trety countries and explaining China's stand on the German issue, declared that China would not consider herself bound by any agreements concluded without her participation.[20] The following year she declined to send an observer to participate in the work of the Warsaw Treaty agencies. Since the mid-1960s the Chinese leaders had done their utmost to hamper and torpedo any European settlement. In 1964 Mao revealed to a group of Japanese Socialists his doubts concerning the borders that had appeared in Europe as a result of the Second World War. And in December 1969 *People's Daily* lamented the circumstance that the Soviet idea of European security was designed to maintain the status quo in Europe.[21] It was thus hardly surprising that Peking attacked the treaty between the USSR and the Federal Republic of Germany containing a clause relating to the Oder-Neisse border. On September 13, 1970, *People's Daily* denounced this treaty as a ''betrayal'' of the interests of the German and of the Soviet peoples and criticized similarly the four-power agreement on West Berlin (September 9, 1971).[22] The hostility of Peking was based upon the apparent fear that these treaties, according to Pavlov, would improve the political climate and exert a positive effect on the course of European affairs. It rather was set to frustrate or at least hamper the possibility of a détente in Europe.

While the Soviet Union had long been proposing an all-European conference on security and cooperation, this idea was attacked by Vice Premier Li Hsien-nien as an attempt to ''share out the spheres of influence with U.S. imperialism and to control and enslave Eastern Europe.[23] The Chinese leadership aimed at reversing the tide of détente in Europe and at intensifying the confrontation between the U.S.A. and the USSR to the greatest possible extent. It wished to switch America's main attention from Asia to Europe. In that way the Soviet Union would be able to pursue its goals in Asia, undisturbed by adverse trends in Europe. On November 6, 1968, reporting on Nixon's victory in the presidential elections in the U.S.A., Hsinshua News Agency commented favorably on his promise to reduce American commitments in Asia and shift American interests to

20. *People's Daily*, Feb. 6, 1960 (*PR*, Feb. 9, 1960, pp. 6-9).
21. *Ibid*., Dec. 22, 1969 (*PR*, Dec. 26, pp. 44-45).
22. *Ibid*., Sept. 13, 1971 (*PR*, Sept. 17, 1971, p. 18).
23. *Ibid*., Dec. 2, 1969 (*PR*, Dec. 5, 1964, p. 7).

priority areas, of which Europe was considered the first. As early as November 26, 1968, Peking had proposed to Washington the conclusion of an agreement on the peaceful coexistence of the two countries on the basis of five principles. In the words of Pavlov, "the Chinese leaders' idea is to offer peaceful coexistence with the U.S.A. in return for a switch in the center of gravity in U.S. aggressive policy from Asia to Europe."

The Maoists, according to Pavlov, no longer confined themselves to propaganda attacks on Soviet efforts regarding a European settlement. In an interview given by the premier of the CPR State Council to a correspondent of the British *Sunday Times*, published on December 5, 1971, Peking advanced the idea of "five centers" of world politics: the USSR; the U.S.A.; Western Europe; an intermediate zone, highly industrialized Japan being the fourth power; and China, the fifth "potential power." This scheme, incidentally, lacked the class approach and, rather, considered international relations as a clash of narrow state interests. The Chinese leaders regarded the conversion of Western Europe to an independent political, economic, and military unit as the alternative to all-European cooperation. The latter, which would include Soviet Russia and Russian-dominated Eastern Europe but exclude a trans-Atlantic power like the U.S.A., appeared, of course, an attractive project to the USSR. In addition, the Maoists toyed also with encouraging micro-European associations, a Mediterranean alliance, a Balkan bloc, and so on. Mediterranean countries were advised by the Maoists to extend the boundaries of their territorial waters to 200 miles, which, in Peking's words, would "automatically remove all foreign fleets from the Mediterranean." China had, since October 1970, pursued an activist foreign policy with regard to Western European countries, having established diplomatic relations with five more NATO members.

While Peking was concerned with the "unification" of the West European capitalist countries and praised the "tendency to cohesion" in their policies, it was avowedly hostile to the European socialist community and encouraged, in striking contrast to its attitude to the aforementioned countries, splitting operations against their collective organizations—the council for Mutual Economic Assistance and the Warsaw Treaty Organization. China thus practiced a policy in accordance with the following slogans: "Capitalist countries, unite," "Socialist states, divide."

The attitude of the Chinese leaders to the Common Market similarly showed their "blatant lack of principle and feverish swings from side to side in search of short-term advantages." Their original assessment of the Common Market, following the signing of the Treaty of Rome in 1957, had hardly differed from the judgment of the Soviet Union. But gradually this view underwent radical changes. During the previous two years, after the end of the isolationist era of the "Cultural Revolution," Peking had adopted new tactics for its global strategy of fighting the Soviet Union. At the end of 1971, the CPR State Council Premier had called the Common Market "a first step towards Europe's independence" and "a positive fact." The Common Market was now credited with carrying on more effectively a "fight against the monopoly of the two super-powers." *Peking Review* wrote, in connection with Britain's entry into the EEC: "Such a new situation in Western Europe will constitute a serious obstacle to the U.S. and the Soviet Union on pushing their policies for hegemony in Europe."[24] Finally, with expansion of Peking's trade with capitalist countries and especially Western Europe, Communist China had acquired special interests in the strengthening of Western Europe. Peking also seemed to hope that the economic alliance would lead to "a defense and diplomatic alliance of the Western European countries." The Chinese leadership since the early sixties had also urged the West European countries not to play the role of pawns in the "strategic nuclear force game" but to try to penetrate the "nuclear club." Even today they hold to the view that the more atomic states there are, the better.

In conclusion the writer of the article pointed out that Peking's foreign policy had come to parallel closely that of Washington, D.C. Washington too had long taken a favorable view of the economic and military consolidation of Europe vis-à-vis an alleged "Soviet menace."

Peking's Reversal of Isolationism and the Soviet Assessment

When Communist China terminated the policy of the "Cultural Revolution," she also shed her isolationist skin and once again reached out for the world. During the years 1970 and 1971 the Chinese leadership radically changed its tactics with regard to the U.S.A., the U.N., and the national liberation movement, as well as to interstate relations with the developing countries of Asia, Africa, and Latin America, attempting to increase the "confidence" of the Third World countries in China.[25] It pursued these tactics by resorting once more to the principles and formulas adopted at the Bandung Conference and by establishing all around contacts with many countries, irrespective of their political, social, or economic orientation.

In the Soviet view, Peking retained the basic characteristics of its policy, though it partly resurrected earlier tactics and partly adopted some novel ones, thus displaying "flexibility." In Soviet opinion, the foreign policy of the CPR had, since the 19th Congress in April 1969, continued to exhibit its strongly nationalist character and great-power ambitions, as both

24. *PR*, July 2, 1971, p. 36.
25. *CDSP* 23, no. 36 (Oct. 5, 1971).

theory—the decisions of the September 1970 Second Plenary Meeting of the Party's CC—and the practice of the last years have demonstrated.

Anxious to reestablish diplomatic and other ties with the outside world, China had to "dampen down" the propaganda of ultra-"leftist" slogans of a "people's war." Now the Chinese leadership adopted the role of the champion of détente and peaceful coexistence. The truth of the matter was that Peking had suffered a number of setbacks in its foreign and domestic policies. Its attempt to introduce the methods of Red Guards' violence and armed pressure into international relations had backfired and had alienated both the liberation movement of the developing countries and the progressive democratic movement in capitalist countries.

Peking's new tactics, according to the Soviets, were based upon betrayal of the international revolutionary movement. Communist China has become "the Trojan horse of imperialism" in the revolutionary movement. Her diplomatic flirtation with the imperialist countries headed by the U.S. has resulted in the restoration of her rights in the U.N., including permanent membership in the Security Council. For this purpose Peking has thought it necessary to ingratiate itself with the West and to conceal its participation in the activities of pro-Maoist groups in the revolutionary and liberation movements. In radically changing their tactics regarding the U.S.A. as well as developing countries, devising new catchwords, and resorting to camouflage, they were demonstrating their opportunism and their abandonment of the anti-imperialist struggle.

The very key of Peking's recent foreign policy was the so-called two superpowers concept, the two powers of course being the U.S.A. and the USSR. Against them Communist China was striving to marshal the support of the medium and small countries by manipulating anti-American and anti-Soviet catchwords. Her real goal, however, was to pursue hegemonistic aims and to become "the third super-power" herself. Though playing both melodies, anti-Sovietism and anti-Americanism, the CPR in practice flirted with imperialism, while continuing its anti-Soviet policy. She attempted to strike a bargain with the U.S., especially in regard to East and Southeast Asia. Though the U.S. since 1963 had repeatedly proposed to normalize U.S.-China relations, the Chinese leaders had responded positively to the American initiative only early in 1971. Once its military-bureaucratic dictatorship in the wake of the "Cultural Revolution" was established, Peking could meet the American "bridge-building" policy half-way.

The Chinese leadership, the Soviets asserted, not only displayed inconsistency in approach, but also demonstrated outright betrayal of the pro-Maoist followers in Africa, Ceylon, and the Arab world. Peking also wanted to use Europe as a means of pressure on the U.S.A. and the USSR. The CPR had established diplomatic relations with Italy, San

Marino, Austria, Turkey, and Belgium, ignoring that these states were part of the capitalist and imperialist system but exploiting the common ideological principles of bourgeois nationalism. The Chinese press was also ignoring that most of these states were members of the NATO aggressive bloc, which was hostile to the Soviet Union. Actually, the governments and reactionary circles in some NATO countries were anxious to create a "military complex directed against the USSR."

The Chinese leadership wished to hamper a détente in Europe and to bring "pressure on the USSR from the West." Peking had sharply condemned the Soviet-West German treaty of August 2, 1970, as a betrayal of both the German and the Soviet peoples. To prevent the lessening of Soviet Russia's preoccupation with Europe, China had also come out against the Soviet proposal of convening an all-European security conference. As the Chinese ambassador to Paris, Huang Chen, put it on November 5, 1970, through such a conference the Soviet Union aimed at ousting the Americans from Europe, "so that she may bring greater pressure to bear on China and to fetter her satellites more than ever before." China had also entered into a lively exchange with the capitalist world, which had become a major supplier of plant equipment, including military equipment. Though China had increasingly criticized the resurgence of Japan's militarism and imperialism, and the Sato government in particular, she still tried to normalize relations with Japan and to strike a bargain with her.

The conclusions of Vostokov about the methods and objectives of Mao's foreign policy were confirmed the following month in an article by N. Kapchenko.[26] During the "Cultural Revolution" Mao and his followers, according to Kapchenko, had "voluntarily" withdrawn China from the political arena. They had wished to strengthen the foundations of the Maoist regime at home, to put down the resistance of their political opponents, and to prepare the way for a foreign policy aimed at making broad deals with the imperialist powers. Since early 1970 Peking had sharply increased its activities in virtually every international sphere. But its anti-Soviet policy had by no means relaxed. The leaders of the CPR were still resorting to both threats and promises to stir up anti-Soviet feelings in a particular country. The anti-Soviet line of the present Chinese leadership was not a tactical, but a strategic line.

There were spread in China slanderous inventions about an imaginary "threat from the North," a military threat to China from the Soviet Union. Chinese propanganda thus aimed at scaring the population, so as to facilitate the implementation of the Maoist line.

The far-reaching plans and ambitions of China's present leaders in world

26. *CDSP* 23, no. 27 (Aug. 3, 1971).

politics were clearly at variance with the true potentialities for realizing them. The country's economic potential, to say nothing of moral and political factors, set definite limits to Peking's hegemonistic aspirations. But it was apparently Peking's ambition to use all kinds of political combinations and bloc-arrangements to convert China into an independent center of power. At the moment the CPR hoped to frustrate any positive solution of pressing world problems until such time as China would be able to deal from a position of strength.

The CPR took a sharply negative attitude on virtually all important international problems, to block not only their solution but even any discussion of them. In regard to the disarmament problem, they actively resisted the recent Soviet proposals for a five nuclear-power conference and the convocation of a World Disarmament Conference. Behind the Chinese high-handed preachings to the European peoples about the way they should tackle their various current problems lurked a poorly veiled desire to extend the geographic framework of Peking's great-power chauvinistic policy. The Maoists still considered an atmosphere of tension and instability as a factor favorable to promoting their foreign policy aims. Most important from the Soviet point of view, Peking had shed not a single one of its doctrines, all of which were obnoxious to Moscow, and none of its hostility to the USSR and her policies. In view of its unchanged outlook and persistent practical anti-Sovietism, the new tactics Peking had adopted —all-round contacts instead of remaining in her isolationist shell—made little difference to Moscow and did not alter her long-range critical assessment. Peking demonstrated its new tactics and continuing anti-Soviet hostility when it rushed into the United Nations.

The belated entry of the CPR into the U.N. was a tremendous triumph for Chinese Communism. Though the USSR in the past had led the fight for admission of Peking into the U.N., its enthusiasm in this cause had cooled considerably once the differences between the two Communist giants increased in scope and depth. Though officially the Soviet Union had continued the struggle for the entry of the CPR into the U.N., a clue to Communist China's true sentiments can be seen in *Peking Review's* studied coldness to Soviet Russia after China marched through the doors of the U.N. *Peking Review* listed all the welcoming speeches in the U.N. made in Communist China's behalf except the one by the Soviet Union's representative![27] Also, the statement of the government of the CPR of October 29, 1971, singled out the governments of Albania and Algeria for having made outstanding contributions to the struggle in behalf of the admission of China, and the Royal Government of Cambodia and many other

27. *PR*, Nov. 19 and 26, 1971.

friendly governments for having played an important role in the restoration of the legitimate rights of Communist China in the U.N.[28] The USSR was mentioned, but in no complimentary context: the statement asserted that the voting in the U.N. General Assembly demonstrated that the peoples of the world desired friendship with the Chinese people, and then continued: "At the same time [the outcome of the voting] indicates that one or two [sic!] superpowers are losing ground daily in engaging in truculent acts of imposing their own will on other countries and manipulating the United Nations and international affairs." On entering the U.N., from which it had been excluded for so long, Peking banged the doors with a heavy sideswipe at both the U.S.A. and the USSR—a harbinger of things to come. Once in the U.N., Peking was quick to assail the two superpowers for their alleged "collusion" in the Middle East[29] and for their support of Indian "aggression" against Pakistan.[30]

People's Daily, in a concluding comment on the 26th Session of the U.N. General Assembly, of course stressed its restoration of the legitimate rights of the CPR as well as the increasingly important role played by the Third World states in international affairs.[31] The bankruptcy of the U.S. scheme to create "two Chinas" in the U.N. aside, the writer of the article castigated the "disgusting performance" by the Soviet revisionists in the U.N. on the occasion of India's armed aggression against Pakistan. *Peking Review* welcomed the defeat of the U.S. and the USSR on some issues before the U.N. To Peking it was obvious that the two powers "colluded," while still contending with each other. It was necessary for the medium and small states and all countries and peoples upholding justice to strengthen their unity and smash the control of the U.N. by the two superpowers. China herself "will never be a superpower aggressing against, subverting, controlling, interfering with and bullying others," The author painted the face of a future angelic Communist China, apparently expecting his readers at home and abroad to strike from their memory all recent brutalities and excesses committed by the CPR against its own people and the non-Han minorities.

The Twenty-Fourth Congress of the CPSU, March-April 1971

Since the Moscow Conference of July 1969, minor improvements in the relations between the USSR and the CPR had been accomplished. After

28. *PR*, Nov. 5, 1971, p. 6.
29. *PR*, Dec. 17, 1971, pp. 7-10.
30. *PR*, Dec. 10, 1971, pp. 11-13, 16.
31. *PR*, Dec. 31, 1971, p. 10.

border clashes ceased in the summer of 1969, a certain normalization along the frontiers took place. The heads of the two governments met in September 1969. This meeting was followed by talks of government delegations in Peking concerning the settlement of border questions, though no definite agreement was reached. Late in 1970, the USSR and the CPR exchanged ambassadors. The two countries finally signed commercial agreements, and since then trade between them somewhat increased.

In his major speech at the 24th Congress of the CPSU, held between March 30 and April 9, 1971, Brezhnev called for nuclear-free zones and for winding up military bases in foreign countries and proposed the simultaneous abolition of the Warsaw Pact and the NATO military organizations and the reduction of military expenditures.[32] He also proposed a five-power conference to discuss nuclear disarmament, though the Chinese Government had long made known its opposition to such a conference. Brezhnev's criticism of Communist China's leadership was somewhat subdued, but he made no bones about the non-Leninist, even anti-Leninist, position of the CPC. The accusations against the leadership of the CPC ran the gamut from the charge against Peking of mounting a hostile propaganda campaign against the Soviets, presenting claims on Soviet territory, fomenting dissent in the international Communist movement, to forming outright schismatic groups in several countries to undermine the unity of the Communist movement.

Brezhnev referred to the Chinese leaders' special ideological-political platform—which he declared incompatible with Leninism—and to Peking's insistent demand that the CPSU renounce the line of the all-important 20th Congress (1956). He thus clearly underlined the irreconcilability of the positions of the two parties. Though he admitted that in the past year and a half a number of useful steps had been taken, he pointed to the continuance of the anti-Soviet line in China's propaganda and policy. The suspicious and hostile attitude on both sides persisted and the major problems that divided them continued unresolved. It underlay the policy recently reaffirmed by the 9th CPC Congress. Brezhnev angrily rejected the slanderous fabrications concerning the policy of the CPSU and the Soviet Union that were disseminated from Peking and instilled in the Chinese people—points that hardly differed from those he had made at the July 1969 Moscow Conference of Communist Parties. To sow discord between China and the USSR was all the more absurd and harmful since the imperialists were stepping up their aggressive actions. Therefore the Soviet leadership was prepared to further not only the normalization of relations, but also the restoration of good-neighbor relations and friendship between the USSR and the CPR.

32. *Pravda*, March 31, 1971, pp. 2-10 (*CDSP* 23, no. 12 [Apr. 20, 1971]: 3f.).

While Brezhnev continued to advocate the line of peaceful coexistence with the West, he blasted, on the other hand, American imperialism and allegedly aggressive forces in West Germany, Great Britain, and Japan. The speech continued to reflect the Soviet dilemma of holding out an olive branch to the West, while at the same time rattling the sabre to keep the militant units of the world Communist movement in the Soviet camp and to lessen the attractiveness of the seemingly more militant Chinese Communists. As far as relations with other socialist states were concerned, Brezhnev, hardly surprisingly came out for "economic integration," while avoiding the very word "sovereignty." The representatives, however, of the national Communist Parties, such as the Italian, Yugoslav, and Rumanian Communist Parties, firmly restated the principles of sovereignty and independence. Brezhnev once again offered justification for the intervention in Czechoslovakia, and so did Husak, the representative of Czechoslovakia. The mere circumstance of bringing this touchy issue up again testified, of course, to the continuing dispute over one of the most divisive moves ever made by the CPSU and one of the most controversial policies ever adopted.

But in spite of the restatement of the Brezhnev doctrine of the right of intervention if socialism within the socialist bloc was in danger, the representatives of the French and Italian Communist Parties extolled the principles of the independence and inviolability of all socialist states, principles that had been agreed upon at the Conference of Communist Parties in Moscow in June 1969. The rift between Moscow and the influential Western Communist Parties, and the apparent insistence of the latter on their contrary point of view, were obvious. While these parties did not openly reproach the Soviets for their philosophy and policy, Ceausescu, leader of the Rumanian Communist Party, and the Yugoslav delegate both stressed the concept of the variety of roads to socialism. The Sino-Soviet dispute thus cast its long shadow over the 24th Party Congress of the CPSU.

It was obvious that the Soviets were unable to muster sufficient support among foreign parties to condemn China even verbally. It was widely observed that even the French and East German parties, so far docile toward the Soviet point of view, passed over in silence the delicate topic of Sino-Soviet relations. By emphasizing the right of each party to follow an independent path, both the Italian and Rumanian Communist Parties, by implication, continued to criticize Soviet policy on Czechoslovakia in 1968, thus making clear their opposition to any comparable Soviet move against Communist China in 1971. Thus the Soviet attempt to isolate China still failed to materialize. Soon after the Ussuri river clashes, Moscow, in June 1969, had proposed to contain China by arranging a collective security agreement in Asia through the mobilization of all Asiatic countries. The following month, at the July Moscow Conference of Communist Parties, it continued to press this policy, aiming, vainly, at the excommunication of the CPC from the Communist fellowship.

The India-Pakistan War, November-December 1971, and Its Aftermath

The war between India and Pakistan began on December 3, 1971, with a surprise attack by Pakistani planes upon eight Indian airfields and India's retaliation against nine airfields in East and West Pakistan. The Pakistani attack, designed to strike a crippling blow against the Indian air force, was said to protect East Pakistan from Indian troops that had begun to move against it in support of the native rebel army, the Mukti Bahini. On December 17 the war came to its end, with all of East Pakistan being occupied by the Indian Army. An independent state, Bangladesh, was proclaimed; Pakistan was humiliated and reduced in territory and power, and India was now dominant on the Indian subcontinent. China suffered a tremendous loss of face and the U.S., through blundering and moralizing, a similar loss of prestige. Only the USSR was triumphant. As far as the two Communist colossuses were concerned, the India-Pakistan war was a conflict by proxy. Yet, the possibility of a dangerous simultaneous confrontation of China with the USSR and a strengthened India had become a distinct reality.

The military dictatorship in Pakistan, established by Mohammad Ayub Khan in 1958, had been replaced in 1969 by another military regime, one under the leadership of Mohammad Yahya Khan. Hostility to Yahya's government became particularly pronounced in East Pakistan, where Bengalis complained of maltreatment at the hands of the Punjabi leaders of West Pakistan. In elections held in December 1970, the Awami League, based mainly in East Pakistan, had gained an absolute majority in the National Assembly.

The Awami League, which was hostile to Yahya, demanded autonomy, and advocated withdrawal from the CENTO and the SEATO alliances. When Yahya thereupon postponed the opening of the National Assembly, he once again encountered violence in East Pakistan and dispatched West Pakistani troops into the region to crush the rebellion. The Punjabi troops resorted to indescribable atrocities and outright massacres, killing perhaps one million people and causing almost ten million, mostly Hindus, to flee into West Bengal. The unprecedented terror aroused indignation in India and placed an intolerable financial and psychological burden upon its government. New Delhi, crushed by these obligations and deeply affected by the fate of coreligionists and kindred people, protested vainly, demanding an end to the repressive measures in East Pakistan.

On April 3, 1971, President Podgorny of the USSR, in a message to Yahya Khan, voiced regret over the many casualties in East Pakistan and the arrest of Sheik Mujibur Rahman, the leader of the Awami League. Expressing support for East Pakistani autonomy, he suggested that a peaceful political settlement be reached.[33] In his reply Yahya pointed to six Indian divisions that were poised on the boundaries of East Pakistan and represented a direct threat to his country's security, thereby rejecting what he apparently considered Soviet meddling. *People's Daily* similarly accused Indian "reactionaries" of interference in Pakistan's internal affairs, and the Soviets of their support of India's policy.[34]

Though in early May a Pakistani military delegation arrived in Peking for consultations, the Chinese press maintained an ominous silence about the Indian subcontinent through the spring and summer months of 1971. On the other hand, the Soviet Union and India achieved a rapprochement that found its climax in the signing of a treaty of friendship and alliance on August 9. A similar pact had been offered to India by the USSR in 1969 in the form of collective security zones, but India, then upholding its traditional policy of nonalignment, rejected it. But by 1971, India, increasingly fearful of China's military aid to Pakistan, which would enable China to persist in the repression of East Pakistan and to resume the fight over Kashmir, had changed her mind. Following the signing of the Russo-Indian pact, Mrs. Gandhi visited Moscow on September 27, 1971.

The Soviets were less reticent than the Chinese about the mounting crisis on the Indian subcontinent. On October 9, *Pravda* accused the Peking government of being controlled by reactionary forces, and on November 16 it called for a political settlement of the crisis on the Indian subcontinent. On November 23 it continued to caution Karachi that solution of the conflict by military means would only bring on new difficulties. The Soviets called upon Pakistan to stop her repressive actions and create the necessary conditions for the safe return of the refugees.

Peking's silence during the critical months must have raised doubts in the minds of Pakistan's leadership as to the reliability of China's support. A Pakistani delegation to Peking, headed by Ali Bhutto, apparently returned to Karachi without a firm Chinese commitment, though the CPR was soon to send as many as 400 new fighter and bomber planes to Pakistan.

A number of factors combined to lure India onto the warpath. The apparent willingness of Peking to give stronger pledges of support to Pakistan was not lost on India. New Delhi may also have calculated on the

33. *PR*, Apr. 16, 1971, pp. 8-10.
34. "What are the Indian expansionists trying to do?" *People's Daily*, April 11, 1971 (*PR*, Apr. 15, 1971, pp. 7-8).

Himalayan passes being closed off by the winter snows. Finally, Soviet Russia apparently acquiesced to India's decision to resort to direct military intervention. When on December 3 Yahya, pressed by nationalist groups that urged launching a military operation against India to preserve national unity and Islamic solidarity, yielded to them and ordered a military attack on Indian airfields, India quickly retaliated with air attacks of her own and a full-scale invasion of East Pakistan was begun. Each side charged the other with having started the war. Pakistan insisted that her own attack on December 3 had been unleashed in response to Indian incursions into East Pakistan.[35] As could be expected, Peking and Moscow came out in support of their respective allies.

Tass issued a Soviet government statement that warned that fighting on the subcontinent was occurring in direct proximity to Soviet Russia's borders and that this affected her security! (This probably was no less believable than the U.S.A.'s claim that her security was being threatened in Indo-China.) The statement cautioned other countries not to become involved in the conflict. China, on the other hand, attempting to pin the responsibility for the outbreak of hostilities on India, preferred to ignore the flight of millions of refugees from East Pakistan and the policy of repression and even extermination in that region. Peking, rather, pointed the accusing finger at Indian attacks against Pakistan that had taken place on November 21, and even claimed that the Mukti Bahini rebels operating in East Pakistan were only Indian troops in disguise.[36]

On December 10, *People's Daily* charged that the Indian government, backed by social-imperialism, had in the last few days brazenly expanded its armed aggression against Pakistan. Through direct invasion by Indian troops, New Delhi was seeking to achieve its long-planned aim to annex East Pakistan. The fact was clear: the Indian government was the naked aggressor. The struggle between the Indian reactionaries, the government, and the people of Pakistan was between the former's interference, subversion, and aggression and the latter's fight in defense of integrity. The so-called refugee question was precisely the product of flagrant interference in Pakistan's internal affairs by the Indian government. More than ten years ago the Indian reactionaries had similarly created a refugee question, that of the Tibetans.[37]

After war broke out, both China and Russia dropped the masks of restraint they had worn during the preceding months of the crisis when they had verbally attacked Pakistan and India. The Kremlin now directly ac-

35. *New York Times,* Dec. 4, 1971.
36. "Indian Reactionaries launch armed aggression against Pakistan," *PR*, Dec. 10, 1971, pp. 12-14.
37. *People's Daily*, Dec. 6, 1971 (*PR*, Dec. 10, 1971, p. 6).

cused China's leadership of indifference to the national-liberation movement and of having joined hands with the opponents of this struggle.[38] Peking's anti-Soviet campaign was only a smokescreen to distract attention from the liberation struggles in Indo-China and the Middle East and divert it from the internal political crisis going on in China.[39] The Maoists had sent their agents into East Pakistan to preach a people's war, while at the same time supporting the military regime in West Pakistan.

The split between Moscow and Peking was highlighted in the U.N. Before Peking's recent entry into the world organization, the Sino-Soviet quarrel could be followed in the Russian and Chinese press and its outlets in the English language. After Peking joined the U.N., the dispute was bared to the public at large through the world press, which had always focused on the debates and wrangles in the main agencies of the U.N. In the Security Council the American move for a cease-fire in the war on the Indian subcontinent and the immediate withdrawal of armed personnel on both sides was supported by Communist China but vetoed by the Soviet Union. The leaders of the Chinese and Russian delegations, Huang-Hua and Yakov Malik, crossed swords, the first likening Soviet support for Bangladesh to earlier Soviet aid for a rebellion in Sinkiang in 1962. Malik in turn pointed to China's alleged links with imperialism and denounced the Chinese leadership for having betrayed socialism.

At the urgent meeting of the Security Council on the evening of December 4, 1971, Huang-Hua, Permanent Representative of the CPR on the Council, asserted that the question of East Pakistan was purely an internal affair of Pakistan and rejected the Indian government's claim that it had sent troops into East Pakistan for purposes of "self-defense" as sheer gangster logic.[40] The following day, Huang Hua again criticized the Soviet government for having supported, encouraged, and protected India's aggression against Pakistan with the aim of gaining control over the Indo-Pakistan subcontinent and the Indian Ocean, and of "enlarging its sphere of influence" in its contention with the other superpower for hegemony.

The Soviet representative then suggested that the Council invite a representative of Bangladesh. But the Chinese delegation saw therein nothing but an attempt to subvert and dismember Pakistan, a sovereign member of the United Nations. Since 1962, Huang Hua asserted, when the Soviet government had engineered a counterrevolutionary rebellion in China's Sinkiang province, several tens of thousands of Chinese civilians had remained in Soviet hands and some were used by them for their anti-China

38. "The Indian-Pakistani Conflict and Peking's anti-Sovietism," *Pravda,* Dec. 8, 1971 (*CDSP*, 23, no. 49, [1971]: 2).
   39. *Ibid.,* p. 4.
   40. *PR*, Dec. 10, 1971, p. 19.

schemes and endeavors. India, similarly, was accused of using the East Pakistani refugees as a pretext for launching armed aggression against China!

The Soviet representative, Huang Hua continued, liked to speak of lending a "friendly hand" to other peoples. But, like gangsters, Soviet troops had moved into Czechoslovakia deep in the night. In its recent Tass statement the Soviet government had fixed its security borders on the Indo-Pakistan subcontinent and the Indian Ocean. The Chinese representative indignantly countered that the Soviet theory on security was "completely identical" with the security borders that the Israeli government tried to impose on Arab countries. He also pointed to the circumstance that, while after the outbreak of the Israeli "aggressive war" in 1967 the Soviets had proposed cease-fire and troop withdrawal, they now refused to apply the same principle to the Indo-Pakistani subcontinent. They were resorting to delaying tactics to coordinate with the military action of the Indian aggression against Pakistan in a vain attempt to change the military situation of Pakistan.

In the General Assembly of the U.N., a cease-fire resolution was passed by 104 to 11 votes, with Pakistan and China voting for the resolution, while Russia voted against it. India, however, rejected the suggested truce terms. Thereupon Pakistan's representative Bhutto denounced U.N. action and dramatically marched out of the Security Council.

The Sino-Soviet contest in the United Nations was accompanied by a heated press campaign in Soviet and Chinese journals. While New Delhi blamed Karachi for collaboration with world imperialism,[41] the latter accused the Soviets of abusing their veto power in the United Nations to shield Indian aggression.[42] On December 7, 1971, *People's Daily* dismissed the Soviet claim that the security of the USSR was affected by the developments on the Indian subcontinent in view of its proximity to its own borders as an "unheard-of-absurdity."

While Indian troops invading East Pakistan in December were greeted as liberators and the East Pakistan military regime was in its death throes, the CPR, on December 16, issued a statement once more blasting both India and the Soviet Union. The Indian government, it asserted, had brazenly launched a large-scale war of aggression against Pakistan with the active encouragement and energetic support of the government of the Soviet Union.[43] It was continuing to expand this war, moving massive troops to press on the capital of East Pakistan, Dacca, and blockading the ports and

41. "Flames over South Asia," *Izvestiia*, Dec. 12, 1971 (*CDSP* 23, no. 50 [Jan. 11, 1972]: 8-10).

42. "Refuting the Tass Statement," *People's Daily*, Dec. 7, 1971 (*PR*, Dec. 10, 1971).

43. Statement of the Government of the CPR, Dec. 16, 1971 (*PR*, Dec. 17, 1971).

sea lanes in East and West Pakistan with its naval forces. Cherishing the dream of a Greater Indian Empire, India wanted not only to swallow up East Pakistan, but also to destroy Pakistan as a whole—an apparently extreme view which, however, was virtually shared by some American experts close to the White House.

The Soviet government had played a "shameful role" in India's war of aggression against Pakistan. The representative of the Soviet government in the U.N. Security Council had time and again used the veto to obstruct the cease-fire and troop withdrawal demands embedded in the resolution of the U.N. General Assembly on December 7, 1971. The Soviet government had wantonly vilified China, alleging that it was China that had stirred up the conflict between India and Pakistan. Actually it was the Soviet government itself that had really and truly "set Asians to fight Asians." The present sudden invasion of Pakistan by India with the support of the Soviet Union was precisely a repetition on the South Asian subcontinent of the 1968 Soviet invasion and occupation of Czechoslovakia.

In the Security Council Huang Hua, the Chinese representative, castigated the government of Bangladesh as a "Quisling government."[44] And on December 8 the *People's Daily* denounced the new government as a "gimmick carried in the pocket of the Indian reactionaries." The collusion between these people and Soviet revisionist social imperialism had aroused the indignation of the people of Asia and of peoples all over the world.[45]

Though the war had ended and the crisis subsided, neither Peking nor Moscow was in the mood to let bygones be bygones. This time the outcome of the war—the "consequences of aggression," as Moscow liked to refer to the aftermath of the Israeli-Arab war of 1967—did please the Soviet Union, while Peking's stand rather paralleled the position of the USSR in the Middle East, where the Soviets sanctified the prewar status quo and demanded a return to it. On December 28 *Pravda,* glancing back, accused Peking of having worked to isolate India ever since the Sino-Indian conflict in 1959.[46] It charged it with having split the democractic forces in India by supporting "adventurist and extremist groups," a reference, apparently, to the support given to the pro-Peking faction of the CPI. Peking had inflated the Kashmir dispute to whip up anti-Indian feelings in Karachi and secure the latter's friendship. The CPR finally was charged with a "long premeditated deal with the U.S.A." at the expense of the national liberation movement and of the defense of developing countries.[47]

---

44. *PR*, Dec. 17, 1971, p. 15.
45. *People's Daily*, Dec. 8, 1971 (*PR*, Dec. 10, 1971, pp. 14-15).
46. *Pravda,* Dec. 28, 1971.
47. "Peking and the Third World," *Izvestiia*, Dec. 30, 1971 (*CDSP* 23, no. 52 [Jan. 25, 1972]: 4).

Communist China in turn reiterated her contention that Russia wanted to control the subcontinent in order to challenge the U.S. for control of the Indian Ocean and was exploiting the Indian-Pakistani conflict for her own selfish imperialist goals.[48] In a joint Chinese-Pakistani communiqué, issued after a visit of new Pakistani President Bhutto in Peking on January 31, 1972, the two governments adopted what was hardly a realistic line and foreshadowed a prolonged diplomatic struggle rather than a prompt acceptance of the new status quo. The communiqué condemned Indian aggression, demanded the withdrawal of Indian forces from East Pakistan, and restated support for the Kashmiri people in their demand for national self-determination.[49] A *People's Daily* editorial on January 31 charged that Soviet recognition of Bangladesh represented an attempt to legalize aggression. Peking predicted that Indian aggression in December merely represented "the starting point of endless strife on the subcontinent."[50] The prediction was no doubt an expression of its political wish and had the character of a self-fulfilling prophecy.

Communist China's fury and frustration over the defeat of Pakistan and the victory of India had brought Peking's hostility against Moscow to the boiling point. Soon, however, the CPR resumed her normal stance of carefully balanced, "equal" opposition to both superpowers. Peking's tacit temporary "alliance" with the U.S., their joint opposition to India, friendliness to Pakistan, and anger at the USSR were replaced by the propagandistic necessity of opposing capitalism and imperialism. The CPR could not permit a situation in which the USSR might monopolize the anti-American and anti-imperialist stance. In the curious triangular relationship between Peking, Moscow, and Washington, Peking had at all times to appear to be independent and not tied to or intimidated by any "paper tiger." It had to attempt to balance its lesser weight in world affairs as compared with either of the two superpowers by wresting the leadership of the countries of the Third World. It could not afford to be surpassed in radicalism, to be outflanked at the left. It was thus compelled to appeal to the anti-imperialist, anti-Western nationalist sentiments of the "Third World" countries and occasionally to inject a racial bias into its campaign.

In the article "U.S.-Soviet Scramble for Hegemony in South Asian Subcontinent and Indian Ocean," *Peking Review* charged the "two overlords" with stepping up their maneuvers in that part of the world.[51] The U.S. had dispatched the aircraft carrier *Enterprise* into the Bay of Bengal to "show

48. "U. S.-Soviet scramble for hegemony in South Asian Subcontinent and India," *PR*, Jan. 14, 1972, pp. 16-17.   .
49. "President Bhutto Visits China," *PR*, Feb. 4, 1972, pp. 5-8.
50. "It is impermissible to legalize India's Invasion and Occupation of East Pakistan," *PR*, Feb. 4, 1972, pp. 8-9.
51. *PR*, Jan. 14, 1972, pp. 16-17.

the flag"; spokesmen for the U.S. Defense Department had indicated that the nuclear-powered aircraft carrier would remain in the Indian Ocean indefinitely and that U.S. military authorities had always regarded that sea as an important and strategic part of the world. A U.S. Navy announcement also stressed the strong continuing American interest in the Persian Gulf. On the other hand, Soviet revisionists, following the example of the Russian tsars, especially that of Peter, who dreamed of sending the Russian navy into the Indian Ocean, had donned the old tsars' mantle. They were anxious to establish a sea lane stretching from the Black Sea to the Sea of Japan, linking Europe, Asia, and Africa in order to attain naval hegemony.

After Brezhnev took office, the Soviets secured the right to use naval bases and ports of certain countries on the shores of the Indian Ocean by furnishing economic and military "aid" and other bait. In 1969 a Soviet fleet began to be permanently stationed in the Indian Ocean. In the opinion of the Japanese newspaper *Yomiuri Shimbun,* the India-Pakistan situation offered the USSR a golden opportunity to use India as a pawn to ensure passage through the Indian Ocean for the purpose of expansion in Southeast Asia. Twenty-seven Soviet warships were reported to be deployed in the Indian Ocean. While Soviet revisionism accused U.S. imperialism of pursuing a "gunboat policy" and protested the American view of the Indian Ocean as an American lake, it actually carried out a "gunboat policy" of its own and regarded the Indian Ocean as a Soviet lake.

China, anxious to pose as spokesman "of medium-sized and small countries" such as Ceylon, Pakistan, and Zambia, and to secure their support, assured them and the world at large that no domination of the area by U.S. imperialism or Soviet revisionism would be tolerated—without, of course, specifying the methods Peking would employ to prevent such a contingency.

From Nixon's Journey to Peking to his Visit to Moscow

In 1972 Sino-Soviet relations were deeply affected by the diplomatic initiatives taken by President Nixon. Each of the journeys was jealously watched in the other Communist capital.

The communiqué published at the end of the visit to China contained statements by both the Chinese and the American governments. There was, of course, no public reference to the USSR or to the Sino-Soviet rift. While the communiqué stressed the essential differences between China and the U.S. in their social systems and foreign policies, it proclaimed their agreement in regard to respect for the sovereignty and territorial integrity of all states, nonagression against other states, noninterference in the internal affairs of other states, and peaceful coexistence; it disclaimed resort to the use or threat of force. The reference to territorial integrity may have been reassuring to Peking in regard to Taiwan, but less so in regard to the Sino-Soviet frontier, since the CPR had put forth extensive claims to Soviet territory. Both sides disclaimed seeking hegemony "in the Asia-Pacific region," which, in view of the relative strength of both powers, was likely to impose greater restraint on the U.S.A. than on China. In view of frequent earlier charges by Peking relating to Soviet-American collusion, the pledge in the communiqué of both China and the U.S.A. to refrain from "colluding" with another major country against other countries and from dividing up the world into spheres of interest was of significance, though there were, of course, no possible sanctions in case of violation of such solemn promises.

The Sino-American rapprochement would not have come about without Peking's conviction that the U.S.A. was resolved to withdraw the bulk of her forces from South Vietnam and Indochina in general. The removal of the American threat in the south in combination with the American failure to make in Shanghai any pledge of assistance to South Vietnam or Taiwan comparable to that given to South Korea thus diminished if it did not completely eliminate, the possibility of China's facing a simultaneous confrontation in the south, north, and northwest, the possibility of conflict and war on two fronts, against the U.S.A. and the Soviet Union. China's interest in the American attempt to reestablish ties with herself was thus quite palpable. America's willingness to make far-reaching concessions in the Taiwan question, the "crucial question," in the Chinese view, that obstructed normalization of relations between the two countries, represented, of course, a striking reversal of American policy and removed a major obstacle to further rapprochement between Peking and Washington.

The Sino-American communiqué in Shanghai, dated February 27, 1972, is one of the most important documents in the diplomatic history of our era.[52] Its silence about the USSR, of course, should not mislead one for one moment into believing that it was not relevant to or had no bearing upon the Sino-Soviet relationship. The opposite is true.

China, the largest nation on earth and one of the most ambitious, publicly disdains the superpowers and disclaims any intention of wishing to become one. In the joint Sino-American communiqué, the Chinese side said this specifically, and also proclaimed that it opposed hegemony and power politics of any kind. "All nations, big or small, should be equal: big nations should not bully the weak." Peking had clearly erased from her memory her invasion of India in 1962.

52. Sino-American Communiqué, Feb. 27, 1972.

Communist China was evidently making a bid for the support of the many small and middle-sized states. She hoped to reap vast propagandistic benefits from posing as champion of many of these states, which were fearful, envious, and resentful of the two superpowers.

This Chinese line, reasserted in the joint Sino-American communiqué, has continued to be pressed since. It found especially clear expression in an article "Medium-sized and small nations united to oppose two superpowers' hegemony."[53] Fifty million Indochinese people, the author asserted, had united and set a brilliant example that a small nation can defeat a big one and a weak nation can defeat a strong one. In the Middle East the two superpowers had made deals behind the scenes, betraying the interests of the Palestinians and other Arab peoples. But the waves of the anti-imperialist struggle of the 100 million Arab people from the Persian Gulf to the Atlantic coast were rolling forward. The aggression and expansion by Soviet social imperialism had likewise been jointly condemned and opposed by many medium-sized and small countries. The struggle initiated by Chile, Peru, Ecuador, and other Latin American countries to safeguard their 220-nautical mile territorial waters and protect their ocean resources was favorably responded to by many medium-sized and small countries. Yet, proceeding from their imperialist interests, the two overlords, the U.S. and the Soviet Union, tried to impose on other countries a territorial water limit they had agreed upon.

There was also developing, the author of the article asserted, opposition by middle-sized and small countries along the Indian Ocean and the Mediterranean Sea to both the U.S. and Soviet contention for hegemony. The leaders of Ceylon, Pakistan, and Zambia had strongly denounced the superpowers for expanding their military forces and establishing military bases in the Indian Ocean. Similarly, Boumedienne of Algeria had sternly pointed out that the Mediterranean Sea belonged to the Mediterranean countries. Albania, Libya, Yugoslavia, and other Mediterranean countries had demanded that the U.S. and the Soviet fleets "go home." In the 70s the "two overlords" who had been overbearing and arrogant, were bound to head for a decline and complete defeat.

The February agreement of 1972 between the U.S. and China has not, of course, buried the propaganda war on the part of the CPR either against the USSR or against the U.S.[54] The ink used in signing the treaty had not yet dried when the war of words flared up again. Peking wished to remind the world that the U.S. was still a "tiger" that must be mistrusted —though it need not be feared—and that Peking did not follow in Moscow's footsteps of betraying the sacred cause of Revolution.

53. *PR*, March 31, 1972.
54. There is already strong evidence of this in the Chinese press for March and April 1972.

In mid-April 1972, the escalation of the war against North Vietnam resulted in bitter denunciation of the latest American military moves by both Peking, which the American President had just visited, and by Moscow, to which he was soon to travel. Even prior to the blockading of North Vietnamese ports and in spite of the continued withdrawal of American troops from South Vietnam, the Chinese press, hardly in a mood different from that prior to Nixon's visit, criticized the claim of the U.S. government that its raids on North Vietnam were "in response to" the North Vietnamese "invasion" of South Vietnam. This argument was "ridiculous." North Vietnam was "one country," "the Vietnamese nation is a whole."[55] Then came President Nixon's order to cut off land and water communications of North Vietnam and to intensify air and naval strikes. In "The Statement of the Government of the CPR," published on May 19, 1972, Peking referring to President Nixon's "brazen" order to mine the ports of North Vietnam, denounced "the pretexts used by U.S. imperialism to escalate the war" as "most absurd."[56] It was known to all that the U.S. was the aggressor and Vietnam the victim of aggression. Though the statement reaffirmed the often-made pledge that "700 million Chinese people provide a powerful backing for the Vietnam people," Peking failed to react to the latest American military escalation as it had failed previously to render effective help to Hanoi. It spoke harshly, but wielded no stick.

In another official statement issued by the Foreign Ministry on June 12, 1972, it was pointed out that the steady American expansion of the sphere of bombing up to areas close to the Sino-Vietnamese borders "threatened" the very security of China.[57] However great the threat Peking judged the most recent American moves to be, they apparently produced no diplomatic rapprochement between the CPR and the USSR. America's provocative activities in China's backyard had not generated such a rapprochement between the two Communist superpowers in the hey-day of America's invasion of Indo-China. They were not likely to have such a result at the stage when the U.S. seemed to be at the point of winding down the war in Vietnam.

Soviet Russia's denunciation of the latest American military moves against North Vietnam was as sharp as Communist China's. A Tass statement in *Pravda*, April 17, asserted that the Soviet people "angrily condemned" the acts of U.S. aggression in Vietnam.[58] The further build-up

55. *PR*, Apr. 14, 1972.
56. "The Statement of the Government of the CPR," published May 19, 1972.
57. "Statement of the Foreign Ministry of the CPR," June 12, 1972 (*PR*, June 16, 1972.
58. "A month's press coverage of Vietnam," Tass Statement, *Pravda*, Apr. 17, 1972 (*CDSP* 24, no. 16 [May 17, 1972]: 1-6).

of American air and naval forces in the Indochina region, the resumption of raids on DRV territory, Washington's decision to interrupt the Paris talks for an indefinite period—all these actions were in irreconcilable contradiction with the official statements about the U.S.A.'s desire to achieve a peaceful settlement in Vietnam and Indochina.

The Soviet government denounced Nixon's order to mine the entrances to North Vietnamese ports and to step up the bombing of DRV territory: "To past barbaric acts and crimes, new and graver acts are added." After pointing out the lawlessness of the American acts, judged by principles of international law, the Soviet statement urged the U.S.A. to return to the negotiating table in Paris and warned that it would continue to give the heroic Vietnamese people the necessary support. But the USSR refrained from calling off the impending Russo-American meeting in Moscow.[59]

Then followed the visit of President Nixon to Moscow, beginning on May 22, and the signing of numerous treaties pledging cooperation between the USSR and the U.S.A. in many fields.[60] There was, of course, no reference to Communist China whatsoever in these treaties, though it is questionable whether without the deep rift between Peking and Moscow the President's journey to both capitals would have materialized at all. Whatever the American interest in both journeys, the national interests of both the CPR and the USSR required at least settlement of some minor questions and accommodation in regard to some weighty international issues. Both Peking and Moscow wanted to begin removing some differences with the U.S.A.—ideologically supposed to be the archenemy, but geographically distant—in order to concentrate its efforts upon the immediate hostile heighbor, ideologically supposed to be a comrade-in-arms, but having become increasingly the archheretic himself.

In the final evaluation of the significance of the many treaties concluded with the U.S., the Soviet leadership, in a statement on "The Results of Soviet-American Talks," was careful to point out that the Soviet Union had neither abandoned its Marxist-Leninist principles nor its friends in the Middle East and Vietnam.[61] It had shown, the statement asserted, that disputed international questions could not be resolved by methods of a "position of strength" policy. At the same time, however, as if to assure the revolutionary Communist movement everywhere, the Soviet leadership pointed out that the "might" of the USSR was "constantly gaining strength." This ritualistic Soviet declaration was probably less than reassuring to Communist China.

59. *Pravda* and *Izvestiia*, May 12, 1972, p. 1 (*CDSP*, 24, no. 17, p. 5).
60. *New York Times*, May 28, 1972.
61. *Pravda*, June 2, 1972, p. 1 (*CDSP* 24, no. 22, [June 22, 1972]: 25).

From the Cease-Fire in Vietnam to the Tenth National Congress
of the CPC, 1973

The cease-fire in Vietnam and the apparent end of the war was widely
hailed in the Soviet press. While credit was given "above all" to the
heroic efforts of the entire Vietnamese people in both the North and the
South, the restoration of peace was considered "also a great victory for the
socialist commonwealth." The world was reminded that the "Soviet people have always stood shoulder to shoulder with the Vietnam patriots."[62] At
the same time the Soviet press denounced the imperialist propaganda that
tried to defame the "principled and consistent position of the Soviet Union
and its comprehensive assistance and support to the Vietnamese people's
courageous struggle" and to discredit the Soviet Union. "In this respect,
the Maoist groups, acting hand in glove with the imperialists," seconded
them by resorting to infamous slander of the USSR.[63]

The agreement on Ending the War and Restoring Peace in Vietnam,
signed in Paris on January 27, 1973, was also welcomed by the Chinese
press, which especially hailed the prospect of unification of North and
South.[64] Like the Soviets, the Chinese Communists promised to extend
"firm support" to the just cause of the fraternal people of Vietnam. Differently from the USSR, however, they recalled that the Chinese and Vietnamese peoples were "of the same family." It was evident that Peking
was pleased about the definite removal of the American threat to the south
of their border and that it was laying the groundwork for a special relationship with Hanoi, based not only on recent assistance and common outlook,
but also on revolutionary militancy, geographic proximity, and racial kinship. The latter claims could not be matched by Moscow.

Racial and ethnic kinship have long been an important weapon in
Peking's arsenal. At a banquet a few months later in honor of Prince
Sihanouk, Chou En-lai underscored that the Chinese and the Cambodian
peoples belonged to the same ethnic group.[65] Marxism-Leninism, or better,
Mao Tse-tung Thought, has come full circle to pay respect to nationalism
and racialism!

Throughout 1973 Peking continued to play the role of champion of the
smaller and middle-sized states, which are poorer in industrial and natural
wealth and inferior in military strength, against both superpowers. In striking this pose, it hoped for strong support on the part of the many against
the few powerful and richer states. This was the major theme of the speech
on "the struggle in defense of maritime rights" by Chuang Yen, chief rep-

62. *PR*, Feb. 21, 1973, also Feb. 28, 1973, p. 17.
63. *Pravda*, March 7, 1973.
64. *PR*, Feb. 28, 1973, pp. 6-7; also *People's Daily* editorial, Jan. 28, 1973.
65. *PR*, Apr. 20, 1973, pp. 16-17.

resentative of the Chinese delegation to the meeting of the U.N. Seabed Committee.[66] The speaker criticized the position of the two superpowers in the one's allowing other maritime states only a three-mile, the other a twelve-mile zone. As a developing country, he asserted, China extended her "profound sympathy" for the measures taken by the Asian, African, and Latin American countries to protect their resources. He castigated the Soviet Union for insisting on delimitation of the breadth of her territorial sea at twelve nautical miles, which was designed to realize her ambition to dominate the oceans. The two superpowers tried to outdo each other in advanced techniques and high-tonnage vessels for excessive fishing, thus seriously undermining the world's fishery resources.

The struggle to win the favor of the great majority of the peoples and states of the world and enlist their support against the two superpowers remained throughout 1973 a main theme of Chinese Communist propaganda. The Chinese representative An Chih-yuan, addressing a plenary session of the U.S. on April 12, attacked the USSR, though without mentioning her by name.[67] The Soviet Union was "making a show of force everywhere in the vast region extending from West Asia to the Far East and from the Indian Ocean to the Pacific, infringing on other countries' sovereignty and peddling the so-called Asian collective security system." Chiao Kuan-hua, Chairman of the Delegation of the CPR, addressing the U.N. General Assembly on October 2, 1973, raised the question why the Soviet Union, a "European country," should be so eagerly concerned about Asian "collective security," this "long-ignored trash,"[68] and suggested that the ghost of John Foster Dulles had moved to the Kremlin.

While anxious to remove the threat of an encirclement by Asian peoples gathering under the flag of Asian collective security, the CPR was bent on marching at the head not only of all Asian but also of the African and Latin American peoples against the two superpowers. The CPR played up to the Fourth Conference of Heads of State and Government of Nonaligned Countries; in her view, the conference revealed a further "awakening" of the Asian, African, and Latin American peoples, which aimed at independence, liberation, and revolution. In the economic field, according to Peking, the gap was widening between the rich and developed countries and poor and developing states. Peking also suggested a revision of the U.N. charter to give expression to the numerous small- and medium-sized countries and to the principles of equality of all states, big or small, and to terminate control by the superpowers.[69] Clearly, Peking saw itself already as leader of the great majority of states, the small and middle-sized, the un-

66. *PR*, March 30, 1973, pp. 9-11.
67. *PR*, Apr. 20, 1973, pp. 13-15.
68. *PR*, Oct. 5, 1973, pp. 1-13, 17.
69. *Ibid.*

derdeveloped and poor nations, against the two world powers, one capitalist, the other claiming to be "socialist," but both irretrievably imperialist.

China, An Chih-yuan continued, had come to realize the importance of self-reliance. This did not preclude international economic and trade relations on the basis of equality, but the CPR was firmly set against big powers' seeking hegemony and aiming at economic plunder of other countries in the name of "regional cooperation." China would never be a superpower, subjecting others to aggression or bullying. On the other hand, the Chinese representative stressed that the people of the CPR were "closely bound with other peoples of Asia and the Far East by common struggles of opposing imperialism, colonialism and building our own countries."[70]

The Soviets, commenting on Sino-American relations, took comfort in American assurances that there was no "anti-Soviet motivation" in their agreements with the Chinese, especially in the reassurance at a press conference by then Presidential Advisor Henry Kissinger that the normalization of relations between the U.S. and the CPR would never be directed against a third country, a statement similar to one made earlier by President Nixon himself. Those who asserted that the Soviet Union was preparing a "surprise attack against China," that a "Soviet menace" loomed over China, talked "gibberish," according to *Pravda*.[71] Soviet leaders clearly and definitely had stated time and again that the USSR had no territorial or economic claims against the CPR.

While disavowing any Soviet aggressive designs on Communist China, Moscow suspected intensely Peking's policy and diplomatic moves. On February 25, V. Yermakov in *Pravda* accused Chinese diplomacy of supporting activities of those forces which spoke out against the détente, against the convocation of a European conference, and against disarmament. Peking was favoring all closed political, economic, and military blocs in the western part of Europe, whether it was the Common Market or a revived so-called Western Europe Defense Community, planned by some people in NATO circles.[72] Communist China has actually endorsed Western strength against the USSR in the hope of drawing Soviet forces away from the Chinese border and now was trying to head off a détente between the West and the Soviets.

On August 26, *Pravda* accused Peking of seeking to discourage the relaxation of tension between East and West by asking the Western nations to be distrustful of Soviet overtures. China's "own efforts to improve rela-

70. See n 67 above.
71. L. Zamyatin, ". . . .American-Chinese Dialogue," *Sovetskaya Rossia, CDSP* 25, no. 9 (March 28, 1973): 13.
72. *Pravda*, Feb. 25, 1973; *CDSP* 25, no. 8 (March 21, 1973): 20.

tions [with the West] could be welcome if she pursued the same aims as the Soviet Union." But instead, the article charged, Peking was trying to make common cause with the imperialists against Moscow.[73]

In 1973 the Soviet Union, concerned about Chinese diplomatic moves anywhere, continued to suspect anti-Soviet scheming. B. Krymov in *Literaturnaya gazeta* reported of Chou's having given Japan military assurances in the event of an attack by the Soviet Union on Japan. He had also voiced his support of a "reasonable growth" of Japanese military strength as a potential counterweight to the USSR's "aggressive designs." The disavowals of Japan and China were dismissed as meaningless.[74]

The CPR, on the other hand, was equally convinced of the Soviet Union's aggressive plans. It raised questions as to the presence of Soviet naval units in the Sea of Japan and came out in behalf of the return of northern territories to Japan. *Peking Review*, in an article "Doubts on European Security," quoted approvingly the words of Leber, Defense Minister of the Federal Republic of Germany, that the USSR was "an expansionist world power," had "a fundamental inclination to expansion" and presented "worldwide claims." Western Europe, in the view of Leber, needed close support by the U.S.[75] In the Sino-French Communiqué, dated September 14 in Peking, the two sides, examining the situation in Europe, stated: "China supports the efforts made by the European peoples to safeguard the independence, sovereignty and security of their respective countries and, on this basis, to unite themselves for the preservation of their own security."[76] The sovereignty and security of European countries, including capitalist ones such as France, were in Chinese eyes obviously threatened, primarily, if not exclusively, by the USSR! According to Chiao Kuan-hua, Chairman of the Chinese Delegation to the U.N., Europe was the "focus of contention between the two superpowers" and the European security conference was "nothing but one of the forums of contention." European security in turn was tied to the security of all Mediterranean countries and was endangered when the Mediterranean region was under the armed threat of, and contention by, the two superpowers. The USSR, it was strongly implied, sought to divide and disintegrate Western Europe.[77]

The Chinese press also demonstrated a lively interest in the twentieth session of the Council of Ministers of the CENTO in Teheran on June 11, which was to strengthen the defense posture of their member states against

73. *Pravda*, Aug. 26, 1973.
74. B. Krymov, "A New Guardian?" *Literaturnaya gazeta*, Jan. 1973, p. 9 (*CDSP* 25, no. 3 [Feb. 14, 1973].
75. "Doubts on European Security, "*PR*, June 29, 1973, pp. 18-19.
76. *PR*, Sept. 21, 1973, pp. 4-5.
77. *PR*, Oct. 5, 1973, p. 12.

the Soviet Union. Another time, sympathy was expressed for Iran which, it was said, felt "uneasy" about the Soviet presence in the Middle East. Peking also continued to show considerable interest in Rumania's maverick attitude toward the Soviet Union.[78] It also continued to woo the Arabs and to discredit the USSR: it especially criticized the Soviet Union for permitting the emigration of Soviet Jews.

To denounce Israel, the Chinese Communists indulged in superlatives ("mad" and "shocking crime," "criminal act," "aggressive nature and extremely ruthless features of the Israeli Zionists," "capable of savage crimes," "height of arrogance," etc.), but blamed not only the U.S., but also the USSR for the woeful situation of the Arabs. "It is plain to all that one superpower supplies an uninterrupted flow of money and weapons to Israel, while the other superpower through continual emigration provides it with massive manpower and sources of troop recruitment and even technical specialists." While denouncing the USSR on account of the alleged betrayal of the Arab countries, the Peking press at other times, not quite consistently, criticized Soviet revisionism for "poking its nose into the Middle East."[79]

The common denominator of all these comments and positions was the underlying conviction that the Soviet Union, because of its overweening imperialist ambitions and designs, was a menace to the security of all her neighbors and of the world at large.

The Chinese press quoted approvingly the statement of Lord Carrington, British Secretary for Defense, that "the Soviet threat was growing" and the evaluation of E. F. Hill, Chairman of the Marxist-Leninist Party of Australia, that the Soviet Union was an "imperialist power." The Peking press expressed commiseration for all European peoples, including the Germans, who had suffered greatly from the two world wars, but ridiculed the Soviets, who made so big a fuss about European détente, peace, and security, but had "not eased up in their military build-up."[80]

On the other hand, Peking had sacrificed, as Moscow often charged, all principles of revolutionary consistency to the demands of opportunism. Chou boasted: "We are prepared to develop normal relations with any country on the basis of equality."[81] In 1973 the CPR even established diplomatic relations with Franco's Spain. In spite of the diplomatic rapprochement with the U.S., however, Peking, in and outside the U.N., continued to denounce not only Moscow but also Washington for alleged aggression. As Chou elaborated: "Relaxation is but a superficial phenome-

78. *PR*, June 22, 1973, p. 18 and July 16, 1973, p. 19.
79. *PR*, July 20, 1973, p. 11; Apr. 20, 1973, p. 19; Aug. 3, 1973, p. 7.
80. *PR*, Aug. 10, 1973, p. 20, pp. 7-8, 9-10.
81. *PR*, Sept. 7, 1973, pp. 17-29.

non.''[82] While China officially denied that she was against détente, she denounced at the same time what in her view was "only a travesty of peaceful coexistence" in the world. "The substance is coexistence in rivalry." In a speech on October 2 the Chairman of the Delegation of the CPR to the U.N. ridiculed the "absurd theory of the so-called 'peaceful transition' '' that was advocated by the USSR.[83] Again and again Peking reminded the world that it was still dedicated to the spread of revolution and remained intransigent.

Each Communist superpower directed broadside attacks on the other. The CPR made a direct assault on Moscow with the article "Two tactics with one purpose: Soviet revisionists' ugly design in renaming towns in the Far East."[84] The Soviets had issued a decree that was to change the names of a number of towns in the Han and Manchu dialects in the Soviet Far East into Russian ones. The "Iman" District and Town had been renamed "Dalnerechensk" (distant river), the town "Suchan" called "Partizansk" (town of the guerrillas), and "North Suchan Workers' Settlement" renamed "Uglemkamensk Workers' Settlement." The Chinese writer quoted approvingly the *New York Times* to the effect that the Soviet Government's decision to rename these towns would appear to be "aimed at removing evidence that the region was once Chinese." However, the Chinese writer concluded that renaming places could in no way alter history and Brezhnev's "despicable trick" of attempting this would only further reveal the Soviet leader's "wild ambitions for aggression."

The territorial claims and border disputes remained inextricably linked up with nationality problems within both countries, but especially in the broad belt along the 4,000-mile border. In April 1973 the deputy representative of the Chinese delegation to the twenty-ninth session of the U.N. Economic Commission for Asia and the Far East pointed out that in densely populated areas with high birth rates, the Chinese government generally advocated late marriage and also birth control; "in national minority areas," however, it had adopted appropriate measures "to help increase population,"[85] though guidance and help were also given to those who desired to practice birth control. This Chinese claim of discrimination in reverse, a bias in favor of national minorities, must be taken with a grain of salt, though the mere assertion of it and the admitted contrast to China's general policy are clear indications of the vulnerability of the Chinese position in this area and have special significance in view of the massing of troops on both sides of the long frontier.

82. *Ibid.*
83. *PR*, Oct. 5, 1973, pp. 10-17.
84. *PR*, March 16, 1973, pp. 9-10.
85. *PR*, Apr. 27, 1973, p. 21.

In 1973 the Chinese press deliberately tried to closely associate well-known opponents of Mao, for years targets of ceaseless denunciation by the CPC, with alleged Soviet attempts to infiltrate the Chinese Party and to impose revisionist views on it. In the New Year message of 1973 of *People's Daily* and *Red Flag,* Liu Chao-chi "and other political swindlers" were violently denounced on account of their revisionism; they were accused of wishing "to capitulate to Soviet revisionist social imperialism and to oppose China, Communism and the revolution."[86] Later in the year, Lin Piao was similarly branded as a Soviet tool. The Soviets in turn spoke frequently of "healthy" elements, though at the moment these were reduced to impotence, in the CPC.[87] It was apparent that while both sides had burned bridges as far as the opposite current leadership was concerned, they still entertained some hope for a favorable change beyond the border some time in the future; or for apparent tactical reasons, they had to give the impression that they continued to nourish such hopes.

Each Communist superpower considered the position of the other on nuclear weapons reprehensible, if not inexcusable. The CPR blamed the USSR for her determination to keep all nuclear weapons intact, not sharing them with her; the USSR in turn accused the CPR of wishing to become a nuclear power, in her judgment an unmistakable sign of her hegemonic ambitions. The Soviets were especially aroused over what they considered the hypocrisy of the CPC. Referring to the June 27 Chinese explosion of a nuclear device, *Pravda* wrote: "While regularly conducting nuclear tests in the atmosphere and on the ground, the Maoists have been voting in the U.N. against resolutions calling for a halt of nuclear and thermonuclear testing." Peking was opposing relaxation, but made desperate efforts to become a nuclear and missile superpower. She would "like to decide the fate of countries and peoples."

In a speech on August 15, 1973, Brezhnev directed a sharp attack against Peking, denouncing Maoism as alien to Leninism.[88] At that very time high-level Party and government meetings were taking place in Peking and Brezhnev may have intended to influence policy decisions in the CPR in the Soviet Union's favor. Brezhnev's address might also have been geared to influencing an impending gathering of about seventy nonaligned countries that were scheduled to meet in Algiers on September 5. The Chinese delegate at the conference of the nonaligned nations then portrayed the USSR as a "dangerous friend."[89] For years both Communist superpowers have directed their propagandistic campaign at the countries of the

86. *PR*. Jan. 5, 1973, pp. 9f.
87. *PR*, Sept. 7, 1973, p. 19.
88. *Izvestiia,* Aug. 16, 1973.
89. *New York Times,* Sept. 8, 1973.

Third World to boost their own image and to detract from that of the other. The net result has been to wound each other.

If in August 1973 it was still possible to escalate the Sino-Soviet conflict beyond the high level it had already attained, this was achieved at the Tenth National Congress of the CPC. In his report to the Congress, delivered on August 24 and adopted four days later, Chou En-lai revealed for the first time the full extent of Lin Piao's traitorous moves against Mao and the current leadership; he had attempted a coup that had failed, in the course of which he had been killed. In March 1971 he had drawn up his plan for an armed coup and on September 8, 1971, he had launched it, "in a wild attempt to assassinate our great leader Chairman Mao" and to set up a rival Central Committee.[90] Lin Piao, the formerly widely hailed heir to Mao and always referred to as his "close comrade-in-arms," was now bitterly denounced by Chou on account of his "conspiracy and sabotage." On September 13, after the conspiracy had collapsed, Lin Piao had surreptitiously boarded a plane and "fled as a defector to the Soviet revisionists in betrayal of the Party and the country." He had died in a crash at Undur Khaun in the People's Republic of Mongolia.

Chou considered the "shattering of the Lin Piao anti-Party clique"* the CPC's "greatest victory since the Ninth Congress and a heavy blow dealt to the enemies at home and abroad." China's masses had expressed their intense proletarian indignation "at the bourgeois, careerist, conspirator, double-dealer, renegade and traitor Lin Piao." "A movement to criticize Lin Piao and rectify the style of work" was then launched throughout the country. The whole Party, Army, and people were conscientiously studying "Marxism-Leninism-Mao Tsetung Thought," "conducting revolutionary mass criticism of Lin Piao and other swindlers."

Chou dwelled on the alleged ties between the Lin Piao clique and the CPSU. As early as January 13, 1967, Brezhnev, the chief of the Soviet revisionist renegade clique, had frantically attacked China's Great Proletarian Cultural Revolution at a mass rally in the Gorky region and had openly declared that the USSR stood on the side of the Liu Chao-chi renegade clique, saying that the downfall of this group was a "big tragedy for all real Communists in China and we express our deep sympathy to them." At the same time Brezhnev publicly announced the continuation of the policy of subverting the leadership of the CPC and struggling "for bringing it back to the road of internationalism." Other Soviet chieftains had

90. *PR*, Sept. 7, 1973, p. 18.

*The "anti-Party" group was a concept invented by Khrushchev in dealing with his domestic opponents in 1957. The Chinese leaders, in spite of their dislike of Khrushchev, had apparently no hesitation in borrowing this concept from him, applying it, no doubt "creatively," to the CPR.

anticipated that "sooner or later the healthy forces expressing the true interests of China will have their decisive say" and that Marxism-Leninism would triumph. What they actually wanted was to reduce China to a colony of Soviet revisionist social-imperialism. The Brezhnev renegade group had revealed the "ultra-Rightist nature of the Lin Piao anti-Party clique."

Lin Piao and his "handful of sworn followers were a conspiratorial clique who never had shown up without a copy of [Mao's] *Quotations* but who " 'stabbed you in the back.' " They wanted to betray the line of the Ninth Congress and turn the CPC "into a revisionist, fascist Party, subvert the dictatorship of the proletariat and restore capitalism." They wanted to institute a "feudal-comprador-fascist dictatorship." Lin Piao had engaged in machinations within the CPC not just during the last decade, but for several decades.

In the last fifty years the CPC, according to Chou, had gone through ten major struggles. Such struggles would occur again and again: "Ten, twenty or thirty times, Lin Piaos will appear again and so will persons like Wang Ming, Liu Shao-chi, Peng Teh-huai and Kao Kang." Chou might have added that virtually all of them had, at one time or the other, been accused of pro-Soviet leanings.

According to Chou, the current international situation was one "characterized by great disorder on earth." The great disorder was "a good thing for the people, not a bad thing," since it threw the enemies into confusion and caused division among them, while it aroused and tempered people, "thus helping the international situation develop further in the direction favorable to the people and unfavorable to imperialism, modern revisionism, and all reaction." Modern revisionism, most revealingly, was placed right in the middle between "imperialism" and "reaction."

There could be no misunderstanding about whom Chou considered "enemies." It was those against whom the countries of the Third World and the CPR herself were pitted, the two nuclear superpowers, the U.S. and the USSR, who were contending for hegemony throughout the world. While they fought each other, they were also colluding with each other. Contention was "absolute and protracted," whereas collusion was "relative and temporary." "The West wants to urge the Soviet revisionists eastward to divert the peril towards China. China was an attractive piece of meat coveted by all. But this piece of meat was very tough. For years no one has been able to bite into it," and with Lin Piao, the "super-spy," having fallen, this would be even more difficult now. At present, the Soviet revisionists were "making a feint to the east, while attacking in the west," and were stepping up their contention in Europe and their expansion in the Mediterranean, the Indian Ocean, and every place their hands could reach. The U.S.-Soviet contention for hegemony is the cause of world intranquility.

Peking thus pointed to U.S.-Soviet differences as the major root of international tension, though on many other occasions it of course underlined the Sino-Soviet confrontation. But to make the latter the main or even a major source of international dispute in the world would have increased world pressure upon China to do her part to remove this source of world tension. While both superpowers were ambitious, it was another thing whether they could achieve their ambition. "They want to devour China, but find it too tough even to bite." Both superpowers are thus portrayed as deadly enemies of Communist China. The U.S.-China rapprochement was here simply ignored.

The apparent propagandistic need to have, next to Soviet revisionism and social-imperialism, a real capitalist and imperialist enemy, may account for the careful balancing of Washington and Moscow as the two major foes of Peking. For Communist Peking, the hoped-for center of world Communism, a capitalist enemy, next to the Soviet arch-enemy, is plainly an imperative!

There followed a bitter denunciation by Chou of "the Soviet revisionist clique from Khrushchev to Brezhnev" that made a socialist country degenerate into a social-imperialist country. The ruling group "had restored capitalism, enforced a fascist dictatorship and enslaved the people of all nationalities." Externally, it "has invaded and occupied Czechoslovakia, massed its troops along the Chinese border, sent troops into the People's Republic of Mongolia, supported the traitorous Lon Nol clique, suppressed the Polish Workers' rebellion, intervened in Egypt, causing the expulsion of the Soviet experts, dismembered Pakistan, and carried out subversive activities in many Asian and African countries." This series of facts, according to Chou, profoundly exposed the USSR's ugly features as the new Tsar, and also its reactionary nature, namely "socialism in words, imperialism in deeds. The more evil and foul things it does, the sooner the time when Soviet revisionism will be relegated to the historic museum by the people of the Soviet Union and the rest of the world." The speech was one of the sharpest ever directed against the Soviet leadership.

Recently, the Brezhnev clique, Chou continued, had talked a lot of nonsense on Sino-Soviet relations. "It alleges that China is against relaxation of world tension and unwilling to improve Sino-Soviet relations." This was designed to alienate the friendly feelings of the Soviet people for the Chinese people and to disguise the true features of the new Tsars." Chou challenged the Soviets to show their good faith "by doing a thing or two," for instance by withdrawing troops from Czechoslovakia or from the People's Republic of Mongolia, or by returning the four northern islands to Japan. "China has not occupied any foreign countries' territory. Must China give away all the territory north of the Great Wall to the Soviet revisionists in order to show that we favor relaxation of world tension and are willing to improve Sino-Soviet relations? The Chinese people ar not to be deceived or cowed.'' Though Chou did not hold to be favorable the prospect for China and the USSR to settle their ideological differences, he held the improvement of state relations to be not impossible. ''The Sino-Soviet controversy on matters of principle should not hinder the normalization of relations between the two states on the basis of the Five Principles of Peaceful Coexistence. The Sino-Soviet boundary question should be settled peacefully through negotiations free from any threat.'' The improvement of state relations was obviously contingent on the Soviets' returning extensive Chinese territories, though these were not specified. Any Soviet ''threat'' regarding the boundary question prior to or during possible ''negotiations'' would take the form of insistence on respect for the territorial status quo. While apparently conciliatory in words, Chou was adamant on Soviet territorial concessions, if not on outright surrender of vast territories, in the name of ''peaceful coexistence,'' without holding out any chance of settling other outstanding issues, or ideological and Party differences.

Why should Khrushchev and Brezhnev, ''both betrayers of Lenin,'' ''colluding and compromising with'' U.S. imperialism, ''restorers'' of capitalism, if not of fascism, in the Soviet Union, be prepared to make any concessions to the CPR? Chou's speech actually revealed the utter hopelessness of an early settlement of the outstanding issues that divide Peking and Moscow. Actually, the Soviet threat loomed definitely larger in this speech than any posed by the U.S. While he was talking about the need of liberating Taiwan and of unifying ''our great motherland,'' it did not occur to Chou to warn the U.S. But while recalling Mao's admonishments to be prepared against the contingency of war, he stressed the need of high vigilance ''against any war of aggression that Imperialism may launch and particularly[!] against a surprise attack on our country by Soviet revisionist social-imperialism.'' It took the CPC many years to concede that it considered the threat from the USSR as dangerous as that from U.S. imperialism. In the meantime, the expansionism of the Soviet Union was elevated to one by ''revisionist social-imperialism,'' and Chou put the threat posed by the USSR even higher than that of the U.S. which has relinquished South Vietnam and has retreated from Asia. The Soviet threat is felt to be serious and immediate! What other reasons would Chou and the Chinese Communist leadership have to trumpet their controversy with the Soviet Union to the world?

Domestic considerations might, of course, be adduced. A saying of Confucius has frequently been quoted: ''Without the menace of foreign aggression, a country is doomed.'' But with Soviet and Chinese troops massed along the border and facing each other in the most serious confrontation, the mutual threat is quite real and no illusion.

Chou's apparent view that the Soviet Union represents a greater threat to the security of China than even the U.S. is from a Marxist perspective inexplicable unless, of course, one denied that the USSR was still a socialist country; the CPC had indeed moved toward this position ever since it proclaimed that the ruling revisionist clique in the Soviet Union had "restored capitalism." To counter the Chinese accusations of a Soviet threat to Peking, Brezhnev revealed that the Soviet Union had repeatedly, and again recently, proposed a nonaggression pact to the CPR, but that Peking had turned it down.[91] It was characteristic that the leaders of the CPR, who "screamed throughout the world about some Soviet threat supposedly hanging over them, did not even bother to reply to the concrete proposal of the Soviet Union." Brezhnev called the CPC's "frenzied anti-Sovietism" the only "bar" to a nonaggression pact, accusing China of "false harangues" and "raving concoctions" of a Soviet military threat to China. He challenged Premier Chou to follow up his recent comments about desiring normal relations with Moscow by taking concrete actions.

In Tashkent Brezhnev also warned the Western powers against trying to extract advantages from the Sino-Soviet disputes, "whipping up passions," and "aggravating disagreements" between the USSR and China. "Such a policy is myopic." "One cannot proclaim oneself a champion of détente and cooperation in one part of the world and, in another part, fan the spark of tension and mistrust." In a generally moderate speech, Brezhnev's remarks drew attention to the Kremlin's deep uneasiness about being unable to patch up the relationship with Peking and its frustration at failing to block the rapprochement of Peking with some West European nations.

By disclosing the offer of a nonaggression pact, Brezhnev attempted to answer those who accused Moscow of not being flexible enough in bargaining with Peking. He thus also weakened the case of the CPR, which, it was now revealed, had spurned a seemingly reasonable Soviet offer. The speech also revealed Brezhnev's anger directed at Western and other politicians who were attempting to "warm their hands" at the fire of Sino-Soviet differences and trying to draw profit therefrom. This may have been an allusion especially to the recent visit of French President Pompidou to Peking and perhaps also to that of the Vice-President of Egypt, Hussein el-Shafi.

Moscow's attempt to disarm Peking by the offer of a nonaggression treaty and at the same time to convince the rest of the world of its peaceful intentions was of course directly related to its status quo stance. A Sino-Soviet nonaggression treaty without prior redrawing of frontiers would be equivalent to Peking's renunciation of its extensive territorial claims. It thus would directly play into Moscow's hands without giving Peking real

91. *New York Times*, Sept. 25, 1973; see also *PR*, Sept. 7, 1973, pp. 17f.

security. The USSR must have recalled Hitler's violation in 1941 of the Russo-German nonaggression pact of August 1939 and her own disregard in 1945 of the Soviet-Japanese nonaggression pact of 1941. While Moscow has proposed such a nonaggression treaty to Peking, it has continued to champion an Asian collective security treaty that would deter the CPR from unleashing aggression against any Asian state at the threat of instant Soviet retaliation.

From the Fourth Arab-Israeli War to a New "Cultural Revolution"?

The outbreak of the war in the Mideast in October 1973, which took Israel by surprise, caught most of the world, including China, unawares. Peking, however, quickly denounced the surprise attack allegedly launched by Israel, which was accused of plotting new territorial expansion. (But who does not recall the treacherous "attack" by South Korea almost a quarter of a century ago upon innocent North Korea?) Israel dared to resort to new military adventure only because it had "the support and connivance of the superpowers[!]."[92] While claiming "consistent support" for the Arab cause, Soviet revisionist social-imperialism had actually "allowed large numbers of Soviet Jews to emigrate to Israel as manpower support" and was also prepared to restore diplomatic relations with Israel. The Soviets had given the Arab countries "some arms," but restrained them from recovering their lost territories. Soviet revisionism and U.S. imperialism were both "contending and colluding with each other in the Middle East" and exploiting the situation to preserve and expand their spheres of influence. While the CPR expressed its conviction that the Arab countries would close their ranks and persevere in fighting, Peking, unlike in the 1967 war, did not promise direct and immediate Chinese assistance but, rather, limited itself to voicing "strong indignation."

On October 15 *People's Daily* continued its criticism of the two superpowers. Both attempted to reimpose a "no war, no peace" situation on the Arab people. Peking was also furious about the joint Soviet-American resolution placed before the U.N. Security Council on October 22. The scheme of the two superpowers was to "work together to put out raging flames of the Arab people's just war against aggression." What the Soviet revisionist renegade clique actually wished when it talked about peace in the Middle East was "no more than wanting the victims of aggression to lay down their arms so that the Israeli aggressors [might] place a knife to

92. *People's Daily*, Oct. 8, 1973, *PR*, Oct. 12, 1973, p. 3 (*PR*, Oct. 15, pp. 6-7).

the neck of the people of the Arab countries."[93] Such apparent distortions were not likely to enhance Chinese prestige and diminish Arab gratitude for the mass deliveries of Russian arms and for the timely Russo-American intervention that produced the cease-fire and saved Egypt's Third Army.

At the U.N. Security Council, Chiao Kuan-hua, Chairman of the Chinese Delegation, similarly minimized the Soviet dispatch of weapons to Arab countries as a mere attempt to "control the development of the Middle East situation so that it [would] not go beyond the limits it agreed to with the other superpower," and went so far as to accuse the Soviet Union of "partiality toward Israel"![94] Yet, as far as the 700 million Chinese were concerned, he held out to the Arabs only the assurance of "sympathizing with them" and supporting them, apparently only diplomatically and morally—a faint echo of the lavish promises made in the 1967 war.

If the Chinese in and outside of the U.N. proved to be masters of innovative invective and childish exaggeration, the Soviets did not lag far behind. The Soviet representative Malik talked unabashedly of China and Israel's having concluded a so-called alliance.[95] Huang Hua, the Chinese Permanent Representative to the U.N., countercharged, not without reason, that this was "making a mockery of the common sense of the representatives," though this description equally fitted Peking's own verbal excesses. According to Huang Hua, however, it was the USSR and not the CPR that in the past had had diplomatic, economic, trade, cultural, and other relations with Israel. The CPR had never entered into any relations with her. To Peking it was apparent that the Soviet Union wished to make a future ally of Israel. Over the past six years the Soviet Union in the Middle East had "turned on the tap at one time and turned it off at another time," saying that she was concerned about the bloodshed and the sacrifices of the Arab people and that she has loyally supported their struggle.[96] This, hoever, was 100 percent hypocrisy. An article in *Peking Review* dated November 16, 1973, reminded the Arabs that it was the Soviet Union that had originally, in November 1947, voted for the partition of Palestine in the U.N. General Assembly.[97]

Moscow, of course, was furious over Peking's interpretation of the Mideast War and of the role of the Soviets in it. On October 30 the Soviet analyst A. Bovin commented thus: "By egging on the Arab peoples to war"[98]—which was exactly Soviet policy the moment Egypt and Syria un-

93. *People's Daily*, Oct. 15, pp. 7-8 (*PR*, Oct. 19, pp. 7-8; also Nov. 2, pp. 4-5).
94. *PR*, Nov. 2, pp. 5-6.
95. *Ibid.*, p. 7.
96. *Ibid.*, pp. 7-8.
97. "Israel's Four Wars of Aggression," *PR*, Nov. 16, p. 13.
98. "Who profits from this?" *Izvestiia*, Oct. 30, p. 4 (*CDSP* 25, no. 44 [1973]: 7).

leashed their attack on Israel—Peking was instilling in them the thought that in the name of independence they must refuse Soviet assistance. Moscow, however, claimed that continuation of the war would not necessarily bring a just peace closer, but would only increase the number of casualties. Yet Arab casualties had not been on the Soviets' mind prior to nor immediately after the start of hostilities, not so long as the Arabs, due to the element of surprise, seemed to be scoring. When the Israeli troops approached Damascus and when the Israeli thrust on the western side of the Suez Canal rapidly grew, however, Moscow grew both alarmed and pacific, and jointly with the U.S. moved rapidly toward the cessation of hostilities. The hypocrisy of Soviet criticism of Peking's policy aside, the CPR was reminded that it had not helped the Arab liberation struggle except by mouthing platitudes.

According to another article of *Izvestiia,* "Peking and the Near East Crisis," which revealingly also focused upon the policy of the CPR in the Mideastern crisis, Peking had greeted the news of the outbreak of war in the Near East almost with exultation. The Chinese leaders had aimed at bringing about, if possible, a direct military clash between the Soviet Union and the U.S. They were, according to *Izvestiia,* not interested in ascertaining who was whinning or what casualties each day of the war would cost. Against the Chinese implied accusation of Soviet-American collusion in the Mideast, Moscow as usual countercharged that in the final analysis Peking's leaders feared "falling out of the good graces" of the U.S. They were giving the Arabs provocative advice to fight "to the end," regardless of casualties. Peking's reaction to the new Arab-Israeli war also revealed, more than anything else, "frantic "anti-Sovietism." The Chinese press was especially criticized because the critical comments about the Israeli aggressors and their imperialist accomplices did not take up even one percent of the space given to unbridled attacks against the Soviet Union.[99]

Indeed, the guns in the Middle East were hardly silent when American Secretary of State Henry Kissinger once again visited China, staying from November 10 to 14. Foreign Minister Chi Peng-fei referred then to differences of views between the two governments on a series of questions. But in toasts at the banquet welcoming the American guests, the Chinese representatives spoke of the continuing striving toward the goal of normalizing relations, first stated in the Shanghai communiqué, and completely omitted any public mention of the Middle Eastern War![100] While Peking deliberately exacerbated its relations with the USSR during the Mideast conflict,

    99. Koloskov, "Peking and the Near East Crisis," *Izvestiia*, Nov. 20, pp. 4-5 (*CDSP* 25, no. 47 [Dec. 19, 1973]: 11-12.
    100. Communiqué, *PR*, Nov. 16, 1973, p. 10.

it was, revealingly enough, unwilling to sacrifice the recent détente with the U.S. on account of the Arab-Israeli war, though, for foreign and domestic consumption, the recent American attitude did not escape Peking's criticism. Yet it was mild compared to the denunciation of Moscow.

On the occasion of a visit by the Algerian President Houari Boumedienne to Peking, Chou claimed that the crux of the Middle East question was the fierce rivalry between the two superpowers, accused the Soviet Union of "obstructing" the struggle of the Arab people "lest the flames of war should engulf her," but promised no direct assistance to the Arab struggle—which might involve the CPR in direct military clashes. Both superpowers were ridiculed as "paper tigers," which the war allegedly had shown, "while it is the people of the Arab world who are really powerful." In spite of this profuse flattery however, Chou held that the struggle of the Arab people would be "long and complicated" and their road "tortuous."[101] Speeches like these emanating from Peking do not, of course, reinforce the thesis of a genuine détente between Peking and Washington, though the exchange of pleasantries with Kissinger indicates the prevalence occasionally of a more diplomatic mood. The contradiction in tone and substance is self-evident and revealing of Peking's ambivalence toward the U.S. Yet there is little ambivalence on Peking's part in regard to Moscow. Chou's foregoing references to Moscow show clearly the continuing unmitigated hostility toward it.

In his address to the Tenth Party Congress of the CPC, Chou En-lai had referred to a widespread movement of criticism of Lin Piao. Soon thereafter, in October 1973, this mass criticism was widened to include Confucius, often before made the target of critical remarks, but never of a concerted and sustained massive attack. The criticism now embraced the unlikely combination of two personalities, separated from each other by two and a half millennia and not truly comparable in historic significance, Confucius (551-479 B.C.) and Lin Piao. Lin Piao, formerly considered the heir and successor to Mao himself, was later called "traitor," a renegade who perished in the attempt to overthrow Mao in 1971. The new massive propaganda campaign was mounted against Confucius allegedly because of his reactionary thought, in particular his stubborn support of the slave system.[102] The essence of Confucian thought, it was alleged, was to prove that laboring people could be exploited, enslaved, and ruled. Opposed by the feudal landlord class and the bourgeoisie, these strata, once they had seized power, had praised Confucius as the "most holy sage" for more than two thousand years.

101. *PR*, March 8, 1974, pp. 6-7.
102. Yang-Jung-kuo, "Confucius. . . ," *PR*, Oct. 12, 1973, pp. 5-9.

Red Flag, raising the question why it was necessary to combine criticism of Lin Piao with criticism of Confucius, replied that Lin Piao, "like all reactionaries in history. . .was every inch a devout disciple of Confucius." To deepen the criticism of Lin Piao *and* Confucius was now, the daily insisted, "a major issue for the whole Party, the whole army and the entire Chinese people." Failure to engage in criticism, the paper warned in an unmistakable manner, meant "failure to grasp class struggle, failure to continue the attacks on revisionism[!] and the bourgeois world outlook," and would inevitably "slip into revisionism."[103] Thus, not only were Confucius and Lin Piao associates in reaction, but the denunciation of and struggle against both were imperative in the interest of the fight against the main enemy of the CPC, Soviet revisionism. Confucius, Lin Piao, and Soviet revisionism were all enemies of Chinese Communism, marching in unison against Peking.

Thus criticism of the doctrine of Confucius and Mencius was now necessary in order "to see the more clearly the counter-revolutionary crimes of the Lin Piao anti-Party clique," as well as the ultra-Rightist nature of his revisionist line. Only by digging out the reactionary ideology of Lin Piao and Confucius would it be possible "to carry out the Great Proletarian Cultural Revolution so as to consolidate and develop[!] its tremendous achievements."[104] The struggle against Confucius and Lin Piao is seen as a continuation and renewal of the Cultural Revolution.

While the present line of the CPC is traced back to the 1958 Big Leap Forward in the national economy and the Great Proletarian Cultural Revolution, Lin Piao's views, on the other hand, are traced far back to the German revisionist Eduard Bernstein and are allegedly rooted in the erroneous concepts of Karl Kautsky, Trotsky, Zinoviev, and Bukharin, as well as of the more recent Soviet revisionist renegade clique. "In China, the mantle of Bernstein and others was donned by Chen Tu-hsiu, Liu Shao-chi and Lin Piao."[105] The attacks of all of these men were spearheaded against the proletarian revolution and the dictatorship of the proletariat. Lin Piao is pictured as only the last and most prominent representative of the counterrevolutionary and revisionist forces in China.

These charges were elaborated in an article by Szu Hua-hung, "Lin Piao Anti-Party Clique: Sworn Enemy of the Dictatorship of the Proletariat." Lin Piao had followed the path of Liu Shao-chi as well as of Khrushchev and Brezhnev, had put up a false front by speaking highly of the high his-

103. "Broaden and deepen the struggle to criticize Lin Piao and Confucius," *Red Flag*, no. 2, 1974 (*PR*, Feb. 15, 1974, pp. 4-6).

104. *Ibid.*; see also "Lin Piao. Doctrine of Confucius and Mencius," by the Mass Criticism Group of Peking University, *ibid.*, pp. 6-12.

105. Li Cheng, "Theory of Productive Forces. . . ," *PR*, Nov. 30, 1973, pp. 11-15, esp. 13.

torical significance of the Great Cultural Revolution. But Lin Piao and company had thrown themselves into the arms of imperialism, "particularly of Soviet social-imperialism." The dictatorship of the proletariat was the "protective talisman for a victorious people." But the Lin Piao anti-Party clique had wanted to establish a state in which the landlord and comprador-capitalist classes in power would exercise dictatorship over the laboring people." In other words, it was a Hitler type of "socialism" or social-fascism like that of the Soviet revisionist renegade clique.[106]

The evidence produced to link Lin Piao's thought and final attempt at a coup to the revisionist camp across the border would appear rather unsubstantial, but there can be no doubt about the repeated attempts of Peking to tie Lin Piao in thought and deed to Soviet revisionism and play not only upon extant antirevisionist practices and sentiments but, perhaps more effectively, upon xenophobia, in particular anti-Russian prejudices.

The accusations against the USSR raised in connection with both the resumption and cessation of hostilities in the Mideast and the charges leveled against Lin Piao as in league with revisionism across the border did not abate, but sharpened the Sino-Soviet tension. This tension was further increased by continuation of the earlier charges hurled back and forth on both sides of the border.

On September 13, 1973, *People's Daily* hailed the Fourth Conference of Heads of State and Government of Non-Aligned Countries, which had terminated its work in Algiers.[107] On the eve of this conference Brezhnev had written a letter to President Boumedienne of Algeria, warning against dividing the world into big nations and small nations, rich countries and poor countries, and especially against putting the U.S. and the USSR "on a par."[108] *People's Daily* asserted as usual that China, a developing socialist country, belonged to the Third World, and also claimed that the unity and growth of the Third World had made the superpowers "panic-stricken." Peking admonished the countries of the Third World to keep themselves aloof from the superpowers, which were only striving toward big-power hegemony, imperialism, and colonialism, and to "rely on their own strength," persevere in struggle, and close their ranks.[109] This, of course, would automatically rally them under Peking's leadership. Peking's seeming modesty in considering the CPR as just one of the countries of the Third World thus placed her in a position of strategic advantage against the superpowers and against the Soviet rival in particular.

The Chinese Communist press continued to discredit this rival, attempt-

106. *PR*, Dec. 28, 1973, p. 6; about Lin Piao see also *ibid.*, Jan. 11, 1974, pp. 7f; *Red Flag*, no. 12 in *PR*, Jan. 25, 1974, pp. 5f; and *PR*, Feb. 15, 1974, pp. 4-16.
107. *People's Daily*, Sept. 13, 1973 (*PR*, Sept. 21, 1973).
108. *Ibid.*
109. *Ibid.*

ing to unmask him as an enemy of the Third World, while pretending that
the CPR was her true friend, older brother, and champion in the struggle
against both the USSR and the U.S. The Soviet Union was accused of interfering in the Middle East for selfish purposes and of exploiting Iran by
paying a very low price for her natural gas and of dishing up a fantastic
"theory of international property" in speaking about Arab oil, which it occasionally pictured as an "international asset."[110]

The Soviet Union continued to be castigated on account of her
imperialism.[111] Brezhnev's previous disclaimer that the USSR was a superpower was discounted; facts testified to the truth of the anti-Soviet charges.
The Hsinshua correspondent pointed on October 7, 1973, to the USSR's
organizing military blocs and everywhere setting up military bases. She
was stationing "scores of divisions in Eastern Europe so as to control this
area and threaten Western Europe." She had sent troops to Mongolia, posing a threat to China and other Asian countries, and had grabbed naval and
air bases and the right to use ports in some Asian and African countries
and sent military "advisers" to lord over these countries. "These are the
behavior of imperialism and superpower pure and simple." The Soviet
Union, while calling for disarmament day after day, is claimed actually to
be engaging in arms expansion daily. Since 1963 the USSR had increased
the number of her intercontinental missiles "and surpassed the U.S." The
Soviet Union had resorted to undisguised nuclear threat against the world's
people. She had admitted that she was in a scramble for hegemony with
U.S. imperialism in the Mediterranean and other oceans. Judging by the
boasts of Soviet naval chieftains, it was clear that the USSR "wants to
replace Britain and the U.S. as an overlord ruling the sea."

The Hsinshua correspondent dismissed the Soviet Revisionists' disarmament proposals as sanctimonious and hypocritical.[112] He accepted the estimates produced by the London-based International Institute for Strategic
Studies regarding the huge amounts of Soviet military spending and contrasted them with the recent Soviet proposal to cut the military expenditures of the permanent members of the U.N. Security Council by ten to
fifteen percent to provide assistance to the underdeveloped countries. The
two superpowers were not trying to prevent nuclear war; they were rather
contending for nuclear superiority.[113] In spite of numerous agreements
signed between them, the nuclear arms race was taking a big stride forward. The Soviets, Peking charged, had in the first ten months of 1973

110. Chiu Pei-chiang, "Energy Crisis'. . . ," PR, Sept. 28, 1973, p. 13.
111. "Soviet Union-Imperialism and Superpower, Concoction or Fact?" PR, Oct. 19,
1973, pp. 18-19, 23; also PR, Nov. 30, 1973, pp. 21-22 and Oct. 12, 1973, pp. 12-14.
112. PR, Oct. 12, 1973, pp. 11-12.
113. PR, Nov. 16, 1973, pp. 17-18.

conducted fifteen underground nuclear explosions. Soviet intercontinental ballistic missiles had increased over fifteen times in the last ten years.

In a vote on November 15, 1973, of the Political and Security Committee of the U.N. the Chinese representative Chuang Yen, denouncing the Soviet-U.S. nuclear monopoly policy, charged the superpowers with aiming at preventing the nonnuclear countries and countries with few nuclear weapons from possessing and developing their own nuclear weapons for self-defense and with intimidating people of various countries.[114] When the Soviet representative in turn accused China of negativism and lack of interest in the Soviet disarmament proposal, the Chinese delegate countered by warning the USSR that she would not succeed "in muzzling us with a few slanderous labels" and that Peking was resolved "to expose your fraud and oppose your maneuvers and tricks." He followed up this speech with one on November 21 at the plenary meeting of the U.N. General Assembly, charging against the USSR that her arms race had the sole purpose of "ordering other countries about [and] overwhelming and replacing her rival and ruling supreme in the world." The Soviet proposal that the permanent members of the Security Council reduce the military budget by ten per cent would be utterly meaningless in view of the great disparity between China's defense capabilities and those of the superpowers. (Considering China's relative poverty as compared to the other four powers, Peking was probably also furious about the Soviet proposal, which was likely to set China's development plans further back). The Soviet Union, which sold weapons at high prices to the Arab countries and others, should also stop "seizing upon others' difficulties as a means of extortion" and cease being a merchant of death.

Such accusations hurled by China in the light of full publicity from the world forum of the U.N. against the Soviet "comrades" was more acrimonious than simultaneous charges raised by the CPR against the U.S.; these, as a matter of fact, have become relatively subdued. The same must be said about Soviet charges leveled publicly against the U.S. since the beginning of the détente policy, though there are of course occasional bursts of polar air emanating from the USSR, recalling the worst storms of the Cold War era. It nevertheless remains true that in the curious triangular relationship between Washington, D.C., Moscow, and Peking, the most violent and abusive language is reserved by Moscow for Peking and by Peking for Moscow.

Peking looks with utter skepticism, if not with outright ridicule, upon the Soviet-American "détente" and restraint" that both sides pledged at the Soviet-U.S. summit talks in 1972.[115] Peking's interest in military bal-

114. *PR*, Nov. 30, 1973, pp. 17-20.
115. "Soviet Revisionist 'Detente' Smokescreen in Europe," *PR*, Dec. 21, 1973, pp. 4-5.

ance in Asia and the Far East aside, the CPR continues to pay great attention to European developments. Europe, after all, as seen from the Great
Wall, is the backyard of the USSR; more exactly, it is historically the area
of primary Russian interests and, as Peking concedes, is also of primary
interest to the U.S. In recent years, according to Peking, Soviet revisionism has drastically reinforced its military strength on the seas at both
the southern and northern links of Europe. Peking quoted data to this effect
released by the London International Institute for Strategic Studies as well
as *Le Monde's* observation that the Soviet grab of naval and air bases in
the eastern Mediterranean was an attempt to form a pincer movement
against the West by attempting to turn Europe's southern flank. While paying endless lip service to "peace" and "détente," the Soviet revisionists
and the military bloc under their control had carried out about ten joint
military exercises in Eastern Europe every year since 1966.

Since Europe, according to the anonymous writer of this article, has
long been regarded as a key area by the two superpowers in their contention for world hegemony, the Soviet revisionists have for many years deployed most of their troops there. Even though the Soviets since the
mid-1960s have been "stretching their claws into Asia, Africa and wherever they could and carrying out military threats against China" by steadily
increasing their forces along the Sino-Soviet border, Soviet troops in
Europe, according to the Western press, have since 1968 gone up almost
twenty percent and the tactical air force by fifty per cent. Three-fifths of
the Soviet ground forces and over three-fourths of their air force are
massed now in Eastern Europe and the Soviet Union. It is quite obvious why
Peking is interested in seeing to it that both Soviet preoccupation with
Europe and Europe's countermeasures against the rising Soviet threat continue, thus preventing the USSR from focusing her expansionist thrusts
against China and Asia.

Peking has continued to denounce Soviet thrusts in the Mideast and
Europe—which are detrimental to the interests of Western Europe, especially Great Britain and France—and also her expansionist efforts elsewhere, into the Indian Ocean through Afghanistan and Pakistan, particularly through the mountainous regions of Pakistan's Baluchistan province,
and into Southeast Asia.[116] In an article in October of 1973, Novosti Press
Agency voiced the view that the "two Chinas" would remain a reality for
a long time and seemed to favor the prolongation of this situation.[117] The
feverish Soviet propaganda in 1973 of a system of security for Asia made

116. "Superpower Rivalry in the Middle East Expedites West European Unity," *PR*, Dec.
7, 1973, pp. 13-14, and "Social Imperialism's Expansion in South Asia and Indian Ocean,"
ibid., pp. 15-16.
117. "Soviet Revisionism's 'Two Chinas' Fallacy," *PR*, Dec. 21, 1973, p. 21.

Peking wonder why the USSR, "a European country," showed such unusual concern for peace and security in Asia.[118] The USSR since 1969 had,
according to Peking, signed some bilateral "peace and friendship" treaties
with Asian countries and had praised them as "first bricks" in the "edifice
of collective security in Asia," but these agreements were invariably followed by armed aggression and conflicts, such as, for instance, the war of
aggression against Pakistan that closely followed the Soviet-Indian treaty of
1971.

The Soviet revisionist clique asserted, according to *Peking Review,* that
collective security in Asia and Europe was "inconceivable" without rec-
ognizing the "immutability of existing frontiers."[119] It thus opposed all attempts to redemarcate postwar borders in regard to her East European
neighbors, stubbornly refused all attempts to return to Japan the four
northern islands, and opposed the settlement of the Sino-Soviet boundary
question on the basis of a series of unequal treaties, "insisting on occupying territory seized from China in violation" of even these treaties. The
retention of all her territory was one of the important objectives in the
Soviet move to establish a system of collective security in Asia. The
Chinese contention of being willing to settle on the basis of the foregoing
treaties, which they at the same time brand "unequal," has obviously not
enhanced Soviet confidence that cession of some territories—those seized
"in violation" of the foregoing treaties—would appease China for very
long.

According to Peking, the Soviets' real aim in proposing the system of
collective security in Asia was, under the pretext of maintaining security,
to "consolidate their vested interests and step up infiltration and expansion
so as to contend with the other superpower for hegemony in Asia." The
Soviet revisionists openly declared that their proposed system of collective
security in Asia could best replace the Asian military blocs rigged up by
the U.S. In other words, "they want to replace the U.S. and exercise ex-
clusive hegemony in Asia, that is, to 'fill the vacuum' there." But Asia
belongs to the Asian people, and there is no vacuum.

While the debate with the Soviets in the course of 1973 became, if possible, even bitterer, Peking's criticism of the U.S. tended somewhat to
abate. This criticism became increasingly a weak second to the mounting
and furious exacerbation of the exchange of words with the USSR.
Peking's apparent approval of the strengthening of Western Europe, which
in spite of the dissonances within the Western Alliance is militarily still

118. "System for 'Security' or for Aggression and Expansion?", *PR*, Dec. 28, 1973, pp.
7-9.
119. Commentary by Hsinshua Correspondent, "World in Great Disorder: Excellent Situation," *PR*, Jan. 9, 1974, p. 11.

tied to the U.S., means that Peking no longer puts the U.S. and the USSR on the same plane. The latter, in Peking's eyes, is clearly the more dangerous foe.

The manner in which *Peking Review* gave prominence to Chairman Mao's meeting with Secretary of State Henry Kissinger—in the obvious absence of any corresponding encounter between Peking and Moscow—is very revealing, as is the fact that immediately after the outbreak of hostilities in the Mideast China stood aside when a threatening confrontation between Washington and Moscow was in the making.[120] Though ceaselessly accusing both superpowers of being imperialistic, Peking seemed pleased about Kissinger's visit and, contrary to its loud propagandistic proclamations designed for public consumption at home and abroad, seemed satisfied with the assurance that the U.S. was not seeking hegemony in the Asia-Pacific region or any other part of the world, as was confirmed in the joint communiqué. China on this occasion noted "progress made during 1973" in relations with the U.S. and was apparently gratified by the reaffirmation of the American, at the moment rather theoretical, acknowledgment that there was only one China and that Taiwan was part of it. It also noted "with satisfaction" that the liaison offices in Peking and Washington were functioning smoothly and that they would be expanded. The communiqué also noted that trade had "developed rapidly" during the past year and that exchanges had "deepened" understanding and friendship between the two peoples. Surely, whatever the real significance of such diplomatic pleasantries, the mere fact that they were given expression by the CPC and the U.S., while at the same time no comparable rapprochement took place between Communist China and the USSR, speaks volumes!

The Soviets have of course duly taken notice that the USSR has in Peking's eyes moved up to be the number-one enemy of the CPR. It took some developments to arrive at this stage. The CPC had first worked out the "theory of so-called intermediate zones, "according to which, between the USSR on the one hand and the U.S. on the other, there was an intermediate zone that included all other countries. This put Peking between the superpowers, assigning to it the natural role of leader of most of the rest of the world. But soon even this theory no longer suited the CPC in its rising dispute with the CPSU. In 1971 and 1972 *Hung Chi*, the organ of the Central Committee of the CPC, developed a theory that still assumed two world poles, but placed both superpowers, the USSR and the U.S., not at opposite poles but rather cozily at one end—and at the other end, China and some socialist countries. Two intermediate zones between them included first the countries of Asia, Africa, and Latin America, and the sec-

120. "Chairman Mao Meets Secretary of State Kissinger," *PR*, Nov. 16, 1973, pp. 6-7, 10.

ond, the main capitalist countries of the West and East.[121] In Peking's view, the two superpowers are now hardly distinguishable from each other—a view that infuriates the Soviet Union.

The Soviets had already criticized the first theory, charging that it had nothing in common with the Marxist-Leninist analysis of the present epoch and that it was based upon the inexcusable error of placing the Soviet Union and American imperialism on the same plane. But, understandably, they were even more aroused by the theory of "China's chief enemies," represented by the U.S. and themselves, a theory that had been proclaimed at the Ninth Party Congress in 1969. According to Moscow, the anti-Soviet campaign in China, however, further escalated when the Maoists late in 1972 called the USSR "the most dangerous enemy," simultaneously opened a campaign in which they distinguished between "chief and secondary enemies" of China and began to lay the groundwork for lining up with the latter enemies against the most formidable foe, the USSR. The Polish newspaper *Sztandar Mlodych* has recently held that there is now only one enemy for the Maoist leaders today—the Soviet Union and other socialist countries.

The escalation of the struggle with Moscow was bound to be accompanied by a toning down of the struggle against the CPR's "secondary" foes. This explains the virtual withdrawal from their propaganda arsenal of odious extremist slogans that were popular only a few years back. Yet Chinese Communists hardly want a true détente with the West, "secondary" enemies, or a stable world situation, and the Western press, in the Soviet view, has become increasingly aware of Peking's double-dealing tactics. China has characteristically refused to participate in any of the existing international agreements on disarmament. "One general aim behind the Chinese leaders' approach to international problems such as European security, the situation in the Middle East and the settlement in Hindustan, namely to destroy any détente, is to aggravate existing contradictions and to find a common platform with the anti-Soviet forces."

The Soviets have complained that the Chinese mass media have unleashed a campaign against the USSR to "brainwash [its] population in the spirit of anti-Sovietism." In 1972 two major newspapers alone [*People's Daily* and *Kuangming Jihpao*] carried 505 articles containing attacks on the Soviet Union, while the twelve issues of *Hung Chi* carried thirty-one similar articles. The same three publications contained more than one hundred anti-Soviet articles in the first three months of 1973. The USSR was portrayed as China's worst enemy. To create a war psychology, the Chinese leaders exploited the "prepare for war" slogan.

During the last years Maoist foreign policy, according to Moscow, was

121. *Hung Chi*, no. 9, 1971, p. 21, and no. 11, 1972, quoted by L. Alexeyev, "Anti-Sovietism in Peking's Strategy," *International Affairs*, no. 7, 1973, pp. 21f.

marked by a switch to the Right by the former "ultra-revolutionaries."[122] One of the reasons for this move of the Maoists from one extreme to the other lies in the objective contradiction between Peking's extravagant pretensions and its actual possibilities for achieving these pretensions and in the petty-bourgeois psychology that nourishes the Leftist adventurism and Right-opportunist trends springing from a "lack of faith in the revolutionary forces." Leftist adventurism has crystallized in Peking's propaganda campaign. In 1973 Peking's propagandistic line was spelled out by the directive "Dig deep trenches, lay in stocks of wheat, never aspire to hegemony."[123] The emphasis is clearly on military and economic preparedness coupled with shrewd speculation on the widespread opposition to the hegemony of the supoerpowers.

"Right-opportunist trends," in the Soviet view, were also clearly noticeable in Peking's policy. In Latin America Peking had also quickly revealed its true colors by granting the fascist junta of Chile de facto recognition.[124] China is repeatedly accused of political opportunism; her ties, *Pravda* charged, with colonial and racist regimes such as the governments of Portugal, the Republic of South Africa, and Southern Rhodesia were actually widening.[125]

Defending their own policy of détente and rejecting Peking's criticism with an accusation of their own against China's "collusion" with the U.S. the Soviets have charged the CPC with having taken the side of reactionary extremists everywhere against the USSR. Both sides in the dispute have agreed that it has escalated during the last years and both have charged that, while their own ideological and political course had proved steadfast, the other side had made a radical shift to the Right. Each side has accused the other of having set up a fascist, Hitler type of regime.

Both Moscow and Peking have revealed deep pessimism about "converting" in the foreseeable future the opposing side to the true religion, or rather, to adopting the correct interpretation of Marxism-Leninism. Yet each Party, claiming to be in possession of the full truth, condemns the alien heresy, though not the mass of the alien heretics. Each side insists that there are still true believers in the other camp, that in due time conversion will save them, and that a lifting of the oppression will come about. O. B. Borisov and B. T. Koloskov in *Soviet-Chinese Relations, 1945-1970: An Outline* (Moscow, 1972) point out that even before 1949

122. G. Apalin, "A Policy Inimical to Peace, Democracy and Socialism," *International Affairs*, no. 11, 1973, pp. 22f.

123. A. Pamor and V. Trifonov, "Maoist Slogans and Facts," *New Times*, no. 2, Jan. 1974, p. 22.

124. H. Novikov, "Against the Tide," *Izvestiia*, Jan. 20, 1974, p. 2 (*CDSP* 26, no. 3 [Feb. 13, 1974]: 3-4).

125. *Pravda*, Jan. 18, 1974, p. 5 (*CDSP* 26, no. 3 [Feb. 13, 1974]: 4).

there had always raged a struggle of two lines in the CPC, the Marxist-Leninist, internationalist, and the petty-bourgeois nationalist[126] one, and that this struggle had continued to the present—which furnishes the Soviets a theoretical base for an optimistic outlook, at least over the long stretch.

126. O. B. Borisov and B. T. Koloskov, *Sovetskoi-kitaiskie otnosheniia. 1945-1970, Kratkii ocherk* (Moscow, 1972), p. 470; also E. F. Kovalev, "A New Step in the Study of Sino-Soviet Relations. . . ," *Voprosy istorii*, no. 11, 1972.

10
Conclusion

The "Stalin Group" in the Soviet Union recently issued a leaflet "Take the Road of Stalin." It calls on the proletariat and other working people in the Soviet Union to rise up to overthrow the Soviet revisionist renegade clique's rule and to reestablish the dictatorship of the proletariat.
—Peking Review

"O, if Marx could see
  how pitifully, vilely they play
The tragic farce
  of the brazen-faced pseudo-Communist
What becomes
  of even a sacred idea
In the hands of a scoundrel!"

—Yevg. Yevtushenko,
"On the Red Ussuri Snow"

The origins of the Sino-Soviet dispute, as pointed out previously, must be traced back to the twenties, when the CPC was founded, and, at the advice of the Moscow government and the Comintern, took part in the work of reunification of China under the leadership of the Kuomintang. This study, however, has been confined to tracing the complex and involved relationship between the Communist Parties of China and the USSR from the proclamation of the Chinese Communist victory in 1949, especially from the Eighth Congress of the CPC and the Twentieth Congress of the CPSU in 1956, to the present. By 1956 the CPC had been in power for almost seven years, the CPSU for almost forty years. The very difference in age, and the deradicalization that inevitably followed from it for the Soviet Union, its leaders, and its people, had a decisive bearing upon some of the differences beetween Peking and Moscow in philosophy, tactics, perhaps even ultimate goals, and deepened the clash of interests and the conflict between them.

Communist China's "Great Leap Forward" and Moscow's critical reaction, the Soviet change of mind in the matter of helping Peking to develop nuclear weapons, and the withdrawal of Soviet technical aid raised the first serious questions as to the solidity of the Sino-Soviet friendship and alliance. But it was the Sino-Indian war and the simultaneous Cuban missile crisis of 1962, and the differences between Moscow and Peking that these events revealed, that finally opened the eyes of the West. There followed in 1963 a wide-ranging debate and vicious accusations and counteraccusations, unheard of among comrades and allies; they related to down-to-earth territorial, economic, and political problems, and to tactical questions of war, peace, and coexistence, of differences on methods of the revolutionary struggle and of strategies regarding national liberation. Some of the acid exchange also focused on highly esoteric topics of Marxist-Leninist exegesis.

The USSR accused the CPR of paying mere lip-service to "peaceful coexistence" of states with different social systems, while actually toying with the possibility of a hydrogen war. Moscow charged Peking with underestimating the horrors of such a war and its potential for destruction, a war that would kill not only a handful of capitalists, but also millions of toilers. The Soviet leaders asserted that revolution could make headway without resort to military conflict. Peking, however, accused Moscow of sacrificing both the proletarian revolution and the national liberation movement on the altar of "peaceful coexistence" and at the price of betraying Marxism-Leninism, all for the sake of undisturbed economic growth.

The Chinese leaders claim that Soviet society under the false tenets of "revisionism" had become "bourgeoisified," soft, and "degenerated." The leaders of the USSR, however, have vigorously denied that improvement of their living standard was identical with "restoring capitalism." On numerous occasions the government of the CPR has also officially asserted that the USSR was not an Asian power, while Peking was the political center of Asia. The Soviet leaders saw in such attempts apparent maneuvers to push the Soviet Union out of Asia and back to the Ural mountains and to "estrange" the countries of Asia, Africa, and Latin America from the USSR. They saw in it a propagandistic device to wrest the leadership of the National Liberation Movement from Moscow and to use blatant racism to further Peking's own territorial and political ambitions.

The complex phenomenon of the "Great Proletarian Cultural Revolution," which began late in 1965 and lasted until 1969, brought long-extant trends in the CPR to the fore and shook Communist China to her foundations. It worsened, if possible, the Sino-Soviet relationship by aggravating their differences in regard to political, ideological, cultural, and foreign policy issues.

The objective differences between Peking and Moscow were undoubtedly deepened by the sharp personal animosities between the leaders of the two Communist superpowers, though to a large extent even personal differences were an outgrowth of diverse national approaches and of the adaptations of fundamental ideology to different national conditions. Chinese resentment of the Soviet leadership was not to abate, but rather to increase after Stalin's death. The eclipse of one man's overwhelming power and prestige, and the disarray following the struggle between the rival epigones, were bound to reduce Moscow's role in international Communism, especially vis-à-vis China. Mao, on the other hand, had been the dominant figure in Chinese Communism for about half a century, an era which, on the Soviet scene, comprised the political life times of Lenin, Stalin, Khrushchev, and Brezhnev taken together. It would have taken a much more modest man than Mao was, and greater disinterestedness than he possessed, not to assert vis-à-vis Khrushchev his immense political and intellectual stature in China and world Communism, as compared to Khrushchev's own relatively meager credentials.

The sharply critical Soviet views on the Cultural Revolution, Mao, and Maoism have found clear expression in numerous articles in the Soviet press and journals. According to them, the "Cultural Revolution" had actually created a new Party, Chairman Mao's Party and had replaced the principles of Marxism-Leninism with "Mao's ideas." In the contemporary Chinese view, Mao strides across the stage not as a semigod, but as Savior or God himself.

Worship of Mao aside, Maoism extolled the eminent importance of China as a model for the revolution of undeveloped countries of the world and stressed the revolutionary role of the peasantry. Moscow charged that Peking, differently from the Soviet Union, spurned rational economic planning. The CPC in turn claimed that it had found a shortcut to Communism, laid stress on immediate egalitarianims in China, and challenged the Soviet Union's primacy in international Communism. It also questioned her domestic policies, charging her with having abandoned the Marxist-Leninist doctrine and of having embraced a pseudo-revolutionary creed and going to the absurd extreme of accusing the USSR of having restored capitalism.

Both Communist parties, the CPSU and the CPC, considered Moscow and Peking respectively as the new Mecca of world Communism, claimed to be the true guardians and interpreters of Marxism-Leninism, and would have liked, if possible to excommunicate the heretics on the other side of the border and to extirpate the heresy.

The war in Vietnam has figured large in the Sino-Soviet dispute. If by the time of the Tonkin Gulf incident in August 1964 and of the American attack on North Vietnamese targets on February 7, 1965, the Sino-Soviet conflict had not already reached greatest intensity, the logical and unavoidable result of the American escalation of war would have been to push the Soviet Union and the CPR into each other's arms. But instead, though both denounced American aggression and snarled at American imperialism, the war in Vietnam had the curious result of widening rather than narrowing the gulf between the two Communist giants.

Peking denounced Moscow for limiting its assistance to Hanoi and attempting to avoid a conflict with the U.S. "aggressor" over Vietnam. She had thus shirked her internationalist duties and betrayed revolution. The Soviets in turn countercharged that Peking itself was braver in words than in deeds. They accused Peking of needing "a long conflict" in Vietnam in order to keep up international tension and to picture China as a besieged fortress, and charged that the political objective of the Chinese leaders was to provoke a military conflict between the USSR and America.

Moscow has accused the CPC of having abandoned Leninism. Peking, while denying the charge, has boldly countered that it alone was the true heir of Leninism. If one attempts to cut through the thicket of charges and countercharges of betrayal and heresy, one arrives at the conclusion that Leninism is deeply anchored in Mao's thought, though some Leninist concepts have definitely been shed or drained of their original content.

Nor can Moscow's claim that it has loyally adhered to Lenin's scriptures be taken at face value, though it has perhaps not reversed his thought in some areas as Peking has done. Leninism, of course, does not constitute a logically consistent body of ideas, and thus Peking and Moscow have been able to claim that they have remained faithful to Lenin's legacy even in the face of outright abandonment of some of its features.

The Chinese Communist concept of political consciousness as being instilled by an elite or vanguard among the proletariat is certainly Leninist.[1] Mao's thoughts about theory and practice of organization, his theory of imperialism, and the concept of common interests of even hostile classes in dependent, colonial countries against the imperialist foe testify similarly to Mao's Leninism. Leninist also is the idea of an alliance between the proletariat and certain other classes, especially the peasantry, during the pre-socialist, democratic, phase of the revolution. Mao's precept for a "four-class bloc"—of workers, peasants, the petty bourgeoisie, and the national bourgeoisie—is of Stalinist origin and is the very foundation of his theory of the people's democratic dictatorship.

But Mao's thought has its own peculiarities. To Mao nationalism was not a necessary evil as it was to Lenin, but a genuine value. Tied up with this view, the four-class bloc—which for Stalin was only a passing

1. Schram, pp. 134-37.

phenomenon—was considered by Mao, at least until the Cultural Revolution, an alliance that might continue until Communism was reached. Similarly, Mao's stress on extreme voluntarism, virtually reversing economic foundation and ideological superstructure by claiming that "the subjective creates the objective" and that politics takes precedence over economics, reversed the traditional Marxist relationship between them and represented not just a deviation but an actual break with Marxism-Leninism. It established Maoism as something novel and different in character from the matrix from which it sprang.

The same might be said especially about the role of the CPC. The Cultural Revolution has seen the clear subordination of the Party hierarchy to the army and its subjection to terrorism by the Red Guard, a phenomenon without parallel in the Soviet Union. The downgrading, finally, of organization and technical knowledge in China, the extolling of the "poor and blank thesis" (of the alleged advantages for China of being poor and ignorant), was a complete departure from Marxist-Leninist concepts. The rebirth of populist prejudices in China resulting in the glorification of the peasants in the countryside as the genuine seat of revolutionary consciousness likewise constituted a complete reversal of Marxist-Leninist revolutionary concepts.

The Sino-Soviet dispute has escalated from the early state of suppression of what must at first have seemed to both sides only minor ideological differences of an abstruse nature to the stage of blunt, rude, exchanges of recriminations and later outright abuse, in which the hostile brethren accused each other of having abandoned the most cherished ideals of Communism and having betrayed the socialist idea. It has reached the climax of physical clashes and of continuing military confrontation. The border incidents of 1969 portent to both sides the ultimate threat of atomic war and destruction. Though both continue to denounce imperialism and especially U.S. expansionism and alleged neo-colonialism as the great threat to world peace, each has explicitly conceded that the other Communist giant represents at least as great, if not a greater, threat to peace and to its own security as U.S. imperialism.

In actuality, Peking and Moscow are probably more fearful of the possibility of war with each other than with the distant United States. While each looks at the white of the eyes of the other Communist superpower, both sides repeat without end their familiar anti-capitalist and anti-imperialist inprecations. Both are devotees and at the same time prisoners of the Marxist-Leninist world view. They each believe and assert that the other Communist super-power is "in collusion" with capitalism and imperialism and that the United States in particular aims at "encircling" it. Peking has asserted that in the Soviet Union the rule of the bourgeoisie and of capitalism has been "restored." Moscow has claimed that a new military-bureaucratic clique has come to rule in the CPR and that a new Party, the Mao Party, has emerged.

The ideological blinkers of both Communist superpowers have tended to distort, at times perhaps to magnify, the all-too-real differences between the two Communist giants. One Chinese newspaper charged Moscow with looking at Peking through "crooked mirrors"; yet, this accusation can be leveled with equal justification at Peking. The leadership of both countries have become captives of their own ideological concepts and distortions and their own peculiar Russified or Sinicized version of Marxism-Leninism. Beyond it, both have resorted to propagandistic exaggerations and have become ensnared in their own lies.

The dispute between the Chinese and Soviet Russian Communist Parties is in some respects comparable to the religious disputes of hostile sects in the Middle Ages and the Age of Reformation and Counter Reformation, though it has, of course, both global and secular aspects. It is also a clash of rival states and power centers with far-reaching territorial and ideological aspirations. The legacy of the past, a past reaching beyond the Russian October Revolution and the founding of the CPC, beyond 1917 and 1921 respectively, lies heavily on both Peking and Moscow and adversely affects their relationship. The dispute, whatever its modern, Marxist-Leninist, external appearance, has excessive nationalism, imperialism, and power struggle as its old-fashioned core. National ambitions and insecurity and fear are closely intertwined.

The Chinese nationalist concept of their country as the "Middle Kingdom," the center of the universe, is of course irreconcilable with the idea of accepting a role subordinate and inferior to the USSR or any other power. For centuries it was the Chinese view that their civilization and culture were superior to those of the surrounding and more distant barbaric nations. These notions, never abandoned in the twentieth century, have—in combination with Chinese frustration born of national humiliation, over-sensitivity, and past grievances, and the Soviets' insistent and arrogant counter-claims as the leaders of the Communist camp—added an abrasive character to the twentieth-century rift and lent it a distinct national and psychological dimension.

The fact of plain Chinese national resentment about overbearing Russian behavior should not be overlooked. As early as 1936 Mao told Edgar Snow: "We are certainly not fighting for an emancipated China in order to turn the country over to Moscow." And once in 1943 he referred to the past "meddling" by the Comintern in the internal affairs of the CPC. Leading cadres of Communist Parties in various countries had already grown up and attained political maturity, while the Comintern, "far removed from the concrete struggle in each country,'' had, in his view, become obsolete. Chinese resentment at the "feudal-patriarchal" relationship between Moscow and other Communist parties later boiled over in the polemical outburst of 1963 and clearly revealed the strong emotional aspects and personal and national acrimonies of the dispute, which had embittered the Moscow-Peking relationship even further.

Finally, the difference in age, alluded to before, between the Russian and Chinese Revolutions also accounts for the deep rift between the two countries. For Soviet Russia in the late fifties and sixties, the October Revolution and the Civil War were past history; for Communist China the victory in her Civil War and the proclamation of the CPR were glorious recent events. In the USSR few old Bolsheviks survived as living witnesses to the October Revolution (most of them had been eliminated by Stalin) and the early revolutionary enthusiasm had worn thin; no Soviet propaganda was able to revive it. In China a supreme effort was made to reawaken the spirit of the Revolution and of the heroic exploits of the Civil War. This effort had greater chances of success in China, due to the longevity of many of her revolutionary leaders; the proximity of the year of victory, 1949; the poverty of China and the asceticism that it bred; and, last but not least, the revolutionary zeal of Mao himself.

Since 1917 Soviet Russia has made vast industrial strides and, in Chinese eyes, has become settled, satiated, and "bourgeoisified," while China's own more modest accomplishments in the field of industrialization in combination with her egalitarian drives at home and abroad and her militant past have made her a more resolute enemy of the status quo everywhere in the world. For all these reasons the spirit of Yenan is thus a greater reality in China than that of the October Revolution in the USSR. The industrial and managerial establishment and its imperatives of technical rationality play an immensely greater role in the USSR than in China. In China they are more likely to be subordinated and are often lost in the internecine struggle for power and for revolutionary orthodoxy.

The CPSU came to the fore through a successful seizure of power by a determined minority. It moved unchallenged into what was a political and military vacuum; it preserved its power in a short civil war. It was very different in China; there the Civil War was protracted and the CPC attained power not prior to it, but in consequence of it. In China, power indeed, as Mao claims, grew out of the barrel of the gun. The role of the army in Soviet politics has been a subordinate one as compared to the Party, while that of the army in contemporary Communist China has been preeminent.

The notion that China would be the revolutionary model for many, especially the politically dependent peoples is deeply rooted in Mao's thought. He was convinced, he revealed to Edgar Snow in July 1936, that many colonial countries would follow the example of China. The CPC, extend-ing the Chinese revolutionary experience to the global scene, has stressed the role of Revolution in underdeveloped countries as a catalyst for more advanced countries, and especially the importance of the Chinese example for the rest of the world of Revolution by peasant-based guerrilla warfare.

Encirclement of the cities from the countryside was the essence of the Chinese revolutionary guerrilla experience. Mao transposed this experience to the world scene, claiming that Asia, Africa, and South America were comparable to the countryside in China, and Europe and North America to the Chinese cities. This doctrine put China conveniently on the winning side and the USSR on the losing end; for apparent reasons it has not been acceptable to the Soviets. The Soviet leaders responded by deriding Mao's new geopolitics. China's appeal, they pointed out, was also deliberately racial, directed at the nonwhite and also at the undeveloped nations and was in violation of the Marxist-Leninist world view. The USSR understood that she could not match the CPR's appeal to racial prejudices and resented it the more since propagandistically it placed her at a disadvantage, under-lining the circumstance that she belonged to the white peoples, the "beati possidentes," a minority among the peoples of the globe.

The Communist Parties in the CPR and the USSR, in their endless cam-paign of vituperation against and vilification of each other, and in their massing of troops along the border, are an unquestionable menace to each other. They have uttered special threats against the opposing ruling clique and are unmistakably appealing to the people and Party members beyond the border to shake off the ruling "capitalist" and "imperialist" or military-bureaucratic and "fascist" ruling groups. The resolute fight against the Soviet "revisionist renegade clique" and heretic and chauvinis-tic Maoism, respectively, apparently justifies revolutionary appeals and ruthless tactics, which differ little from those applied against Western capitalism and "imperialism."

Selected Bibliography

Dailies, Journals, and Digests

China Digest
China Reconstructs, Peking
China Quarterly
Current Abstracts of the Soviet Press
Current Background (American Consulate General), Hongkong
Current Digest of the Soviet Press (CDSP)
Current History
Encounter
Foreign Affairs
The Hindu, Madras
International Affairs
International Press Correspondence (Inprecor, 1922-38)
Izvestiia
Kommunist, Moscow
Kommunisticheskii Internatsional
Die Kommunistische Internationale
Krasnaya Zvezda
Literaturnaya gazeta
Le Monde, Paris
Neues Deutschland
The New China News Agency, Peking
New Times (Novoe vremia)
New York Times
Observer, London
Partiinaya Zhizn
Peking Review (PR)
People's Daily (Renmin Ribao), Peking
Pravda
Problems of Peace and Socialism

Problemy dalnevo vostoka
Red Flag (Hongqui), Peking
Review of the Hongkong China Press
The Russian Review
Soviet News
Soviet Studies in History
Survey of the China Mainland Press
Times
Voprosy istorii
Die Welt
World Marxist Review
Yearbook of World Affairs
Za rubezhom

General Works (some of the books listed here include collections of
    primary sources)

Acheson, Dean G. *Present at the Creation; My Years in the State Depart-
    ment*. New York, 1969.
Ambroz, Oton. *Realignment of World Power, The Russo-Chinese Schism
    under the Impact of Mao Tse-Tung's Last Revolution*. New York,
    1972.
An Analytical Survey of Moscow-Peiping Relations. Published by the
    World Anti-Communist League. Taipei, Taiwan, 1971.
Astaf'ev, G. A., Nikiforov, V. N. and Sladkovskii, M. I., eds.
    Noveishaia istoriia Kitaia, 1917-1970 gg. (Contemporary History of
    China, 1917-1970). Moscow, 1972.
Baby, Jean. *La grande controverse sino-soviétique, 1956-66*. Paris, 1966.
Barnett, A. Doak. *Communist China and Asia; Challenge to American
    Policy*. New York, 1960.
———, ed. *Communist Strategies in Asia*, New York, 1963.
Beloff, Max. *Soviet Policy in the Far East, 1944-51*. London, 1953.
Bettati, Mario. *Le Conflit Sino-soviétique*. Paris, 1971.
Bolshaya Sovetskaya Entsiklopediya (s.v. Stalin). Moscow, 1938.
Boorman, H. L. and others. *The Moscow-Peking Axis: Strengths and
    Strains*. New York, 1957.
Borisov, O. B. and Koloskov, B. T. *Sovietskoi-kitaiskie otnosheniia.
    1945-1970. Kratkii ocherk*. (Soviet-Chinese relations. 1945-1970. A
    brief outline). Moscow, 1972.
Borkenau, F. *World Communism: A History of the Communist Interna-
    tional*. New York, 1939.
Boyle, J. Hunter. *China and Japan at War, 1937-1945*. Stanford, Calif.,
    1972.

Brandt, Conrad, *Stalin's Failure in China, 1924-27*, Cambridge, Mass. 1958.

Brandt, C., Schwartz, B. and Fairbank, J. *A Documentary History of Chinese Communism.* Cambridge, Mass. 1952 (rpt. 1959).

Brzezinski, Z. K. *The Soviet Bloc; Unity and Conflict,* Cambridge, Mass., 1967.

Callis, H. G. *China, Confucian and Communist,* New York, 1959.

Caroe, Olaf *The Turks of Central Asia and Stalinism. London, 1953.*

——— *Soviet Empire.* London, 1953.

Carr, E. H. *The Bolshevik Revolution, 1917-1923.* vol. 1. New York, 1951.

Ch'en, Jerome. *Mao and the Chinese Revolution.* Oxford, 1965.

Cheng Tien-fong. *A History of Sino-Soviet Relations.* Washington, D. C., 1957.

Cherepanov, A. I. *Severnyi pokhod Natsionalnorevolyutsionnoi Armii Kitaya* (The Northern March of the National-Revolutionary Army of China). Moscow, 1968.

Chiang Kai-shek. *Soviet Russia in China: A Summing-up at Seventy.* New York, 1957.

Chin Szu-k'ai. *Communist China's Relations with the Soviet Union, 1949-57.* Hongkong, 1961.

Clemens, Walter. *The Arms Race and Sino-Soviet Relations.* Stanford, Calif., 1968.

Clyde, P. H. *The Far East.* New York, 1958.

Clubb. O. Edmund. *Twentieth Century China.* New York, 1964.

———. *China and Russia; the "Great Game."* New York, 1971.

Cohen, Arthur. *The Communism of Mao Tse-tung.* Chicago, 1964.

Columbia University Russian Institute. *The Anti-Stalin Campaign and International Communism; a Selection of Documents.* New York, 1956.

Committee of Concerned Asian Scholars. *China. Inside the People's Republic.* New York, 1972.

Compton, Boyd. *Mao's China: Party Reform Documents.* Seattle, 1952.

Crankshaw, Edward. *The New Cold War; Moscow versus Peking.* Baltimore, Md. 1963.

———, ed. *Krushchev Remembers.* Boston, 1970.

Creel, H. G. *Chinese Thought from Confucius to Mao Tse-tung.* Chicago, 1953.

Cressey, G. B. *Land of the 500 Million: A Geography of China.* New York, 1955.

Dahm, Helmut. *Abschreckung oder Volkskrieg. Strategische Machtplanung der Sowjetunion und Chinas in internationalem Kräfteverhältnis.* Freiburg i. B., 1968.

Dallin, A., ed. *Diversity in International Communism.* New York, 1963.

Dallin, David J. *Soviet Russia and the Far East.* New Haven, 1948.

————. *The Rise of Russia in Asia*. New Haven, 1949.

Davidson-Houston, J. V. *Russia and China from the Huns to Mao Tse-tung*. London, 1960.

Davies, J. Paton. Jr. *Dragon by the Tail*. New York, 1972.

Dedijer, V. *Tito Speaks*. London, 1953.

Degras, Jane, ed. *Soviet Documents on Foreign Policy*. 3 vols. London, 1951-53.

Deutscher, I. *Russia, China, and the West, A Contemporary chronicle, 1953-1966*. Edited by F. Halliday. London, 1970.

Djilas, Milovan. *Conversations with Stalin*. London, 1962.

———— *Lenin über die Beziehungen zwischen sozialistischen Staaten*. Belgrade, 1950.

Documents on the Sino-Indian Boundary Question. Peking, 1960.

Doolin, Dennis, Jr. *Territorial Claims in the Sino-Soviet Conflict; Documents and Analysis*. Stanford, Calif., 1965.

Dulles, Foster Rhea. *American Foreign Policy toward Communist China, 1949-69*. New York, 1972.

Dutt, V. P. *China and the World*. New York, 1966.

Editorial Collegium: L. P. Delyusin, M. A. Persits, A. B. Rezhikov, Prof. R. A. Ulyanovskii, chief ed. *Komintern i Vostok, Borba za Leninskuyu Strategiyu i Taktiku v Natsionalno-osvoboditelnom Dvizhenii*. (The Comintern and the East. Struggle for the Leninist Strategy and Tactics of the National Liberation Movement). Moscow, 1969.

Efimov, G. *Ocherki po novoi i noveishi istorii Kitaia* (Studies on the Recent and Contemporary History of China. Moscow, 1951.

Elegant, Robert S. *China's Red Masters*. New York, 1951.

Floyd, David *Mao against Khrushchev*. New York, 1964.

Friters, G. M. *Outer Mongolia and Its International Position*. London, 1951.

Foreign Policy of the United States, 1931-1942. Washington, D. C., 1949.

Fairbank, J. K. *The United States and China*. New York, 1963.

Fedoseev, P. N. *Marksizm i voliuntarizm* (Marxism and Voluntarism). Moscow. 1968.

Feis, H. *The China Tangle. The American Effort in China from Pearl Harbor to the Marshall Mission*. Princeton, N. J. , 1953.

Fessler, L. *The Party Comes of Age*. American University Field Staff, East Asia, 16, no. 8 n.d.

Feuerwerker, A., ed. *History of Communist China*. Cambridge, Mass., 1968.

Fischer, L. *The Soviets in World Affairs*. 2 vols., Princeton, N. J. 1951.

Fitzgerald, C. P. *The Birth of Communist China*. Baltimore Md., 1964.

————. *The Chinese View of their Place in the World*. London, 1964.

Friters, G. M. *Outer Mongolia and Its International Position*. London, 1967.

Garaudy, R. *Le grand tournant du socialisme*. Paris, 1969.

Garthoff, R. L. *Sino-Soviet Military Relations.* Washington, D.C., 1966.

Ginsburgs, G. and Mathos, M. *Communist China and Tibet.* The Hague, 1964.

Gittings, John. *Survey of the Sino-Soviet Dispute; a Commentary and Extracts from the Recent Polemics, 1963-1967.* London, 1968.

———. *The Role of the Chinese Army.* Oxford, 1967.

Goodman, E. R. *The Soviet Design for a World State.* New York, 1960.

Gray, J. *Maoism and the Cultural Revolution.* New York, 1968.

Gray J. and Cavendish, P. *Chinese Communism in Crisis.* New York, 1966.

Griffith, Samuel. *The Chinese People's Liberation Army.* New York, 1967.

Griffith, William E. *World Communism Divided.* New York, 1964.

———. *The Sino-Soviet Rift.* Cambridge, Mass., 1964.

———. *Sino-Soviet Relations, 1964-1965.* Cambridge, Mass., 1967.

———. *Albania and the Sino-Soviet Rift,* Cambridge, Mass., 1963.

———. *Cold War and Coexistence, Russia, China and the United States.* Englewood Cliffs, N.J., 1971.

Gubelman, M. I. *Borba za Sovetskii Dalnii Vostok, 1918-1922* (The Struggle for the Soviet Far East, 1918-1922), Moscow, 1958.

Halperin, Morton H. *Sino-Soviet Relations and Arms Control.* Cambridge, Mass., 1967.

Halpern, A. M., ed. *Policies toward China: Views from Six Continents.* New York, 1966.

Hamm, Harry and Kun, Joseph. *Das rote Schisma,* Cologne, 1963.

Hinton, H. C. *Communist China in World Politics.* London, 1966.

——— *The Bear at the Gate; Chinese Policymaking under Soviet Pressure.* Washington, D.C., 1971.

Hoetzsch, Otto. *Russland in Asien, Geschichte einer Expansion.* Stuttgart, 1966.

Ho Kan-chih. *A History of the Modern Chinese Revolution.* Peking, 1960.

Hostler, Charles W. *Turkism and the Soviets.* New York, 1957.

Hsio-Hsia, ed. *China: Its People, Its Society, Its Culture.* New Haven, Conn., 1960.

Hsiao Tso-liang. *Power Relations within the Chinese Communist Movement 1930-34.* Seattle Wash., 1961.

Hudson G. F. and others. *The Sino-Soviet Dispute Documented and Analyzed.* London, 1961.

Isaacs, H. *The Tragedy of the Chinese Revolution.* Stanford, Calif., 1961.

Isenberg, I., ed. *The Russo-Chinese Rift: Its Impact on World Affairs.* New York, 1966.

Jackson, W. A. Douglas. *The Russo-Chinese Borderlands.* New York, 1962.

Joxe, A. *El conflicto chino-sovietico en america latina.* Montevideo, 1967.

Kapitsa, M. S. Sovetsko-kitaiskie otnosheniia v 1931-45 (Sino-Soviet Rela-

350   THE SINO-SOVIET DISPUTE

tions, 1931-1945). Moscow, 1956.

Kapur, Harish. *Soviet Russia and Asia, 1917-1927: A Study of Soviet Policy Towards Turkey, Iran and Afghanistan,* Geneva, 1966.

Kardelj, Edward. *Socialism and War: A Survey of Chinese Criticism of the Policy of Coexistence.* Translated from the Serbo-Croatian by Alec Brown. London, 1961.

Karnow, Stanley. *Mao and China from Revolution to Revolution* (Introduction by J. King Fairbank). New York, 1972.

Kautsky, J. H. *Moscow and the Communist Party of India:* A Study in the postwar Evaluation of International Communist Strategy.

Keesing Research Report. *The Cultural Revolution in China: Its Origins and Course.* New York, 1967.

Kirsch, Botho. *Sturm über Eurasien. Moskau und Peking im Kampf um die Weltherrschaft.* Stuttgart, 1970.

Kiuzadzhan, L. S. *Ideologicheskie kampanii v KNR (1949-1966)* (Ideological Struggles in the People's Republic of China, 1949-1966). Moscow, 1970.

Klein, D. W. and Clark, A. B. *Biographic Dictionary of Chinese Communism.* 2 vols. Cambridge, Mass., 1971.

Klochko, M. A. *Soviet Scientists in Red China,* London, 1964.

KNR:dva desiatiletiia-dve politiki (The People's Republic of China: Two Decades-Two Political Courses). Moscow, 1969.

Kolarz, W. *Russia and her Colonies.* London, 1952.

———. *The Peoples of the Soviet Far East.* New York, 1954.

Kommunisticheskii internatsional pered vii vsemirnyn kongressom: materialy (The Communist International on the Eve of the Seventh World Congress: Materials). Moscow, 1935.

Krakowski, Eduard. *Chine et Russie: L'Orient contre la civilization occidentale.* Paris, 1957.

Krylov, G. M. ed. *Vneshniaia Politica KNR* (The Foreign Policy of the People's Republic of China). Moscow, 1971.

Labedz, Leopold, and others, eds. *The Sino-Soviet Conflict;* eleven radio discussions. London, 1965.

Lattimore, Owen. *Inner Asian Frontier of China.* New York, 1951.

———. *Nationalism and Revolution in Mongolia.* New York, 1955.

———. *The Mongols of Manchuria.* New York, 1934.

———. *Manchuria, Cradle of Conflict.* New York, 1935.

Lenin i problemy sovremennogo Kitaia (Lenin and the Problems of Contemporary China). Moscow, 1971.

Leninskaia politika v otnoshenii Kitaia (Leninist Politics and Relations with China). Moscow, 1968.

Lensen, George A. *Russia's Eastward Expansion.* New York, 1964.

Levenson, J. *Confucian China and its Modern Fate.* 3 vols. Berkeley, Cal. 1958-65.

Levi, Werner. *Modern China's Foreign Policy.* Minneapolis, Minn., 1953.

Lobanov-Rostowsky, A. *Russia and Asia.* Ann Arbor, Mich. 1951.

London, Kurt, ed. *Unity and Contradiction: Major Aspects of Sino-Soviet Relations*. New York, 1961.

Low, A. D. *Lenin on the Question of Nationality*. New York, 1958.

Lowenthal, Richard. *World Communism. The Disintegration of a Secular Faith*. Oxford, 1964.

Macfarquhar, R. *The Hundred Flowers Campaign and the Chinese Intellectuals*. New York, 1960.

———, ed. *Sino-American Relations, 1949-1971*. New York, 1972.

Mackintosh, J. M. *Strategy and Tactics of Soviet Foreign Policy*. London, 1962.

Mao Tse-tung. *Selected Writings from the Works of Mao Tse-tung*. Peking, 1967.

———. *Little Red Book* (Quotations from Chairman Mao Tse-tung). Peking, 1967.

———. *Selected Military Writings of Mao Tse-tung*. Peking, 1963.

May, E. R. and Thomson, J. C., Jr. *American-East Asian Relations*. Cambridge, Mass., 1972.

McLane, C. B. *Soviet Policy and the Chinese Communists, 1931-1946*. New York, 1958.

———. *Soviet Strategies in Southeast Asia;* An Exploration of Eastern Policy under Lenin and Stalin. Princeton, N.J., 1966.

Mehnert, Klaus. *Peking and Moscow*. (Translated from the German). London, 1963.

Mendel, D. *The Politics of Formosan Nationalism*. Berkeley, Calif., 1970.

Mezhdunarodnye otnosheniia na Dal' nem Vostoke 1870-1945 (International Relations in the Far East, 1870-1945). Prepared by the Soviet Academy of Sciences. Moscow, 1951.

Metaxas, Alexandre. *Pekin contre Moscou*. Lausanne, 1959.

Michael, Franz H. and Taylor, G. E. *The Far East in the Modern World*. New York, 1956.

Nikiforov, V. N. *Sovietskie istoriki o problemakh Kitaia* (Soviet Historians about the Problems of China). Moscow, 1970.

North, R. C. *Kuomintang and Chinese Communist Elites*. Stanford, Calif., 1952.

———. *Moscow and the Chinese Communists*. Stanford, 1953 (rpt. 1963).

Ojha, I. C. *Chinese Foreign Policy in an Age of Transition*. Boston, 1969.

Padick, Clement and others. *Russia and China, Non-ideological Aspects of Their Relationship*. Los Angeles, Calif., 1966.

Park, A. G. *Bolshevism in Turkestan 1917-1927*. New York, 1957.

Payne, Robert. *Portrait of a Revolutionary: Mao Tse-tung*. New York, 1961.

Perevertailo, A. S. (chief ed.), Glunin, V. I., Kukushkin, K. V., and Nikiforov, V. N. *Ocherki Istorii Kitaya v Noveishee Vremya*. (Outlines of the History of China in the Most Recent Period). Moscow, 1959.

Piao, Lin. *The Polemic on the General Line of the International Com-*

munist Movement. Peking, 1965.

Pierce, R. A. *Russian Central Asia 1867-1917*. Berkeley, Calif., 1960.

Pipes, R. *The Formation of the Soviet Union: Communism and Nationalism, 1917-1923,* Cambridge, 1954.

Pomerennig, Horst. *Der chinesisch-sowjetische Grenzkonflikt*. Freiburg i.B., 1968.

Pye, Lucien W. *The Spirit of Chinese Politics: A Psychocultural Study*. Cambridge, Mass., 1968.

Pyn Min. *Istoriia kitaisko-sovetskoi druzhby* (The History of Sino-Soviet Friendship). Moscow, 1959.

Rees D. *Korea: The Limited War*. New York, 1964.

Rice, E. E. *Mao's Way*. Berkeley, Calif., 1972.

Ronchey, Alberto. *The Two Red Giants; an Analysis of Sino-Soviet Relations*. New York, 1965.

Roy, M. N. *Revolution and Counterrevolution in China*. Calcutta, 1956.

Rowland, J. *A History of Sino-Indian Relations*. Toronto, 1967.

Rubinstein, A. Z. *The Foreign Policy of the Soviet Union*. New York, 1960.

Rue, J. E. *Mao Tse-tung in Opposition, 1927-1935*. Stanford, Calif., 1966.

Rumiantsev, A. M. *Istoki i evoliutsiia "idei Mao Tszeduna"* (The Origins and the Evolution of the "Ideas of Mao Tse-tung"). Moscow, 1972.

Salisbury, H. E. *War between Russia and China*. New York, 1969.

———. *To Moscow–and Beyond*. New York, 1959.

Saran, V. *Sino-Soviet Schism. A Bibliography, 1956-1964*. Bombay, 1971.

Schram, Stuart R. *The Political Thought of Mao Tse-tung,* New York, 1963 (rpt. 1969).

———. *Mao Tse-tung*. New York, 1967 (rpt. 1969).

———. *Documents sur la théorie de la 'révolution permanente' en Chine*. Paris, 1963.

———. ed. *Quotations from Chairman Mao Tse-tung*. New York, 1969.

Schurman, Franz. *Ideology and Organization in Communist China*. Berkeley, Calif. 1966.

Schwartz, Benjamin I. *Chinese Communism and the Rise of Mao*. Cambridge, Mass., 1958.

Schwartz, Harry. *Tsars, Mandarins, and Commissars;* A History of Chinese-Russian relations. Philadelphia, 1964.

Shabad, Theodore. *Geography of the USSR. A Regional Survey*. New York, 1951.

———. *China's Changing Map*. New York, 1956.

Seton-Watson, Hugh. *From Lenin to Malenkov,* New York, 1953.

Simon, S. W. *The Broken Triangle: Peking, Djakarta, and the PKI*. Baltimore, Md., 1968.

Skachkov, P. E. *Bibliografiia Kitaia* (Bibliography of China). Moscow, 1960.

Snow, Edgar. *Red Star over China*, New York, 1938.

———. *Mao's Autobiography*. New York, 1939.

Sovetsko-Kitaiskie otnosheniia, 1917-1957 (Soviet-Chinese Relations, 1917-57). Moscow, 1957.

Stalin, I. V. *Sochineniia* (Collected Works). 13 vols. Moscow, 1946-51; for China, especially vols. 8 and 9, 1948 and 1949.

Steiner, H. A. *The International Position of Communist China*. New York, 1958.

Swarup, Shanti. *A Study of the Chinese Communist Movement*. Oxford, 1966.

Tang, Peter S.H. *Communist China Today*, Washington, D.C., 1961-1962.

———. *Russian and Soviet Policy in Manchuria and Outer Mongolia, 1911-1931*. Durham, N.C., 1959.

Tang Tsou. *America's Failure in China*. Chicago 1963.

Thiel, Erich. *The Soviet Far East*. New York, 1957.

Treadgold D. W. *Twentieth Century Russia*. Chicago. 1959.

———. *The West in Russia and China,* Cambridge, Mass., 1973.

———, ed. *Soviet and Chinese Communism, Similarities and Differences,* Seattle, 1967.

Treaties and Agreements with and concerning China, 1919-1929 Washington, D.C.: Carnegie, 1929.

Trotsky, L. *Problems of the Chinese Revolution*. New York, 1932.

Tuchman, Barbara. *Stillwell and the American Experience in China 1941-45*. New York, 1970.

Ulam, A.B. *Expansion and Coexistence. The History of Soviet Russian Foreign Policy 1917-1967*. Washington, D.C., 1968.

———. *The Rivals. America and Russia since World War II*. New York, 1972.

USSR: Ministry of Foreign Affairs. *Dokumenty Vneshnei Politiki SSSR.* (Documents of the Foreign Policy of the USSR) Moscow, 1958.

U.S. Dept. of State. Foreign Relations of the United States. *United States Relations with China, with Special Reference to the period 1944-1949*. Washington, D.C., 1949.

Van Slyke, L. P. *Enemies and Friends: the United Front in Chinese Communist History*. Stanford, Calif., 1967.

Vucinich, Wayne S., ed. *Russia and Asia. Essays on the Influence of Russia on the Asian Peoples*. Stanford, Calif., 1972.

Watson, Francis. *The Frontiers of China*. New York, 1966.

Wei, H. *China and Soviet Russia*. New York, 1956.

Wheeler, G. E. *The Modern History of Soviet Central Asia*. New York, 1965.

Whiting A. S. *Soviet Policies in China, 1917-1924*. New York, 1954.

——— and General Sheng Shihts'ai. *Sinkiang: Pawn or Pivot*. East Lansing, Mich., 1958.

Wilbur, C. M. and Julie Lien-ying How. *Documents on Communism,*

Nationalism and Soviet Advisors in China, 1918-1927. New York, 1956.

Wittfogel, K.A. *Oriental Despotism. A Comparative Study of Total Power.* Chapter 9. New Haven, Conn., 1957.

Wolfe, T. W. *Soviet Power and Europe, 1945-1970.* Baltimore, Md. 1970.

Wu, Aitchen K. *China and the Soviet Union. A Study of Sino-Soviet Relations.* New York, 1950.

Yakhontoff, V. A. *Russia and the Soviet Union in the Far East.* London, 1932.

Zablocki, Clement J., ed. *Sino-Soviet Rivalry: Implications for U.S. Policy.* Washington, D.C., 1966.

Zagoria, Donald S. *The Sino-Soviet Conflict 1956-1961.* Princeton, 1962.

————. *Vietnam Triangle, Moscow, Peking, Hanoi.* New York, 1967.

————, ed. *Communist China and the Soviet Bloc* (American Academy of Political and Social Science). Philadelphia, 1963.

Zimmerman, William. *Soviet Perspectives in International Relations.* Princeton, N.J. 1969.

Zinner, Paul E., ed. *National Communism and Popular Revolt in Eastern Europe;* a Selection of Documents. New York, 1956.

Periodical Articles

American Consulate General, Hong Kong. "Sino-Soviet Border Clashes." *Current Background,* no. 876 (April 11, 1969).

————. " 'Soviet Revisionist Social-Imperialism' or US-Soviet Collaboration.' " *Current Background,* no. 883 (June 26, 1969).

Alexeyev, L. "Anti-Sovietism in Peking's Strategy. *"International Affairs,* no. 7, (1973), pp. 21-26.

Apalin, G. "Peking: A Policy Inimical to Peace, Democracy and Socialism." *International Affairs,* no. 11 (1973), pp. 22-28.

Avakumovic, I. "The Communist Party of Canada and the Sino-Soviet dispute," *Pacific Affairs* (Winter 1964-65), pp. 426-35.

Baum, R. "Revolution and Reaction in the Chinese Countryside: the Socialist Education Movement in Cultural Revolutionary Perspective." *The China Quarterly* (April-June 1969), pp. 92-119.

Berton, P. "Background to the Territorial Issue." *Studies in Comparative Communism* 2, nos. 3-4 (July/October 1969): 131-382.

Borisov, V. "Peking and the Détente." *International Affairs,* no. 12 (1973), pp. 31-35.

Brzezinski, Z. K. "Threat and Opportunity in the Communist Schism." *Foreign Affairs,* 40, no. 3 (April 1963): 513-26.

Chai, W. "The reorganization of the Chinese Communist Party, 1966-1968." *Asian Survey* (Nov. 1968), pp. 901-10.

Charles, D. A. "The Dismissal of Marshal P'eng Teh-huai." *The China*

Quarterly, no. 8 (Oct.-Dec. 1961), pp. 63-76.

Hinton, H. C. "Conflict on the Ussuri: A Clash of Nationalisms." *Problems of Communism* 20, nos. 1-2 (Jan.-April 1971): 45-59.

Hoeffding, O. "Sino-Soviet Economic Relations 1959-1962." *Annals of the American Academy of Political Science* (Sept. 1963), pp. 94-105.

Hudson, G. F. "Mao and Moscow." *Foreign Affairs* (Oct. 1957), pp. 78-90.

———. "Mao, Marx and Moscow." *Foreign Affairs* (July 1959), pp. 561-72.

———. "Russia and China: The Dilemmas of Power." *Foreign Affairs* (Oct. 1960), pp. 1-10.

Ito, K. and Shibata, M. "The Dilemma of Mao Tse-tung." *The China Quarterly* (July-Sept. 1968), pp. 58-77.

Johnson, C. "The Cultural Revolution." *Far Eastern Economic Review* (Feb. 1968), pp. 187-96.

Kovalev, E. F. "A New Step in the Study of Sino-Soviet Relations between 1945-1970." *Voprosy Istorii,* no. 11 (1972).

Lacqueur, W. A. "The End of the Monolith World Communism in 1962." *Foreign Affairs* (April 1962), pp. 360-73.

——— and Labedz, L. "Polycentrism, the New Factor in International Communism." *American Political Science Review* (Dec. 1963), pp. 1019-21.

Lee, W. Rensselaer, III. "The Hsia Fang System: Marxism and Modernization." *China Quarterly,* no. 28 (Oct.-Dec., 1966).

Low, A. D. "Soviet Nationality Policy and the New Program of the CP." *The Russian Review* (Jan. 1963), pp. 3-29.

Lowenthal, R. "Russia and China: Controlled Conflict." Foreign Affairs 49, no. 3 (April 1971): 507-18.

———. "The World Scene Transformed." *Encounter* 15, no. 4 (Oct. 1963): 3-10.

Macfarquhar, R. "The Chinese Model and the Underdeveloped World." *International Affairs* (July 1963), pp. 372-85.

Mancall, M. "The Persistence of Tradition in Chinese Foreign Policy." *The Annals* 349 (Sept. 1963).

Michael, F. "Twenty Years of Sino-Soviet Relations." *Current History* (Sept. 1969).

Mosely, P. E. "The Chinese-Soviet Rift: Origins and Portents." *Foreign Affairs* (Oct. 1963), pp. 11-24.

Nikolayev, L. and Mikhailov, Y. "China's Foreign Economic Policy." *International Affairs,* no. 9 (1973), pp. 44-52.

"On the Tenth Congress of the Communist Party of China." *International Affairs,* no. 12 (1973), pp. 73-79.

Pamor, A. and Trifonov, V. "Maoist Slogans and Facts." *New Times,* no. 2 (Jan, 1974), pp. 22-26.

Robinson, J. "The Cultural Revolution in China." *International Affairs* (April 1968), pp. 214-27.

Robinson, T. W. "The Sino-Soviet Border Dispute: Background, Development, and the March 1969 Clashes." *The Rand Corporation* (August 1970).

————. "The Border Negotiations and the Future of Sino-Soviet-American Relations." *The Rand Corporation* (August 1971).

Rupen, R. A. "Inside Outer Mongolia." *Foreign Affairs* (Jan. 1959), pp. 328-33.

Sapiets, Janis "The Twenty-fourth Congress of the Soviet Communist Party." *Russian Review,* 31 (Jan, 1972), no. 1.

Scalapino, R. A. "Moscow, Peking and the Communist Parties of Asia." *Foreign Affairs* (Jan. 1963), p. 323.

Schecter, J. L. "Khrushchev's Image inside China." *China Quarterly* (April-June 1963), pp. 212-17.

Seton-Watson, H. "Differences in the Communist Parties." *Annals of the American Academy of Political and Social Science* (May 1958), pp. 1-7.

————. "The Great Schism." *Encounter* 15, no. 5 (May 1963) pp. 3-10.

Schram, P. "Unity and Diversity of Russian and Chinese Industrial Wages Policies." *Journal of Asian Studies* (Feb. 1964), pp. 245-51.

Schram, S. R. "The Party in Chinese Communist Ideology," *China Quarterly* (April-June 1969), pp. 1-16.

Snow, E. "Talks with Chou En-lai: The Open Door." *The New Republic* (March 27, 1971), pp. 20-23.

Thomas, J. R. "Sino-Soviet Relations." *Current History* (Oct. 1971), pp. 210-15.

Tikhvinskii, S. L. "On Problems in the Recent History of China. *"Voprosy istorii,* no. 2 (1973); also in *Soviet Studies in History* 12, no. 2 (Fall 1973): 3-58.

Várnai, F. "Whither China?" *International Affairs,* no. 8 (1973), pp. 82-90.

Wittfogel, K. "The Influence of Leninism-Stalinism on China." *Annals of the American Academy of Political and Social Science* (Sept. 1951).

————. "The Legend of 'Maoism,' " *China Quarterly,* nos. 1-2 (1960).

————. "The Russian and Chinese Revolutions: "A Socio-Historical Comparison." *Yearbook of World Affairs* 15 (London, 1961): 41.

Unpublished Materials: Seminar Papers, Marquette University

Kollaparambil, J., Father. "The Indo-Chinese Border Dispute, 1962, and the Sino-Soviet Rift." (24 pages)

Roebke, Ruth D. "War, Revolution and Peaceful Coexistence, and the Sino-Soviet Dispute, 1962-64." (25 pages)

Sobocinsky, Harvey J. "The Beginnings of the Sino-Soviet Dispute, 1956-57. (21 pages).

Index

357